OXFORD THEOLOGICAL MONOGRAPHS

OXFORD THEOLOGICAL MONOGRAPHS

'WORKING THE EARTH OF THE HEART'
The Messalian Controversy in History, Texts, and Language to AD 431
Columba Stewart, OSB (1991)

THE LORDSHIP OF CHRIST
Ernst Käsemann's Interpretation of Paul's Theology
David V. Way (1991)

BEAUTY AND REVELATION IN THE THOUGHT OF SAINT AUGUSTINE
Carol Harrison (1992)

THE MURATORIAN FRAGMENT AND THE DEVELOPMENT OF THE CANON
Geoffrey Mark Hahneman (1992)

CHRISTOLOGY AND COSMOLOGY
Models of Divine Activity in Origen, Eusebius, and Athanasius
J. Rebecca Lyman (1993)

KIERKEGAARD AS NEGATIVE THEOLOGIAN
David Law (1993)

EARLY ISRAELITE WISDOM
Stuart Weeks (1994)

THE FATHERHOOD OF GOD FROM ORIGEN TO ATHANASIUS
Peter Widdicombe (1994)

RIGHT PRACTICAL REASON
Aristotle, Action, and Prudence in Aquinas
Daniel Westberg (1994)

JOHN NEWTON AND THE ENGLISH EVANGELICAL TRADITION
between the Conversions of Wesley and Wilberforce
D. Bruce Hindmarsh (1996)

ST GREGORY OF NAZIANZUS
POEMATA ARCANA
C. Moreschini and D. A. Sykes (1997)

Universal Salvation

Eschatology in the Thought of Gregory of Nyssa and Karl Rahner

MORWENNA LUDLOW

OXFORD
UNIVERSITY PRESS

This book has been printed digitally and produced in a standard specification in order to ensure its continuing availability

OXFORD
UNIVERSITY PRESS

Great Clarendon Street, Oxford OX2 6DP

Oxford University Press is a department of the University of Oxford.
It furthers the University's objective of excellence in research, scholarship,
and education by publishing worldwide in

Oxford New York

Auckland Cape Town Dar es Salaam Hong Kong Karachi
Kuala Lumpur Madrid Melbourne Mexico City Nairobi
New Delhi Shanghai Taipei Toronto
With offices in
Argentina Austria Brazil Chile Czech Republic France Greece
Guatemala Hungary Italy Japan South Korea Poland Portugal
Singapore Switzerland Thailand Turkey Ukraine Vietnam

Published in the United States
by Oxford University Press Inc., New York

Reprinted 2007

ISBN 978-0-19-827022-5

To my parents

ACKNOWLEDGEMENTS

This book is based on my D.Phil. thesis, for the funding of which I have primarily to thank the British Academy. I am also grateful to the president and fellows of Trinity College, Oxford, for their support during the early stages of my thesis, to the provost and fellows of the Queen's College, Oxford, for the award of a Holwell studentship and to the committee administrating the Denyer and Johnson studentship in theology. I completed the thesis and its later metamorphosis into a book as a junior research fellow at St John's College, Oxford. I would like to thank the president and fellows for electing me to this position and for their support throughout my fellowship.

I owe many thanks to Prof. Keith Ward and Dr. Mark Edwards. Many of my ideas have been developed under the influence of their pertinent and sympathetic questioning (although of course the final conclusions I draw are my own); my transition from reading greats to reading theology was much helped by their patience and theological rigour. Keith Ward supervised me throughout my graduate study and has been a constant source of infectious enthusiasm and friendly support throughout the writing and rewriting of my thesis. Mark Edwards kindly agreed to take on the supervision of the chapters on Gregory of Nyssa, but in fact went far beyond this in reading and commenting very helpfully on the whole work and generally in encouraging my research.

My thanks are due to the Oxford Theological Monographs committee for setting me on the path of rewriting my thesis and especially to Prof. Maurice Wiles, who has been most generous with his time and advice. He has not only paid detailed attention to the text, but has encouraged me to move on from the conclusions of my D.Phil. to view my research from a wider perspective. Thank you also to my editor at the Oxford University Press, Georga Godwin.

To my husband Piers, I owe warm thanks for casting an historian's eye over this book in all its myriad forms, but also for his enthusiasm and humour, and most of all for the fact that he has never had to ask why I was writing it.

Finally, this book is dedicated with gratitude and affection to my parents, who have supported and encouraged my study at every stage.

M.L.

Oxford

CONTENTS

KARL RAHNER

ABBREVIATIONS AND CONVENTIONS

ET	English translation
GNO	*Gregorii Nysseni: Opera* (E. J. Brill, Leiden)
NPNF	*A Select Library of Nicene and Post-Nicene Fathers of the Christian Church*, 2nd series, ed. P. Schaff and H. Wace (T&T Clark, Edinburgh)
PG	*Patrologiae: Series Graeca Prior*, ed. J.-P. Migne
SC	*Sources Chrétiennes* (Éditions du Cerf, Paris)
SM	Karl Rahner et al. (eds.), *Sacramentum Mundi*, tr. W. J. O'Hara (Herder & Herder, New York, 1968–70)
ST	Karl Rahner, *Schriften zur Theologie* (Benziger, Einsiedeln, 1954–84)
TI	Karl Rahner, *Theological Investigations*, tr. various (Helicon Press, Baltimore; Darton, Longman & Todd, London, 1961–92)

Abbreviations of the titles of other works by Karl Rahner and those of Gregory of Nyssa and other Patristic authors are given in the bibliography.

All other abbreviations follow the conventions of *The Oxford Dictionary of the Christian Church*, ed. F. L. Cross and E. A. Livingstone, 3rd edn. (Oxford University Press, Oxford, 1997).

CONVENTIONS

Biblical citations are from the Revised Standard Version, unless they come within a quotation, in which case the original author's own wording is retained.

Inclusive language has been used where possible, but the words of texts cited have not been altered.

Finish then Thy new creation,
Pure and spotless let us be;
Let us see Thy great salvation,
Perfectly restored in Thee,
Changed from glory into glory,
Till in heaven we take our place,
Till we cast our crowns before Thee,
Lost in wonder, love and praise.

Charles Wesley

Introduction

Then comes the end . . . And when all things have been subjected unto him, then shall the Son also himself be subjected to him that did subject all things unto him, that God may be all in all.[1]

God will be all in all, and all persons will be united together in fellowship of the good, Christ Jesus our Lord, to whom be glory and power for ever and ever. Amen.[2]

this single real and uniquely fulfilling consummation that is the fullness of finality: God—all in all.[3]

For nearly two thousand years theologians and mystics, scholars and simple men and women of prayer have sought to find meaning in Paul's evocative but mysterious words at the end of 1 Corinthians 15. In particular, the passage has appealed to those who have faith in a 'wider hope'—that in the end no person will be lost from God's love. Indeed, many argue, if God will be 'all in all' surely this indicates that the whole cosmos will be saved?

Clearly, such hopes for universal salvation are at variance with much of Christian tradition. Mainstream theologians have tended to emphasize the possibility, if not the certainty, of hell. Yet, since Origen, if not before, there has been a minority of Christian thinkers who have proposed that God will bring everything to fulfilment. Indeed, in the early Christian Church there were two important streams of eschatological thought: a universalist stream, which asserted that all people would be saved, and a dualistic stream, which stressed the two parallel fates of eternal heaven and eternal hell. However, the dualistic current in eschatology was always the stronger, particularly in the West, and since about the fifth or perhaps sixth century it has been overwhelmingly powerful.[4] This dominance was due partly to the theology of Augustine of Hippo: he denied universal

[1] 1 Cor. 15: 24, 28.

[2] Gregory of Nyssa, *In canticum canticorum* xv: McCambley, 276; *GNO* vi. 469.

[3] Karl Rahner 'Immanent and Transcendent Consummation', *TI* x. 289.

[4] Although there is much to be said about attitudes to eschatology in the East after Gregory of Nyssa's time, this book will restrict itself to developments in the West.

salvation with a forcefulness which had a profound influence on both Catholic and Reformed traditions. It was due also to the anathematizing of various Origenistic doctrines, including an extreme version of universal salvation, by the Fifth Ecumenical Council in 553.[5] Furthermore, in the following centuries the supremacy of the dualistic stream of eschatology became connected with the increasing institutional and political power of the Church: assertions of universal salvation were treated as threats not only to true Christian doctrine, but also to the authority of the Church and to the stability of society.

This is not to say, however, that the Church extinguished all interest in the idea of universal salvation. A series of factors encouraged the second stream of eschatology to flow on, albeit as a trickle. Perhaps the most important of these occurred around the time of, or as a result of, the Reformation. The humanist reformers, above all Erasmus, revived interest in Greek patristic authors and ensured that the works of Origen not only became known, but were available in new editions. The Reformation also represented a response to the perceived exclusivity of the doctrines and practices of the Roman Catholic Church, which was expressed by some theologians in terms of a wider eschatological hope. Although the mainstream Protestant Reformers did not advocate universal salvation, a few sectarian groups or individual preachers believed in it (or at least were accused of believing in it).[6] In the following centuries, a substantial number of advocates of universal salvation came from perhaps the most unexpected angle: Calvinists reacting against their own tradition's exclusivist doctrine of double predestination.[7]

The years between the Reformation and the Enlightenment

[5] Much controversy surrounds these fifteen anathemas, which do not mention Origen by name and condemn the idea of universal salvation only in association with other doctrines (such as the pre-existence of souls, the nature of Christ, and the qualities of the resurrection body). The important point is that they were later commonly *assumed* to anathematize both Origen himself and the idea of universal salvation as such. (See below Chapter 1, section d.)

[6] Various groups loosely called 'Anabaptist' were so accused. Hans Denck (1495–1527) was formally charged with believing in universal salvation. (See: A. Coutts, *Hans Denck 1495–1527: Humanist and Heretic* (Macniven and Wallace, Edinburgh, 1927), 46 and Chapter 15; F. L. Weiss, *The Life, Teaching and Works of Johannes Denck* (published independently at Strasbourg, 1924), 29.) However, although his extant writings strongly emphasize God's universal saving will, they make no claims as to its ultimate success.

[7] See Geoffrey Rowell, 'The Origins and History of the Universalist Societies in Britain 1750–1850', *Journal for Ecclesiastical History* 22 (1971), esp. 54–5.

saw a large number of protracted debates over whether the doctrine of hell was rationally coherent with other theological claims. Perhaps partly in reaction to the increasing trend towards rationalism, an increasing number of people turned to mystical writers, such as Jacob Boehme, who emphasized the universal revelation of God through the Spirit. While this idea does not logically entail universal salvation (and Boehme himself was not a universalist), it greatly influenced universalist thought.[8]

Gradually, loyalty to the teachings of a church became less important to many writers than the submitting of religious beliefs to rational scrutiny, or had been overtaken by other more personal and spiritual priorities. Nevertheless, anxieties remained that the doctrine of universal salvation would cause general immorality and social upheaval. Thus, the writings of authors who were persuaded of the truth of universal salvation were often published anonymously or posthumously and in many cases it is likely that their beliefs were not written down at all. In addition to this self-censorship, there were still also some external pressures to conform. As late as 1853, F. D. Maurice lost his position at King's College, London, for espousing a view which was taken to be a straight affirmation of universal salvation—although his actual opinions were somewhat more subtle than that.[9] It has been perhaps only since the late nineteenth century that theologians have really felt free to suggest that God will save all people, without being in fear of losing their jobs, reputations, or even their lives. By this period there also seems to be a consensus that the doctrine of hell has never been a particularly effective moral deterrent, and thus that its removal would not threaten public order.

A fundamental reason, then, for the extent and vigour of the current debate about universal salvation is the openness with which it is now conducted. However, besides this freedom from the fear of actual or perceived consequences of advocating universal salvation, there are other reasons why the idea is discussed more than ever before. Above all there is an increasing sense of moral unease at the notion of God consigning people to

[8] For universalism in this period see D. P. Walker, *The Decline of Hell* (Routledge & Kegan Paul, London, 1964) and M. A. Ludlow, 'Universal Salvation and a Soteriology of Divine Punishment', *Scottish Journal of Theology* (forthcoming).

[9] Geoffrey Rowell, *Hell and the Victorians: A Study of the Nineteenth-Century Theological Controversies concerning Eternal Punishment and the Future Life* (Clarendon Press, Oxford, 1974), 76–84.

an eternal hell. Such an attitude of disquiet has a long history, but it has become much more prevalent since the beginning of the twentieth century—despite an acute awareness of the potential of humans to do evil to each other. Interestingly, although there has been a trend away from 'optimistic' theologies based on notions of human progress, this has not noticeably reduced the breadth of theologians' eschatological hope: on the contrary, theologians of hope like Jürgen Moltmann take their starting-point precisely from human evil but look to God to redeem it thoroughly. Is the torture of prisoners in a totalitarian state truly *redeemed* if the torturers are subjected to eternal torture? Perhaps the horrors of the twentieth century have only strengthened the resolve of theologians not to bring God down to humanity's level. Furthermore, since the concept of an eternal hell is based on the assumption of the justice of retributive punishment, recent debates about the nature of punishment, reflecting a growing interest in reformative punishment and restorative justice, seem to have encouraged the move away from the idea of God imposing an eternal hell.

Related to this general moral disquiet are several other more specific concerns. First there is a changing perception amongst many in the Church about the role of Christianity in the world: the growing encounter with and knowledge of other religions has intensified the question of whether Christianity is the only means to salvation. Similarly, an increasingly secular world has forced believers to question the Church's traditional teaching about those who practice no religion at all. Allied to these considerations is an awareness of the complexities of human intentionality. A deeper comprehension of the influence of biologically inherited tendencies and of the social and cultural environment on human behaviour has raised doubts about the degree of ultimate responsibility people have for their decisions—particularly with regard to decisions of faith. The disciplines of evolutionary biology and scientific cosmology have also played an important role. A growing understanding of the place of human beings within the development of life on our planet has caused many thinkers to question the supposed Christian doctrine of the moral supremacy of humanity among other species; likewise the idea of the uniqueness of the earth is challenged by discoveries about the age and vastness of the cosmos.

All these concerns question the justice of God's privileging one group of humans above the rest of creation. Such considerations challenge the divisions which have characterized much of Christian eschatology: between the elect and the non-elect; between those with faith and those without it; between the good and the wicked; between humans and the rest of creation. If these distinctions now seem more fluid, how can we speak easily of the salvation of one group and not another? Some theologians have responded to this question by suggesting that since the choice of any particular group for salvation would indeed seem arbitrary, consequently God will save at least all humanity and perhaps the whole universe.

For these reasons, the stream of belief in universal salvation, for much of its life weak and flowing underground, has once again come up into the daylight. Although it has not yet become a mighty river, nevertheless a significant number of mainstream theologians have at least countenanced the idea. Discussions of it have taken several very different forms. Compare, for example, Karl Barth's rethinking of the doctrine of election[10] with Moltmann's political-ecological eschatology;[11] or Gustavo Gutiérrez's liberation theology[12] with Hans Urs von Balthasar's exploration of the Greek fathers and the image of Christ's descent to hell on Easter Saturday.[13] In Britain, John Hick's view of universal salvation has developed from an encounter between the philosophy of religion (especially as applied to theodicy) and the comparative study of religions.[14]

[10] See Karl Barth, 'The Humanity of God', in *God, Grace and Gospel*, tr. J. S. McNab, Scottish Journal of Theology Occasional Papers (Oliver and Boyd, Edinburgh, 1956) and his treatment of election: *Church Dogmatics* ii/2 (T & T Clark, Edinburgh, 1957) ch. 7, pp. 3–506. Scholars are divided as to whether Barth believed in universal salvation: although his theology tends in that direction, he merely says one should hope for it (e.g. *Church Dogmatics* ii/2. 417–18).

[11] Jürgen Moltmann, *The Coming of God: Christian Eschatology* (SCM Press, London, 1996), 235–55. Moltmann expresses his belief that all will be saved much less ambiguously than either Barth or von Balthasar.

[12] Gustavo Gutiérrez, *A Theology of Liberation: History, Politics and Salvation*, 2nd edn. (SCM, London, 1988), ch. 9.

[13] Hans Urs Von Balthasar, *Pneuma und Institution* (Johannes Verlag, Einsiedeln, 1974) tr. in M. Kehl and W. Loser, (eds.) *The Von Balthasar Reader* (T & T Clark, Edinburgh, 1982); *Mysterium Paschale* (Ressourcement, T & T Clark, Edinburgh, 1990); *Dare We Hope 'That all Men be Saved'?* with *A Short Discourse on Hell* (Ignatius Press, San Francisco, 1988). Von Balthasar hopes for universal salvation and warns against asserting it outright (e.g. *Mysterium Paschale*, 177–8, 262–6; *Dare We Hope . . .*, 148–57, 236–54).

[14] John Hick, *Death and Eternal Life* (Collins, London, 1976), 242–61; *Evil and the God*

More recently, Keith Ward has explored universal salvation in the context not only of comparative religion but also of the cosmology and evolutionary theory of modern natural science.[15] Other writers have been more directly interested in the biblical evidence for the doctrine: J. A. T. Robinson's *In the End, God . . .* and Jan Bonda's *The One Purpose of God* are two good examples of the very different ways in which such a treatment of universal salvation can proceed.[16] Finally there are those eschatologies which, although not proposing universal salvation in a strict sense, not only emphasize a holistic approach but also have cosmic scope. They thus have affinities with some of the concerns of theologians who have asserted a more conventional doctrine of universal salvation. Most obviously, one can point to Teilhard de Chardin's famous conception of the Omega point,[17] but less frequently noted are the holistic and potentially universalistic elements in the treatments of eschatology by a few feminists[18] and some process theologians.[19]

of Love, 2nd edn. reissued with a new preface (Macmillan, Basingstoke, 1985), 341–5. Although Hick talks in terms of faith and hope, for him the salvation of all is a 'practical certainty' (*Evil and the God of Love*, 345).

[15] Keith Ward, *Religion and Creation* (Oxford University Press, Oxford, 1996), 261–5; *Religion and Human Nature* (Oxford University Press, Oxford, 1998), ch. 14. Although Ward asserts that one cannot guarantee that God's love will succeed in every case, he emphasizes that one can rightly hope and pray that it will and he excludes the possibility that '*all* free creatures should choose evil' (*Religion and Creation*, 265).

[16] J. A. T. Robinson, *In the End, God . . .* (James Clarke, London, 1950); Jan Bonda, *The One Purpose of God: An Answer to the Doctrine of Eternal Punishment* (Eerdmans, Grand Rapids, Mich.; Cambridge, 1998).

[17] Pierre Teilhard de Chardin, *The Phenomenon of Man* (Collins, London, 1959), *passim*; the idea of the Omega point seems to suggest universal salvation, although J. A. Lyons emphasizes that Teilhard thought that damnation was always a possibility: J. A. Lyons, *The Cosmic Christ in Origen and Teilhard de Chardin* (Oxford Theological Monographs, Oxford University Press, Oxford, 1982), 74.

[18] Rosemary Radford Ruether, *Sexism and God-Talk: Towards a Feminist Theology* (SCM, London, 1983), 250–8; see also her *Gaia and God: An Ecofeminist Theology of Earth Healing* (SCM, London, 1992), ch. 9 (in which she comments on both Teilhard and process theology). Ruether's eschatology emphasizes the unity of the whole world; all death is identification with 'that great matrix that supports the energy-matter of our individuated beings', 'the Holy Being into which our achievements and failures are gathered up, assimilated into the fabric of being, and carried forward into new possibilities' (*Sexism and God-Talk*, 256). Sallie McFague, while also emphasizing the unity and interconnectedness of creation, expresses more of a hope for redemption and transformation: Sallie McFague, *The Body of God: An Ecological Theology* (Fortress Press, Minneapolis, 1993), ch. 7.

[19] On process theology, see e.g. Norman Pittenger, *After Death, Life in God* (SCM, London, 1980), 72; A. N. Whitehead, *Process and Reality* (Cambridge University Press, Cambridge, 1958), 496–7; Charles Hartshorne, *Reality as Social Process* (Free Press, Illinois,

There is, however, by no means a consensus over the orthodoxy of the idea of universal salvation: its espousal by some theologians has provoked a variety of responses. This has perhaps been most evident in the evangelical tradition.[20] Evangelical discussions of universal salvation have led some to assert with renewed enthusiasm a position which is in effect double predestination, but which is usually referred to as the Reformed teaching.[21] Others continue to assert the reality of hell, but justify it not only by emphasizing the role of human free will but also sometimes by claiming that God's saving revelation will be presented at some stage or other, or in one form or other, to all people.[22] Thus they believe that all people will have the opportunity freely to respond to God and that those who do not do so deserve to go to hell. The notion of being in hell is sometimes mitigated either by taking it to mean psychological suffering or the pain of eternal separation from God (rather than a place of physical torture), or by asserting that those who do not turn to God will ultimately cease to exist.[23] A few evangelicals accept the doctrine of universal salvation, when expressed in terms of hope rather than prediction.[24]

1953), 41–2; Schubert Ogden, *The Reality of God* (Harper & Row, New York, 1963), 223, 226.

[20] A good range of evangelical views is to be found in Nigel M. de S. Cameron, *Universalism and the Doctrine of Hell.* Papers presented at the Fourth Edinburgh Conference in Christian Dogmatics, 1991 (Paternoster Press, Carlisle; Baker Book House, Grand Rapids, 1992) and in K. E. Brower and M. W. Elliot, (eds.) *'The Reader Must Understand': Eschatology in Bible and theology* (Apollos, an imprint of Inter-Varsity Press, Leicester, 1997). See also T. J. Gray, *Hell: An Analysis of Some Major Twentieth Century Attempts to Defend the Doctrine of Hell* (D. Phil. Thesis, University of Oxford, 1996) and Kendall J. Harmon, *Temporally Excluded from God? Some Twentieth Century Theological Explorations of the Problem of Hell and Universalism with Reference to the Historical Development of these Doctrines* (D. Phil. Thesis, University of Oxford, 1993) chs. 6 and 7.

[21] See Paul Helm, *The Last Things: Death, Judgment, Heaven and Hell* (Banner of Truth Trust, Edinburgh, 1989) and John Blanchard, *Whatever Happened to Hell?* (Evangelical Press, Durham, 1993).

[22] See John Sanders, *No Other Name: Can Only Christians be Saved?* (C. S. Lewis Centre, SPCK, London, 1994) chs. 5, 6, and 7.

[23] The view that those who do not choose for God will not live for ever is often known as conditional immortality—on the grounds that immortality is not natural, but conditional on God's grace, and will not be granted to all. This view is sometimes also known as 'annihilationism', although strictly speaking that word better applies to the view that humans are naturally immortal but that God will actively cause the wicked to cease existing. See, for example, John Wenham, 'The Case for Conditional Immortality', in Cameron, *Universalism and the Doctrine of Hell.*

[24] For example, Nigel Wright in *The Radical Evangelical* (Gospel and Culture, SPCK, London, 1996), chs. 3 and 7.

From this brief survey of the history of the idea of universal salvation it is plain that there are many currents and cross-currents within this one stream of eschatological thought and that various different sources flow into it along the way. Universalism is restricted to no particular denomination or wing of Christianity. It is connected to no single philosophical system. One may question whether it is fair to imply that it is one coherent 'stream' at all. This diversity, however, encourages the student of Christian doctrine to make comparisons: How has the idea changed? To what extent is its expression affected by the theological and cultural milieu? Whose arguments for it are the most convincing? This book intends to raise such questions by embarking on a comparative study of just two of the influential theologians who have examined the idea of universal salvation: Karl Rahner and Gregory of Nyssa. It will compare the ways in which each thinker deals with the theological and philosophical problems involved and will highlight which ones remain for future theologians to tackle.

The choice of one theologian from the patristic era and one from the twentieth century reflects the fact that these are the periods in which the concept of universal salvation has most freely been discussed, but it will also enable this study to examine how the idea has been treated in two very different cultural and philosophical contexts. Indeed, although there are twentieth-century theologians, such as Hans Urs von Balthasar, whose reflections on universalism have been directly influenced by patristic discussions, Karl Rahner has been chosen as a subject for this book precisely because his eschatology is not so closely related to the early debate. By comparing two theologians who have genuinely different methodologies and philosophical approaches, one can attempt two tasks. First, one can try to abstract the bare bones of a doctrine of universal salvation from the surrounding ideas with which it is expressed. If this is possible, one can then highlight this skeletal idea as that which has the strongest claim to be truly Christian. If two versions of Platonism, for example, reach the same sort of conclusions about universal salvation, it is easy to suppose that it is merely Platonism that is responsible, not reflection on Scripture and other sources of the Christian tradition. However, if two very different systems, both claiming to be Christian, pick out the same elements of a doctrine as important and truthful, then it is at least more likely that these ideas do indeed express something which is genuinely central to Christianity.

It is important, however, not to divorce any discussion of universalism entirely from its context. An examination of the different ways in which Gregory and Rahner treat universal salvation will be the foundation of the other task of this study: to assess the relative effectiveness of each in dealing with the problems associated with the idea. The conclusions arising from this comparison will raise a whole host of wider questions concerning the development of doctrine. If Rahner deals better with universalistic eschatology, is this because modern theology actually possesses a greater body of relevant information or uses better theological arguments? Or is it that patristic theology is out of date merely in its expression? Or, if it is Gregory who solves more satisfactorily some or all of the problems associated with the idea of universal salvation, why is this? In either case, what insights can modern theology draw from the patristic treatment of eschatology?

Despite the differences between them, there are also several affinities between Gregory and Rahner. Obviously it is important that both theologians are broadly sympathetic to the idea of the salvation of all things: Gregory of Nyssa expresses this more forthrightly than Rahner (who insists that it must only remain a hope, not an assertion), yet the acknowledgement by each thinker that it is at least a possibility and one which would accord with the Christian understanding of God's nature means that they both engage with the difficulties which this possibility raises.[25]

Secondly, both theologians approach eschatology with philosophical rigour. Despite using philosophy in a slightly different way from each other and being educated in different philosophical traditions, both men are certain that philosophy is a necessary theological tool—although of course secondary to

[25] Rahner's hope for universal salvation should not be underestimated: in an interview late in his life he revealed that he would have liked to have written something on universal salvation that was 'orthodox' and 'acceptable' (interview by Leo O'Donovan published as 'Living into Mystery: Karl Rahner's Reflections at 75', *America*, 10 March 1979, 179; cited in P. Phan, *Eternity in Time: A Study of Karl Rahner's Eschatology* (Susquehanna University Press, Selinsgrove; Associated University Press, London and Toronto, 1988), 153). See below Chapter 5, section B.

Scripture. Especially with regard to eschatology, both Gregory of Nyssa and Karl Rahner try to construct an anthropology which is not only fully Christian (based on Scripture and, in Rahner's case, Catholic teaching) but also philosophically acceptable. The philosophical expression of their theology is facilitated in each case by the fact that they shun a purely literal approach to exegesis: both have a sophisticated approach to scriptural interpretation, with their eyes more on the overall import of the Bible than on individual verses. This is particularly the case with Rahner, who cites biblical texts with much less frequency than Gregory; but even in his commentaries on Scripture Gregory is careful to interpret each verse in the context of the book, and indeed the Bible, as a whole. This is not to say that Scripture, tradition, and philosophy are perfectly blended in either case: for both men the fusion of these elements sometimes creates tensions in their thought, including in their reflections on eschatology.

Thirdly, neither Gregory nor Rahner writes about eschatology in a vacuum separate from the rest of his theology. Both theologians have a broadly systematic approach, although none of their works can be strictly described as a systematic theology. Gregory's *Catechetical Oration*, for instance, is too short to be considered a systematic expression of the whole of his theology; rather it sets out just the basics of the Christian faith in a form suitable for new believers. Nevertheless, although Gregory did not write any work which one can compare in style to a modern systematic theology, he was influenced by Origen's inclination to systematize and harmonize the elements of Christian tradition—particularly Scripture. Consequently, Gregory's work demonstrates a fundamental coherence, despite its wide range of topics and genres and despite the presence of contradictions and changes of direction over some particular ideas. The basic harmony is to be found even in his shorter *ad hominem* writings, allowing one to refer to these—and to Gregory's commentaries and homilies—as sources for his eschatological views with as much confidence as one cites his more obviously doctrinal works.

Karl Rahner's work on Christian doctrine for the most part takes the form of short articles and is very different from the systematic writings of a theologian like Barth. Despite the fact that his theological interests are very wide-ranging, and despite the fact that he too often directed himself to the solution of a very particular theological problem, there is a coherence to Rahner's thought and patterns of development can be traced within it. Like Gregory he wrote what might be described as a handbook of Christian theology: the *Foundations of Christian Faith.* This work is much longer, more complex and intended for a more theologically-aware readership than Gregory's *Catechetical Oration*, nevertheless both works are best seen as summaries of the grounds for Christian faith, rather than full-scale systematic theologies which express the last word of the author on every doctrine.

The fact that they write for a more general audience as well as for their more specialized theological contemporaries is a reminder that these two theologians, both ordained priests, in no way treat theology as a purely intellectual discipline. Both men took part in an important ecumenical church council—Gregory at the Second Ecumenical Council in Constantinople (381) and Rahner at the Second Vatican Council (1962–5, regarded as ecumenical by the Roman Catholic Church, at least). Although eschatology itself was not on the agenda of the former and only one topic among very many at the latter, the involvement of each theologian in such events shows their willingness to discuss theology in a public forum. Nevertheless, Rahner was not interested in church high politics for their own sake and Gregory was certainly a very reluctant churchman in that respect. Furthermore, both had a somewhat ambivalent relationship with church authority: Gregory underwent exile because of the influence of the opposing party in the Arian disputes, and Rahner more than once met the disapproval of the Vatican. Neither was loyal to the church establishment *per se*, but rather to what they regarded as the truth of the Church's faith: both seem to share an overriding desire to see church doctrine clarified for the ordinary believer. This desire connects closely with their pastoral concerns. Rahner not only paid great attention to pastoral duties throughout his life, but wrote much on spirituality and often focused an article on a specific pastoral problem. There is little evidence about Gregory's life as a priest and bishop (besides his clear unsuitability for ecclesiastical administration); however, his homilies too show a concern for the spiritual welfare of his readers and there are glimpses of more specific concerns.

Finally, one of the most important factors which unites Gregory of Nyssa and Karl Rahner is their attitude to writing theology. Rahner's approach to eschatology is to reinterpret doctrines with two aims in mind: first to pick out the essential aspects of the doctrine (and if necessary to set aside those non-essential elements which are misleading) and secondly to express them in a way which is relevant to the modern believer and which engages with secular issues and ideologies. Doctrines develop, Rahner believes, not in their essence, but in their expression; hence he attempts innovatory expression, whilst remaining within the bounds of orthodoxy.

Gregory, like Rahner, has an exploratory instinct in his theology. He, of course, lived in an era in which orthodoxy—particularly in eschatology—was much less well-defined; nevertheless, there are clearly some interpretations of Christian doctrine to which he feels especially committed and some pressures upon him to conform to others. The result is not a slavish following of any particular party line (at least in respect of eschatology), but writings in which speculative theology is employed with great creativity within certain boundaries. So, for example, although Gregory is indebted to Origen for much of his eschatological thought and shares his love of speculation, he rejects both the idea of the pre-existence of souls and Origen's interpretation of the resurrection. Gregory also introduces innovatory concepts of his own, such as the idea of the two creations, and he is constantly seeking to express traditional Christian beliefs in a new way which will be more illuminating for his readership. (This aim is evident, for example, in his frequent use of scientific analogies.)

It is clear that whereas Rahner is consciously attempting to renew theology within the bounds of orthodoxy, Gregory shows no signs of having such a task explicitly in mind. Nevertheless, both are engaged in the same project: to express Christian eschatology in the most convincing, relevant, and meaningful way possible to their audience. This, of course, immediately raises the question of how convincing, relevant, and meaningful their respective discussions of eschatology are to today's reader—one of the questions which this book will seek to answer.

Before beginning a comparative study of Gregory and Rahner, it will be useful first to clarify the problems associated with the idea of universal salvation. The first difficulty is that the claim that God will save the whole world is far from being obviously true, if it is true at all. Scripture is notoriously inconclusive on the matter: whichever side one takes in the issue of universalism there are difficult passages which require explanation.[26] Alternatively, one must accept that inconsistencies in the scriptural evidence cannot be perfectly resolved.

Some biblical passages emphasize a division between the blessed and the rest of humanity; hence, the history of Christian eschatology in both the Catholic and the Protestant churches has long been dominated by a dualistic conception of heaven and hell. This comprises two fundamental assertions: first, that after judgement (whether that is immediate upon the individual's death, or is a general judgement following the resurrection) some will go to heaven and others to hell, and, secondly, that this division is permanent. If there were the possibility of repentance after death (or indeed a second Fall), this strictly dualistic scheme would break down. Although some theologians have asserted degrees of bliss in heaven and varying punishment in hell according to individual merit, this does nothing to break down the fundamental division between heaven and hell. Similarly, although the Catholic doctrine of purgatory might appear to blunt the sharp edges of the division between the blessed and the damned by suggesting that some will suffer only temporarily before entering heaven, even this concept relies upon a rigid distinction between those who will enter heaven (either immediately or eventually) and those who are damned from the moment they die.

However, the biblical support for the dualistic view has been questioned. There are other biblical passages—notably Paul's

[26] John Hick surveys such passages (*Death and Eternal Life*, 243–50) distinguishing those which mention punishment in general (e.g. Luke 6: 23–4; Matt. 23: 14; 5: 26; 18: 34–5) from those which refer specifically to eternal punishment (Matt. 25: 41, 46; John 3: 36; 5: 29; probably Mark 3: 29 and parallels, and possibly Matt. 25: 30). He suggests that 1 Cor. 15: 22; Rom. 5: 18; 11: 32; Eph. 1: 10; 1 Tim. 2: 4 point to universalism. Jan Bonda argues for universal salvation both from the general direction of Scripture (e.g. the stories of Abraham and Moses, Jesus Christ as the revelation of a compassion Father) and from a detailed study of the Epistle to the Romans, emphasizing Rom. 5: 18 (Bonda, *The One Purpose of God*, chs. 2–8).

words in 1 Corinthians 15—which seem to suggest that God's ultimate plan is the salvation of the whole world. Those who argue for the overriding importance of these passages often assert that references to the division between saints and sinners refer only to divine judgement, not punishment, or else to a finite period of punishment, not an eternal existence in hell. Many argue that those biblical words usually translated 'eternal' do not mean everlasting, but extremely long or of ultimate importance: the terms stress the seriousness and significance of God's judgement, rather than its permanence. In other words, they are challenging not the belief that divine judgement will divide humanity, but the belief that this division is permanent.

Those who argue for universal salvation often appeal to two other types of evidence besides Scripture. One is theological evidence of a general kind, such as the doctrine of God's nature and of the incarnation. For example, it might be argued that if God is perfectly good and perfectly powerful, it follows that he will not allow part of his creation to be punished for ever (or annihilated), even if it is thought to deserve it. Thus the doctrine of eternal hell is criticized for emphasizing God's justice to the exclusion of his mercy: Is everlasting retribution coherent with the nature of a God whose essence is declared to be love? If, by contrast, hell is seen as a *reformative* punishment, then it might be more in keeping with the divine nature which wills and is able to achieve good in everything. As a matter of logic, if an omnipotent God sets out to reform people in hell, hell cannot be thought of as eternal. Furthermore, there are theological problems not only with the eternity of hell, but with the nature of the original division: in its extreme form, when dualistic eschatology is coupled with a doctrine of double predestination, God's judgement might be seen as arbitrary rather than just. On the other hand, when merit (either in the form of moral virtue or in the form of faith) is cited as the factor which divides the blessed from the damned, one might well ask whether individuals in all their variety are simply too heterogeneous a group to be divided neatly into two. Finally, it has occasionally been claimed not only that Christ died in order that all *could* be saved, but that the *actual* effect of his death and resurrection is that all will in fact be saved. These points, although usually derived from Scripture, are better described as general theological considerations, rather than direct scriptural warrant for universal salvation.

A further sort of evidence is more philosophical; for example, some argue that evil is necessarily impermanent. Again, there are arguments based on the nature of punishment: some have argued (sometimes with an eye to human administration of justice) that the only justification for punishment is reform. Others have affirmed a retributive justification of punishment with its notion of proportionality, but have denied the traditional argument that all sin against God is infinite and thus deserves a punishment of infinite duration.

Beyond the issues of the truth of universal salvation and the grounds for asserting it lies a further problem: if all will be saved, *how* will they be saved? The problem may be set out systematically as follows. Broadly speaking, Christian theologians have answered the question of what is necessary for human salvation in three ways: an emphasis primarily on free conscious decision (faith), or on moral effort (good works, moral purity), or on God's grace. Theologies which emphasize the importance of the individual's relationship to God tend to stress either faith or works, and theologies which place more value in the collective relationship of humanity to God stress God's grace. In fact, most theologians have tried to achieve a balance between the three elements, but despite this a tendency to emphasize one aspect rather than another is frequently evident. The implications of such a bias are particularly problematic when it is universal salvation that is being discussed. For example, the insistence upon faith—if it means that each individual must knowingly and freely make a decision for God—creates a specific problem for universalism, for, besides those who appear not to have decided for God in their lifetime, there are others who seem never to have had even the opportunity to make such a decision (for example infants who die shortly after birth, or people with a severe mental or psychological handicap). A believer in universal salvation could claim that a decision can be made after death; however this suggestion would run contrary to most teaching in both the Catholic and Protestant churches, largely because the possibility of a decision after death has been commonly thought to diminish the importance of this life (in both its positive and negative aspects), making it seem merely an ante-room to life after death. The notion of a decision after death has also often been ruled by those who consider that a decision (i.e. a mental change) is logically incompatible with the supposedly traditional Christian notion of life after death as a timelessly eternal (i.e. changeless) state. The theologian who asserts the salvation of all must therefore investigate these philosophical issues of decision in relation to death and time.

A second answer to the question 'if all will be saved, how will they be saved?' is to claim that it is primarily moral purity and not faith which matters. In the past, this view has often been attributed to ascetic movements; it now has a certain appeal for those modern theologians who want to assert the possibility of the salvation of those who are either not Christian or not religious at all. However, an excessive emphasis on moral purity, which conveys the impression that humans *earn* salvation and seems to devalue divine grace, has been unattractive to most Christian theologians, especially after Augustine's attack on Pelagius and the condemnation of Pelagianism at several church councils.[27] (An emphasis on decision tries to avoid this problem by seeing it more as a *response* to God's grace, not the *cause* of being awarded it.) For a universalist, an emphasis on moral effort carries with it the additional problem that many people seem to have grave moral failings: either universalism must affirm the possibility of moral development after death (again causing problems regarding change and timelessness) or assert that the level of moral effort required is so minimal that all have already achieved it. The latter option seems to be both improbable and offensive: it would suggest that even those who died unrepentant of the greatest cruelty need not change in order to be saved, would make a nonsense of the notion of divine judgement and would leave humanity with no theologically based moral criteria—for if all types of behaviour are ultimately acceptable to God, how are humans to make meaningful ethical distinctions between them?

[27] Pelagius and Celestius were condemned by the African bishops in 416; Celestius was condemned by the 3rd Ecumenical Council at Ephesus in 431. (F. L. Cross and E. A. Livingstone (eds.), *The Oxford Dictionary of the Christian Church*, 3rd edn. (Oxford University Press, Oxford, 1997), 'Pelagianism'.)

A third possible answer to the question of how all people will be saved is to take a collective approach: in other words to assert that personal action and faith are insignificant with regard to salvation, because individuals are saved (through God's grace) by virtue of being part of humanity as a whole. The obvious objection to this is that it appears to diminish the intrinsic value of each person by suggesting that God does not care for humans as individuals. It also appears to deny humans the freedom to affect their ultimate destiny; although this is not the only sort of human freedom, it has been commonly supposed to be very valuable. Furthermore, the suggestion that humans will be saved *en masse* raises questions about what else might be saved. For if the criterion for salvation is no longer personal decision or moral worth, but merely membership of a biological species, then it is not clear why salvation should be restricted to humans alone. Given that the ability to make decisions or act morally is no longer relevant, why should not other animals or inanimate matter be saved? Thus the argument that the salvation of the whole of humanity is less arbitrary than the gracious election of a few is weakened by this counter-argument which points out that the choice of the human species is equally arbitrary. On the other hand, if the whole of the universe is saved this might be said to weaken the significance of salvation, levelling out the meaning of the word to the lowest common denominator of all its possible applications and ruling out, for example, the concept of salvation as a fulfilled spiritual and personal relationship with God.

In sum, the question of *how* all people will be saved leads to a complex theological discussion of human nature: its freedom, knowledge, ethical character, temporal condition, and relation to the rest of the world. The question of *whether* all people will be saved, on the other hand, raises difficult issues regarding the nature of God, revelation, scriptural exegesis, and the use of philosophy. The following chapters will examine the eschatologies of Gregory of Nyssa and Karl Rahner in their respective contexts in order to discover exactly what each writes about universal salvation and to assess how well each responds to the problems outlined above. The concluding chapter will compare their responses and will return to the more fundamental questions raised by this Introduction: is the idea of universal salvation a truly Christian one? Are we now in a better position to deal with the concept? What can we learn from patristic writers such as Gregory? What difficulties remain?

Gregory of Nyssa

1

Gregory of Nyssa's Eschatology in Context

A. THE LIFE OF GREGORY OF NYSSA (c.335–95)[1]

Gregory of Nyssa's early development was shaped by both pagan and Christian influences. His grandmother was a convert of Gregory Thaumaturgus and several members of Gregory's family were not only Christians but entered the priesthood or a monastic community. Gregory himself was particularly indebted to his sister Macrina for Christian spiritual teaching, referring to her as 'teacher' (διδάσκαλος).[2] His work, the *Life of Macrina*, perhaps exaggerates the effect she had over the religious lives of her family, but it does give some indication both of this remarkable woman's influence and of the sort of Christian environment in which Gregory grew up. With regard to pagan influences, it seems that Gregory was not educated in Athens like his brother Basil and Gregory of Nazianzus; in fact, he once claims that he had no teachers other than Basil and 'Paul and John and the rest of the Apostles and prophets'.[3] This indicates the degree to which he felt indebted to Basil for his

[1] For the historical background to Gregory's life and works, see Anthony Meredith, *The Cappadocians* (Outstanding Christian Thinkers Series, Geoffrey Chapman, London, 1995), chs. 1 and 2; and id., *Gregory of Nyssa* (Early Church Fathers, Routledge, London, 1999), Introduction, esp. 1–6.

[2] See: *De anima et resurrectione* (= *De an.*): Oehler, 319: 7 (The editor is referred to as Oehler by Altenburger and Mann in their *Bibliographie zu Gregor von Nyssa*, although he is named as Dehler in some other literature.) The dialogue form of the treatise mirrors that of the *Phaedo* and Macrina's role parallels that of Socrates: the teacher explains the reasons for serenity in the face of death to grieving friends. Her authoritative role also echoes that of Diotima in Plato's *Symposium*. The word διδάσκαλος is also used by Gregory to refer to Basil.

[3] Gregory's comment must be treated with caution because it is an excuse for paying an elaborately constructed compliment to Libanius, Basil's former tutor: 'for if Basil was the author of our oratory, and if his wealth came from your treasures, then what we possess is yours, even though we received it through others' (*Letter to Libanius*: *NPNF* v. 533: Letter 10).

education, but is surely an exaggeration, for Gregory's works show much erudition and in particular a more impressive grasp of pagan philosophy than Basil's do. His writings also show that he was strongly influenced by pagan intellectual culture in general and his friendly correspondence with the pagan Libanius reveals an openness to those of his contemporaries who were not Christians.

Although his general background is clear, specific events in Gregory's life are difficult to pin-point with accuracy. Ordained bishop of Nyssa by Basil, *c.*371, he was later deposed and forced into exile *c.*375 by opponents of the Nicene formula; he returned about three years later. It has been argued that at one stage in the decade before his consecration as bishop he left the Church to pursue rhetoric as a career, but this is uncertain, as is the question of when (or indeed whether) he married. The general consensus is that he was more fitted to theology and oratory than to the administrative and political demands of a career in the Church—a view shared even by his own brother who consecrated him.[4] Accordingly, the highlights of his career were his contribution to the Second Ecumenical Council at Constantinople, which reaffirmed the Nicene Trinitarian formula and, most of all, the production of his writings, many of which were first delivered as sermons or speeches.

B. PHILOSOPHY, MYSTICISM, AND EXEGESIS

Gregory writes in a variety of genres: treatises, commentaries, homilies, sermons and letters. Even the treatises differ in style—for example: dialogue, extended comment on one verse of Scripture or one narrow dogmatic point, and systematic defence of orthodoxy.[5] However, running through this variety there is a similarity of theme: an unshakeable belief in the infinity of God's nature and a consequent emphasis on divine incomprehensibility, the ultimately all-pervasive quality of God's goodness and the infinity of the journey of the soul towards the divine. In

[4] J. Quasten, *Patrology*, iii: *The Golden Age of Patristic Literature* (Newman Press, Westminster, Md., 1960), 255 ff.

[5] For example, *De anima et resurrectione*; *In illud: tunc et ipse Filius*; *De infantibus praemature abreptis*; and *Contra Eunomium*, respectively.

homilies the latter theme is often connected with Gregory's encouragement to his audience to pursue virtue, that is to perfect the soul. All of these themes are central to his eschatology and will be discussed in the following chapters.

Partly because of the diverse genres in which Gregory writes, however, it is difficult to gain a coherent overview of the style of his theology. In particular, it is tempting to view him as either a 'Christian philosopher', or a 'mystical writer', when in fact his theology—and above all his eschatology—unites the two.

It is immediately clear that Gregory is greatly influenced by pagan philosophy and this is particularly evident in treatises such as *Contra Eunomium* and *De anima et resurrectione.* There are two questions which are raised by Gregory's use of such philosophy, however: first, the question of whether he is a philosopher or a theologian, and secondly, the more specific problem of which pagan philosophy, if any, is dominant. With regard to the latter question, the greatest pagan influence on Gregory of Nyssa was certainly Plato (and later forms of Platonism). Gregory makes use of quasi-religious as well as strictly philosophical Platonic concepts: of particular importance for Gregory's eschatology are Plato's image of the soul rising to God as its proper goal and his idea that this rise required effort and that the effort involved both moral and intellectual growth.[6] Moreover, the dependence on Plato is not only conceptual but literary, the most obvious example being the echoing of the *Phaedo* in the form, subject-matter, and setting of Gregory's treatise *De anima et resurrectione.*[7] As this parallelism suggests, Gregory must have read at least some of Plato's works in their entirety although he may also have used later commentaries or compilations.[8]

Some of the Platonic concepts in Gregory, however, are filtered through the writings of later Platonists. In particular, one may point to Plotinus: his themes of the dependence of all creation upon God and the purification (κάθαρσις) of the soul are

[6] See Meredith, *The Cappadocians*, 12; Harold F. Cherniss, 'The Platonism of Gregory of Nyssa', in J. T. Allen, H. C. Nutting, and H. R. W. Smith (eds.), *University of California Publications in Classical Philology,* xi: *1930–3* (University of California Press, Berkeley, Calif., 1934), 47; W. Jaeger, *Two Rediscovered Works of Ancient Christian Literature: Gregory of Nyssa and Macarius* (Brill, Leiden, 1954), 73–9.

[7] See n. 2.

[8] Cherniss, 'The Platonism of Gregory of Nyssa', *passim*, but esp. 20.

important motifs in Gregory's work.[9] Gregory seems also to have been influenced by Plotinus' mysticism.[10] Scholars disagree as to whether Gregory had read the *Enneads* himself, but von Balthasar points out at least one instance in which Gregory echoes a Plotinian model closely, which would suggest a fairly close familiarity with the work.[11] It is likely that Gregory was also influenced by other Neoplatonists and in particular by their exegetical theory—a point which will be discussed later.[12]

The Greek philosophical influence in Gregory is not merely Platonic, or Neoplatonic, however. He often uses Stoic language, sometimes with its original connotations, sometimes changing its meaning to fit it to Christian doctrine. For example, he uses Stoic words for the unity of the cosmos—συμφωνία, συμπάθεια, συμπνοία—either to affirm the unity of the universe itself or to express the unity of the body of Christ, of the Church, of the good, and eschatological unity foreshadowed in the cross.[13] In his specifically Christian usage of these words he is perhaps deliberately surprising the reader, or it may be that in his day the words had lost their specific Stoic association. Gregory's attitude to Aristotle is more ambiguous: his terminology is sometimes echoed, but Aristotelianism in general is condemned by its association with Eunomius.[14] In the *Contra Eunomium* Gregory asserts that he can understand Aristotle and Epicurus better than his opponent and his arguments against pagan views elsewhere certainly show that he was concerned to understand those Greek

[9] See Casimir McCambley, Introduction to his translation of *St. Gregory of Nyssa: Commentary on the Song of Songs* (Hellenic College Press, Brookline, Mass., 1987), 9, where he cites *Enneads* 4. 7, 4. 9, 5.4.1. (on dependence) and 1. 6. 5. (on κάθαρσις). For suggestions that Gregory drew on aspects of Plotinus' philosophy which were different from previous Platonist thought see Frances Young, 'Adam and Anthropos', *Vigiliae Christianae* 37 (1983), 119; and Cherniss, 'The Platonism of Gregory of Nyssa', 26.

[10] See Hans Urs von Balthasar, *Presence and Thought: An Essay on the Religious Thought of Gregory of Nyssa*, tr. Mark Sebanc (Communio Books, Ignatius Press, San Francisco, 1995), 16–17; and Colin Macleod, 'Allegory and Mysticism in Origen and Gregory of Nyssa' in his *Collected Essays* (Oxford University Press, Oxford, 1983).

[11] Daniélou is certain that Gregory had read the *Enneads*; Cherniss is less sure: Jean Daniélou, *L'être et le temps chez Grégoire de Nysse* (Brill, Leiden, 1970), p. vii; Cherniss, 'The Platonism of Gregory of Nyssa', 61. Von Balthasar: 'Plotinus' famous image of the "heliomorphic" eye is taken up by Gregory' (*Presence and Thought*, 114).

[12] See below p. 29.

[13] McCambley, Introduction to *St. Gregory of Nyssa: Commentary on the Song of Songs*, 10 f; Paulos Mar Gregorios, *Cosmic Man: The Divine Presence: The Theology of Gregory of Nyssa* (A New Era Book, Paragon House, N.Y., 1988), 10 f.

[14] Cherniss, 'The Platonism of Gregory of Nyssa', 6.

philosophical ideas which he clearly did not agree with.[15] It is important to stress, however, that he only rejects specific views, not Hellenistic philosophy as a whole. When he addresses the question of the value of pagan learning, it is clear that Gregory usually thinks that some of it has intrinsic value and he once claims that even the worst can serve as a means to a good end, that is, true faith.[16]

In addition to these strictly philosophical sources, Gregory is familiar with some pagan scientific works: he often uses astronomical or technical phenomena as illustrative examples or analogies—almost, it seems, in a self-conscious effort to prove his erudition. But he is also interested in scientific questions at a more serious level. For example, in his eschatological discussions he deals both with human anatomy and with the relation of soul to body (with regard to the resurrection of the body) and wider cosmological issues.[17] He affirms the value of pagan scientific learning whilst seeing it as an entirely human enterprise (and thus implicitly regarding it as inferior to revelation).[18]

Thus, although Gregory's primary philosophical influence was Platonism, he made wide use of other philosophical and scientific concepts. Because of this diversity Gregory has been described (sometimes dismissively) as an eclectic; this is unfair, if by 'eclectic' one means someone whose philosophy is a casual miscellany of others. That he uses vocabulary from a variety of philosophical schools was in fact typical of his day: in Jaeger's words, 'Gregory speaks the common philosophical language of late ancient philosophy, but that does not make him an "eclectic"'.[19] Certainly Gregory is a slavish follower of no

[15] This is apparent in *De anima et resurrectione*, for example, in which Macrina argues against Epicurus for the immortality of the soul (*NPNF* v. 432; Oehler, 322) and against unnamed pagan philosophers for the resurrection of the body (*NPNF* v. 453 ff; Oehler, 356 ff).

[16] The most famous example is *De vita Moysis*: Malherbe and Ferguson, ii: 115. Cherniss cites others: 'The Platonism of Gregory of Nyssa', 1 and 10, including the comment about the worst of pagan philosophy from Gregory's *De vita b. Gregorii Thaumaturgi* (*PG* 46, 901a–b).

[17] See Young, 'Adam and Anthropos'; and W. Telfer, 'The Birth of Christian Anthropology', *Journal of Theological Studies* n.s. 13 (1962) for Gregory's use of science in *De hominis opificio*. In *De anima et resurrectione* Gregory uses such analogies from, for example, medical diagnosis, from the waxing and the waning of the moon (both *NPNF* v. 434; Oehler, 325–6), and the functioning of a water-organ (*NPNF* v. 435; Oehler, 328).

[18] See Mar Gregorios, *Cosmic Man*, 5.

[19] W. Jaeger, *Two Rediscovered Works*, 80.

single philosophical school: indeed, his use of a broad range of reference is very creative and was perhaps also aimed at encouraging respect for the author in his readers.[20] Ultimately, the factor which makes Gregory neither a 'Platonist' nor an 'eclectic' is a coherent nucleus of theological views most of which are directly dependent on Scripture.[21] Philosophical and scientific language is used when he attempts to express this theological nucleus systematically and comprehensibly. Gregory's use of scientific language in particular reinforces this view: it is used to press home, illustrate, or expand upon a theological point, not to prove it. It also may have served in an apologetic function: so for example, when he discusses the resurrection of the body in the *De anima et resurrectione* he attempts a scientific explanation of how such a resurrection might be possible; his belief in the resurrection, however, is firmly grounded in biblical texts such as 1 Corinthians 15. There are indeed differences between the ways in which Gregory uses scientific and philosophical language: the former is most often used for illustration, frequently in the form of analogies, whereas the latter usually has a straightforward literal sense and is employed in an unselfconscious manner which suggests that it was the natural means of expression for scholars at that time. But one can say that Scripture is the foundation of all Gregory's thought and that he used both philosophical and scientific concepts to express, clarify, explain, and (to a certain extent) systematize it. So—to answer our earlier question—Gregory is above all a theologian: attempts to see him as a philosopher usually end up frustrated by his lack of philosophical 'system'.[22]

Whereas some of his works, like the *Contra Eunomium*, give an

[20] This breadth of reference may be due to the influence of Origen, who was also noted for his wide learning: see J. W. Trigg, *Origen* (SCM Press, London, 1985), 244.

[21] Cf. *De an.*: *NPNF* v. 439; Oehler, 333: 22–4; 'we make the Holy Scriptures the rule and the measure of every tenet; we necessarily fix our eyes upon that, and approve that alone which may be made to harmonise with the intention of those writings' (cited by Mar Gregorios, *Cosmic Man*, 3).

[22] See, for example, Cherniss, who praises Gregory as 'the most learned and subtlest thinker of the Church', but castigates him for his timidity in always choosing orthodox Christian views when they clashed with philosophy. Such timorousness led, according to Cherniss, to contradictory views, although for the most part 'Gregory has merely applied Christian names to Plato's doctrine and called it Christian theology' ('The Platonism of Gregory of Nyssa', 62). Most other commentators see theology as more important than this in Gregory's writings—and view it more positively.

impression of Gregory as a 'Christian philosopher', some others, like *The Life of Moses*, are often referred to as 'mystical' works. However, this is misleading in two ways: it wrongly suggests that there are two distinct aspects to Gregory's writings and that he writes explicitly about his own spiritual experience or gives exercises in contemplation. While there is a strong didactic element to his theology, it is ethical not technical, consisting in encouraging virtue which he considers necessary for the soul's advance towards God. It is this advance which is the heart of Gregory's so-called 'mystical' writings and he is more interested in the theological and philosophical framework of the soul's progress than in how one might achieve a mystical experience and what that might feel like. (For this reason, writings which deal with the theme of the soul's progress towards God will be described in this book as 'spiritual', rather than 'mystical', writings.) As *The Life of Moses* demonstrates, the soul advances throughout—and indeed beyond—its lifetime and not merely in occasional moments of contemplation.

In this context, the eschatological importance of Gregory's writings on the soul becomes clear. If the progress is a necessary aspect of the salvation of the individual, then the possibility of all souls making this progress becomes the condition for the salvation of all people. In addition, Gregory's description of the eschaton is dependent on his concept of the soul's perpetual progress: because God is infinite and the human soul finite, the latter can never reach the former; hence Gregory's concept of heaven is not static but dynamic. Doctrines such as the infinity of God's nature arise in Gregory's thought through Scripture and through *theological* debate (in this case his encounter with Eunomius) and not, it seems, out of Gregory's own mystical experience.[23] Just as theology, and ultimately Scripture, is the key to Gregory's apparently philosophical works, so it is also for his spiritual writings.

Since Scripture is Gregory's criterion for the veracity of doctrine it is most important to understand his approach to it. In the prologue to his homilies on the Song of Songs Gregory admits that his method of exegesis is contentious and defends it on the grounds that it is not arbitrary but is aimed at drawing a

[23] See Meredith, *The Cappadocians*, 78–9, citing Langerbeck in agreement on this point.

useful meaning from the text.[24] He does not denigrate the literal meaning of Scripture, but rejects it only when it is immoral, logically or practically impossible, or incoherent with the rest of theology.[25] For justification he turns to Scripture itself: in particular to examples of non-literal exegesis from the practice of Jesus (particularly the parables and his new interpretations of the Law) and of Paul.[26] With the air of someone who is tired with debates over the minutiae of terminology, Gregory seems unwilling to draw close distinctions between different sorts of non-literal methods of exegesis in order to reject some and keep others: rather, 'immaterial and spiritual interpretations' in general are valid (when no literal reading is possible) for they are used within Scripture themselves.[27] He also explicitly acknowledges Origen as the source of this approach to exegesis.[28]

In addition other general assumptions guide Gregory's exegesis, whether it be literal or not. Most importantly he believes that all parts of Scripture are God-inspired and have something important to say: he follows some previous exegetes in countering the suggestion that the Old Testament has an inferior status to the New, or is not divinely inspired at all.[29] Secondly, when Gregory comments on a particular book of the Bible in depth (for example the Psalms and the Song of Songs), he treats each as a coherent whole with a single aim (*skopos*)—usually the encouragement of the reader to rise to God by means of virtue.[30] Heine

[24] *In cant.*, Prologue: *GNO* vi. 4–5. Gregory was probably defending himself against exegetes of the Antiochene school: see Ronald E. Heine, 'Gregory of Nyssa's Apology for Allegory', *Vigiliae Christianae* 38 (1984), 366–8.

[25] Heine cites Monique Alexandre as finding four criteria in the prologue—theological impropriety, physical\logical impossibility, immorality, uselessness—however, the last of these seems to be Gregory's main criterion and the other three explanations of what is not useful. Heine, 'Gregory of Nyssa's Apology for Allegory', 360, citing Monique Alexandre, 'La théorie d'exégèse dans le De Hominis Opificio et l'In Hexameron', in M. Harl (ed.), *Écriture et culture philosophique dans la pensée de Grégoire de Nysse* (Brill, Leiden, 1971).

[26] *In cant.*, Prologue: *GNO* vi. 5–6 (Paul) and 8–10 (Jesus Christ).

[27] *In cant.*, Prologue: *GNO* vi. 4–6. Some members of the Antiochene school of exegesis rejected certain forms of non-literal exegesis, e.g. allegory, but accepted some higher level of meaning which they called *theoria*. Gregory, however, uses *theoria* for non-literal meaning in general. See Manlio Simonetti, *Biblical Interpretation in the Early Church*, tr. John A. Hughes, ed. Anders Bergquist and Markus Bockmuehl (T & T Clark, Edinburgh, 1994), ch. 3, §4; also Heine, 'Gregory of Nyssa's Apology for Allegory', 368.

[28] *In cant.*, Prologue: *GNO* vi. 12.

[29] See *In cant.*, Prologue, passim. See Simonetti, *Biblical Interpretation* on Clement of Alexandria and Philo (p. 35) and on Origen (p. 39).

[30] See, for example, *In insc. pss.*: Heine, 83 (1. 1); *GNO* v. 24: 'For you enjoined us to

suggests that this sort of exegesis is indebted to Iamblichus, whose method is described in words which could equally apply to Gregory's own technique:

[it is a] consideration of the larger significative perspective of the text which yields the more profound meaning of the text. . . . It consists in seeing how a particular passage in a text relates to the whole and how the passage ought to be evaluated philosophically.[31]

Thirdly, it is not just the coherence and single purpose of a text which is significant for Gregory but the order:

well does the divine Scripture of the Psalter point the way to [the truly good] for us through a skilful and natural sequence in teaching . . . by setting forth systematically in various and diverse forms the method for acquiring the blessing.[32]

Hence, some of Gregory's works which appear at first sight to be commentaries do not progress through detailed line-by-line remarks on the text, but rather in a more discursive fashion draw from the words a meaning which is always related to the central *skopos* and to the progression of the text.[33] The result is that Gregory's 'commentaries' are more correctly to be seen as ordered sets of homilies on a key topic. This feature of Gregory's exegesis is particularly important in relation to eschatology: the rise of the soul to God through virtue is a central eschatological theme and the emphasis on the importance of order in the text means that he often sees a text as indicating the progress of the soul from its current state to its final eschatological state. As a result, the conclusions of his writings on the inscriptions of the Psalms and on the Song of Songs are particularly important sources for his eschatology.[34]

investigate the meaning to be observed in these inscriptions, so that their capacity to lead us to virtue might be obvious to all.'

[31] Heine, Introduction to *Gregory of Nyssa's Treatise on the Inscriptions of the Psalms*, 34. Like Gregory after him, Iamblichus called this method *theoria*.

[32] *In insc. pss.*: Heine, 84 (I. 7); ; *GNO* v. 26; see also ibid.: Heine, 83 (I. 3); *GNO* v. 24–5. The same emphasis on order or *akolouthia* is also evident in Gregory's use of logical or historical arguments. See Meredith, *The Cappadocians*, 54; Mar Gregorios, *Cosmic Man*, ch. 3, esp. §3 (pp. 57–61) on Scripture.

[33] Gregory's work on the life of Moses, although it is not based on a single book of the Bible, nevertheless shows a similar preoccupation with the theme of the ascent of the soul and with the order of the text.

[34] It is curious that although both of these works are unfinished, in the sense that they have not covered the whole biblical book, they both end on an eschatological note.

In his treatises, Gregory uses Scripture in a very different way. He rarely embarks on an extended commentary on a text,[35] but uses short biblical passages to establish the truth of a doctrine, or to elucidate a particular point. Frequently, parts of key eschatological texts are used to remind the reader of the wider import of that text—for instance, the phrase 'God will be all in all' recalls the whole of 1 Corinthians 15. In relation to Gregory's eschatology, the latter text is, for obvious reasons, a favourite; he refers also to other Pauline passages, to the Gospels (particularly John) and to the Psalms. Gregory's use of Scripture in the treatises will become clearer through the discussion of his eschatology in the following chapters.

C. PATRISTIC ESCHATOLOGY

Christian eschatological beliefs appear to have been very fluid in the first four centuries of this era. Although it makes sense to say that Gregory of Nyssa's doctrine of universal salvation is at odds with what was later regarded as orthodox eschatology, it is by no means possible to say with certainty that it was regarded as heterodox in his own day. However, it does seem that there were two broad types of eschatology by the time that Gregory was writing: a brief outline of each will follow.

The first type of eschatology is dualistic. Systematic expressions of this view can be found in those theologians of the second century who envisaged that the just would live in eternal bliss and the unjust in eternal damnation.[36] There was some confusion over the timing of the judgement: as the parousia came to be expected less imminently, so there appeared the idea of a judgement immediately after death or a double judgement (after death for the individual and upon the resurrection for mankind as a whole—sometimes accompanied by a conception of an 'interim state' the character of which depended on one's virtue). Already the tension between an individual and a universal perspective was becoming evident. The second-century

[35] Unless a particular text is the object of a treatise, e.g. *In illud: tunc. . . .*

[36] For accounts of eschatology of this period see J. N. D. Kelly, *Early Christian Doctrines* (A&C Black, London, 1958), ch. 17; and Brian Daley, *The Hope of the Early Church: A Handbook of Patristic Eschatology* (Cambridge University Press, Cambridge, 1991), ch. 2.

apologists were particularly concerned to combat Platonist ideas of the inherent immortality of the soul and its superiority over the body. They therefore stressed the God-given unity of man as soul and body together and asserted that the resurrection was of the whole person and came about only through God's grace. Millenarians believed in a blissful life on earth for the just before the final judgement, which also forcefully emphasized the goodness of God's material creation.

Irenaeus inherited the dualistic schema and the emphasis on the goodness of creation and developed them in reaction to Gnostic beliefs.[37] He taught that after death the soul will be temporarily separated from one's body and will descend to the dead.[38] At Christ's parousia there will be a resurrection for the just and the unjust alike: because of the resurrection of Christ it is emphatically the resurrection of the body, and the just will enjoy for one thousand years the kingdom of God on earth, the whole of creation being renewed for their use.[39] The resurrection is very clearly a progression to a new state of fulfilment and perfection, which, if we are receptive to God's Spirit here on earth, is a process which starts now.[40] This period will be followed by universal judgement, after which the good enjoy communion with God and the unjust are doomed to eternal separation from God ('death'), because they lack the divine Spirit.[41] Irenaeus stresses that this fate, though harsh, is freely chosen and is an inevitable consequence of departure from God—he does believe that the fire of punishment can purge some sins, but not all.[42] The Devil himself is described as being bound and committed to eternal fire.[43]

A contemporary of Irenaeus, Clement of Alexandria, reacted somewhat differently to Gnosticism and Platonism and it is in his theology that the roots of the second broad type of eschatology can be found. He was sympathetic to Gnostics' and Neoplatonists' intellectualist and speculative concerns,

[37] Daley, *The Hope*, 27.

[38] *Adversus haereses* (= *Adv. haer.*) 5. 31. 2.

[39] Resurrection of body: *Adv. haer.* 5. 7. 1., 5. 14. 1; millennium: *Adv. haer.* 5. 32. 1–2, 5. 33. 3, 5. 35. 1.

[40] *Adv. haer.* 5. 3. 2, 5. 12. 6, 5. 8. 1.

[41] Judgement: *Adv. haer.* 5. 15. 3; fate of the just: ibid. 5. 27. 1, 5. 17. 1, 5. 35, 1–2; fate of the unjust: ibid. 5. 27. 2, 5. 22. 2, 5. 11. 1.

[42] Ibid. 5. 27. 2, 5. 28. 3.

[43] Ibid. 5. 21. 2–3, 5. 26. 2.

especially to their emphasis on the role of knowledge and learning in believers' attempts to perfect themselves.[44] Clement sees the eschaton as the culmination of the 'true Gnostic's' efforts: an eternal contemplation of God in full understanding.[45] Although he did not see the material world as evil and did assert the resurrection of the body, he viewed death as a welcome release from the earthly body.[46] Perhaps most influential was his doctrine of punishment: this he saw as medicinal and pedagogical, vindictive punishment being alien to God's perfectly good nature.[47] Since it is medicinal, at least some punishment after death is temporary. This had two important consequences. First, Clement asserted that sins committed by believers would be cleansed in this way, thus becoming the first Christian writer to assert categorically that even the just would undergo punishment after death, albeit of a purgatorial kind.[48] Secondly, he suggested that the punishment might be enough to purify or turn unbelievers to God after their death. It is unclear whether he thought that this would in fact lead to universal salvation, although his thought tends in that direction.[49] It is also unclear whether the purgatorial punishment constrains sinners to repent against their will or works in harmony with human freedom.[50]

Origen developed Clement's eschatology in a specifically universalistic direction and is the most influential exponent of the second type of patristic eschatology. His basic view of the last things is set out in *De principiis*. Upon death the individual's earthly body will be transformed into a spiritual body and the whole person will be judged and punished immediately.[51] The

[44] See Daley, *The Hope*, 44. [45] Ibid., 45. [46] Ibid., 46.

[47] John R. Sachs, 'Apocatastasis in Patristic Theology', *Theological Studies* 54 (1993), 618.

[48] Daley, *The Hope*, 47: 'Clement can be regarded as the first Christian exponent of the doctrine of purgatorial eschatological suffering'; see also Sachs, 'Apocatastasis', 619.

[49] Daley, *The Hope*, 47.

[50] Daley, citing *Stromateis* (= *Strom.*) 7. 12. 78. 3, argues that some repent against their will (*The Hope*, 47); Sachs notes that *Strom.* 7. 2. 12. 5 asserts that sinners will be 'constrained to repent by necessary chastisements' but cites *Strom.* 7. 2. 12. 3 as evidence that 'somewhat paradoxically, [Clement] suggests that God's omnipotence can accomplish this without curtailing human free will' ('Apocatastasis', 619).

[51] *De principiis* (= *De princ.*) 3. 6. 4–6, Preface 5. Mark Edwards argues convincingly (against Henri Crouzel and others) that Origen had no concept of a disembodied soul in an intermediate state: Mark Edwards, 'Origen's Two Resurrections', *Journal of Theological Studies* n.s. 46/2 (1995).

kingdom of God consists of a gradual accumulation of those individuals who have been purified in their life and through medicinal punishment after their death.[52] He also speaks on a cosmic level of the restoration of the whole of humanity to its original state:

So then, when the end has been restored to the beginning, and the termination of things compared with their commencement, that condition of things will be restored in which rational nature was placed, when it had no need to eat of the tree of knowledge of good and evil.[53]

Although Origen sometimes establishes a linear, not a cyclical, view of humankind's development, his usual schema emphasizes the aspect of return, summed up by the repeated assertion that 'the end is always like the beginning'.[54]

Origen's eschatology has several controversial aspects, all of which are significant for Gregory's interpretation of the same themes. First, although Origen stresses the continuity of the spiritual body with the earthly one, saying that it will be 'raised from the earth' and that its nature will 'undergo a change into the glory of a spiritual body' he does not think that identity with the physical atoms of the corpse is necessary for that continuity.[55] Instead the soul retains the form (or *eidos*) of the body, which is more than just the body's appearance but seems to be the bearer of the body's essential characteristics.[56] From this *eidos* the spiritual body is built up. It is clear that Origen thinks that it is impossible for any soul to be entirely disembodied, for more than once he states that only God is utterly incorporeal.[57]

Unfortunately, Origen's doctrine of the resurrection was later famously misinterpreted by Methodius (d. *c.*311)—with great significance for Gregory of Nyssa's eschatology. Thinking that by *eidos* Origen meant merely the external appearance of a body,

[52] Daley, *The Hope*, 49; Edwards, 'Origen's Two Resurrections', 515.

[53] *De princ.* 3. 6. 3.

[54] *De princ.* 1. 6. 2; cf. ibid. 2. 1. 3. For the linear model, see ibid. 3. 6. 1: 'man received the dignity of God's image at his first creation; but . . . the perfection of his likeness has been reserved for the consummation'.

[55] Quotations: *De princ.* 3. 6. 6.

[56] Edwards suggests that the *eidos* is 'both the substrate of corporeal functions and a superficial form': 'Origen's Two Resurrections', 517.

[57] Daley, *The Hope*, 52 (citing *De princ.* 2. 2. 1, 3. 6. 1, Preface 9); Edwards, 'Origen's Two Resurrections', 504 (citing *De princ.* 1. 6. 4).

Methodius claimed that the Alexandrian did not uphold the resurrection of the body.[58] Even if he had correctly understood that Origen too asserted the identity of the earthly and risen bodies, Methodius' criteria for that identity were far stricter: arguing from his belief that Christ's risen body was composed of flesh and bones, Methodius insisted that the risen body was in every sense the earthly one.[59] Epiphanius of Salamis (c.315–403) followed Methodius closely in his own doctrine of the resurrection and attack on Origen, and it was probably his writings which stimulated Gregory's own reaction.[60]

The second area of controversy is Origen's view of punishment and his consequent advocacy of universal salvation. He followed Clement in viewing punishment as medicinal and in recognizing that most believers would not die perfect and would need some form of purification after death. He saw this process largely in intellectual terms and even speaks of a 'school for souls' after death.[61] He stated more clearly than Clement that the medicinal and pedagogical nature of divine punishment meant that even the punishment of the wicked would be temporary. The scriptural description of the punishment of sinners as αἰώνιος Origen therefore interprets as 'lasting for an age', not as 'lasting for ever'.[62] Furthermore he interprets the 'submission' of God's enemies in 1 Corinthians 15: 28 as meaning that they will repent, not that they will be destroyed.[63] In several places Origen asserts that these enemies include the demons, while in other places he is more circumspect; in his *Letter to Friends in Alexandria* he even denies that he ever taught the doctrine of universal salvation.[64] However, the whole tenor of his eschatology tends in a universalistic direction and the *De Principiis* view was certainly the one most commonly attributed to him by later

[58] Daley, *The Hope*, 62, citing Methodius, *De resurrectione* 3. 17 f.

[59] Daley, *The Hope*, 62.

[60] Ibid., 90; see Epiphanius, *Panarion* 64.

[61] Daley, *The Hope*, 57; *De princ.* 2. 11. 6. This should not be taken to mean that souls are indoctrinated: Origen emphasizes that their education will be 'by word, by reason, by teaching, by exhortation to better things . . . and also by . . . merited and appropriate threatenings' and not by 'the pressure of some necessity that compels [them] into subjection' (*De princ.* 3. 5. 8).

[62] Daley, *The Hope*, 56; Edwards, 'Origen's Two Resurrections', 511, Müller, 'Origenes und die Apokatastasis', *Theologisches Zeitschrift* 14 (1958), 184.

[63] Sachs, 'Apocatastasis', 621–2, esp. n. 27, citing *De princ.* 3. 6. 5.

[64] Daley, *The Hope*, 58.

theologians, both those sympathetic and those inimical to his cause.

A third problem with Origen's eschatology is that his schema shares similarities with the pagan doctrines of successive worlds, each summed up by a restoration (ἀποκατάστασις—indeed Origen even uses this word for the restoration of humanity to its original state).[65] If the end will be like the beginning, there is surely the possibility that mankind will fall in the future as it did in the past: this would seem to cast doubt on God's power or on the efficacy of Christ's incarnation and resurrection.[66] In one place Origen offers a suggestion as to why an indefinite series of falls and restorations is not possible: alluding to his key eschatological text, 1 Corinthians 15: 28, he asserts that when God will be 'all in all' evil will not exist and that therefore those who are in full possession of the good will have no urge 'to eat from the tree of the knowledge of good and evil'.[67] There seems to be the suggestion that the end will not be *exactly* like the beginning—either because of some metaphysical change in the condition of the world or because of greater human intellectual maturity.[68] Another reason perhaps lies in Origen's stress on the creating and saving power of the Logos. His dictum that the end will be like the beginning is not so much a philosophical principle as an assertion that just as the cosmos began in its creation through the Logos, so it will end in its submission to God in the Logos—again a reference to 1 Corinthians 15: 28.[69] His emphasis on the divine power to save may seem to clash with human freedom: Origen acknowledges this, but asserts that only God knows how the divine plan for humanity will be accomplished in a manner which is consistent with 'the preservation of free will in all rational creatures'.[70] There is clearly a tension in

[65] See section D. below for a discussion of the term ἀποκατάστασις.

[66] Origen asserts that if there were future worlds they would not necessarily be identical, because of human free will; however for precisely this reason there would still be the possibility of a fall. Müller suggests that Origen was led to acknowledge the possibility of future worlds through this emphasis on human freedom—humans must be free to fall again (at least once). Müller, 'Origenes', 188–189.

[67] *De princ.* 3. 6. 3.

[68] At *De princ.* 2. 11. 6, Origen makes it clear that even the saints will participate in the post-mortem educational process.

[69] On this verse Müller cites Bigg: 'These words were *never* out of Origen's mind.' Bigg, *The Christian Platonists of Alexandria* (1866), 299, cited in Müller, 'Origenes', 184.

[70] *De princ.* 3. 5. 8.

Origen's eschatology here which he never resolves; nevertheless Daley's comment that 'an endless cycle of alternating falls and redemptions is almost certainly foreign to his thought' is probably the fairest conclusion to draw from the general tenor of Origen's theology, particularly his emphasis on the redeeming power of God's love and the universal scope of Christ's incarnation and resurrection.[71]

As the compilers of the *Philokalia*, Basil and Gregory of Nazianzus were amongst those who were more sympathetic to Origen. However, neither wrote much about eschatology and what they did say was usually in the context of homilies, where the emphasis was more on stressing the unwelcome consequences of sin rather than on a systematic treatment of the issues. So, for example, Gregory of Nazianzus sometimes speaks of an eternal and avenging fire but he also asserts that punishment after death is medicinal.[72] On the whole he seems inclined to believe that evil will ultimately be consumed by God and that the goal of the universe is the union of all creatures with God:

> God will be all in all at the time of the restoration (τῆς ἀποκατάστασεως) . . . We shall then be wholly like God, receptive of God as a whole and of God alone. This . . . is the perfection towards which we strive.[73]

Although this appears more sympathetic to an Origenistic approach to eschatology, his highly pictorial and poetic style prevents one from drawing any conclusion with certainty. It is clearer, on the other hand, that Basil was much less enthusiastic about Origen's universalistic eschatology. He seems to have believed that punishment after death was eternal and that each sin will be punished with equal severity because each is an act of disobedience against God.[74]

It will be seen from the following chapters that in his own eschatology Gregory of Nyssa rejects the dualistic type of patristic eschatology, as exemplified by Irenaeus and Basil, and opts for the universalistic schema, as expounded by Origen. In particular his clear rejection of Basil's views on eschatology should be noted. The facts that the majority of

[71] Daley, *The Hope*, 58.
[72] See ibid., 83–5.
[73] Gregory of Nazianzus, *Theological Oration* 4 (= *Or.* 30) §6.
[74] See Daley, *The Hope*, 81 ff.

Gregory's works were written only after Basil's death (*c.*371) and that some of these were intended to complete specific theological tasks which Basil had begun do indeed indicate the brothers' close teacher-pupil relationship. However, it is very likely that some of Gregory's commentaries—*In inscriptiones Psalmorum*; *De beatitudinibus*; and *De oratione dominica*—were written before Basil's death; these are by no means immature works and the extensive and sophisticated work on the Psalms in particular sets the tone of much of Gregory's later work, including his universalistic eschatology.[75] So, although most of his works were written late in his life, the idea that Gregory at first lived under Basil's shadow should not be exaggerated.[76]

Furthermore, the originality of his own position *vis-à-vis* Origen will also become clear. Origen was the most important influence on Gregory's theology in general and certainly on his eschatology: they both share, for example, the general idea of a universal *apokatastasis* and Gregory was also very influenced by Origen's re-expression in Christian terms of the Platonic concept of the soul's rise to God. Nevertheless, he did reject several main theological doctrines held by Origen, including the concept of the finitude (and ultimate comprehensibility) of God's nature, the pre-existence of souls and their fall into fleshly existence. Moreover, it has already been seen that he rejects Origen's view of the resurrection, so that an assessment even of his eschatology as Origenistic does not do it full justice. In his theology in general and in his eschatology in particular Gregory was indebted as much to the example of Origen's systematic method and scholarship as to specific Origenistic doctrines.

In summary, all the evidence brought forward in this chapter about Gregory's influences, theological and philosophical, has gone to show that he transformed previous writers' work in an original and highly creative manner to his own ends. The following chapters will examine his eschatology in detail, after a note on the most controversial term which he uses: ἀποκατάστασις.

[75] *In insc. pss.*: Heine, 211–12 (2. 16. 282); *GNO* v. 174–5.

[76] Meredith, for example, notes that despite his claim to be Basil's pupil, Gregory's grasp of theological issues seems superior to his brother's. Meredith, *The Cappadocians*, 52.

D. *APOKATASTASIS*—A NOTE ON TERMINOLOGY

The word *apokatastasis* is now usually used to refer to a specifically Origenistic doctrine of universal salvation.[77] However, in Gregory of Nyssa's time the Greek word had not yet assumed this very specific, almost technical meaning—although some modern commentators seem to suggest that it had.[78] It is true that the word was sometimes used by Gregory's contemporaries with particular reference to Origen's universalism and to the question of whether the resurrection would be spiritual or bodily.[79] It is also true that later, in the anathemas of Justinian (543) and of the Fifth Ecumenical Council (553), ἀποκατάστασις had virtually become a technical term connected with the Origenistic doctrines of the pre-existence of souls and the salvation of demons.[80]

However, until the mid-sixth century usage was very flexible. A brief look at the history of the word's use will illustrate this and

[77] In this book the word *apokatastasis* (in Latin script) will be used with this universalistic meaning, however the use of the word ἀποκατάστασις (in Greek script) is to be understood as not necessarily having these implications—as the following discussion will make clear.

[78] For example, Daley speaks of Gregory's 'hope for universal salvation or "Apokatastasis", the restoration of intellectual creatures to an "original" unity with God in contemplative beatitude'. Daley, *The Hope*, 85.

[79] e.g. see references to Jerome (pp. 160, 436), to Epiphanius (p. 400), to Evagrius (pp. 422 f.) and to Theophilus (p. 443), in Jon F. Dechow, *Dogma and Mysticism in Early Christianity* (Mercer University Press, Macon, Ca., 1988).

[80] See Dechow, *Dogma and Mysticism*, 450 and 458. Brian Daley notes that although the anathemas mention no-one by name and were provoked by a contemporary controversy over Origenism amongst monks in Palestine, most Greek writers from the sixth century onwards took the condemnations to refer to Origen himself and to his followers Didymus the Blind and Evagrius of Pontus (Daley, *The Hope*, 190). Didymus (*c.*313–98) appears to have taught the *apokatastasis* in a much more extreme form than did either Origen or Gregory of Nyssa: he saw the resurrection as purely spiritual, the restoration as part of a cyclical movement of the universe and salvation as being the unity of all souls in God, beyond all multiplicity (ibid., 90). Evagrius (346–99) taught the destruction of human bodies at the Last Judgement and the transformation of the soul alone in the future life. No clear pronouncement on universalism is extant, but he does speak of all rational beings bowing to God and of there being a time when there will be no more evil (ibid., 91). Two theologians who were involved in the sixth-century Origenist debate were Philoxenus of Mabbug (*c.*440–523) and Stephen bar Sudaili (*c.*480–*c.*543): the former taught a universal and spiritual resurrection and the latter a far more extreme doctrine of the final substantial union of all creatures with God (ibid., 183–4). It seems likely, then, in view of the later more extreme developments of Origenism in both the fourth and the sixth centuries, that the proponents of the 553 anathema were really condemning those—not the theology of Origen and certainly not that of Gregory of Nyssa.

will illuminate Gregory's eschatology by showing that it is mistaken to think that the word's central meaning is universalistic.[81]

The root meaning of the word *ἀποκατάστασις* is 'restitution' or 'restoration to a previous state of affairs'. In classical Greek usage its precise meaning alters according to the context: hence, in medicine it means 'healing' and in law the restoration of property or the restoration of a hostage to his home town. In political contexts it signifies the re-establishment of a state's constitution or a new political foundation. In astronomy it is the technical term for the restoration of a star or constellation to its former position in the heavens. From this last meaning, gradually the word came to be applied to the cosmos as a whole as theories developed which postulated that after a particular period the universe would end and then restart from the beginning. In Greek philosophy the use of the word developed from this astronomical meaning. The Stoic school taught that when the planets reached the place in the heavens which they occupied when they were created there would be a world conflagration (*ἐκπύρωσις*) followed by the recreation or restoration of the old world (*ἀποκατάστασις* or *παλιγγενεσία*). There is little mention of possible ethical or soteriological aspects of the restoration, although Plutarch wrote (of the conflagration) that 'when this will have burnt the universe, nothing mean will remain; everything will then be reasoned and wise'.[82] Later, Neoplatonist thought gave the word a more religious meaning than previous Greek philosophy: unlike the Stoics who used the word in relation to theories about the cosmos, some Neoplatonists spoke of the restoration (*ἀποκατάστασις*) of the individual soul. However, because salvation for the Neoplatonists consisted not in rebirth in another body but in complete release from matter altogether, their use of the word *ἀποκατάστασις* rarely had soteriological overtones because it meant reincarnation into a tedious cycle of further lives.[83] In

[81] The sources for this discussion are *Reallexikon für Antike und Christentum*; *Theologisches Wörterbuch zum N. T.*; *Lexikon für Theologie und Kirche* and Lampe's *Patristic Greek Lexicon* (in each case under the entry 'Apokatastasis').

[82] Plutarch, *Moralia*, no. 72: *De communibus notitiis adversus Stoicos* 1067A, cited in *Reallexikon für Antike und Christentum*, col. 511.

[83] e.g. Proclus seems to have used the word *ἀποκατάστασις* to mean reincarnation (*Institutio theologica* 199).

contrast, the word did have a soteriological meaning among the Gnostics: for example Valentinus uses it for the return of the non-material reality to its original state and Herakleon uses it almost synonymously with σωτηρία (salvation).[84]

The word does not appear at all in the Septuagint and rarely in Jewish literature of the first centuries AD.[85] This absence can be partly explained by the fact that the Jewish linear model of history in which God was expected to break in and establish an entirely new era was inimical to the Greek philosophical concept of a cyclical return to an original state. Only Philo (who was notably sympathetic to Hellenistic thought) uses it more philosophically when he links the Hebrews' deliverance from Egypt to the mystical restoration of the soul.[86]

Christian use of the word ἀποκατάστασις reflects this wide range of meaning, and not just the philosophical/astronomical usage. There appear to be two broad strands of meaning: first a return to an original location and secondly a return to an original condition. Within the first strand, the word ἀποκατάστασις is often used to indicate the return of people to their home town, and particularly is used of the return of the Jews to Jerusalem, either in the past or in the eschatological future.[87] It is also used by Gregory of Nazianzus for the ascent of Christ into heaven.[88] When non-human subjects are being referred to, the astronomical meaning is dominant and the word ἀποκατάστασις has one of four related meanings: the simple return of a heavenly body to its original position, the revolution of that body between its start and end points, the end of an astronomical 'great year' or the end of the world. These meanings appear to occur most in Christian writers' accounts of Gnostic

[84] On Valentinus: Daley, *The Hope*, 26. He cites Valentinus' *Treatise on the Resurrection [Epistle to Rheginus]* 44. 31; *Origin of the World* 127. 14–17; *Gospel of Philip* 67. 15–18; *Tripartite Tractate* 122. 19–23. ἀποκατάστασις is not by any means the only word used: other characteristic words are ἀνατρέχω in Greek and 'ascendere' and 'resipere' in Latin (Kelly, *Early Christian Doctrines*, 467).

[85] It is found in Aristeas (*Epistula* 123) and Josephus (*Antiquities* 11. 63) but with the meaning of a return to a home town.

[86] Philo, *Quis rerum divinarum heres sit* 293.

[87] e.g. Clement of Alexandria, *Stromateis* 1. 21; Origen, *Contra Celsum* 4. 22. The transitive use of the verb ἀποκαθίστημι in Acts 1: 6 seems to be related to this meaning in an eschatological sense: 'Lord will you at this time restore [ἀποκαθιστάνεις] the kingdom to Israel?'

[88] *Or.* 41. 11.

heresies where they sometimes refer to an eschaton in a religious sense.[89] The divinely appointed end of the world seems also to be the meaning of the word ἀποκατάστασις in Acts 3: 19–21, in Peter's sermon in the Temple:

> Repent . . . that [God] may send you the Christ . . . whom the heaven must receive until the times of restoration of all things (ἄχρι χρόνων ἀποκαταστάσεως πάντων), whereof God spoke by the mouth of his holy prophets which have been since the world began.

There is much controversy over the interpretation of the passage, particularly because it is the only time that a New Testament author uses the word ἀποκατάστασις. Peter seems to be using the word simply to refer to the end of time (which will be a time of judgement) and in this context πάντων would refer to the restoration of all things (i.e. of the whole cosmos) not of all people.[90] It should not be taken in a universalistic sense: notably Origen and Gregory of Nyssa do not use the verse as clear scriptural evidence for universalism, although they do borrow from it the expression ἀποκατάστασις πάντων.[91] Thus, to sum up this first meaning of ἀποκατάστασις: although derived from the concept of a return to an original location, it primarily came to mean the end of the world, that is, it is eschatological.

The second broad area of meaning is that of a return to an original or proper condition. Origen and Gregory of Nyssa both use the word ἀποκατάστασις for the restoration of sight to the blind. Although the word in its strict sense means a restoration to a previous state, here in its extended sense it can in fact be prospective or teleological: there is no necessary implication that the blind ever had sight, just that they ought to have sight. The word ἀποκατάστασις is also used to refer to the resurrection: that of Lazarus, that of Christ, and that of Christians.[92] In the last of these

[89] e.g. Irenaeus *Adv. haer.* 1. 17. 1; Hippolytus, *Refutatio omnium haeresium* (ed. Marcovich) 99. (7)8; 260. 40; 300. 22; 306. 39. The last three refer to the end of the world and seem to be soteriological in the very broad sense that they imply the elimination of evil, or the achievement of unity in the cosmos.

[90] Rhetorically, it would diminish the impact of Peter's call to repent if he were asserting in the same breath that all will be saved.

[91] The expression ἀποκατάστασις πάντων either can have an explicitly universalistic sense in Origen (see later) or can simply mean the end of the world: see *Fragmenta in Lucam* 14. 19–20 (*PG* 8, 1168a).

[92] Lazarus: Origen, *In Jo.* 28. 6; Christ: Origen, *In Jo.* 20. 11; Christians: Methodius, *De resurrectione* 3. 2.

uses, again there is a strong forward-looking aspect to the word: the resurrection is the establishing of people in their *proper* state, which is also a *better* state than they were ever in before. From this last meaning is derived Clement of Alexandria's typical use of the word ἀποκατάστασις. For him it means fulfilment or consummation of individual Christians—for example, consummation of their faith or hope or relationship of sonship to God.[93] Whether it has a forward-looking focus (consummation, fulfilment) or a backward-looking one (restoration), this second strand of meaning can be characterized as being soteriological.

Although Origen uses the word ἀποκατάστασις in other contexts, his usage is frequently dependent on both of these two broad strands of meaning—eschatological and soteriological. He clearly means to refer to an event in which the whole of the cosmos is involved and indeed unified, yet he is also referring to the perfection or healing both of the cosmos and of the individual spiritual beings within it. This perfection includes the resurrection of the body and the consummation of non-material human qualities such as knowledge and love. For Origen, of course, this does mean the restoration of humanity and the cosmos to an actual previous state, because he believes that the end will be like the beginning. He used the word ἀποκατάστασις particularly in connection with his concept of universal salvation, but that was not the meaning of the word in itself.[94]

Gregory of Nyssa's own use of the word is surprisingly flexible and reflects the range of meanings which have just been described. As Daniélou points out, ἀποκατάστασις is used by him several times simply to mean a restoration to a previous state of perfection, with no cosmological or eschatological significance at all.[95] In particular, Gregory uses it to signify a return to health, or the hoped-for return of a sinner to the Church.[96] All these meanings share the central idea that the return is to an original,

[93] All these examples come from *Strom.* 2. 22; see also *Strom.* 10. 56.

[94] For the use of ἀποκατάστασις in a universalistic context, see e.g. *De princ.* 2. 10. 8.

[95] Jean Daniélou, 'L'apocatastase chez Saint Grégoire de Nysse', *Recherches de Science Religieuse* 30/3 (1940), 328.

[96] e.g. the miraculous restoration of sight to a diseased eye by Macrina (*De vita Mac.*: *SC* 178, 264. 1); Gregory expresses his aim to restore Eunomius to the true Church (*Contra Eun.* 1: *GNO* i. 23. 24). Daniélou also cites a return to health (*frg. PG* 46, 1161a) and the reconciliation of sinners with the Church (*Test. adv. Judaeos*: *PG* 46, 232c): Daniélou, 'L'apocatastase', 328.

proper and perfect (or at least much preferable) state. Nevertheless, Gregory does also frequently use the word to mean an eschatological consummation—although his emphasis is often less on the notion of a *cosmic* cycle as in Origen, and more on the idea that *humanity in particular* will ultimately be restored to the original state of perfection which it possessed before the Fall.[97] A typical example of Gregory's use of the word is the following description of the soul's progress through life:

> The goal and the end of the journey . . . is the restoration to the original state (ἡ πρὸς τὸ ἀρχαῖον ἀποκατάστασις), which is nothing other than similarity to the divine.[98]

Sometimes this goal is expressed in terms of the restoration of the image of God.[99] At other times, Gregory talks of the return of humanity to heaven: for instance, he writes that the eighth Beatitude indicates the 'restoration to heaven of those who had fallen into slavery' [τὴν εἰς τοὺς οὐρανοὺς ἀποκατάστασιν].[100] Frequently this restoration is linked to—or even identified with—the resurrection from the dead:

> For the resurrection is nothing other than the complete restoration to the original state [οὐδὲ γὰρ ἄλλο τι ἐστιν ἡ ἀνάστασις, εἰ μὴ πάντως ἡ εἰς τὸ ἀρχαῖον ἀποκατάστασις].[101]

This brief assessment of his terminology has thus shown that ἀποκατάστασις is not always used as an eschatological term by

[97] The lack of cosmic emphasis is attested to by the fact that when referring to the end of the world, Gregory usually uses other words: e.g. συντέλειαν (completion: *De hom. opif.*: *PG* 44, 185d1); συμπληρώσεως (fulfilment: *De hom. opif.*: *PG* 44, 204c4); ἀναστοιχειώσις (summing-up: *De hom. opif.*: *PG* 44, 205c12; see also: ἐν τῇ τοῦ παντὸς ἀναστοιχειώσει, *De hom. opif.*: *PG* 44, 221c6; ἐπὶ τῆς δευτέρας ἀναστοιχειώσεως, *In cant.* 15: *GNO* vi. 458. 20). In fact when Gregory uses the word ἀποκατάστασις in an astronomical context, it appears to have a narrow technical meaning, for example, the return of light after eclipse. *In cant.*: *PG* 44, 933a, cited in Daniélou 'L'apocatastase', 328; see also an astronomical meaning in *Contra Eun.* 2: *GNO* i. 247. 19.

[98] *De mortuis*: Lozza, §60. 26–7; see also *De hom. opif.* 30.

[99] See, for example, *De virg.*: SC 119, 416. 10–13 (= *GNO* viii/1. 302). For a detailed discussion of the theme of restoration of the image of God, see Chapter 3.

[100] *De beat.*: *PG* 44, 1292b11–15. See also *De orat. dom.*: *PG* 44, 1148c: ἀποκαταστσει σε τῇ οὐρανίῳ πατρίδι. Note: from what Gregory says elsewhere, this is clearly not meant to imply that humans pre-existed as disembodied souls.

[101] *In Eccles.*: *GNO* v. 296. 16–18. In *De anima et resurrectione*, the resurrection is standardly defined in similar terms: e.g. *De an.*: *NPNF* v. 464; Oehler, 371. 23–4; *NPNF* v. 467; Oehler, 375. 13–14. See also *De hom. opif.* 17. 2; *De mortuis*: *GNO* ix. 51. 16 ff; *De orat dom.*: *PG* 44, 1148c.

Gregory but that, when it is, the primary idea behind the word is that of a restoration to a perfect original state. As it does in Origen's writings, ἀποκατάστασις in Gregory's works often has both of the two broad strands of meaning which were identified above: eschatological and soteriological. Additional to (and not included within) these is the idea that the restoration will be universal. As it will be seen in Chapter 3, Gregory clearly does believe that all humanity, indeed the whole cosmos, will be saved and purified of evil; however, he does not appear to think that the word ἀποκατάστασις necessarily carries with it any universalist implications.[102] Thus he should not be seen as using ἀποκατάστασις as a technical term with one specific meaning and the word should not be regarded as having *exactly* the same implications as it does in Origen, although it is often used in a similar way.

The above is not just a semantic discussion: it has highlighted the two major themes of Gregory's eschatology: restoration to a perfect original state and universalism. The following two chapters will examine each of these in turn, in order to answer the question of whether Gregory did assert a universal restoration to perfection throughout his eschatology and to clarify exactly what he meant by this. The questions raised in the Introduction will therefore be borne in mind. Does Gregory's description of humanity's restored state illuminate the fate of the human body and the material universe? If perfection will be restored to all people, how will that affect humanity's individual and collective relationship to God and what role will human freedom play in the achievement of that perfection?

[102] A possible exception is *De vita Moysis*: Malherbe and Ferguson 2. 82 (= *GNO* vi/1. 154. 5), for a discussion of which see below, Chapter 3, section A. i. Gregory tends to refer to the 'restoration *of everything*' [τῇ τοῦ παντὸς ἀποκαταστάσει] when he writes about universal salvation, echoing the phrase from the Acts of the Apostles (*De an.*: *NPNF* v. 444; Oehler, 341. 15–16; Acts 3: 21).

2

Perfection in Resurrection

The previous chapter closed by highlighting restoration to perfection and universalism as the two major themes in Gregory of Nyssa's eschatology. By looking at the former concept, one can determine what Gregory thinks the future state will be like, particularly with regard to the nature of the resurrection body and humanity's ideal relationship with God. However, this chapter will attempt more than a mere description of Gregory's view of the future state; it will also reveal his belief that, despite the Fall, the whole of human nature (that is, each individual human) is perfectible. He has a strongly teleological concept of human nature—humans were created for an eschatological relationship with or participation in God—which is best expressed by the notion of the image of God. This image was marred, but not completely destroyed, by the Fall. Since it exists, to some degree, in each individual, it can be perfected in all. Thus, Gregory's anthropology reveals the possibility of universal salvation, even though it does not directly assert it.

It will be seen that Gregory's anthropology is not naturalistic: rather he learns about human nature from the doctrines of the creation, Fall and resurrection, as he takes them to be revealed in Scripture. From the first two he draws conclusions about the perfectibility of human nature (see section A. below); from the doctrine of the resurrection and direct scriptural references to the future life he makes more precise claims about the nature of humanity's eschatological state (sections B. and C., respectively).[1] Although the main point of this chapter is to show that Gregory's view of human nature in itself commits him only to the assertion that universal salvation is possible (not inevitable), some evidence

[1] Gregory not only argues from scriptural accounts about humanity before the Fall to make conclusions about the afterlife, but also draws inferences about the prelapsarian state from scriptural passages about the resurrection. Both sorts of argument are frequently (and sometimes confusingly) interwoven.

will be examined which suggests a belief not only that each human is potentially directed towards fulfilment in God, but also that human fulfilment is collective and possibly even universal. The following chapter will deal with more explicit evidence for his belief in universal salvation.

A. RETURN TO PARADISE?

The resurrection promises us nothing other than the restoration of the fallen to their ancient state. For the grace we look for is a certain return to the first life bringing back again to Paradise him who was cast out of it.[2]

This key extract from *De hominis opificio* clearly shows that Gregory equates the resurrection state with the original state of humanity and the latter with the existence of humans in Paradise before the Fall. But how does he characterize this prelapsarian way of life? Is a restoration to this state possible for *all* the fallen? In answer to these questions several broad themes emerge with consistency across Gregory's writings whether they be early or late, doctrinal or exegetical. These issues will be dealt with after briefly clarifying his particular doctrine of the two creations and the Fall.

i. Creation and the Fall

Working from the text of Genesis 1: 27, Gregory takes it to refer to not one but two creations:

Thus the creation of our nature is in a sense two-fold: one made like to God, one divided according to this distinction [of sex]: for something like this the passage darkly conveys by its arrangement, where it first says, 'God created man, in the image of God created he him', and then, adding to what has been said, 'male and female created he them'—a thing which is alien from our conceptions of God.[3]

The second creation was not the consequence of the Fall—it did not come after it; however it *was* the consequence of God

[2] *De hom. opif.*: *NPNF* v. 17. 2; *PG* 44, 188c–d: ἡ δὲ τῆς ἀναστάσεως χάρις οὐδὲν ἕτερον ἡμῖν ἐπαγγέλλεται, ἢ τὴν εἰς τὸ ἀρχαῖον τῶν πεπτωκότων ἀποκατάστασιν, ἐπάνοδος γάρ τίς ἐστιν ἐπὶ τὴν πρώτην ζωὴν ἡ προσδοκωμένη χάρις, τὸν ἀποβληθέντα τοῦ παραδείσου πάλιν εἰς αὐτον ἐπανάγουσα.

[3] *De hom. opif.*: *NPNF* v. 16. 8.

foreseeing the Fall. Gregory believes that humanity in its fullness consists of a specific number of individuals (the *pleroma*). Had there been no Fall, humanity would have expanded to this ordained size by procreating like the angels.[4] However, knowing that humanity would sin and that sin would lead to mortality and the impossibility of such procreation, God made humanity to share sexual procreation with animals 'in order that the multitude of human souls might not be cut short'.[5] Humans also share with the animals another feature of irrational animal nature—that is passions, which are not characteristics of God:

> For it is not allowable to ascribe the first beginnings of our constitutional liability to passion (τῆς ἐμπαθοῦς διαθέσεως) to that human nature which was fashioned in the Divine likeness; but as brute life first entered into the world, and man, for the reason already mentioned, took something of their nature (I mean the mode of generation), he accordingly took at the same time a share of the other attributes contemplated in that nature . . .[6]

The doctrine of the two creations is introduced in the *De hominis opificio* as a means of explaining how humankind can truly be said to be in God's image. Gregory's answer is to distinguish humanity's original state—the first creation—from the state of Adam and Eve before the Fall—the second creation. It is the humanity of the *first* creation which can truly be said to be in the image of God, for like God it has no sexual differentiation, no desires. Only in the first creation is humanity perfect.[7]

It is important to note that Gregory strenuously denies the concept of a disembodied original state and is committed to asserting a bodily resurrection, so one must assume that embodiment *per se* does not obscure the image of God in humans. Further, although the second creation brings *sexual* differentiation, presumably some differentiation between persons must exist in the first, despite the fact that Gregory only talks of humanity *en masse* in that context.

[4] *De hom. opif.*: *NPNF* v. 17. 2. Gregory reasons this from his assumption that the original state was like the resurrection state combined with Jesus' response to the Sadducees in Luke's Gospel (20: 35–6): 'in the resurrection they neither marry nor are given in marriage, for they are equal to the angels'. He offers no explanation as to what angelic procreation might be.

[5] *De hom. opif.*: *NPNF* v. 17. 4.

[6] *De hom. opif.*: *NPNF* v. 18. 1; *PG* 44, 192a–b.

[7] *In cant.* 15: *GNO* vi. 458. 10–12, 17–19.

There is much more that could be said about Gregory's understanding of the two creations, not least because of the problematic notion of God foreseeing that humans would fall and creating them with a different nature because of this: it can be argued that sometimes Gregory sounds as if God caused humans to sin, by creating them with a nature with a tendency to sin.[8] Nevertheless, it is important to note four points with particular relevance to his belief in eschatological restoration. First, at the eschaton humanity will return not just to its prelapsarian state, but more precisely to its original state in the *first* creation, when it truly possessed the image of God. Secondly, Gregory claims that humanity as a whole was created perfect and this would seem to suggest that the return to perfection will be of humanity as a whole.[9] Thirdly, passion is not a characteristic of the original human nature in the first creation. Simple animal passions (e.g. the urge for sex, for food and drink) on the other hand, although they are characteristics of humans before the Fall, are only shared by humans because God foresaw the Fall and are not essential to humanity. They belong to humanity in the second creation. The more corrupt human desires are the result of a pattern of human sinfulness established by the Fall.[10]

Finally, and most importantly, Gregory does not appear to view the two creations as temporally successive: they are only consecutive in logical terms. By writing that 'in the Divine foreknowledge and power all humanity is included in the first creation' Gregory indicates that the first creation is ideal and the second actual.[11] This is not only because it does not make sense to say that all humanity (the *pleroma*) exists before any actual humans exist but also because the first creation exists in God's

[8] The problem is that God apparently created humans with the passions which in part caused the Fall: Eve's choice of the fruit is said to be the result of a misjudgement which is influenced by pleasure (*De hom. opif.*: *NPNF* v. 20. 4). Although this does not mean that God *caused* Eve to fall, for she had free will and could have done otherwise, it does raise a logical problem about the status of desires. For passions are both the effect of the Fall (due to God foreseeing the Fall) and the partial cause of the Fall. It may be preferable to interpret Gregory as believing that the Fall was also due to ignorance: see below, Chapter 3, section C. ii. and iii.

[9] This argument will be examined further in Chapter 3, section B. i. and ii.

[10] There are problems connected with Gregory's concept of passion and desire which will be discussed later in this chapter (section A. iii.).

[11] *De hom. opif.*: *NPNF* v. 16. 16; cf. 29. 1.

foreknowledge. Gregory asserts that God could not create anything indefinite (for in his infinity he alone is indefinite); hence instead of creating two individuals as the beginning of an indefinite series, he 'created' the whole of humanity, or *pleroma*, first. Gregory seems to be thinking of the first creation almost as an idea or plan in God's mind. The significance of this for Gregory's eschatology is that when he talks of humanity being 'restored' to its original state, he is in one sense speaking metaphorically: humankind is achieving, rather than returning to, perfection. Hence there is absolutely no question of Gregory's eschatology resting on the assumption of a cyclical view of history, in which the end of human history is its beginning (a significant departure from Origen). Amongst other problems, this circular view of history carries the unwelcome suggestion that if humanity is returning to its prelapsarian state there is the possibility that humanity might fall again, an idea which is completely alien to Gregory's eschatology. Hence, Jean Daniélou warns the reader not to take the notion of 'return' too literally in Gregory's theology:

> C'est une concession à ce mirage psychologique, inscrit dans le vocabulaire, que fait que le Paradis vers lequel nous sommes en marche nous apparaît toujours comme un Paradis perdu.[12]

Gregory's is a teleological view of humanity, setting out clearly humanity's goal in terms of God's intention as he created us: 'because creation exists from the very beginning by the divine power, the end of each created being is linked with its beginning'.[13] In this sense, then, Gregory's idea of the perfection of humankind is more a forward-looking attainment of an ideal than a retrospective restoration to an actual previous state.

However, because the ideal state which God held in his foreknowledge from the very beginning is something more in Gregory's metaphysics than a mere plan, in another sense the language of restoration is not entirely metaphorical. It is almost as if Gregory thinks that ideal humanity or human nature (*ἡ ἀνθρωπίνη φύσις*) is akin to a Platonic form in the mind of God. It thus already in a sense exists: 'everything created from nothing

[12] Jean Daniélou, 'L'apocatastase chez Saint Grégoire de Nysse', *Recherches de Science Religieuse* 30/3 (1940), 342.

[13] *In cant.* 15: *GNO* vi. 457. 21—458. 1.

comes into existence with its beginning'.[14] The concept of the first creation indicates something about the true nature of humankind, which cannot be expressed by simply talking of the state of Adam before the Fall, as previous theologians had done. At the eschaton humanity is in a sense regaining the ideal, although it is only then and not at the beginning that the ideal and actual states coincide. So it is true to say that in Gregory's eschatology humanity does not excel itself, rather it gains its proper self.

ii. Creation in the Image of God

Having distinguished the first and second creations and having established that human nature is truly perfect only in the first, what can one say about Gregory's concept of this perfection? Like his predecessors, Gregory stresses that the state of humanity in the first creation was sinless and free from evil. For example, he notes that at the eschaton, 'everything which had its beginning through God will be such as it was from the beginning, when it never received evil'.[15] There being no sin, there were none of the consequences of sin (or of God forseeing sin): no old age, disease, disability, sexual procreation, feeding—and above all no death.[16] The absence of these qualities left humans in a state of passionless existence completely free from tempting desires. So, Macrina reassures Gregory in *De anima*, this will also be true of the future life.[17] This freedom from sin, desire, and the consequences of sin Gregory frequently describes as beatitude or a life of grace.[18] He makes it clear that humans were from the beginning created with bodies, therefore he is implicitly disassociating sin and its consequences from embodiment as such. The Fall brought

[14] *In cant.* 15: *GNO* vi. 458. 1–2.

[15] *In illud: tunc . . .*: *GNO* iii: 2. 14. 5–7.

[16] *De an.*: *NPNF* v. 464; Oehler, 371. 24 ff. See also *NPNF* v. 466; Oehler, 374. 40–375. 7, where humans are said to abandon in death those properties which are acquired through a passionate disposition (*διὰ τῆς ἐπαθοῦς διαθέσεως*), properties such as dishonour, corruption, weakness, and ageing.

[17] In *De an.*: *NPNF* v. 466–7. For the sake of clarity, when referring to *De anima*, 'Gregory' will refer to Gregory of Nyssa's assumed persona in the dialogue and 'the author' to Gregory as writer. In fact, the arguments which Gregory puts into Macrina's mouth are ones which he as author would agree with, Macrina being the authoritative figure in the work and Gregory being the sceptic.

[18] Beatitude: e.g. *De mort.*: Lozza, 78. 7 (*τῇ ἀκηράτῳ ἐκείνῃ μακαριότητι*); *In cant.* 15: *GNO* vi. 439. 18–19 (*τὴν πρώτην τῆς φύσεως ἡμῶν μακαριότητα*); *De an.*: *NPNF* v. 464; Oehler, 371. 38 (*τὴν ἀπαθῆ μακαριότητα πάλιν ἀναδραμοῦσα*). Grace: e.g. *De hom. opif.*: *NPNF* v. 21. 4; *PG* 44, 204a (*τῆς εἰκόνος ἡ χάρις*); *Cat. or.* 8: Srawley, 47. 8–9 (*πρὸς τὴν ἐξ ἀρχῆς . . . χάριν*); *Cat. or.* 16: Srawley, 71. 5 (*ἡ πρώτη περὶ τὸ ἀνθρώπινον χάρις*).

with it not embodiment, but the physical consequences of sin: it is the latter, not the former which Gregory in his later works equates with the scriptural mention of 'coats of skin'.[19]

Particularly in his exegetical works and the more rhetorical of his orations the perfection of the original state is described in metaphorical terms. For example, in his commentary on the Song of Songs Gregory talks of Christ the bridegroom 'restoring [human] nature to virginal incorruptibility' (*εἰς ἀφθαρσίαν παρθενικὴν ἀναστοιχειώσας τὴν φύσιν*) and of a soul regaining its 'proper beauty' (*τὸ ἴδιον κάλλος*).[20] In *De mortuis*, Gregory as part of an extended analogy refers to humanity's 'original health' (*τὴν ἐξ ἀρχῆς εὐεξίαν*).[21] In his commentary on the inscriptions of the psalms, Gregory asserts that 'the first humans . . . used to sing in chorus with the angel powers' but that because of the Fall 'man was separated from connection with the angels'.[22]

Although the perfection, goodness, and freedom of humanity's original state are expressed by Gregory in general terms, the most systematic treatment focuses on the concept of the image of God. This theme is most important, for it indicates not only the qualities humans will have, but also the relationship they will have with God. It is taken from the words of the first creation account in Genesis:

> And God said, let us make man in our image, after our likeness . . . So God created man in his own image, in the image of God he created him; male and female he created them.[23]

So Gregory writes:

> we will return to our proper beauty (*τὸ οἰκεῖον κάλλος*), in which we were formed from the beginning, becoming like the form of our archetype (*κατ' εἰκόνα τοῦ ἀρχετύπου*).[24]

[19] See *Cat. or.*: Srawley, 43: 10–11; Srawley ET, 46; *In cant.* 11: *GNO* vi. 327–32; McCambley, 204–6.

[20] *In cant.* 11: *GNO* vi. 318. 9–10; and 15: *GNO* vi. 439. 18. See also *De mort.*: Lozza, §11, 52. 3 (*τὸ οἰκεῖον κάλλος*).

[21] *De mort.*: Lozza, §15, 64. 27. This metaphor is particularly apt, for although it deals with the 'disease' of sin, Gregory thought also that physical disease was literally the result of the Fall.

[22] *In insc. pss.*: Heine, 139 (2. 6. 60); *GNO* v. 86. Despite the musical metaphor, the reader should take the reference to angels literally: according to Gregory, humanity originally not only was closely associated with the angels, but shared many of the qualities of angelic life: see e.g. *De hom. opif.*: *NPNF* v. 22. 4; *PG* 44, 204d.

[23] Gen. 1: 26–7.

[24] *De mort.*: Lozza, §11, 52. 3–4.

This naturally raises the question of how created, material, mutable humanity could possibly be like God, the immaterial, immutable, Creator—a question which Gregory himself asks in *De hominis opificio*.[25] As we have seen, to a certain extent that question is answered by the distinction between first and second creations: it is difficult to envisage humanity in the image of God partly because human nature is so different from the perfection of the first creation. Nevertheless, because humanity in the first creation is not a purely spiritual creation, the question still remains of how embodied humans can in any way bear God's image.

At first in *De hominis opificio* Gregory appears to suggest that the whole of humankind was created in the image of God, the soul having regal qualities and the body, with its unique upright stance, signifying human superiority over the rest of creation.[26] However, later in *De hominis opificio* and also in his other works, Gregory consistently emphasizes that humans are created in the image of God in respect of their immaterial part alone—that is, the soul (ψυχή).

What is the divine quality to which the soul is similar? Not mass (σῶμα), nor shape, nor form (εἶδος), nor surface, nor weight, nor space, nor time . . . rather one must know that it is that which is left when all these have been removed, [that] it is intelligible, immaterial, impalpable, without body and extension.[27]

Hence, when Gregory is urging his reader to become more godlike, it is the soul—not the whole person—which requires purification and significantly this purification consists in the cleansing away of any effects of materiality on the soul:

Thus [the soul] must cleanse itself of every material deed and thought and be transformed into that which is spiritual and immaterial (πρὸς τὸ νοητόν τε καὶ ἄϋλον), a splendid image of the archetype's beauty (ἐναργεστάτην εἰκόνα τοῦ ἀρχετύπου κάλλους).[28]

Similarly, in *De anima* it is the soul which must liken itself to God, so that 'having become simple and single in form and so

[25] *De hom. opif.*: *NPNF* v. 16. 3–4 and 6.
[26] *De hom. opif.*: *NPNF* v. 4. 1.
[27] *De mort.*: Lozza, §10, 50. 21 ff.
[28] *In cant.* 15. *GNO* vi. 439. 8–11; see also ibid. 440.

perfectly godlike, [it] finds that perfectly simple and immaterial good'.[29]

In *De hominis opificio* the emphasis is specifically on the mind (νοῦς) or reason (λόγος) rather than on the soul in general. This is because in Gregory's terminology, strictly speaking, plants and animals too have souls: the aspect which makes human souls distinctive and in which their likeness to God resides is their rationality.[30] Also, in *De infantibus praemature abreptis* Gregory says that humanity was created in God's image in respect of its 'godlike intellectual essence'.[31] In fact, Gregory tends to use the words ψυχή and νοῦς almost interchangeably, the only discernible difference being the functions which he wants to emphasize at the time: reason (in the case of νοῦς) or love (in the case of ψυχή).

Given that the soul is immaterial and intellectual, it is thus in principle able to share other divine qualities: it is said in *De anima* to be unconnected with matter, yet to be able to pervade and to influence it, just as God is immaterial but is in control of all creation.[32] Furthermore, and again because of its immateriality, the soul—like God—is simple and unknowable.[33] In addition to these qualities, which one might say are qualities necessary to any immaterial object, the soul has certain other qualities which are apparent only when it is truly the image of God. The most obvious of these is immortality: Gregory writes in his *Catechetical Oration* that since humanity was created in God's image and one of God's essences is immortality, then it was necessary that human nature 'should have within it an element that is immortal'.[34] Although Gregory sometimes sounds as if he is talking about a soul which is naturally and inevitably immortal (especially in *De anima*), in most places it is clear that he thinks that immortality was lost as a result of the Fall.[35] Possibly he is

[29] See, for example, *De an.*: *NPNF* v. 450; Oehler, 351. 1 ff.

[30] *De hom. opif.*: *NPNF* v. 8. 4; 5. 2; 11. 4.

[31] τῆς θείας τε καὶ νοερᾶς οὐσίας: *De infant.*: *NPNF* v. 375; *GNO* iii: 2. 77. 17.

[32] *De an.*: *NPNF* v. 437; Oehler, 330. 23 ff.; see also *De hom. opif.*: *NPNF* v. 12. 6.

[33] Simplicity: e.g. *De an.*: *NPNF* v. 437; Oehler, 331. 5 (τὴν ἁπλῆν ἐκείνην καὶ ἀσύνθετον φύσιν); *De hom. opif.*: *NPNF* v. 11. 1; incomprehensibility: e.g. *De hom. opif.*: *NPNF* v. 11. 2–3.

[34] *Cat. or.* 5: Srawley, 23: 18–24. 2 (ET, p. 36); see also *De hom. opif.*: *NPNF* v. 4. 1, where human nature is described as being clothed with immortality because it is in God's image.

[35] It has already been seen that death is absent from the original state (above p. 50). Part of the problem is that, since Gregory insists that the soul is simple and therefore indivisible, it is difficult to see how the soul *could* die.

distinguishing in his own mind between the immortality of the *soul* (retained after the Fall) and the immortality of the *human being as a whole* (lost). Gregory's exegesis of the incident from the book of Exodus in which Moses first breaks the tablets of the Law and then replaces them with new ones is that the tablets represent human nature: it was once unbroken and immortal, but sin led to the tablets being broken. Christ, the true lawgiver, by becoming incarnate, cut new tablets of human nature from the earth for himself—a reference, presumably, to the incarnation. Through God's grace (the finger of the Holy Spirit imprinting letters on the tablets) human nature has thus become immortal.[36] The same idea is treated more simply in the first of the Easter sermons: the first human was immortal, sin led to the loss of immortality, but God was moved by pity to restore humanity to its ancient state.[37] Both of these passages thus seem to stress human nature as a whole losing immortality, not the soul.

What other qualities can humanity expect to recover after the resurrection? Gregory frequently lists those which came to humanity through being created in the image of God, but which were lost through sin; for example he concludes *De anima* thus:

> When such [evils] have been purged from it . . . then every one of the things which make up our conception of the good will come to take their place; incorruption, that is, and life and honour and grace and glory and everything else that we conjecture is to be seen in God and in His image, human nature.[38]

Other similar lists can be found in *De hominis opificio*, the *Catechetical Oration*, *De mortuis* and *In sanctum Pascha*.[39] Essentially the perfected soul's characteristics are of four types: intellectual (wisdom and reason);[40] moral (virtue, freedom of will, purity, freedom from passion);[41] denoting imperishability (incorruptibility,

[36] *De vita Moysis*: Malherbe and Ferguson, 2. 215–16.

[37] *In s. Pascha*: Hall, 11; *GNO* ix. 254; cf. *Cat. or.* 5: Srawley, 25: 5–7 (Srawley ET, p. 36).

[38] *De an.*: *NPNF* v. 468 (slightly altered); Oehler, 377. 1–6. The list of qualities: ἡ ἀφθαρσία, ἡ ζωή, ἡ τιμή, ἡ χάρις, ἡ δόξα, ἡ δύναμις.

[39] See *De hom. opif.*: *NPNF* v. 4. 1; 5. 1–2; 12. 9; 15. 11; *Cat. or.* 5; *In s. Pascha*: Hall, 11; *GNO* ix. 253–4; *De mort.*: Lozza, §15, 62. 26–33.

[40] σοφία, λόγος.

[41] ἀρετή, ἐλευθερία, καθαρότης, ἀπάθεια.

life);[42] denoting status (kingship, honour, glory).[43] Finally, the soul reflects its archetype in being good, blessed, and beautiful.[44] All these qualities are the result of the relation of the created soul to its Creator—which is a relation of grace (χάρις).

Sometimes the relationship between the image and the archetype is said to consist not only in the image being created by God, but also in its participation in God:

That nature which transcends everything is first and properly called blessed (μακάριον). Among humans however, that beatitude (τὸ μακάριον), which is the nature of the one participated in, occurs to a certain extent, and is specified by participation (τῇ μεθέξει) in true being. Likeness (ὁμοίωσις) to God, therefore, is a definition of human blessedness (τῆς ἀνθρωπίνης μακαριότητος).[45]

Similarly, Gregory describes the human purpose as looking upon God, which is 'participation in God' (τὸ τοῦ θεοῦ μετέχειν) and 'life nourishment appropriate to intellectual nature' (ζωὴ τῇ νοερᾷ φύσει ἐοικυῖά).[46] Furthermore, as R. Leys remarks, the fact that Gregory emphasizes in *De hominis opificio* that God 'imparted' (μετέδωκεν) not 'gave' (δέδωκεν) mind and reason to humanity again suggests that humans participate in God's νοῦς and λόγος, rather than being completely autonomous in these respects.[47] Like many other qualities properly belonging to humanity as the image of God, participation was impeded, although not completely stopped, by sin. So, Gregory seems to be referring to participation in the goodness of God, when he writes:

The goodness of God is not to be found separated from our nature nor established far away from those who choose God, but it is always in each person; unknown and hidden, whenever it is stifled by the cares and pleasures of life, but found again whenever we turn our thought to Him.[48]

[42] ἀφθαρσία, ζωή.

[43] τιμή, δόξα: Gregory uses no one particular word for kingship, but see *De hom. opif.*: *NPNF* v. 4 for his clearest comments on this quality.

[44] ἀγαθός, μακάριος, καλός (all characteristics also ascribed to God).

[45] *In insc. pss.* Heine, 84 (1. 1. 6); *GNO* v. 26. 6–10.

[46] *De infant.*: *NPNF* v. 375; *GNO* iii: 2. 79. 14 and 3. On this idea Leys also cites *Contra Eun.* 3. 6. 7 (in the Migne edition): R. Leys, *L'image de Dieu chez Saint Grégoire de Nysse: Esquisse d'une Doctrine* (Museum Lessianum: Section Théologique no. 49; L'édition Universelle, Bruxelles; Desclée de Brouwer, Paris, 1951), 69.

[47] Leys, *L'image de Dieu chez Saint Grégoire de Nysse*, 69, citing *De hom. opif.*: *PG* 44, 149b.

[48] *De virg.*: *SC* 119, 412. 2–7; *GNO* viii: 2. 300 (my translation).

Similarly, Gregory writes that humanity was created in the image of God, so that 'the participation in good may be the reward of virtue'.[49]

Gregory's doctrine of participation is not to be taken as implying that God's very self is actually in humans; rather, it seems to indicate that humans share in God's *qualities*. Nor does Gregory claim that all creation participates in God: he clearly thinks that humanity has a privileged position in this respect. Nevertheless it is also apparent that the image was given to human nature as a whole and that, at least potentially, it can be renewed in humanity as a whole.

iii. *Apatheia*, Desire, and Love

The concept of the image of God usefully focuses on the specific qualities which will be restored to humanity at the eschaton; however, one of these qualities raises a problem for Gregory's eschatology: this quality is *apatheia* (ἀπάθεια), freedom from passion (πάθος)—which might seem to imply or include freedom from desire (ὄρεξις). The problem arises because in several passages, notably in Gregory's spiritual works, the soul is described as having a natural and proper desire for God, or the Good. The questions of what this desire is, and whether it is compatible with *apatheia*, are important, for the answers shed much light on Gregory's perception of humanity's future relationship to God and provide an important background to the following chapter's discussion of the purification of the soul.

One resolution to the problem can be found in *De mortuis*, where Gregory differentiates between different objects of desire.[50] First, there is the desire for things which are necessary, given humanity's fallen state: the desire for food, drink, procreation, protection and so on.[51] These are also desired by animals, so a desire for them is not distinctive of humankind and is not intrinsically evil. Secondly, there is desire which springs from the previously mentioned natural and necessary desire but which pursues its objects immoderately: this leads to gluttony, sexual

[49] ὥστε ἆθλον ἀρετῆς εἶναι τὴν τῶν ἀγαθῶν μετουσίαν: *Cat. or.* 5: Srawley, 27. 2–3 (ET, p. 37).

[50] In *De mortuis* Gregory appears to use the words ὄρεξις and ἐπιθυμία synonymously; I translate both 'desire'.

[51] See for example, *De mort.*: Lozza, §17, 68. 13–22.

excess, violence, for example.[52] These varieties of intemperance *are* presumably distinctive of humans, for they are distinctive of humanity's fallen state. However, the Fall does not mean that they are not culpable: people are free to refrain from them.[53] (Like many pagan philosophers before him, Gregory entreats his audience to desire only the necessities of life.[54]) However, he also clearly recognizes a third aspect of desire, which is more profoundly 'natural' than the physical desires above. In an analogy drawn from the smelting of iron, Gregory notes that desire can be directed to materialistic impulses in this life (things like pleasure, wealth, love of glory, and so on).[55] However, in the afterlife the soul will be purified of these impulses (metaphorically portrayed as slag) so that only the pure desire (pure iron) remains:

> Denuded and purified from all these [materialistic impulses], our desire will turn its energy towards the only object of will and desire and love. It will not entirely extinguish our naturally occurring impulses towards such things, but will refashion them towards the immaterial participation in good things. For there shall lie the unceasing love of true beauty, there the praiseworthy greed for the treasures of wisdom, and the beautiful and good love of glory which is achieved in the communion of the kingdom of God, and the fine passion of insatiable appetite which will never be cut short in its good desire by a satiety of these things.[56]

This quotation makes it clear that it is not so much that there are several different human desires but rather that human desire is something which can be rightly or wrongly directed. Gregory

[52] See *De mort.*: Lozza, §17, 68. 23–70. 3. Strictly, these are granted to humanity by God in the second creation, because he foresaw that humanity would fall.

[53] In *De mortuis* Gregory makes it quite clear that it is human free choice which directs one 'away from need to the desire for what is unnecessary' (*De mort.*: Lozza, §17, 70. 5–6). See also *De hom. opif.*: *NPNF* v. 18. 1–4, esp. 18. 4: 'Our love of pleasure took its beginning from being made like to the irrational creation, and was increased by the transgressions of men . . .'.

[54] e.g. *De mort.*: Lozza, §17, 68. 23–6.

[55] *De mort.*: Lozza, §19, 70. 36–72. 2.

[56] *De mort.*: Lozza, §19, 72. 2–9 (my translation). *ὧν γυμνωθεῖσά τε καὶ καθαρθεῖσα πάντων ἡ ὄρεξις πρὸς τὸ μόνον ὀρεκτόν τε καὶ ἐπιθυμητὸν καὶ ἐράσμιον τῇ ἐνεργείᾳ τραπήσεται, οὐκ ἀποσβέσασα καθόλου τὰς ἐγκειμένας φυσικῶς ἡμῖν ἐπὶ τὰ τοιαῦτα ὁρμὰς ἀλλὰ πρὸς τὴν ἄυλον τῶν ἀγαθῶν μετουσίαν μεταποιήσασα. Ἐκεῖ γὰρ ὁ ἔρως τοῦ ἀληθινοῦ κάλλους ὁ ἄπαυστος, ἐκεῖ ἡ ἐπαινετὴ τῶν τῆς σοφίας θησαυρῶν πλεονεξία καὶ ἡ καλή τε καὶ ἀγαθὴ φιλοδοξία ἡ τῇ κοινωνία τῆς τοῦ θεοῦ βασιλείας κατορθουμένη καὶ τὸ καλὸν πάθος τῆς ἀπληστίας οὐδέποτε κόρῳ τῶν ὑπερκειμένων πρὸς τὸν ἀγαθὸν πόθον ἐπικοπτόμενον.* Clearly, Gregory is using the rhetorical technique of emphasizing the change, by the copious use of oxymoron: 'praiseworthy greed', 'fine passion', etc.

holds that humanity does have an inclination (ῥοπή) to the good: the problem is that humans make mistakes in this life as to what the good is, with the result that they align their desire towards their passions (παθημάτα), instead of towards the good.[57] Hence, Gregory appears to be distinguishing desire (ὄρεξις / ἐπιθυμία) from a mere impulse (ῥοπή / ὁρμή) or passion (πάθος / πάθημα).[58] Desire can be aligned with materialistic impulses and passions (the last two sorts of desire), or it can be aligned to an impulse for the good (the first). In the afterlife, when one is purified from all impulses and passions, one's natural desire will reach out to God. Ἀπάθεια is thus not absence of desire (ὄρεξις / ἐπιθυμία) but freedom from any *materialistic* impulse or passion (ῥοπή, ὁρμή, πάθος or πάθημα). Gregory's use of the words ὄρεξις and ἐπιθυμία comes close to meaning 'will'.

Later, in *De anima*, Gregory offers a more complex solution.[59] Here, in response to Gregory's questions about whether anger and appetite are truly characteristics of the soul, Macrina asserts that although they are 'to be observed in the soul' (ἐνορᾶσθαι τῇ ψυχῇ), the principles of appetite and anger (τὸ ἐπιθυμητικόν τε καὶ θυμοειδές) are not essential characteristics of the human soul.[60] She gives three reasons for this.[61] First, she asserts that, according to Scripture, 'there is no excellence in the soul which is not a property as well of the divine nature' and that since the principles of anger and appetite cannot be found in God, neither need one argue that they are necessary elements of the human

[57] *De mort.*: Lozza, §16, 66. 12–13. Sin is caused by an intellectual error (encouraged but not determined by earthly desires) as to what is the true good for humans.

[58] Gregory appears not to draw a significant distinction between urges and passions, beyond the fact that, strictly speaking, the former are active (an urge for something) and the latter passive (an emotional reaction to something).

[59] The dialogue form of *De anima*, and in particular the way in which Macrina's answers are modified in response to Gregory's criticisms, indicate that Gregory is very tentative about drawing any definitive conclusion about the nature of the soul. The following account is an attempt at synthesis which inevitably papers over some of the cracks in the argument of *De anima*. For a similar synthesis with less of an eschatological emphasis, see Rowan Williams, 'Macrina's Deathbed Revisited: Gregory of Nyssa on Mind and Passion', in L. Wickham, and C. Bammel (eds.), *Christian Faith and Philosophy in Late Antiquity* (= *Supplements to Vigiliae Christianae*, 19) (Brill, Leiden, 1993). One of Williams's themes is that Macrina's ambiguity over the status of passions and the soul rests at least partly on the genuinely ambiguous nature of the soul itself.

[60] *De an.*: *NPNF* v. 439; Oehler, 333. 13, 10. In *De anima* Gregory does not use ὄρεξις and ἐπιθυμία synonymously: I will translate the former as 'desire' and the latter as 'appetite'.

[61] See *De an.*: *NPNF* v. 439–40; Oehler, 333. 33–335. 16.

soul.[62] Secondly, she points out that as animals also have anger and appetite these principles are not distinctive to human nature and that what is unique in humans (the intellectual soul) cannot be identical to what is not (anger and appetite). Since it is the intellectual soul which is in God's image, anger and appetite cannot be part of that image.[63] Thirdly, Macrina argues further that anger and appetite cannot be essential human characteristics by pointing to the fact that, even in their earthly life, some people such as Moses have managed to battle with their reason against anger and appetite and to exist without them.

Later, when pressed by Gregory, Macrina admits that, since the intellectual soul is necessarily embodied in sentient matter, humans have both reason and the desire (ὄρεξις) for those necessaries of material existence.[64] The word desire covers anger and appetite and other passions (πάθη) which are neither good nor bad by necessity, but can be directed by reason towards virtue or vice.[65] This is similar to the view found in *De mortuis*, but there are some important differences. By distinguishing the intellectual soul from the sentient/animal aspect of humanity, Macrina is saying that the passions are only *associated with* the soul, not actually *of* it.[66] Also, the meaning of the word ὄρεξις in *De anima* is a general term covering emotions and inclinations (πάθη and κινήματα) and does not mean a faculty of desire which aligns itself with either right or wrong inclinations, as in *De mortuis*. Instead, free choice (προαίρεσις) is given more prominence as the rational faculty which determines whether the inclinations are used rightly or wrongly.

Although she admits that some forms of desire are necessary for this life on earth, Macrina is less clear as to whether they will appear in a future life. Is desire closely connected with embodiment *per se* (including that in the resurrection), or with that

[62] *De an.*: *NPNF* v. 439; Oehler, 333. 33–5.

[63] She also argues on this point that humans are defined according to their unique properties: that is, that what is not distinctive is not essential. The problem with this argument is that although it shows that anger and desire are not essential to a definition of humankind, it does not prove the point in question—that they are not essential in the sense that they do not pertain to humanity in its perfect state.

[64] *De an.*: *NPNF* v. 441; Oehler, 337. 18–24.

[65] *De an.*: *NPNF* v. 442; Oehler, 337. 33–8.

[66] She speaks of the passions being 'mixed with' or 'knit up with' the intellectual soul: ταῦτα τῷ νοερῷ τῆς ψυχῆς κατεμίχθη *De an.*: Oehler, 337. 24; τὰ συννημένα ibid.: Oehler, 337. 32.

embodiment which is animal? One would suspect the latter since there would seem to be no need of material food and so forth in that purified life and thus no need of appetite, nor any need to use anger in the fight against the devil. Her earlier argument that the principles of anger and appetite are not possessed by God would also seem to suggest that they are not part of humanity's perfect state. At one point, Macrina explicitly raises the question of whether appetite at least is absolutely essential to humanity, hypothesizing that the purpose of appetite being sown in us by God was that it would grow up in the direction of the true beauty. She asks:

> If human nature suffered such a mutilation [as the removal of appetite: ἐπιθυμία], what will there be to lift us up to grasp the heavenly heights? If love (ἀγάπης) is taken away from us, how shall we be united (συναφθησόμεθα) to God?[67]

Further on in *De anima*, Gregory echoes this question, challenging Macrina to explain how we will be drawn to God, given that after death all appetite will have been purged away.

> when every unreasoning instinct (κινήσεως) is quenched within the fire of purgation, this principle of appetite (τὸ ἐπιθυμητικὸν) will not exist any more than the other principles; and this being removed, it looks as if the striving after the better way would also cease, no other emotion (κινήματος) remaining in the soul that can turn us up to the appetence (ὄρεξιν) of the Good.[68]

Gregory questions whether this can really be so: Macrina's answer, following the principle that like attracts like, is that humans are drawn to God by their godlike part—that is by the 'speculative and critical faculty' of their soul (τὸ θεωρητικόν τε καὶ διακριτικόν).[69] When earthly passions no longer impede this, the soul will be naturally attracted to God—the more like God the image, the swifter the attraction:

> It will therefore be no detriment to our participation in the Good (τὴν τοῦ ἀγαθοῦ μετουσίαν), that the soul should be free from such emotions (κινημάτων), and . . . should behold the Original Beauty reflected in the mirror and in the figure of her own beauty.[70]

[67] *De an.*: *NPNF* v. 443; Oehler, 339. 22–4.
[68] *De an.*: *NPNF* v. 449; Oehler, 349. 4–8.
[69] *De an.*: *NPNF* v. 449; Oehler, 349. 9–10.
[70] *De an.*: *NPNF* v. 449; Oehler, 349. 23–7.

Macrina now emphasizes several times that, although it may be useful in this life, in fact appetite (ἐπιθυμία) is not *necessary* for this participation in the Good and will not survive in the resurrection-state. Indeed, according to her own earlier definition of appetite this would be impossible:

We should call [appetite: ἐπιθυμία] a seeking for that which is wanting, or a longing for pleasurable enjoyment, or a pain at not possessing that upon which the heart is set, or a state with regard to some pleasure which there is no opportunity of enjoying.[71]

As will be seen below, Gregory's doctrine of progressive participation in God rests on the assumption that at each stage the soul can advance further without feeling dissatisfied.

Thus in *De anima* Gregory and Macrina conclude that appetite by definition cannot be the driving force of the soul's advance towards God. Instead, the dynamism comes from the godlike qualities of the human soul which attract it to the divine.[72] Macrina does not mean only intellectual qualities; she clearly wants to avoid implying that the soul is drawn to comprehend God fully. Rather she speaks in terms of beauty attracting beauty and of the soul's love (ἀγάπη) of God.[73] For example, the soul is said to attach itself to the Good 'by means of the movement and the activity of love'.[74] Hence, Macrina explains the advance of the soul in terms, not of appetite (which implies lack), but of love (which implies fulfilment).

This language of love is also found in *In canticum canticorum*. Gregory's interpretation of the Song of Songs systematically

[71] *De an.*: *NPNF* v. 440; Oehler, 335. 20–23.

[72] However, as Rowan Williams points out, because the soul is embodied in actual human beings who have animal passions (due to God's forseeing the Fall), this dynamic attraction to God is always experienced in this life in the context of these passions. Indeed, he suggests that 'this freedom from instinct is—. . . concretely and historically—unrealisable without the force of desire in our present empirical humanity to "launch" it' (Williams, 'Macrina's Deathbed Revisited', 242). Certainly, it is at least true that Gregory shows a markedly positive attitude to embodiment and its compatibility with the spiritual life (reinforced by his doctrine of the resurrection); but the extent to which the soul's love of God is actually *dependent* on inferior but analogical human desires is perhaps less clear than Williams claims.

[73] 'For this is what love (ἀγάπη) is, the inherent affection towards a chosen object' (*NPNF* v. 450; Oehler, 350. 41–351. 1). For other references to love see *NPNF* v. 450 *passim* and Oehler, 351 *passim*. The word Gregory uses here is ἀγάπη, a choice partly dictated perhaps by his references to 1 Cor. 13 where Paul speaks of ἀγάπη, but also rejecting any connotations of unsatisfied desire which ἔρως might carry with it.

[74] διὰ τῆς ἀγαπητικῆς κινήσεώς τε καὶ ἐνεργείας: *De an.*: *NPNF* v. 450; Oehler, 351. 4–5.

interprets the desire of the bride for the bridegroom as the soul's desire—or love—for God. There are three interesting features of the way Gregory speaks of the soul's love of God in this later work. First, Gregory links love closely with appetite (ἐπιθυμία), but there is no need to assume a change of mind by Gregory on the issue. The difference can be attributed to the type of writing in each case. The *De anima*—a much more philosophical work—defines desire very specifically as something which does not properly belong to the soul and sees love not as an emotional response, but as the natural attraction of the soul to God. In his commentary on the Song of Songs, however, Gregory writes much more colourfully, and though his intention is to interpret the story of the bride and the bridegroom, he does not translate the story into strictly philosophical language. Hence he uses 'love' and 'desire' of the bride and of the soul alike and we are not to assume that these words, even when used of the soul, have the same precise meanings as they do in the *De anima*.

Secondly, the love involved is not just described as ἀγάπη, but also sometimes as ἐρῶς—a word which is much more readily associated with desire or appetite for what one does not have, rather than with fulfilment. However, Gregory sometimes qualifies his use of the word ἐρῶς by saying, for example, that it is a passionless sort of love, or a love according to the spirit, or that divine love is the opposite of physical love.[75] On one occasion, he explicitly defines ἐρῶς as intense ἀγάπη.[76] Thus, although Gregory may be using the word ἐρῶς to emphasize the intensity of the soul's attraction to God, it is clear that he is also disassociating it from any physical meaning.

Thirdly, Gregory's commentary on the Song of Songs emphasizes that desire or love for the divine is dynamic, that it draws the lover towards the beloved: in the Song of Songs this can be seen in the language of pursuit and yearning which it uses. Crucially, since the beloved—God—is infinite, Gregory reasons that the soul's progressive advance towards God must also be infinite.

[75] *In cant.* 1: *GNO* vi. 23. 12: 'Wisdom speaks clearly in Proverbs when it ordains the love (τὸν ἔρωτα) of divine beauty, for this is without reproach, a passionless passion directed at incorporeal things (ἀπαθὲς ἐπὶ τῶν ἀσωμάτων τὸ πάθος).' *In cant.* 1: *GNO* vi. 27. 13: 'It is necessary for [the soul] to quench all corporeal dispositions and seethe with love only in the spirit (μόνῳ τῷ πνεύματι ζέειν ἐρωτικῶς).' *In cant.* 1: *GNO* vi. 192. 1: ἐκ τῶν ἐναντίων τῇ σωματικῇ ἐπιθυμίᾳ τὸν θεῖον ἔρωτα γίνεσθαι.

[76] *In cant.* 13; *GNO* vi. 383: 9: ἐπιτεταμένη γὰρ ἀγάπη ὁ ἔρως λέγεται.

You see how boundless is the path for those rising up to God, yet how it is that what the soul has comprehended is the beginning of something beyond her? [He who looks at] the divine boundless beauty . . . continues to wonder at God's continuous revelation; he never exhausts his desire (ἐπιθυμίας) to see more because what he awaits is always more magnificent and more divine than anything he has seen . . .[77]

The idea of perpetual progress is opposed to a final static beatific vision of God (which in Gregory's view wrongly suggests that the soul is capable of comprehending God). It is important to remember that progress for Gregory is a *necessity* due to God's infinity, but also that it is nonetheless a *blessed* state for the soul.

In his discussion of Gregory's concept of perpetual progress, Richard Sorabji links it to a discussion of the value of philosophical perplexity. He notes that Aristotle and Plato appear to value the contemplation of truth more highly than the seeking of it, whereas for a 'minority tradition' 'happiness consists in *seeking* the truth'.[78] Yet this emphasis on opposing opinions about the essence of true happiness in relation to truth is perhaps slightly misleading. Gregory's famous doctrine of perpetual progress in the future state is based on the twin premisses of God's infinity and the soul's attraction to or advance towards God, which he calls desire. Because of God's infinity even the most perfect experience of God cannot but be a continuous advance. Again, although it is clear in fact that Gregory's vision appeals to some readers and not others, for Gregory himself the experience was *by definition* a happy one, for the desire drawing the soul to God is the deepest and most true expression of humanity and the purifying of oneself so as to allow this desire free rein leads to real freedom and fulfilment.[79] Gregory's most contentious assumption—that desire can simultaneously be fulfilled and yet not sated—is explained by his

[77] *In cant.* 11 (slightly altered from McCambley): *GNO* vi. 320. 8–10 and 321. 16–22. That this doctrine is not confined to Gregory's spiritual writings alone can be seen by reference to a description in *De mortuis* of the soul's insatiable appetite in the future state: *De mort.*: Lozza, §6. Oddly, in one place Gregory asserts the opposite view, stating that the activity of wisdom is two-fold and that whereas we will continue to retain what we have learnt, we will cease inquiring: 'For of what use will inquiry be, when that which is inquired after will be present?' *In insc. pss.*: Heine, 119 (1. 8. 111); *GNO* v. 64.

[78] Richard Sorabji, *Time, Creation and the Continuum: Theories in Antiquity and the Early Middle Ages* (Duckworth, London, 1983), 150.

[79] Similarly, it is Aristotle's and Plato's philosophical presuppositions about the nature of knowledge and the possibility of knowing God, that lead them to associate happiness with θεωρία (contemplation).

doctrine of the soul's participation in the goodness of God. He thinks that our progress is in one sense not so much *towards* God (as if one were chasing an infinitely distant object) but *in* God—towards progressively fuller participation. Provided that it is not masked by evil, any participation in God must, by definition, be satisfying, hence Gregory can assert his paradoxical doctrine of fulfilment without satiety.[80] (This doctrine is much easier to understand in terms of the love of the good, rather than knowledge of the truth, although in fact Gregory uses both types of terminology.) So, the doctrine of perpetual progress is about the soul's relation to God, not its relation to philosophical truth. The importance of this doctrine of perpetual progress for Gregory's universalist eschatology will be examined in the next chapter; for the time being it is merely necessary to emphasize again that infinite progress is for Gregory an *essential* characteristic of the soul's ideal relationship to God.

To conclude this section on love and desire, then, it can be seen that in its perfect, purified state the soul will be naturally attracted to God, as like is attracted to like. Gregory describes this attraction as love (in the *De anima*) or sometimes as desire (in *De mortuis* and in his spiritual works). The soul, however, will be purified both of any vicious impulses and also of those natural impulses and passions which were granted to humanity in the second creation and which are shared by animals.

B. RESURRECTION

The concept of the image of God emphasizes the spiritual perfection of humanity which will be completed at the eschaton. However, as we have seen, Gregory also claims that in the first creation, humankind was physically perfect. The assertion that this perfection will be finally achieved in actuality at the eschaton is conveyed in Gregory's doctrine of the resurrection, which he constantly refers to as the restoration of humanity to its original state.

[80] Sorabji does emphasize the point about God's infinity ('since the distance between us and God is always infinite, there will always be more to understand') but Gregory's second premiss that a human's proper desire is for God and his tacit assumption that this desire can be fulfilled and yet not sated are also needed to explain why perpetual progress can be pleasant instead of endlessly frustrating.

Although he is slightly ambivalent about the nature of the resurrection body in the *De mortuis* (an early work, *c.* 371), by the time of the *De hominis opificio* (*c.* 379) and the *De anima* (*c.* 380) Gregory is firmly committed to the view that people will be resurrected with bodies composed of identically the same physical matter of which their bodies were constituted in their lifetimes.[81] According to Gregory, the body is composed of particles (στοιχ-εῖα—sometimes unhelpfully translated 'atoms'). Each particle is of one of the four elements—fire, earth, water, air. In combination, the particles are in tension and they do not necessarily show the characteristics of their respective elements (fire being hot, for example). In separation, each of the constituent particles returns to its home element: particles of air to the air, those of fire to fire, earth to earth, and water to water.[82] In *De mortuis* this dissolution is seen more as a consequence of death, not as death itself which is the departure of the soul from the body. Hence, the dead, 'being mind and spirit (νοῦς καὶ πνεῦμα), those who are freed from flesh and blood, do not have such a nature as to be seen by those encumbered by the heaviness of the body'.[83] Throughout *De mortuis* Gregory emphasizes that this separation is good—this is the whole rhetorical point of his *consolatio*. His main argument is that since the truly good is immaterial, by being released into immateriality by death, we come nearer to the good in death.[84]

[81] *De mortuis oratio* is an early and highly rhetorical piece, based on the classical *consolatio*, persuading Christians not to mourn over their loved ones by revealing the glories of the next life. *De hominis opificio* is a discourse on the creation of humanity, intended as a sequel to Basil's *Hexaemeron*. *De anima* is one of Gregory's most impressive works. Based in structure on Plato's *Phaedo*, in which Socrates bravely faces death and philosophizes about the immortality of the soul, *De anima* portrays the dying Macrina answering Gregory's queries about the soul and resurrection. The dialogue thus not only emphasizes Macrina's wisdom as *didaskalos* and her saintliness in facing up to disease and death, but also deals with complex doctrinal issues, possibly not just for the reason that they fascinated Gregory, but also because, as in *De mortuis*, he genuinely believed that this sort of philosophy was a succour in a time of bereavement. At the beginning of *De anima* he notes that 'the impulse to mourn for [Basil] was shared by all the churches' (*NPNF* v. 430; Oehler, 319. 5–6) and in *De vita Macrinae* (SC 178, §§26–35) he recounts the grief upon his sister's death; perhaps then *De anima* was in part a response to personal and collective grief over these two figures.

[82] *De mort.*: Lozza, §5: 'the body is separated and dissolved into the elements (στοιχεῖα) from which it was made up'. Cf. ibid., §11, 52. 7–8 and *In s. Pascha*: Hall, 18; *GNO* ix. 263–4, where Gregory emphasizes that the particles of the body are separated, but not completely annihilated.

[83] *De mort.*: Lozza, §7, 48. 14–15; see also §6.

[84] *De mort.*: Lozza, §11, 50. 36—52. 2.

taking off our fleshly covering (τὴν σαρκώδη περιβολὴν) like a horrid mask, we return to our proper beauty in which we were formed from the beginning, becoming like the form of our archetype. . . . For the matter of the body (ἡ τοῦ σώματος ὕλη) is a stranger and foreigner to the bodiless spirit (τῇ ἀσωμάτῳ φύσει); the mind is bound up by necessity in this life and perseveres although it is living an alien (ἀλλοφύλῳ) life.[85]

His second consolatory argument is that since the elements in human bodies are bound together in an uneasy coexistence, death releases people from this battle into peace.[86]

The emphasis upon the release of the soul from the body echoes much of Greek philosophy in the Platonic tradition, particularly perhaps Socrates' arguments in the *Phaedo*.[87] Gregory implies that the important part of the human being is the soul by arguing that what humans truly are is unseen: 'So, looking at what has decomposed, do not think that you see yourself.'[88] However, the emphasis on the soul presents two important theological problems for the Christian. First, it raises questions about the resurrection: if 'I' am truly my soul, then why does my body need to be resurrected? If death is a release, will not resurrection be reimprisonment? Gregory's answer to the first question is that resurrection is testified to by Scripture. The second question is more problematic for the *De mortuis* because Gregory so emphasizes life after death as a release from the body. This problem is only partially resolved by the fact that, when he does mention the resurrection body, he continually stresses how different it is from its earthly counterpart, implying that the new embodiment will not be prison-like:

When [the body] has changed into something more godly (πρὸς τὸ θειότερον) through the rebirth (διὰ τῆς παλιγγενεσίας), the soul will beautify [the body's] superfluous and useless parts for the enjoyment of the future life . . .[89]

[85] *De mort.*: Lozza, §11, 52. 2–4 and 52. 9–11.

[86] *De mort.*: Lozza, §11, 52. 23–4; in death the soul has peace and quiet: εἰρήνην (52. 28) ἡσυχίας (52. 31).

[87] See for example *Phaedo* 64c: 'And by death do we not mean simply the departure of the soul from the body?' Cf. Cherniss, 'The Platonism of Gregory of Nyssa', section ii. Gregory repeats the assertion in the *Phaedo* that those in the body are like prisoners: *De mort.*: Lozza, §7, 46; cf. *Phaedo* 62b.

[88] *De mort.*: Lozza, §8, 48. 26–7.

[89] *De mort.*: Lozza, §18, 70. 7–10.

This desire to stress the difference between this and the next life perhaps explains why Gregory spends more time discussing the qualities of the resurrection body than in later dialogues: for instance he states that it will be light and will move in a different way from an earthly body, that sexual differentiation will disappear, and that the form of the resurrection body will reflect a person's virtuous or bad habits.[90] Sometimes he even speaks in the work as if the resurrection body will be a replacement, not the former body renewed. (The reference to 'change' in the quotation above may imply that there will be some sort of bodily continuity and not a replacement spiritual or heavenly body; however, it is difficult to see in what the continuity consists.) Nevertheless, the main emphasis of *De mortuis* seems to be on the soul as true self.

Secondly, the view that the person is essentially the soul calls into question the value and point of our life here and now. This is very much the weakest point of *De mortuis*: Gregory has been at such pains to emphasize that life without the body is incomparably better, his arguments struggle to show why God subjects humans to embodiment.[91] His first argument that embodiment is part of the natural sequence of life and that it is part of the journey of life, not an end in itself, is coherent, but would have been more convincing if he had not previously depicted embodiment so negatively. Next Gregory appears to argue that embodiment (or at least, the irrationality which comes with physicality) is not bad because it is not a punishment for the Fall, but is rather God's way of ensuring that the evil in humanity caused by the Fall will eventually be purged away without endangering human free will.[92] Embodiment would then seem to be a blessing in disguise, which again would be a satisfactory case had Gregory not originally attempted to portray the body as a prison.

As Daniélou has noted, *De mortuis* is more Origenistic than, for example, *De hominis opificio* and *De anima,* in that in it Gregory

[90] Weight and movement: *De mort.*: Lozza, §20, 72. 26–33; sexual differentiation: ibid., 72. 35 ff; 74. 6 ff; virtue or vice: ibid., 74. 36–7; 75. 5–11.

[91] For these arguments see *De mort.*: Lozza, §§14–16.

[92] See *De mort.*: Lozza, §§14–16. It is unclear here whether Gregory thinks that the 'coats of skin' (ibid. 62. 28; 64. 29) which God gave to humans as the result of the Fall are physical bodies (as in Origen) or mortality and irrationality (as later in Gregory of Nyssa's writings). In this context, I think that the former interpretation makes more sense.

seems ambivalent to the idea of re-embodiment.[93] He suggests that Gregory's move away from this line of thought was influenced by Methodius' *De resurrectione*, because *De anima* in particular shares this work's strong emphasis on the identity of the earthly and the resurrection bodies and a reluctance to make any statement which might be interpreted as Origenistic.[94] The difficulty of the Methodian view of resurrection, however, lies in explaining how one's risen body will be identical and continuous with the body one has in one's lifetime; it is to this challenge that Gregory rises in *De anima* and—to a lesser extent—in *De hominis opificio*. His solution is subtle and imaginative and T. J. Dennis suggests that Gregory's 'one truly original contribution' to the debate over resurrection is his solution to the problem.[95]

Methodius strongly asserts that bodily continuity has to lie in identical bodily substance, form, and structure; Gregory is less emphatic about the latter two, but certainly believes that the earthly and resurrection bodies must share identically the same particles:

> For if the identical individual particle (ἀκριβῶς τὸ ἴδιον) does not return and only something that is homogenous but not identical (ἐκ δὲ τοῦ ὁμογενοῦς ἀντὶ τοῦ ἰδιάζοντός) is fetched, you will have something else in place of that first thing, and such a process will cease to be a resurrection (ἀνάστασις) and will be merely the creation of a new man (καινοῦ ἀνθρώπου δημιουργία).[96]

But this raises the further question of how the particles of the body, which are clearly dispersed in decomposition, are brought back together again. The two most important versions of Gregory's answer rest not only on appeals to the omnipotence

[93] Jean Daniélou, 'La chronologie des oeuvres de Grégoire de Nysse', *Studia Patristica* 7 (= *Texte und Untersuchungen* 92) (1966), 160. He uses this contrast to help date these works. (*De mortuis* is also more Origenistic in that in it Gregory interprets the 'coats of skin' as bodies, suggesting that there was an original state which was not physical.).

[94] For a brief discussion of Origen and Methodius on the resurrection, see above, Chapter 1, section c. Cf. T. J. Dennis, 'Gregory and the Resurrection of the Body', in A. Spira and C. Klock, *The Easter Sermons of Gregory of Nyssa* (Philadelphia Patristic Foundation, Cambridge, Mass., 1981), 55–7. Methodius died in about 311, before Gregory was born; although his work clearly influenced Gregory's change of emphasis the precise stimulus of this change may never be known.

[95] Dennis, 'Gregory and the Resurrection of the Body', 57.

[96] *De an.*: *NPNF* v. 446; Oehler, 343. 42–344. 4; see also *De an.*: *NPNF* v. 453 (Oehler, 355. 34–5), 454 (Oehler, 356. 27–8), 459–60 (Oehler, 364. 29–30); *In s. Pascha*: Hall, 9; *GNO* ix. 251.

of God (as Methodius' solution did), but on analyses of the relation of soul to body and the consequent power of the soul to bring the elements of the body back together again.

In *De hominis opificio* Gregory suggests that this ability lies in the close connection of body and soul in life:

As the soul is disposed to cling and long for the body that has been wedded to it, there also attaches to it in secret a certain close relationship and power of recognition (*τοῦ οἰκείου σχέσις τε καὶ ἐπίγνωσις*), in virtue of their commixture, as though some marks had been imprinted by nature.[97]

Asserting that the body is not in complete flux, he claims that the form (*εἶδος*) of the body is its 'stable and unalterable element (*τὸ μόνιμόν τε καὶ ὡσαύτως ἔχον*)' which is allied to the soul. Using an everyday analogy, he compares the *eidos* to the impression (device or pattern) in a seal, which both leaves its mark on the particles of the body (pieces of wax) and marks the soul (the seal-stone) itself: 'the form necessarily remains with the soul as the impression of a seal remains with what it has impressed'.[98]

Those things which have received from the seal the impression of its stamp do not fail to be recognized by the soul, but at the time of the world-reformation (*τῆς ἀναστοιχειώσεως*) it receives back to itself all those things which correspond to the stamp of the form.[99]

Hence, although Gregory does stress that it is God's omnipotence which guarantees the resurrection (providing the power by which the particles are retrieved), he also suggests a more technical explanation of the means by which they are recognized.[100]

[97] *De hom. opif.*: *NPNF* v. 27. 2; *PG* 44, 225b.

[98] *De hom. opif.*: *NPNF* v. 27. 5; *PG* 44, 228b. My translation, translating *ἐκμαγεῖον* as that which is impressed by a seal (rather than the impression carved in the seal) and *σφραγίς* as the impression carved in the seal (rather than the whole seal itself). It seems to make most sense in this rather tricky analogy to take *σφραγίς* to mean specifically the shape or form of the impression in the seal, so as to obtain a closer analogy with the human *eidos* or form. This approach seems also to fit better with the other analogy which he uses: the owner (soul) of animals (particles of the body) being able to recognize them because of a mark on them (*eidos*) which the owner recognizes.

[99] *De hom. opif.*: *NPNF* v. 27. 5.

[100] It is typical of Gregory's approach to theology, that he is not content merely to say why something is\happens (because it is willed by God, for example) but tries to explain how it is\happens that way. His explanations seem to be motivated partly from a natural fascination with science and partly from a view that belief in the bodily resurrection, for example, can be strengthened by such explanations.

In *De anima* Gregory's argument again rests on the ability of the soul to recognize all the particles of the body, despite the fact that they have been separated from one another and have returned to groups of other particles of the same element. This time, the soul's ability is described as being due to its intimate knowledge of the body, which arises from the fact that it dwells 'in' the body's particles both before death and after—'like a guardian' (οἱονεὶ φύλακα).[101]

> the soul will be near each [atom] by its power of recognition (τῇ γνωστικῇ δυνάμει) and will persistently cling to the familiar atoms until their concourse after this division again takes place in the same way, for that fresh formation of the dissolved body, which will properly be, and be called, resurrection.[102]

Although the soul is immaterial, it is not prevented from existing in the particles any more than it is prevented from existing in the whole body, or any more than God could fail to permeate the whole of material creation.[103]

Dennis argues that these two explanations of the process by which the resurrection is achieved are substantially different, but this is to exaggerate the case.[104] It is likely that in *De anima* Gregory wanted to avoid using the word εἶδος ('form') which might sound too Origenistic: Origen argued that the form of the body remained in the future life whilst the actual atoms were replaced. However, when he uses the word εἶδος in *De hominis opificio* Gregory is clearly asserting that the form which remains in the soul after death is the means by which the identical atoms are restored—a very different theory from Origen's, despite the similarity in terminology. His references in *De anima* to the soul's intimate knowledge of the body are vague and could well be another way of expressing the *De hominis opificio* theory without using the word εἶδος, for it would seem to make sense to suggest that the soul's 'power of recognition' lies in the stamp of the form. Similarly, the statement that the soul remains 'in' the atoms is the result of stating more explicitly the implications of holding that the soul is immaterial, rather than a completely new departure.

[101] *De an.*: *NPNF* v. 446; Oehler, 344. 8.
[102] *De an.*: *NPNF* v. 445; Oehler, 343. 25–31.
[103] *De an.*: *NPNF* v. 445; Oehler, 342. 20–7.
[104] Dennis, 'Gregory and the Resurrection of the Body', 60.

In contrast to the problematic notion of the soul leaving the body, the theory of the *De anima* has three main advantages: it implies that the human person is truly both soul and body, affirms the value of this earthly material life, and provides a clear basis of identity between the earthly and risen bodies.[105] The theological problems are that it is unclear why the resurrection body is an improvement on the present one and that it is now difficult to say what death actually is. With regard to the latter point, if the soul remains 'in' or somehow connected to the atoms, the moment of death cannot be said to be that at which the soul leaves the body; on the other hand, the beginning of the dissolution of atoms seems to be too late to be called the moment of death. Gregory in fact seems implicitly to hold that the soul does not leave the body, but simply ceases to animate it—without making clear what this might mean.

The former problem—as to whether the resurrection body is an improvement—is of more significance. As Gregory comments to Macrina in his sceptical role in the latter piece:

> if our bodies are to live again in every respect the same as before, this thing that we are expecting is simply a calamity: whereas if they are not the same the person raised up will be another than he who died.[106]

Gregory's problem is made worse by his insistence on the exact identity of particles in the two bodies, for if all the particles are restored, surely any marks of disease and age will also be restored? Gregory's answer is that the same matter will have different qualities. His account of what these qualities will be is very similar to his words in *De mortuis*—the body will be lighter and without sexual differentiation, for example, as well as lacking the marks of disease or ageing. The puzzle of how the same particles can have changed qualities Gregory answers with recourse to great faith in the transforming power of the resurrection. Ultimately, Macrina appeals to the fact that the answer is hidden: 'we shall be taught the mystery of the Resurrection by the reality of it'.[107] To supplement this answer, one can perhaps point to Gregory's assumption that different combinations of

[105] For the affirmation that humans are characterized by the conjunction of soul and body see *In s. Pascha* Hall, 21; *GNO* ix. 266.

[106] *De an.*: *NPNF* v. 462; Oehler, 368. 28–30.

[107] *De an.*: *NPNF* v. 464; Oehler, 371. 11.

particles form things with very different qualities: a group of exclusively water particles form water, which is wet, flowing and freezable, yet the body, because the water particles are in combination with particles of the other elements, does not have these characteristics (or at least has a different sort of wateriness). Again, water particles mixed with the other elements in a flower will have different qualities. It is conceivable then that just as different combinations of different particles have different qualities, so (slightly) different combinations of the *same* particles will result in the resurrection body having (slightly) different qualities: the same particles will make up the eye, but because of a slightly different arrangement the eye will not be diseased. Even if this solution were coherent, it does not solve the sort of grotesque problems which pagans traditionally raised for Christian apologists—people who had lost limbs to wild animals, for example, or those born without a body part. It is one occasion where Gregory fails to appreciate the problem, or perhaps silently sets it aside, his ingenuity and imagination having for once failed to rise to a solution.

Although from the point of view of modern science one has to reject Gregory's account of the resurrection, it has much historical and theological interest: it is interesting that Gregory clearly feels compelled to assert the complete material identity of the earthly and resurrection bodies, despite his awareness of the problems that this theory causes and despite his recognition that even in earthly life the particles of the body are in constant flux.[108] Whereas another theologian might be willing to assert identity of form, but not of matter, Gregory avoids this solution as being too reminiscent of Origen.

So the answer to the question of whether a material body is included in Gregory's conception of ἀποκατάστασις is yes—with the qualification that it is clearly a body of a different quality. Hence the restoration will be both physical and spiritual, reflecting the fact that Gregory's conception of humanity in the first creation was perfect in both body and soul. Again it seems clear that resurrection is possible for all human beings and indeed Gregory's powerful defence of the resurrection in *De anima* leaves one with the impression that resurrection is the

[108] *De hom. opif.*: *NPNF* v. 27. 3.

inevitable consequence of death. He does not appear even to consider the possibility that only the saints will be resurrected.

C. VISIONS OF HEAVEN

Besides referring to Scripture for the doctrines of the creation, Fall and resurrection, Gregory also uses it to illuminate his view of the nature of the afterlife. His commentaries on various biblical passages confirm that he sees the resurrection state as one of both spiritual and physical perfection and also hints that it will be collective, and perhaps even universal.

A particularly vivid example can be found in Gregory's treatise on the inscriptions of the psalms (*In inscriptiones psalmorum*). Gregory interprets the Psalter as a coherent whole in which the order of the psalms reflects the order of humanity's pilgrimage. Hence Psalm 150, a hymn of praise, indicates to Gregory the praise of God at the eschaton:

> After this, when humanity (ἡ ἀνθρωπίνη δύναμις) has laid aside everything that is of the earth and noiseless and silent, it joins the sound of its own 'strings' with the loudness of the 'drums' in the heavenly choirs. . . .
>
> For such a combination . . . when human nature (ἡ ἀνθρωπίνη φύσις) is again exalted to its original condition, will produce that sweet sound of thanksgiving through their meeting with one another. And through one another and with one another they will sing a song of thanksgiving to God for his love of humanity which will be heard throughout the universe. . . .
>
> And when [the enemy] has been destroyed completely . . . then praise will be ceaselessly offered fully to God with equal honour by every breathing creature (ἐν πασῃ πνοῇ) forever.[109]

It is worth quoting this passage at length, for it includes four important aspects of the final heavenly state, as Gregory sees it. First, the passage stresses *activity*: the vital energy of Gregory's interpretation reflects that of the psalm, but also reminds one of the ceaseless activity of the perpetual progress of the soul. Gregory makes similar comments on the inscription of Psalms 52 and 87: translating the psalms' inscription '*Maeleth*' as 'by means of a choral dance', he writes:

> For the inscription means that choral dancing and rejoicing await those who have prevailed in the struggles [over evil] . . . The entire spiritual

[109] *In insc. pss.*: Heine, 120–1 (1. 9. 116–18); *GNO* v. 66: 7–9, 16–22; 67: 3–6.

creation (πάσης τῆς νοητῆς κτίσεως) joins in an harmonious choral chant, as it were, with the victors.[110]

The two passages emphasize that the activity is not some aimless bustle, but the specific activity of praising God for his victory over evil.[111] It is not important to ask whether Gregory literally means that there will be singing and dancing in heaven: the essential point is the emphasis on the eschaton as an active, not passive experience. Hence, in *De mortuis* Gregory reminds his audience that the future life will be free from the unwelcome passive experiences of this life, both physical (such as war and earthquakes) and mental (such as anger, fear, and misery); there will be no grief, no orphanhood or widowhood, and no envy or contemptuous superiority, because all will be equal.[112] Furthermore, although Gregory stresses the vitality of the future life, he naturally emphasizes that there will be no labour of the sort that humans are compelled to undertake in this life to feed and clothe themselves, and so on.[113]

Secondly, the passage from *In inscriptiones psalmorum* implies the *beauty* of the victory song. A stronger emphasis on beauty is apparent in *De mortuis* where Gregory writes with a rhetorical flourish of the beauty of heaven—of the movements of the sun, moon, and stars, of the variety of the (new) earth's produce, of the sea, of the grandeur of the public and private buildings of the celestial city.[114] Again, less important than the question of whether there actually will be buildings, for example, is the general tone which emphasizes that humanity's environment will be transformed: in Gregory's theology, beauty indicates perfection. The beauty of the music and of the celestial realm of course reflects the only true and fully perfect beauty of God himself, just as the restored beauty of the image of God in humankind reflects its archetype:

[110] *In insc. pss.*: Heine, 138–9 (2. 6. 59); *GNO* v. 86. 4–5, 13–14.

[111] Gregory notes elsewhere that humanity's purpose is to glorify God in all creation, by means of its intellectual nature.

[112] *De mort.*: Lozza, §6: 'Equality and democracy (ἰσηγορία τίς καὶ ἰσονομία) live together as fellow-citizens through completely peaceful freedom in the populace of souls' (my translation). There is a problem with using this section of *De mortuis* as evidence for Gregory's views on the future life, because it appears to be talking about souls alone—however, I assume that the comments which I have selected would apply to an embodied or a bodiless state.

[113] See e.g. *De vita Moysis*: Malherbe and Ferguson, 2. 145; *De hom. opif.*: *NPNF* v. 18. 9; 19.

[114] *De mort.*: Lozza, §7.

For the beauty excelling these things, which the truthful word says is seen by the pure in heart, is greater than all hope and higher than conjectural comparison.[115]

Thirdly, Gregory's interpretation of Psalm 150 appears to be *universally inclusive* in its reference: Gregory writes of 'humanity', 'human nature', and 'every breathing creature', rather than of the blessed as opposed to the damned.[116] Furthermore, he asserts that the heavenly song will last for ever and will spread throughout the universe.

Finally, one is struck by the passage's emphasis on the *unity* between humanity and the angels and—implicitly—between individual humans too: the harmony of the music is obviously intended to reflect the harmony of the community of heaven.[117] In another work he suggests that this harmony is not only interpersonal but also intrapersonal:

the structure of our bodies [will be] harmoniously set out for the participation in the good things.[118]

This contrasts with the present state of the body, which is composed of elements which are always in tension with, or struggling against each other.[119] Not only does the harmonious unity apply at all levels of the heavenly kingdom, but it seems implicitly to be connected to the universalism of Gregory's claims: in being drawn to God, all are drawn together, ultimately united and not separated by judgement. This is expressed in a passage commenting on the Song of Songs:

If love (ἀγάπη) perfectly casts out fear . . . then will be found unity, the result of salvation, when all have been united with one another in being grafted on to the sole good . . . (*τότε εὑρίσκεται μονὰς τὸ σῳζόμενον ἐν τῇ πρὸς τὸ μόνον ἀγαθὸν συμφυΐᾳ πάντων ἀλλήλοις ἑνωθέντων*) But all will become one, adhering to the one and only good; so that through the

[115] *De mort.*: Lozza, §7; 48. 1–3.

[116] This passage is not conclusive evidence for Gregory's doctrine of universal salvation, for it is compatible with conditional immortality; however, Gregory nowhere appears to consider that doctrine, apparently assuming that all souls are immortal and that all bodies will be resurrected.

[117] See a specific reference to 'harmony': *In insc. pss.*: Heine, 122 (2. 9. 121); *GNO* v. 68.

[118] *ἡ τοῦ σώματος ἡμῶν παρασκευὴ ἁρμοδίως πρὸς τὴν τῶν ἀγαθῶν μετουσίαν διατεθεῖσα* *De mort.*: Lozza, §18, 70. 12–13.

[119] *De mort.*: Lozza, §6.

unity of the Holy Spirit . . . tied with the bond of peace, all will become one body, and one spirit, through one hope to which they were called . . .[120]

This extract makes it quite clear that it is union with God which makes unity with each other possible—indeed, which makes unity of all humanity possible.

Thus, eschatological perfection will be both physical and spiritual. Gregory is at pains in his important dogmatic writings to assert that individuals will be resurrected with the same physical body which they possessed in life—although in other works he sometimes puts greater emphasis on spiritual, rather than physical perfection. According to Gregory's theology of the restoration of the divine image, this ideal relationship of the soul to God consists in the full participation of the soul in God and the perpetual progress of the soul towards and into God through the attraction of love. His direct references to the qualities of the future life suggest activity, beauty, unity and—implicitly—universality. In stressing the creation–resurrection parallel, Gregory also appears to imply that perfection and resurrection can (and perhaps will) apply to all humans created by God.

In the next chapter more direct evidence for the universality of Gregory's concept of salvation will be considered, bearing in mind the themes dealt with so far. In particular, one implication of Gregory's theology of the image of God will be examined: if the image is present in humanity as a whole, and if the image will be restored, does this necessarily entail the restoration of all human individuals? Other bases for Gregory's universalism will also be assessed, including those which imply the salvation of the whole universe.

[120] *In cant.* 15: *PG* 44, 1116; *GNO* vi. 466. 5–8; 466: 18–467. 2. In some places Gregory speaks of a division caused by judgement, but this appears to be a temporary condition. See next chapter.

3

Universal Perfection

From the analysis in Chapter 1 of the way in which Gregory uses the word ἀποκατάστασις it was seen that although the primary meaning of the word is restoration to a perfect state, Gregory also uses it in apparently universalistic contexts. In Chapter 2 the examination of the idea that the resurrection will be a restoration of humanity's spiritually and physically perfect state also suggested that Gregory envisaged the perfectibility and perhaps the actual salvation of all human beings. This chapter will assess whether Gregory's eschatology is indeed universalistic and will then ask whether his arguments for universalism are coherent, given the emphasis which he places on human freedom as a defining characteristic of human nature. The challenge is that it is difficult to see how the most recalcitrant of sinners could be saved without a degree of compulsion from God, which would appear to threaten their freedom.

A. EVIDENCE FOR GREGORY'S UNIVERSALISM

The most obvious evidence for Gregory's universalism is in several passages where he directly states that all will be saved, or in which he pointedly refers to the salvation of even the most sinful. However, these passages rarely explain the reasons for Gregory's belief in universal salvation, so it is also necessary to look at other passages which place the belief in context, or which deal with the theological presuppositions of the belief.

i. Direct Statements

Perhaps the clearest statement of Gregory's universalism is to be found in *De anima et resurrectione*. Macrina has set herself the task of supporting her claims about the resurrection with scriptural references; in fact she goes beyond this and interprets Psalm 118 not only as evidence for the resurrection, but also as supporting universalism.[1] The image is that of the feast of Tabernacles and of celebrations in the Temple, which Macrina interprets as a type representing eschatological celebrations.

Since all the further barriers by which our sin has fenced us off from the things within the veil are in the end to be taken down, whenever the time comes that the tabernacle of our nature is as it were to be fixed up again in the Resurrection, and all the inveterate corruption of sin has vanished from the world, then a universal feast will be kept around the Deity by those who have decorated themselves in the Resurrection; and one and the same banquet will be spread for all, with no differences cutting off any rational creature from an equal participation in it; for those that are now excluded by reason of their sin will at last be admitted within the holiest places of God's blessedness . . .[2]

Macrina then quotes Philippians 2: 10—'that at the name of Jesus every knee should bow, in heaven and on earth and under the earth'. She assumes that Paul means by this 'the accord of the whole universe with the good' (*τὴν τοῦ παντὸς πρὸς τὸ ἀγαθὸν συμφωνίαν*) and therefore that the verse gives universalism a scriptural foundation.[3]

A second place where Gregory emphasizes that sinners will eventually be saved is the famous passage from *The Life of Moses* which mentions a universal *apokatastasis*. It occurs in the middle of Gregory's interpretation of the plagues upon Egypt, which he sees as the effect of sin on sinners, the righteous (the Hebrews)

[1] The reference—to Psalm 118: 27—is somewhat obscure and confused. Macrina takes the psalm to refer to the redecoration and setting up of tabernacles (in the feast of Tabernacles) both of which are interpreted as indicating the resurrection ('the true tabernacle-fixing'). However, she also follows a variant reading of the verse—'keep the Feast among the decorators'—which she takes to mean that one day those who were formerly not allowed to enter the Temple will be given the same privileges as those who decorate the innermost part of the Temple. See Moore's note on *De anima* (= *De an.*): *NPNF* v. 460 n. 2.

[2] *De an.*: *NPNF* v. 461; Oehler, 366. 27–35: *ἀλλ' ἐπειδὴ μέλλει ποτὲ τὰ μέσα ταῦτα παραφράγματα λύεσθαι, δι' ὧν ἡμας ἡ κακία πρὸς τὰ ἐντος τοῦ καταπετάσματος ἀπετείχισεν, ὅταν σκηνοπηγηθῇ πάλιν διὰ τῆς ἀναστάσεως ἡμῶν ἡ φύσις, καὶ πᾶσα ἡ κατὰ κακίαν ἐγγενομένη διαφθορὰ ἐξαφανισθῇ τῶν ὄντων, τότε κοινὴ συστήσεται ἡ περὶ τὸν Θεὸν ἑορτὴ τοῖς διὰ τῆς ἀναστάσεως πυκασθεῖσεν, ὡς μίαν τε καὶ τὴν αὐτὴν προκεῖσθαι πᾶσι τὴν εὐφροσύνην, μηκέτι διαφορᾶς τινος τῆς τῶν ἴσων μετουσίας τὴν λογικὴν φύσιν διατεμνούσης, ἀλλὰ τῶν νῦν ἔξω διὰ τὴν κακίαν ὄντων ἐντὸς τῶν ἀδύτων τῆς θείας μακαριότητός ποτέ γενησομένων. . .*

[3] *De an.*: *NPNF* v. 461; Oehler, 366. 8.

remaining free from the plagues. Moses' outstretched hands banishing the plagues are interpreted as the outstretched hands of Christ on the cross which save sinners. Hence Gregory suggests that just as Moses banished even the plague of darkness, so Christ's salvation might extend even to the outer darkness of hell:

Perhaps someone, taking his departure from the fact that after three days of distress in the darkness even the Egyptians shared in the light (*γίνεται καὶ τοῖς Αἰγυπτίοις ἡ τοῦ φωτὸς μετουσία*), might be led to perceive the final restoration (*τὴν ἀποκατάστασιν*) which is expected to take place later in the Kingdom of heaven of those who have suffered condemnation in Gehenna (*τῶν ἐν γεένῃ καταδεδικασμένων*). For that 'darkness that could be felt' [Exod. 10. 21], as the history says, has a great affinity both in its name and in its actual meaning to 'the outer darkness' [Matt. 8. 12]. Both are dispelled when Moses . . . stretched forth his hands on behalf of those in darkness.[4]

Gregory seems to be distancing himself slightly from this view by reporting it rather than directly stating it himself; however, the claim that Christ can dispel even that effect of sin which is the outer darkness fits so well with his interpretation of the plagues as a whole that it is difficult not to think that Gregory too believed it.[5] The slight diffidence with which it is presented perhaps shows that some disquiet had already been caused by Origen's claims about the *apokatastasis*; but if Gregory was not following his predecessor on the question of the salvation of sinners it seems more likely that he would either not mention the *apokatastasis* at all at this point or deny it—as Gregory denies other aspects of Origenism elsewhere.[6]

It could be argued from some of Gregory's statements about the destruction of all evil that he is asserting a form of conditional immortality: that there is no eternal hell because the sinners are

[4] *De vita Moysis*: Malherbe and Ferguson, 2. 82 (translation adapted); *GNO* vii/1, 57. 8–58. 3.

[5] Jean Daniélou deals with the question of possible tampering by later writers: 'L'apocatastase chez Saint Grégoire de Nysse', *Recherches de Science Religieuse* 30/3 (1940), 331–6. I agree with his conclusion that the *apokatastasis* was mentioned in the original text and that later writers omitted it in order to protect Gregory from charges of heresy after the anathematizing of some of Origen's doctrines (543 and 553).

[6] Gregory explicitly denies Origen's doctrine of the pre-existence of souls in *De hominis opificio* 38. 1: *PG* 44, 229b (where he appears to refer directly to Origen's *De principiis*); see also *De an.*: *NPNF* v. 458–9; Oehler, 362. 39–363. 8.

simply destroyed. The above passage from *The Life of Moses* would seem to rule this out, but should there be any doubt over the force of Gregory's conviction on this point, an extract from another work explicitly denies the possibility of the annihilation of sinners. Commenting on Psalm 59, Gregory writes that in it David 'predicts the economy ordained by God for his own image':

For he says 'do not kill them [sinners]' but 'bring them down' from the height of evil to the level and even region of divine citizenship (τῆς κατὰ θεὸν πολιτείας). . . . We learn from these things that there will be no destruction of humanity (τῶν ἀνθρώπων ἀφανισμός), in order that the divine work shall not be rendered useless, being obliterated by non-existence. But instead of [humanity] sin will be destroyed and will be reduced to non-being (ἀπολεῖται ἡ ἁμαρτία καὶ εἰς τὸ μὴ ὂν περιστήσεται).[7]

It seems clear from the above passages that Gregory asserted the salvation of all human sinners—but does this salvation extend to devils too? Evidence that it does in Gregory's eschatology is provided by a second passage in *De anima* in which Macrina appeals to *Philippians* 2: 10. Here she states that in particular those 'under the earth' are understood by some to refer to a nature 'which is opposed to . . . good and is harmful to human life, having by an act of will lapsed from a better lot'.[8] She remarks that some people draw the following conclusion from the Philippians passage:

when evil shall have some day been annihilated (ἀφανισθείσης) in the long revolutions of the ages, nothing shall be left outside the world of goodness (ἔξω τοῦ ἀγαθοῦ), but that even from those [evil spirits] shall rise in harmony the confessions of Christ's Lordship.[9]

It may seem that Gregory (as author of the dialogue) is distancing himself from this view by attributing it to some

[7] *In insc. pss.*: Heine, 211–12 (2. 16. 282); *GNO* v. 174. 15–175. 2 (translation adapted). For further confirmation that sinners will not be destroyed, but will be reconciled, see *In illud: tunc GNO* iii/2, 26. 16–27. 5 referring to Romans 5. 10.

[8] *De an. NPNF* v. 444; Oehler, 341. 41–342. 2 (translation adapted): τινα φύσιν . . . ὑπεναντίως πρὸς τὸ καλὸν διακειμένην καὶ βλαπτικὴν τῆς ἀνθρωπίνης ζωῆς, ἑκουσίως τῆς κρείττονος λήξεως ἀπορρυεῖσαν.

[9] *De an.*: *NPNF* v. 444; Oehler, 342. 4–7. From the evidence of Gregory's writings as a whole, it is clear that the expression 'long revolutions of the ages' is a figurative one, and should not be taken to imply that he has a cyclical view of time, like Origen.

other unnamed people; however although it is expressed with caution, the idea is clearly one he shares himself. One piece of evidence for this is that the remark is put in the mouth of Macrina, who is clearly the voice of authority in the dialogue and who does not seek to deny the view she reports. Secondly, when he asks his sister about the interpretation of Philippians 2: 10, Gregory says that it means that 'every reasoning creature in the restitution of all things is to look towards him who presides over the whole'; Macrina does not quibble with this interpretation, but merely offers the above refinement specifically referring to fallen angels.[10] Finally, as will be seen below, the salvation not only of sinners but also of devils accords with the direction of the rest of Gregory's eschatology.[11]

It is noteworthy that all of the above passages are, or are derived from, commentaries on passages of Scripture: Gregory clearly thought that his view was biblical. Further examples of Gregory's use of the Bible to back up his assertion of universal salvation can be found throughout his writing. For example, in the Easter sermon *De tridui spatio* he writes that the cross with its beams pointing in four directions signifies the 'breadth and length and height and depth' of God's love, and that these words from Ephesians 3: 19 indicate that 'there is nothing in existence which is not entirely controlled by the Divine Being'.[12] Similarly, in another Easter sermon Gregory gives a universalist interpretation to Psalm 116: 11: 'Praise the Lord all you nations, give him praise all you peoples.'[13]

The most frequent biblical citation which Gregory uses to support universal salvation is 1 Corinthians 15: 28; for example he concludes his commentary on the Song of Songs thus:

> God will be all in all, and all persons will be united together in fellowship of the good, Christ Jesus our Lord, to whom be glory and power for ever and ever. Amen.[14]

[10] *De an.*: *NPNF* v. 444; Oehler, 341. 14–16: (*πᾶσαν λέγοντα τὴν λογικὴν κτίσιν ἐν τῇ τοῦ παντὸς ἀποκαταστάσει πρὸς τὸν τοῦ παντὸς ἐξηγούμενον βλέπειν*).

[11] See p. 85.

[12] *De tridui*: Hall, 46–7; *GNO* ix. 300. From the context it is clear that Gregory is talking about salvation: it is followed by another universalistic interpretation of Philippians 2: 10.

[13] *In s. Pascha*: Hall, 5–6; *GNO* ix. 245–6; cf. ibid.: Hall, 8; *GNO* ix. 250.

[14] *In cant.* 15: McCambley, 276; *GNO* vi. 469 (the first two phrases read in Greek: *γένηται ὁ θεὸς τὰ πάντα ἐν πᾶσι, τοῖς διὰ τῆς ἑνότητος ἀλλήλοις ἐν τῇ τοῦ ἀγαθοῦ κοινωνίᾳ*

Echoes of this verse from Scripture are to be found throughout Gregory's eschatological writing.

ii. Evidence from the Nature of Punishment in Gregory's Theology

A more indirect demonstration that Gregory believed in universal salvation is the fact that he often states or hints that punishment will not be eternal. The corollary of this is that eventually everyone will cease to be punished and will thus be saved.[15] For example, it has already been shown that when he refers to the *apokatastasis* in *The Life of Moses*, Gregory appears to share the view that Christ's death and resurrection will finally cause the end of the outer darkness.[16]

A second passage, in Gregory's commentary on the inscriptions of the Psalms, is much less equivocal, because Gregory makes no attempt to distance himself from the universalistic point of view. Interpreting Psalm 59, Gregory first takes verse 6 (which he reads as '[the enemies] shall return *to* evening') to mean that sinners 'will be forced into the outer darkness' beyond the walls of the city of virtue.[17] This does not refer to a permanent division between heaven and hell, however, because Gregory continues his interpretation of the psalm by asserting that it would detract from the goodness of God's creation if sinners were destroyed or if evil remained.[18] Although Gregory returns again to the theme of punishment, he does not suggest that this is eternal.[19]

The only work in which there is a suggestion that Gregory saw punishment as eternal is his treatise *De infantibus praemature abreptis*, which discusses the question of whether newly-born children will be punished or rewarded in the afterlife. The

συγκεκραμένοις). 1 Cor. 15: 28 reads 'And when all things have been subjected unto him, then shall the Son also himself be subjected to him that did subject all things unto him, that God may be all in all (ἵνα ᾖ ὁ Θεὸς πάντα ἐν πᾶσιν)'. See also *De an.*: *NPNF* v. 452; Oehler, 354. 19 ff.

[15] This is assuming that Gregory thinks that all will be resurrected and that punishment does not end in annihilation. The last chapter showed the former and there is evidence against the latter view in Gregory's writings (see above, p. 80).

[16] *De vita Moysis*: Malherbe and Ferguson, 2. 82 ff. See above, pp. 78–80.

[17] In fact, the verse appears to mean they 'shall return *at* evening'.

[18] See quotation above, p. 80.

[19] *Pace* Daniélou, 'L'apocatastase', 346.

dialogue closes with the argument that part of the blessings of the virtuous will consist in comparing their lot with the 'perdition of the reprobate' (τὴν τῶν κατακρίτων ἀπώλειαν):

not indeed as rejoicing over the laments of those sufferers, but as then most completely realising the extent of the well-earned rewards of virtue.[20]

Although this does not necessarily mean that such perdition is permanent, it might suggest that it is, for otherwise the blessings of the righteous would decrease when the punishment of the wicked ceased (unless their joy at all humanity being united in blessedness compensated for that loss). More problematic than this passage is an earlier reference in the work in which Gregory describes the punishment of the very wicked:

On account of the depth of the ingrained evil, the chastisement in the way of purgation will be extended into infinity (εἰς ἄπειρον παρατείνεται ἡ διὰ τῆς καθάρσεως κόλασις).[21]

One's interpretation of this passage clearly depends on the sense in which one takes εἰς ἄπειρον: does the phrase indicate an infinitely extended period of punishment, or is it a case of hyperbole, emphasizing the extreme duration of the punishment? Given the existence of belief in an eternal hell, the former interpretation might seem the more likely, except for two factors: first that it flies in the face of the rest of Gregory's eschatology, secondly that the punishment is specifically described as purgatorial or purifying (διὰ τῆς καθάρσεως)—surely a purification must stop somewhere, given that evil is finite?

It is this character of punishment as purification or healing that elsewhere gives such force to Gregory's claim that the period of punishment must be finite. Punishment is constantly referred to as purification and Gregory even takes the image of the fire of Gehenna and interprets it as a purifying fire, using the image of refining gold.[22] As suggested above, Gregory's reasoning appears

[20] *De infant. NPNF* v. 381; *GNO* iii/2. 96. 3–5.
[21] *De infant. NPNF* v. 378; *GNO* iii/2. 87: 10–12.
[22] For example: *Cat. or.*: Srawley, 138. 12–139. 8 (Srawley ET, 105–6); *De mort.*: Lozza, 64. 12–15; 66. 8–9; 66. 20–2; *De an.*: Oehler, 349. 4–5; 349. 11–12 (*NPNF* v. 449); Oehler, 373. 10–11 (*NPNF* v. 465); Oehler, 377. 1–2 (*NPNF* v. 468). For a passage talking of the purification by fire in a specifically universalistic context see *In illud: tunc GNO* iii/2. 13. 22–14. 7 (quoted above, p. 79).

to be that no person, however sinful, can be wholly evil—for he or she would then cease to exist. Since God is omnipotent, God will be able to purify each person of their evil through a proportionate punishment after death and eventually all will rise to God in purity. This train of thought can be seen in *De anima* where Macrina remarks that punishment after death will be painful in proportion to the sin left to purge, and will endure for longer in some people than in others:

> according to the quantity of material will be the longer or shorter time that the agonising flame will be burning; that is, as long as there is fuel to feed it.[23]

This is echoed later when Gregory remarks that the difference between the virtuous and sinners is that the former will participate quickly in God after their death, and the latter more slowly.[24] This concept of purification is, however, very different from later doctrines of purgatory which state that some will suffer in an interim state before going to heaven, while others will endure the pains of all eternity. In the *Catechetical Oration*, for example, one can see quite clearly that purifying punishment is envisaged by Gregory as applying to *all* people, except for the blessed who attain heaven immediately. It would be more accurate perhaps to refer to Gregory's doctrine as one of non-eternal hell (with the proviso that hell does not imply retributive punishment). Comparing the purification after death to the refining of gold (which he describes as a 'cure' (θεραπεία)) Gregory writes:

> In like manner, when death, corruption, darkness, and all the other products of vice had attached themselves to the nature of the author of evil (τῷ εὑρετῇ τοῦ κακοῦ), the approach of the Divine power, acting like fire, effects the disappearance of the element which was contrary to nature, and, by thus purging it, benefits the nature (εὐεργετεῖ τῇ καθάρσει τὴν φύσιν). . . . When by these long and circuitous methods the evil, which is now mingled with our nature . . . has been finally expelled from it, and when those who are now plunged in vice are restored to their original state (ἐπειδὰν ἡ εἰς τὸ ἀρχαῖον ἀποκατάστασις τῶν νῦν ἐν κακίᾳ κειμένων γένηται), a chorus of thanksgiving will arise from all creation (πάσης τῆς κτίσεως) . . . This . . . is contained in the

[23] *De an.*: *NPNF* v. 451; Oehler, 353. 14–15.
[24] *De an.*: *NPNF* v. 465; Oehler, 373. 18–20.

great mystery of the divine Incarnation. For by mingling with humanity . . . he effected all the results we have previously described, delivering man from vice and healing the very author of vice (τὸν τῆς κακίας εὑρετὴν ἰώμενος).[25]

This clearly refers not only to the salvation of all sinners (which Gregory significantly calls a 'restoration (ἀποκατάστασις) to their original state') but also to the banishing of evil even from the devil (the author of evil). Crucially, both effects are said to be caused by purification. This passage therefore is ideal evidence that universalism and the purificatory nature of punishment after death are inextricably connected in Gregory's mind. His emphasis on the length of time the purification will take is perhaps evidence that his reference in *De infantibus* to punishment stretching into infinity is an exaggeration intending merely to stress that the lengthiness of punishment will reflect the severity of sin.[26] The fact that the *Catechetical Oration* is clearly intended to be not an exploratory or philosophical work for a limited audience, but a handbook of Christian doctrine, re-emphasizes the point that Gregory is truly committed to the concept of universal salvation as a central aspect of his eschatology. *De infantibus*, on the other hand, seems to be an *ad hominem* work. Although it must be taken seriously, it does not provide conclusive evidence that Gregory believed in eternal divine punishment and even if it did, it would have to be set against the vast majority of Gregory's other writings which suggest otherwise.

However, Gregory can easily be accused of reading his own presuppositions into the biblical text he uses. The above passages give a very good indication that he believed in universal salvation, but to gain a fuller understanding of his doctrine one must look at places in which he discusses it in a more systematic manner. From an examination of these it seems that Gregory justifies his claim that salvation will be universal by appealing to two sorts of evidence: the nature of evil and the concept of the unity of humankind. His arguments based on these will be dealt with in the following section.

[25] *Cat. Or.* 26: Srawley, 99. 12–101. 7; Srawley ET, 82–3.

[26] In the passage from the *Catechetical Oration* cited above, Gregory stresses the 'long and circuitous methods' (ταῖς μακραῖς περιόδοις); earlier in the smelting analogy he noted that 'time is needed for the fire . . . to cause the spurious metal to disappear' (Srawley, 100. 4–5; Srawley ET, 82).

B. GREGORY'S ARGUMENTS FOR UNIVERSAL SALVATION

i. An Argument from the Nature of Evil

> the nature of evil will pass over to non-existence, having been made to disappear completely by being, and the divine and unmixed goodness will contain all rational nature within itself; for nothing which came into being through God will fall short of God's kingdom. When all evil which is mixed with beings . . . has been released through the refinery of purifying fire, everything which had its being through God will be such as it was from the beginning, when it never received evil.[27]

This claim, which Gregory makes in his commentary on 1 Corinthians 15: 28, is based on that verse's assertion that 'when all things are subjected to him, then the Son himself will also be subjected to him who put all things under him, that God may be all in all'.[28]

> Clearly . . . [Paul] asserts the unreality of evil . . . in saying that God who is everything to each thing will be in everything. . . . (*σαφῶς γὰρ τὸ τῆς κακίας ἀνύπαρκτον τῷ λόγῳ παρίστησιν ἐν τῷ εἰπεῖν ἐν πᾶσι γίνεσθαι τὸν θεὸν πάντα ἑκάστῳ γινόμενον*) For indeed it is not proper for God to be in evil. So either he will not be in everything, when something evil is left in beings, or, if it is truly necessary to believe that he will be in everything, the existence of nothing evil is demonstrated together with this belief about him.[29]

Coupled with the premiss that God is totally and infinitely good (a theme that runs throughout Gregory's theology) and the logical premiss that the perfect good can in no way be in anything evil, this assertion that God will be in everything thus proves to Gregory's satisfaction that there will be no evil left.[30]

[27] *In illud: tunc GNO* iii/2. 13. 22–14. 7 (my translation); the first half reads in Greek: *πρὸς τὸ μὴ ὂν ἡ τοῦ κακοῦ φῦσις μεταχωρήσει, παντελῶς ἐξαφανισθεῖσα τοῦ ὄντος, καὶ πᾶσαν λογικὴν φύσιν ἡ θεία τε καὶ ἀκήρατος ἀγαθότης ἐν ἑαυτῇ περιέξει, μηδενὸς τῶν παρὰ τοῦ θεοῦ γεγονότων τῆς βασιλείας τοῦ θεοῦ ἀποπίπτοντος. . .*

[28] Gregory's commentary on 1 Cor. 15: 28 is standardly referred to by the first words of the scriptural text in Latin: *In illud: tunc et ipse Filius* . . . (abbreviated in this book to *In illud: tunc*). The RSV translates the last three words of the verse (*πάντα ἐν πᾶσιν*) 'everything to everyone', but since Gregory clearly takes the Greek *πᾶσιν* to include non-human creation, I depart from the RSV translation on this occasion.

[29] *In illud: tunc GNO* iii/2. 17. 13–21.

[30] For an important statement of God's infinite goodness, see the Prologue to *De vita Moysis* Malherbe and Ferguson, 1. 7.

However, the whole argument leans very heavily both on the assertion that God will be all in all and on Gregory's particular interpretation of what this means. In *De anima* Macrina takes it to mean that 'God will be instead of all other things and will be in all', fulfilling all our needs, being for us our food and drink, so to speak.[31] The assumption is that God cannot fulfil that role in anything which is still 'mixed with evil'.

One is still faced, however, with the question of whether God *will* in fact be in everything. Ultimately, Gregory relies on Scripture for his certainty on this point; nevertheless a Neoplatonic concept of evil does strengthen his assertions. Gregory believes that 'to be in evil is, properly speaking, not to be, since evil itself has no existence on its own but the non-existence of good gives rise to evil'.[32] In Gregory's eyes, this has two consequences. First, God, who is perfect being and the perfect Good, is clearly completely superior to evil, or non-being. He cannot be limited by evil (which is the only thing which could limit the good) and he must therefore be infinite. Being perfectly good, he must also be immutable—in other words unable to become evil. Not only is the good thus much more powerful than evil, which suggests that it will overcome it, but—if Gregory is right in directly opposing the qualities of good and evil—evil is finite and mutable. Gregory takes this to imply that evil is not permanent:

> The nature of sin [= evil] is unstable and transient (ἄστατός καὶ παροδική). It neither came into existence at first with the creation . . . nor does it continue to exist in perpetuity with the things which have being. For some things have being from the One who is Being and continues always in being. But if something is outside the One who is Being its essence is not in being. . . . (τὰ μὲν γὰρ ἐκ τοῦ ὄντος ὄντα καὶ ἐν τῷ εἶναι διὰ παντὸς διαμένει· εἰ δέ τι ἔξω τοῦ ὄντος ἐστίν, οὗ ἡ οὐσία οὐκ ἐν τῷ εἶναι. . .) It will pass away and disappear at the proper times, when the universe is restored to the good (ἐν τῇ τοῦ παντὸς πρὸς τὸ ἀγαθὸν ἀποκαταστάσει), so that no trace of the evil which now prevails over us remains in the life which lies before us in hope.[33]

However, Gregory seems only to show that evil is liable to cease existing, not that it will do so necessarily. A further problem is

[31] *De an.*: *NPNF* v. 452.

[32] *In insc. pss.*: Heine, 117 (1. 8. 106); *GNO* iii/2. 62–3.

[33] *In insc. pss.*: Heine, 196 (2. 14. 232); *GNO* iii/2. 155.

that Gregory has not explained what it is about the future perfect state which will prevent a second Fall, given that evil came about in a previously perfect world.

A second consequence of Gregory's 'negative' conception of evil is pertinent to human moral choice. In *De hominis opificio* he expresses a view which is very similar to the argument from the mutability of evil, except that it is based on the mutability of human nature:

it is absolutely certain that the Divine counsel possesses immutability (τὸ ἀμετάθετον), while the changeableness (τὸ τρεπτὸν) of our nature does not remain settled even in evil.[34]

Gregory argues that the reason for this is that human nature, being mutable, is always on the move. If it moves in the direction of the good, 'it will never cease moving onwards to what lies before, by reason of the infinity of the course to be traversed'.[35] This not only echoes the comments made above about the infinity of the good, but also recalls Gregory's so-called mystical doctrine of perpetual progress in the good, which was mentioned in the last chapter. In other words, it can now be seen that the doctrine does not point merely to a progress in mystical experience or spiritual knowledge, but to a moral progress. In contrast to perpetual progress in the good, if human nature moves in the direction of evil the movement cannot be for ever, since evil is finite and therefore, as Gregory cryptically comments, 'good once more follows in succession upon the limit of evil'.[36] It is very unclear what he means by this. In fact, this metaphysical argument for the finite nature of sin is followed by an ethical argument based on prudence, which will be studied below, but it seems that Gregory is confident in the adequacy of the former: prudence may *explain how* people return to the good, but the finite nature of evil *necessitates that* they will.[37] In *De mortuis* Gregory suggests that a desire for what is not good cannot last for ever, for it will lead to satiety and tediousness (whereas a desire for the good leads to satisfaction without satiety), but it is not clear why this should *necessarily* be so. In addition to this

[34] *De hom. opif.* 21. 1: *PG* 44, 201b.
[35] *De hom. opif.* 21. 2: *PG* 44, 201b.
[36] *De hom. opif.* 21. 2: *PG* 44, 201c.
[37] See below, section c. ii.

difficulty over a lack of explanation for why the soul cannot continue infinitely in evil, the argument from human moral choices suffers from the problem mentioned above, namely that it offers no reason why the soul in its progress towards the good might not fall back.

The argument from the nature of evil thus has major flaws; it remains to be seen towards the end of this chapter whether some of these will be alleviated by Gregory's explanation of the same assertions—that sin is finite but the good infinite—in terms of freedom and choice, rather than by metaphysical concepts.[38]

ii. Arguments from the Unity of Humanity

These arguments are based on the fundamental premiss that in the first creation, humanity was created as a whole:

> Man then was made in the image of God; that is the universal nature, the thing like God (*ἡ καθόλου φύσις, τὸ θεοείκελον χρῆμα*); not part of the whole, but all the fullness of nature together (*οὐχὶ μέρος τοῦ ὅλου, ἀλλ' ἅπαν ἀθρόως τὸ τῆς φύσεως πλήρωμα*) was so made by omnipotent wisdom.[39]

They come in several forms. First, there is the issue of the image. It was seen in the previous chapter that, according to Gregory, humanity truly bears God's image only in the first creation and at the eschaton. Since the first creation was that of humanity as a whole, Gregory appears to think that the image of God is to be found specifically in humanity as a unity; consequently, he seems to be committed to asserting that the image will be restored in humanity as a whole, when the resurrection brings the restoration of the image.

This is suggested by the following passage from *De mortuis*:

> I do not doubt that there will be one race of all people when we will all be one body of Christ, shaped in one form, when the divine image will shine out in all equally . . .[40]

Secondly, there is involved in the concept of the unity of humanity the notion that a specific number of souls (*πλήρωμα*)

[38] See below, section C.

[39] *De hom. opif.* 22. 3: *PG* 44, 204d.

[40] *De mort.*: Lozza, §20, 74. 1–3: *ὅτι μὲν γένος ἔσται τῶν πάντων ἕν, ὅταν ἓν σῶμα Χριστοῦ οἱ πάντες γενώμεθα τῷ ἑνὶ χαρακτῆρι μεμορφωμένοι, οὐκ ἀμφιβάλλομεν πᾶσι κατὰ τὸ ἴσον τῆς θείας εἰκόνος ἐπιλαμπούσης . . .*

make up the human race. As Gregory stresses in a passage from *De hominis opificio*, it is only when this number is fulfilled and humanity completed that all things will be consummated and humanity transformed.[41] Similarly, in *De anima* Gregory writes:

> His end is one, and one only; it is this: when the complete whole of our race shall have been perfected from the first man to the last . . . to offer to every one of us participation in the blessings which are in Him . . .[42]

The clear implication is that the transformation can only occur when every soul has come to life, because every soul must be transformed.

Thirdly, one version of this argument seems to be that, by the very nature of the salvation he effected, Christ saved the whole human race, not certain selected members of it. The two most important places where this view is expressed are in the *Catechetical Oration* and in Gregory's commentary on 1 Corinthians 15: 28.

One of the main aims of the latter is to assert that the submission of Christ to the Father does not support Arian claims that the Son is inferior to the Father, but that it indicates the submission of the body of Christ (that is, humanity in Christ) to the Father at the eschaton. Gregory also seems to be defending himself against the charge of Marcellianism—that is the accusation that he thinks that the kingdom of Christ will disappear at the eschaton. In order to counter these charges, Gregory needs both to explain what 'submission' means and also to elucidate the meaning of 'the body of Christ'. Because Paul's verse ends with the statement that God will be all in all, Gregory concludes that Christ's body is the whole human nature:

> when the whole body of our [human] nature (*παντὸς τοῦ τῆς φύσεως ἡμῶν σώματος*) has been blended with the divine and incorruptible nature, that aforementioned submission of the Son comes about through us . . .[43]

[41] *De hom. opif.* 21. 5: *PG* 44, 205c.

[42] *De an.*: *NPNF* v. 465; Oehler, 373. 8–16: *σκοπὸς δὲ αὐτῷ εἷς, τὸ τελειωθέντος ἤδη διὰ τῶν καθ' ἕκαστον ἀνθρώπων παντὸς τοῦ τῆς φύσεως ἡμῶν πληρώματος . . . πᾶσι προθεῖναι τὴν μετουσίαν τῶν ἐν αὐτῷ καλῶν . . .*; see also ibid.: *NPNF* v. 459; Oehler, 364. 25–8: 'when the completed universe no longer admits of further increase, the whole pleroma of souls will return from their invisible and scattered condition . . .'.

[43] *In illud: tunc GNO* iii/2. 16: 17–19. Two further passages confirm this: ibid. 20: 8–10:'Therefore he made us one with him and he was unified with us and became one with

Gregory assumes that the submission of the body of Christ to the Father achieves the union of humanity with God and that this union is salvific, for by it Christ brings all humanity under God's authority.[44] His conclusion is therefore that 'there is nothing beyond what will be saved' (τὸ μηδὲν ἔξω τῶν σῳζομένων εἶναι).[45]

In the *Catechetical Oration*, a slightly later work, Gregory again uses the concept of union to express the essence of salvation, but focuses more on the resurrection than on submission. He argues that in his resurrection Christ recombined in a permanent union the intelligible and sensible natures which had become separated in human nature.[46] Gregory clearly indicates that this is a salvific act and not simply a physical resurrection to judgement and punishment or reward: he writes that the purpose of Christ's resurrection was 'in order that the primal grace associated with human nature might be recalled, and we might return once more to eternal life'.[47] Because humanity was created as a whole, it will be resurrected as a whole also:

> Inasmuch as the whole of our human nature forms, as it were, a single living being (ἑνός τινος ὄντος ζῴου), the resurrection of the part extends to the whole, and in virtue of the continuity and unity of the nature (κατὰ τὸ συνεχές τε καὶ ἡνωμένον τῆς φύσεως) communicates itself from the part to the whole.[48]

This point is further emphasized by reference to the scriptural assertion that 'as in Adam all die so also in Christ shall all be

us throughout all (διὰ πάντων), and so he builds up all our nature (τὰ ἡμέτερα οἰκειοῦται πάντα)'; ibid. 21. 10–11: 'His [Christ's] body, as has been said clearly many times, is the whole of human nature with which he is mixed (πᾶσα ἡ ἀνθρωπίνη φύσις ᾗ κατεμίχθη)'.

[44] Occasionally, Gregory says that the Holy Spirit has a role in bringing about unity, but such statements are rare and are usually vague. For example: 'If love perfectly casts out fear . . . and if fear changes into love, then unity follows, the result of salvation, for all have been united in the sole good through the perfection symbolised by a dove' (*In cant.* 15: *GNO* vi. 366. 5–9). This would perhaps be more easily taken to mean that the Holy Spirit brings unity after the salvation which is brought by Christ, in which case it is primarily Christ who is seen as the means of universal salvation in Gregory's theology.

[45] *In illud: tunc GNO* iii/2. 21. 2–3.

[46] *Cat. or.* 16: Srawley, 70. 15–71. 13; Srawley ET, 63.

[47] *Cat. or.* 16: Srawley, 71. 5–6; Srawley ET, 63: ὡς ἂν ἡ πρώτη περὶ τὸ ἀνθρώπινον χάρις ἀνακληθείη, καὶ πάλιν ἐπὶ τὴν αἴδιον ἐπανέλθοιμεν ζωὴν . . .

[48] *Cat. or.* 32: Srawley, 117. 4–7; Srawley ET, 93. See also *Cat. or.* 16: Srawley, 72. 2–7; Srawley ET, 64; and ibid. 16: Srawley, 71. 16–72. 1; Srawley ET, 64, where Gregory remarks that Christ mingled intelligible with sensible natures at the level of the genus of humanity (γενικωτέρῳ τινὶ λόγῳ), rather then in the individual alone.

made alive'.[49] The incarnation is important in the sense that in it Christ took on human nature and his death was important as the event which made the resurrection possible, but neither is salvific in itself and both are viewed by Gregory as parts of the divine drama of salvation which are subordinate to the grand eschatological climax of the resurrection.[50]

Thus both *In illud: tunc et ipse Filius . . .* and the *Catechetical Oration* use a concept of universal human nature to imply that salvation will be universal. Because Christ took on human nature and united it within itself and with God, human nature *as a whole* will be saved. However, a note of caution must be sounded with regard to Gregory's use of this concept. There are two closely related problems.[51]

First, it is not typical for Gregory to use the concept of a universal human nature in his soteriology. Usually, he relies on the idea that all individuals can use their free will to purify themselves, so that they become more like God. The dominant concept of salvation is participation (μετουσία), not union, and Christ's role becomes that of the supreme example of one who participated in God through his way of living on earth. This emphasis on the imitation of Christ is to be found particularly in Gregory's ascetic works, such as *De perfectione*. Considering that Gregory does use the concept of universal human nature in his cosmology (with regard to the doctrines both of creation and of the eschaton) it might seem surprising that he does not generally use the same concept in his soteriology. However, the reason for this lies in his belief that universal human nature was created in the image of God and that individual humans still each possess something of that image in them. Gregory believes that individual humans fell, rather than human nature as a whole, so he usually asserts that humans are saved on an individual basis, through the grace of God, but also through their own free effort. This is demonstrated by the fact that, in *De perfectione*, the 'body

[49] 1 Cor. 15: 22; cf. Gregory, *Cat. or.* 16: Srawley, 71. 10–13, Srawley ET, 63–4: 'Now as the principle of death, becoming operative in the case of one man, passed therewith throughout the whole of human nature, in like manner, the principle of the resurrection through one man extends to all humanity (ἐπὶ πᾶσαν διατείναι τὴν ἀνθρωπότητα)'.

[50] See Johannes Zachhuber, *The Universal Nature of Man in Gregory of Nyssa: Philosophical Background and Theological Significance* (Brill, Leiden, 2000), 232.

[51] The following two paragraphs are indebted to Zachhuber, *The Universal Nature of Man in Gregory of Nyssa*, ch. 5.

of Christ' is not, as in *In illud: tunc et ipse Filius . . .*, universal human nature, but rather the Church, of which one becomes a member by personal free decision.[52] However, there is a minor strand in Gregory's thought which does use the notion of universal human nature in a soteriological context, particularly in *In illud: tunc et ipse Filius . . .* and in the *Catechetical Oration*, but also in some other works written in the same half-decade.[53] Why Gregory uses this second strand can be explained convincingly by looking at the context. Because of the debates with Eunomius Gregory is concerned in his Christology to emphasize the full divinity of Christ. This has the consequent effect on his soteriology that Gregory feels the need to emphasize the salvific role of Christ's divinity, rather than his humanity. Hence he stresses the divine Logos taking on humanity and divinizing it, rather than the perfect human life of Jesus of Nazareth. This takes away the emphasis on personal human effort, and by considering humanity as a single item leaves the door open for Gregory to exploit the potential of this concept to suggest universal salvation. Furthermore, because of controversy about Apollinarius' Christology, Gregory seems to have an increasing tendency to emphasize that the Logos was united with the whole of human nature. This meant in the first instance both a human body and a human soul, but Gregory seems to have realized the further potential for bolstering his universalist views by insisting that the whole of human nature also meant the universal human nature, that is, every human individual. Thus arises a distinctive version of so-called 'physical' soteriology: Gregory combines the Irenaean and Athanasian idea of Christ taking on and saving human nature with the Origenistic concept of universal salvation to produce a theory unique to himself.[54]

However, although one might be able to explain why Gregory departs from his normal practice to use the concept of universal human nature in some of his soteriology, a second problem still remains. This is that there is a clear tension not only between these two strands of his soteriology, but also between the main strand of his soteriology and his eschatology.

[52] Zachhuber, *The Universal Nature of Man in Gregory of Nyssa*, 197–8, 210.
[53] Ibid., 204–7.
[54] Ibid., 212, 217, 227–8, 237.

It was seen above that while Gregory does not use the concept of universal human nature for explicating the doctrines of the Fall and salvation, it is consistently used for the doctrines of the creation and the eschaton. This leaves one with a great tension between Gregory's large-scale cosmological theology and his smaller-scale theology of the salvation of the individual. The most important focus of the tension is the concept of free will: if humanity is saved *en masse*, does human freedom play any part at all? If Christ unites himself with and saves universal human nature, how can Gregory also assert that all individuals must perfect themselves? It is important to note that Gregory does mention the role of personal faith and acceptance of Christ in both the Catechetical Oration and *In illud: tunc et ipse Filius* . . ., so the problem is not just one of incompatibility between two sets of texts, but of tension within single texts. Daniélou is too pessimistic when he argues that Gregory's emphasis is only on people as 'l'ensemble de l'humanité' and that this leaves the problem of individual salvation in the shade and ignores the infinite worth of the personal human soul; on the contrary, the problem is precisely that Gregory deals with both the personal and collective sides of salvation, but that these two strands of his eschatology fit together with difficulty.[55] The final section of this chapter will assess how successfully, if at all, Gregory manages to achieve coherence between the two.

Besides this lack of clarity over the relationship between the salvation of the individual and the salvation of all humanity, there is also a problem over the relation of humanity to the rest of creation. Does Gregory's universalism extend merely to the human race or to the whole world? Whereas in the *Catechetical Oration* the emphasis is on the salvation of humanity alone, a passage from *In illud: tunc et ipse Filius* . . . suggests that Gregory perhaps envisages salvation extending not just to human nature but to the entire created world as a whole:

all creation is in agreement (ὁμόφωνος πᾶσα ἡ κτίσις) with [humanity's submission to the divine] and 'every knee shall bow and every tongue will confess that Jesus Christ is Lord'. . . . all creation has become one body and everything is growing together with one another in him

[55] Daniélou, 'L'apocatastase', 346.

through obedience (πάσης τῆς κτίσεως ἓν σῶμα γενομένης καὶ πάντων διὰ τῆς ὑπακοῆς μετ' ἀλλήλων ἐν αὐτῷ συμφυέντων) . . .[56]

While it is clear how a Greek might regard one species as a unity, it is far from clear how the whole world might be considered one. Gregory's occasional references to the unity of all creation run the risk of undermining, or at the very least confusing, his more frequent assertions that humanity is 'one body', because the problems that attend the latter affect the former even more strongly. If the role of human freedom and choice is belittled by the concept of the salvation of humanity *en masse*, it is surely much more endangered by the idea that the whole world is saved as one thing. In fact, although Gregory occasionally talks of the transformation of the world and the whole of creation celebrating at the eschaton, he does not seem to be very interested in the fate of the entirely material parts of creation and he certainly does not face the philosophical problems which would be raised by the assertion that, for example animals, plants or non-living objects are transformed or perfected. Perhaps his comments about the whole world are merely hyperbole, or perhaps they reflect a latent but unformed idea that if human bodies are to be resurrected they must have some sort of environment. In any case, the more central problem of individual freedom remains, regardless of whether Gregory thinks that all humanity or all creation will be saved. It is this problem which will be addressed next.

C. UNIVERSAL SALVATION AND HUMAN FREEDOM

The problem regarding freedom which affects any assertion of universal salvation can be summarized as follows: if all humanity (or the whole cosmos) will be saved, this entails that no-one is free to reject God permanently. It does not, of course, entail that people have no freedom whatsoever—just that they do not have freedom with respect to their ultimate destiny. This has frequently been thought to be a very important sort of freedom. Furthermore, Christianity has often assumed that, even if

[56] *In illud: tunc GNO* iii/2. 20. 11–16.

salvation is granted by God's grace, some participation on the part of the individual (for example, faith or moral purity) is necessary for it to be effective and that this participation must be free. Hence, it can be argued that freedom is intrinsic to salvation and that if human beings are forcibly united with God, they are not truly saved.

There are two possible ways of resolving the dilemma. First, one can change the *assertion* that all will be saved, to the more tentative claim that it is the Christian *hope* that all will be saved. Thus all people are left free to choose or reject God. This is the route which Karl Rahner seems to take, as the second part of this book will show; however, it has been seen already that Gregory was doing more than expressing a hope. If anyone were free to reject God permanently, the devil would be, yet Gregory asserts that the devil *will* be saved.

The second option is to focus on the other horn of the dilemma, that is, freedom, by challenging the notion that human freedom is intrinsic to salvation. The problem is that Gregory regards freedom as an essential characteristic of human nature:

> Thus there is in us the principle of all excellence, all virtue and wisdom, and every higher thing that we can conceive: but pre-eminent among all is the fact that we are free from necessity, and not in bondage to any natural power, but have decision in our own power as we please; for virtue is a voluntary thing, subject to no dominion: that which is the result of compulsion and force cannot be virtue.[57]

Elsewhere freedom is described by Gregory as 'the noblest and most precious of blessings'.[58] It is also one of the qualities of the *imago dei* and as such will be a characteristic of human nature at the eschaton.[59] Furthermore, it seems that Gregory thinks that freedom is necessary specifically for salvation, because he stresses his view that part of the process of salvation is individuals' efforts—aided, but not controlled, by divine grace—to make themselves pure.

[57] *De hom. opif.* 16. 11: *PG* 44, 184b. The second part of the quotation reads in Greek: *τὸ ἐλεύθερον ἀνάγκης εἶναι, καὶ μὴ ὑπεζεῦχθαί τινι φυσικῇ δυναστείᾳ· ἀλλ' αὐτεξούσιον πρὸς τὸ δοκοῦν ἔχειν τὴν γνωμήν. ἀδέσποτον γάρ τι χρῆμα ἡ ἀρετὴ καὶ ἑκούσιον, τὸ δὲ κατηναγκασμένον καὶ βεβιασμένον ἀρετὴ εἶναι οὐ δύναται.*

[58] *Cat. or.* 5: Srawley, 26. 7; Srawley ET, 37.

[59] *De hom. opif.*: *NPNF* v. 4. 1.

Seemingly, then, Gregory can modify neither horn of the dilemma. The only solution to this problem is to suggest that the dilemma is only an apparent one and that another option remains: that is to define freedom in such a way that *true* freedom is characterized as the ability *only* to turn to God, with the consequence that the permanent rejection of God is no longer a criterion for true freedom.[60] The universal salvation of all would thus be God's victory in bringing about true freedom for all people, in releasing them from sin and its consequences. Gregory's theology is such that it is possible to say that he could have at least attempted the beginnings of a defence on these grounds, although he does not consciously defend himself against the problems caused by the dilemma concerning free will and universalism. The remainder of this chapter will assess how successfully Gregory emerges from the dilemma.

i. Three Starting Assumptions

It has already been seen that Gregory's universalism has a certain amount of subtlety in that he does not think that all will be saved simultaneously, but asserts that some will go straight to heaven and that others will have to endure varying lengths of punishment after death. Clearly then one assumption will be that the problem of freedom focuses not on this life but on the next, for Gregory has to be able to show that even those who take the longest to turn to God do so freely.

The second assumption is that Gregory's idea of salvation is not concerned with justification, and consequently avoids the dilemma of whether humans are justified by faith or works. Rather, the dominant concepts used to express salvation are purification, participation in God, and union with God. The first half of this chapter illustrated Gregory's concern with the idea of purification as the eradication of all evil, and purification through punishment. It also revealed Gregory's belief in the union of humanity with God through the Son. Purification, participation, or union are consistent images in Gregory's commentaries on Scripture. The description of these works as 'mystical' all too easily gives the impression that the goal of the

[60] Compare Augustine's 'posse non peccare' (a heavenly state: *City of God* 22. 30) and, in contemporary theology, John Hick, *Death and Eternal Life* (Collins, Glasgow, 1976), ch. 13, section 3.

spiritual life is a 'mystical experience', but in fact the goal is clearly union with God in a much more permanent and eschatological sense. Eschatological and communal images in these works make it quite clear that for Gregory the goal of the spiritual life was not a personal, mystical revelatory experience in this life, but was in fact the *apokatastasis*—an eschatological, universal achievement of perfection in God.[61]

The problem with the concepts of purification, participation, and union (like the similar Greek Christian concept of divinization) is that they might be taken to suggest that the individuals are little involved in their own salvation, whereas the notion of justification by faith or works clearly establishes human involvement. However, our third starting assumption is that it is clear from Gregory's account of those who turn to God in this life that they do so freely. If it is legitimate to draw parallels between the course of salvation in this life and the next, then one may be able to conclude that people turn to God freely in the next life too and that a universal restoration does not threaten human freedom. Gregory certainly speaks of purification before death and after death and his habit of coupling the two together in one phrase is the most obvious evidence that he regarded the two as very similar. A typical example is the following extract from the *Catechetical Oration*:

> Since there was a need that [the soul's] stains too, contracted through sin, should be removed by some remedy, the medicine of virtue (*τὸ τῆς ἀρετῆς φάρμακον*) was applied to it in the present life, in order to heal such wounds. But if it remains unhealed, its cure has been provided for it in the life which follows hereafter.[62]

Similarly, in *De anima* Macrina suggests that our soul may be freed from its emotional attachment to the 'brute creation' 'either by forethought here or by purgation hereafter' and later that some are 'cleansed from evil' in this life, whilst others will be

[61] The goal of the soul's journey is social, e.g. *In cant.* 15: McCambley, 272; *GNO* vi. 459–60, and unites humanity with the angels: *In insc. pss.*: Heine, 121 (1. 9. 117); *GNO* v. 66. 14–15; see also ibid.: Heine, 139 (2. 6. 61); *GNO* v. 87. 4–5. In it, evil will be completely eliminated: *In insc. pss.*: Heine, 118 (1. 8. 110); *GNO* v. 64. 2–14; ibid.: Heine, 196 (2. 14. 232); *GNO* v. 155. 2–14; *In cant.* 15: McCambley, 276; *GNO* vi. 469: 5–6. Punishment may be required before entering it: e.g. *In insc. pss.*: Heine, 139 (2. 6. 61); *GNO* v. 87. 5–6: 'after your soul has been cleansed in the assault of the trials' (*καὶ τὴν σὴν ψυχὴν τῇ προσβολῇ τῶν πειρασμῶν ἐκκαθαρθεῖσαν*).

[62] *Cat. Or.* 8: Srawley, 46. 8–12; Srawley ET, 48.

perfected 'having afterwards in the necessary periods been cleansed by the fire'.[63]

However, it is possible that these pairings of this life and the future life are just rhetorical flourishes. More satisfactory evidence is required to show that Gregory views the two sorts of purification as sufficiently similar for one to draw conclusions about freedom.

ii. Divine Pedagogy

Gregory appears to have two concepts of what is involved in the human advance towards God through purification, one with a more volitional (or moral) emphasis, the other focused on more cognitive aspects—however, these very much overlap and are frequently difficult to separate in analysis. They are certainly complementary rather than alternative ideas in Gregory's theology and it should be stressed that he neither uses the equivalents of the terms 'cognitive' and 'volitional' (which this study will use for the sake of clarity), nor even analyses the two sorts of advance towards God separately. However, it will be useful for the time being to distinguish them in Gregory's thought in order to assess whether freedom and universalism fit together coherently in his theology.

Gregory sometimes sees purification in this life in terms of the distinguishing between good and evil, and the love of wisdom.[64] Hence, the advance of the soul towards God can be expressed in cognitive terms, not so much because the individual learns more about God (for Gregory emphasizes that humans cannot know God's essence) but that he or she learns more about what is good.[65] This clearly overlaps with the question of moral advance, because learning about what is good is obviously vitally important to virtue—one cannot make a virtuous choice if one cannot understand the nature of the options. However, for Gregory knowledge of the good is even

[63] *De an.*: *NPNF* v, 449; Oehler, 349. 11–13 (*εἴτε ἐκ τῆς νῦν ἐπιμελείας εἴτε ἐκ τῆς μετὰ ταῦτα καθάρσεως*); *De an.*: *NPNF* v. 465; Oehler, 373. 9–11 (*τῶν μὲν εὐθὺς ἤδη κατὰ τὸν βίον τοῦτον ἀπὸ κακίας κεκαθαρμένων, τῶν δὲ μετὰ ταῦτα διὰ τοῦ πυρὸς τοῖς καθήκουσι χρόνοις ἰατρευθέντων*).

[64] Love of wisdom: *De mort.*: Lozza, §15, 64. 13–14 (*φιλοσοφίας*); distinguishing right from wrong: ibid., §15, 66. 1–3 (*εἰ μὲν διακρίνοι τοῦ ἀλόγου τὸ ἴδιον*).

[65] Indirectly this is learning about God, because God is the true good.

more vitally important, because he appears to take a Platonic line insisting that humans naturally choose what they think is the good and that sin is essentially due to ignorance. Hence he thinks that Eve took the fruit from the tree in the garden not because she willingly chose evil, but because she incorrectly thought that the fruit was good. (The name of the tree—the tree of the knowledge of good and evil—indicates the dual nature of the fruit: it was evil; it looked good.[66])

Gregory takes this interpretation of sin and develops from it a theory of pedagogy—of God teaching humans not to sin. This is dealt with in the early work *De mortuis*. First Gregory makes it clear that although humans should judge the good 'with the bare eye of the soul', in fact it is inevitable that in this life sense perception is involved in such judgement.[67] This helps to explain Eve's choice of the fruit: it was disguised so as to look attractive, just as the good is frequently disguised in this life.[68] However, although humankind fell through this deceit of the devil, yet Gregory claims that the Fall was willing—in the sense that Eve chose the fruit.[69]

Moving on from the Fall to the current human situation, Gregory asks whether it would not be 'useful' (*χρήσιμον*) to lead people away from evil to the good against their will (*ἄκοντας*).[70] His answer is that to force them to do something against their will would be a deprivation of the dignity which they derive from being made in God's image. Because God is 'self-ruling', humans must be also.[71] Gregory describes God's solution of the problem as follows:

In order, therefore, that authority (*ἡ ἐξουσία*) might remain in [human] nature but that evil might be taken away from it, divine wisdom came upon a design to allow man to do what he wanted, in order that man should taste the evils which he desired and learn from experience (*τῃ πείρᾳ*) what he has preferred to what; and then that he should willingly turn back in his desire towards his original blessedness (*παλινδρομήσῃ διὰ τῆς ἐπιθυμίας ἑκουσίως πρὸς τὴν πρώτην μακαριότητα*), casting off from his nature everything which is passionate and irrational (*ἅπαν τὸ ἐμπαθές τε καὶ ἄλογον*) . . .[72]

[66] *De hom. opif.*: *NPNF* v. 20. 4.
[67] *De mort.*: Lozza, §13, 56. 31 ff.
[68] *De hom. opif.*: *NPNF* v. 20. 2; *PG* 44, 197d–200a.
[69] *De mort.*: Lozza, §15, 62. 33–4.
[70] Ibid., 62. 36–7.
[71] Ibid., 64: 1 ff.
[72] Ibid., 64: 8–13.

The idea appears to be that sin inevitably has bad consequences for the agent, that the agent will gradually learn from these what the good truly is and will subsequently choose the good rather than evil. This doctrine of humans learning not to sin thus relies on a positive view of prudence, for it clearly depends on a belief that the truly good is in the long run beneficial to the agent.

Despite appearing to preserve human autonomy, Gregory's theory of divine pedagogy has its disadvantages. The most obvious is that the theory relies on the assumption that bad consequences *do* always attend the criminal—a claim which simply does not seem to be borne out by experience. Gregory gets round this problem, however, by suggesting that *eventually* (i.e. in the afterlife) bad consequences do always affect the wicked and that they learn from these. This idea is suggested by the fact that Gregory concludes the above quotation by saying that the passionate and irrational should be cast off 'either by purification in this life by attention and love of wisdom, or after leaving here in the melting-pot of purifying fire'.[73] Indeed, Gregory does seem to see punishment not as imposed externally by a vengeful God, but either as a merciful application of pain for a good end, or sometimes as the natural consequence of sin which the wicked bring on themselves. These last two are not necessarily mutually exclusive, for God as creator could be responsible for the fact that the painful consequences of sin affect the wicked.

There are also other indications that Gregory thinks that life after death will bring an experience which will teach the wicked the error of their ways. This is to be found in one of the Easter sermons in which Gregory speaks of the eschaton specifically as a revelatory experience:

> For when 'the pattern of this world' has passed, and Christ is manifested to all (*ἐπιφανῇ πᾶσιν Χριστὸς*) as King and God, having convinced every unbelieving soul and bridled every blaspheming tongue . . . then . . . all the nations and age-old peoples will bow low and offer up the homage of surrender . . .[74]

This may suggest that the recognition of Christ as Saviour will be part of the learning-experience: it could well be terrifying, if not

[73] Ibid., 13–15.
[74] *In s. Pascha*: *GNO* ix. 246; Hall, 5–6.

painful, to experience the revealed glory of God—particularly if one's sin was to reject it in this life. Thus revelation and punishment are not separate, but are one event. In Gregory's commentary on 1 Corinthians 15: 28, he writes that the submission of the Son to the Father indicates 'for all human nature the knowledge of being, and salvation'.[75] This again could be taken to assert that an important feature of the eschaton will be revelation. Nevertheless, he does not assert that it is through the knowledge that salvation comes—indeed, the opposite may be the case: that knowledge is the result of salvation. So, although Gregory has the opportunity to argue that revelation and punishment after death will be educational experiences through which the soul will learn about what is truly good and thus turn to it, he does not actually state this explicitly.

A second disadvantage is that Gregory's concept of divine pedagogy relies heavily on the notion that humans will always choose what they think to be good (or best). This might be challenged by modern views of moral motivation, which draw attention to the irrational nature of some human action. There are also problems with the idea even within Gregory's own system. If sin is caused by ignorance of what is truly good, Gregory does not explain fully what caused this ignorance. In the case of Eve, was it that she had child-like ignorance and that she could not see through the deception of the devil, or was it that she was suffering from culpable ignorance, her reason being clouded by her passions? If the former is the case this commits Gregory to an evolutionary view of human nature, imagining that individuals and the race as a whole grow in the understanding of the good, and in their understanding of the danger of the passions, through God's guidance. This possibility is not denied by the concept of the first, perfect creation, for as has been seen this is in Gregory's theology only an ideal, not an actuality. The problem is to explain why God might have created humans in a state of ignorance such that they were almost bound to sin. One explanation might be that it is better for humans to learn what is good, rather than to be created with the knowledge of what is good: in other words, that life brings a maturity that cannot be achieved in any other way.

[75] *In illud: tunc GNO* iii/2. 23. 15–18: *πάσης ἀνθρωπίνης φύσεως τὴν γινομένην τοῦ ὄντος ἐπίγνωσίν τε καὶ σωτηρίαν.*

If, on the other hand, Gregory believes that it is the case that the Fall was due to culpable ignorance due to the too-strong influence of the passions, then this might seem to confuse his claim that sin is due simply to ignorance. If people have passions for things which are evil, surely this contradicts the claim that they always knowingly choose the good? It is likely that Gregory sees desires as the product of ignorance: one may choose something because it appeals to one's senses, but it is ignorance which causes one to think that something which appeals to one's senses is better than something which one's reason tells one is good. Hence, God's pedagogy may be seen as a training to follow one's reason, not one's senses. This training can be improved by attention in this life to *philosophia* (φιλοσοφία). For Gregory this word indicates not just an academic discipline—although *philosophia* clearly involves reason, the word also often denotes a monastic or ascetic lifestyle. (So, in the *Life of Saint Macrina* the life in her monastic community is consistently referred to as one of *philosophia.*[76]) This is the point at which the cognitive and volitional-moral aspects of the soul's advance towards God overlap: on the one hand, God's pedagogy will result in us learning what the true good is and thus having right desires; on the other, it is clear that human effort in training one's desires will reinforce this process of learning.

Provided that one accepts the assumptions that humans do always choose what they think to be good and that God had good reason to create humans with a degree of ignorance, Gregory's account of divine pedagogy is coherent. There remains, however, a problem with human freedom: even if punishment and revelation in the afterlife are seen as educational, they appear to have such a character that sinners are left in no doubt as to what is good. Divine punishment is always portrayed as effective and the revelation of Christ is decribed as leading to the surrender and submission of the wicked. In the afterlife humans seem to be no longer free to sin and no longer autonomous, whereas they are always free to sin or reject God throughout their lifetime. It must now be asked whether a similar problem affects the volitional aspect of human advance towards God in its post-mortem phase.

[76] *De vita Mac.*: *SC* 178, 1. 27–9; 5. 47; 6. 8–13; 8. 24–6; 11. 14; 11. 48; 37. 10; 37. 21 f. etc. (= *GNO* viii/1. 371. 19–21; 377. 4; 377. 14–19; 379. 18–19; 381. 28; 383. 8; 411. 4; 411. 15 f. etc.).

iii. Moral Perfection: Asceticism and Purification

In Gregory's spiritual works, he advises his readers to order or control their desires in this life through virtue, with the ultimate aim of reaching a true state of *apatheia* at the eschaton. Punishment in the afterlife is also directed at this goal, so one might be tempted to see purification by virtue and by punishment as alternative and mutually exclusive routes to the *apokatastasis*. However, because Gregory clearly believes that there will be different degrees of punishment in the afterlife, perhaps it is truer to his way of thinking to say that the punishment after death makes up for any shortfall in the virtue achieved in this life. Expressed another way, for most people purification after death completes the purification begun in this life; so since the two sorts of purification have the same function in one continuous process it might seem reasonable to assume that this function is performed in similar ways. After looking briefly at how Gregory envisages purification by virtue in this life, it will be asked whether this does in fact illuminate his view of the afterlife.

Gregory describes purification in this life in a variety of ways: for example 'attention and *philosophia*'; distinguishing right from wrong in a noble life; 'putting their spiritual life aright in *apatheia*'.[77] In essence, he seems to be thinking of purification in this life in terms of the pursuit of virtue or of ascetic effort. But in Gregory's theology there is no artificial separation of faith and works, because, since God himself is supreme virtue, to fail to act in accordance with virtue is to turn away from, to reject or deny God. (Hence this version of the soul's advance towards God has here been described as volitional—choosing for/against God—or moral: the two aspects are inseparable.)

Gregory sometimes gives the impression that an individual's progress to God through virtue is by that person's effort alone; for example, he claims:

> well does the divine Scripture of the Psalter point the way to this [beatitude] through a skilful and natural sequence in teaching . . . by

[77] Respectively: *De mort.*: Lozza, §15, 64: 13–14 (διὰ προσοχῆς τε καὶ φιλοσοφίας); ibid., 66. 1–3; ibid., 66. 13–14 (τὸν πνευματικὸν ἐν ἀπαθείᾳ κατορθούντων βίον).

setting forth systematically in various and diverse forms the method for acquiring the blessing (τὴν μέθοδον τῆς τοῦ μακαρισμοῦ κτήσεως).[78]

This impression is reinforced by the dominant metaphor which Gregory uses to describe a virtuous life: the soul following God, which stresses an active human response. He also frequently talks of the effort and struggle of the virtuous life.[79] Looking back to the discussion of desire in the last chapter, it is important to remember that the perfect state of *apatheia* is not, in Gregory's opinion, a passive one.

However, the mention of human involvement should not blind one to the clear contribution made by God to the progress of the soul. First, it is a corner-stone of Gregory's philosophy that, in a very general sense, the source of all good is God; therefore, if one does good, it is inevitably by the grace of God.[80] Secondly, human freedom, which is vital for virtuous action, is clearly granted to us by God: the account of human creation in God's image, with freedom and other divine characteristics, stresses this point: it is only through our creation in the very image of God that we have the grace to be virtuous. Thirdly, Gregory believes that grace has been bestowed upon humanity through the incarnation of Christ and that in particular it is received by faithful Christians in the sacraments. Consequently, one might say—in the terminology of modern theology—that God is the grounds of the possibility of free virtuous action. This is a theme which will also become evident in Karl Rahner's theology.

The relationship between grace and freedom—between divine and human agency—is not at all precisely delineated in Gregory's works. Jaeger stresses the frequent occurrence in the spiritual and ascetic works of the verb συνέργω which he takes as meaning to contribute to the effect of some already existing faculty.[81] Thus he suggests that in Gregory's treatise *De instituto christiano* grace is God's response to human worthiness and

[78] *In insc. pss.*: Heine, 84 (I. I. 7); *GNO* v. 26. 14–19.

[79] All of the *Life of Moses*, but particularly the time in the wilderness, is a metaphor for the struggle of the journeying soul. For references to effort in ascetic works, see: W. Jaeger, *Two Rediscovered Works of Ancient Christian Literature: Gregory of Nyssa and Macarius* (Brill, Leiden, 1954), 78.

[80] *In insc. pss.*: Heine, 109–10 (I. 8: 79); *GNO* v/53. 17–23; *PG* 44, 468b.

[81] Jaeger, *Two Rediscovered Works*, 78.

operates as a consequence of human efforts.[82] However, whilst it does seem to be the case that some grace is such a response—particularly that grace received in the sacraments—grace is also apparent in the creation of humankind in God's image and in Christ's incarnation, neither of which can be properly described as responses to human effort. Hence, Paulos Mar Gregorios stresses the importance of divine agency through human nature, claiming that in Gregory's theology all is grace and that it would be a misinterpretation to impose an artificial distinction between grace and nature on his theology. He concludes that consequently 'Gregory's doctrine of grace is dialectically in tension with the notion of freedom'.[83] However, even the analysis of Mar Gregorios perhaps does not do full justice to Gregory's theology in this assessment of the role of human freedom: because Gregory sees God both as the grounds of the possibility of human virtuous action, and as the one who rewards virtue with further help, this appears to bind both human and divine agency into a harmonious whole, rather than hold them in tension.

The next question is whether this same pattern and harmony can be seen to apply to the purification of sinners in the afterlife. Unfortunately, there appear to be various reasons why it does not. First, punishment in the afterlife often appears to be a passive experience such that it is on the face of it hard to see how free will on the part of the sinner could be involved. In some places, Gregory does move away from the concept of punishment imposed by God the Judge and towards the idea that punishment is the natural consequence of one's sin catching up with one.[84] But the punishment is none the less painful for this:

[82] Jaeger, *Two Rediscovered Works*, ch. 5: 'The Theology of the Treatise'. His assessment of *De instituto christiano* is as follows: 'Gregory's treatise may be characterised as the work in which the theology of the Eastern Church reached the culminating peak of its tendency to bring the two basic elements of the Christian religion, divine grace and human effort into perfect balance. At the same time, the treatise attempted a reconciliation of the Christian concept of grace with the Hellenic ethical tradition, the classical idea of areté' (p. 88).

[83] Paulos Mar Gregorios, *Cosmic Man* (A New Era Book, Paragon House, N. Y., 1988), 130–1.

[84] For example, in *De infantibus* he uses the analogy of two men, one of whom followed his doctor's advice, whilst the other did not; the just and the unjust will experience the 'fruits of their choice' (*τῆς προαιρέσεως αὐτοῦ τοὺς καρπούς*) in the same way that the two men did (*De infant.*: *NPNF* v. 376; *GNO* iii/2. 82. 7–17; quotation from lines 14–15). Similarly in *The Life of Moses* Gregory believes that the Egyptians brought the plagues—

when the soul pines and is wasted away in the reproaches incurred for sin . . . owing to its deeply rooted connexion with evil, there follows of necessity certain deeply inexpressible and indescribable pains . . .[85]

This emphasis on pain conveys the impression of a soul which is helpless to do anything but suffer. It is true that Gregory thought that one of the roles of virtue in this life should be to undergo painful trials patiently; however, this is clearly not the *only* function of virtue in this life, for in many circumstances it has a more active role.[86] The continuous endurance of painful trials after death seems to offer little scope for active response on the part of the soul.

This is even more the case when, in other places, Gregory moves away from the concept of punishment as natural consequence of sin and stresses more the idea that it is a purifying treatment imposed by God: a painful means, justified by a good end.[87] This medicinal view of punishment is compared to medicine in real life:

those who are subjected to the knife or caustics in order to cure them, grow angry with the physicians, smarting under the pain of the incision; whereas if by these means they regain health, and the pain of the cautery passes away, they will be grateful to those who effected the cure in them.[88]

Sometimes Gregory's metaphor is less therapeutic. In *De anima*, for example, the punishment of the soul is compared to the refining of gold: as the gold must be heated along with the dross, so the soul must suffer as it loses its impurities.[89] (The other analogies which Macrina uses in this passage—of a rope losing the clay encrusted around it as it is pulled through a hole and of mangled bodies pulled out of earthquake-shattered buildings—are even more vividly violent.) She sums up the fate of the soul thus:

including that of darkness, which he interprets as hell—on themselves (*De vita Moysis*: Malherbe and Ferguson, 2. 86–7).

[85] *Cat. or.* 8: Srawley, 48. 12–49. 3; Srawley ET, 49.

[86] Lazarus went straight to blessedness, because of his patient endurance of earthly trials: *In insc. pss.*: Heine, 139 (2. 6. 62); *GNO* v. 87. 4–11.

[87] It was seen above that these two views of punishment need not be mutually exclusive (p. 101).

[88] *Cat. or.* 26: Srawley, 99. 20–100: 4; Srawley ET, 82.

[89] *De an.*: *NPNF* v. 451; Oehler, 352. 28 ff.

the Divine force, for God's very love of man, drags that which belongs to Him from the ruins of the irrational and material. Not in hatred or revenge for a wicked life, to my thinking, does God bring upon sinners those painful dispensations; He is only claiming and drawing to himself whatever, to please Him, came into existence. But while He for a noble end is attracting the soul to Himself, the Fountain of all Blessedness, it is the occasion necessarily to the being so attracted of a state of torture.[90]

Besides the emphasis again on pain, the use of words such as 'drags', 'claiming', 'drawing to himself' and 'attracting' further suggests that the soul is a passive object being transformed by God.

A second difference between the perfection in this life and the purificatory punishment of the next rests in the respective results of the purification. As was seen in the last chapter, the goal of virtue in this life, in respect of the passions, is to have the correct attitude to them. Because one cannot survive without the desire for food or drink and so on, the aim is to discipline one's desires so as only to desire what is necessary and to shun what goes beyond that. However, it has also been made clear that, at the eschaton, the 'restoration to the original state' involves not the right ordering but the total eradication of all passion—true *apatheia*. The 'desire' for God which is left is not truly desire but the soul's love of or natural attraction to God. Again, whereas it is easy to see how the disciplining of one's desires is a product of human effort and a free choice, it is more difficult to see a free choice being involved in a punishment which gets rid of earthly desires in the soul and results in the unimpeded rise of the soul to God.

Gregory's concept of the purification in the afterlife as a painful experience to be endured passively and of the result of this as a natural attraction to God thus appears to differ radically from his concept of purification in this life. This is because the afterlife experiences appear to leave little room for free choice, whereas free choice seems to be what virtue is all about.

[90] *De an.*: *NPNF* v. 451; Oehler, 352. 20–7: *ἡ θεία δύναμις ὑπὸ φιλανθρωπίας ἐκ τῶν ἀλόγων τε καὶ ὑλικῶν συμπτωμάτων ἐφέλκηται τὸ ἴδιον. οὐ γὰρ μισῶν, οὐδ' ἀμυνόμενος ἐπὶ τῇ κακῇ ζωῇ κατά γε τὸν ἐμὸν λόγον ἐπάγει τοῖς ἐξημαρτηκόσι τὰς ὀδυνηρὰς διαθέσεις ὁ Θεός, ὁ ἀντιποιούμενός τε καὶ πρὸς ἑαυτὸν ἕλκων πᾶν ὅ τί περ αὐτοῦ χάριν ἦλθεν εἰς γένεσιν, ἀλλ' ὁ μὲν ἐπὶ τῷ κρείττονι σκοπῷ πρὸς ἑαυτόν, ὅς ἐστι πηγὴ πάσης μακαριότητος, τὴν ψυχὴν ἐπισπᾶται, ἐπισυμβαίνει δὲ κατ' ἀνάγκην ἡ ἀλγεινὴ διάθεσις τῷ ἑλκομένῳ·.*

Universal Salvation and Human Freedom according to Gregory of Nyssa

first creation
(ideal)
Humans were perfect and sinless and possessed *apatheia*.

second creation
(actual)
Humans were ignorant/immature: they could be virtuous but could also sin. Foreseeing the Fall, God gave humans material desires.

the Fall
Humans chose what was not truly good—they directed their material desires wrongly.

the history of salvation
This has two aspects: *i. cognitive: learning good, divine pedagogy* and *ii. volitional: rightly ordering desires*
and (for all but the saints) two stages: *this life* and *the next life*.

this life:
Humans act freely through divine grace (*sunergeia*).
Virtuous action (*philosophia*) involves:
i. learning from effects of sin (cognitive) *ii. moral effort, asceticism (volitional).*

next life:
The saints—already perfect—enter life with God.
All others passively experience divine punishment.
This punishment
i. teaches the effects of sin (cognitive) *ii. purifies, heals (volitional).*

the eschaton:
All humans will be perfect and sinless and will possess *apatheia*.
They can no longer sin (or fall).
Is this true freedom?

Figure 1.

Similarly, Gregory's view of pedagogical punishment and revelation in the afterlife seems to imply that it is much more effective than God's teaching in this life and that it will eventually leave humans in no doubt as to what the true good is. Not only is this experience of revelation/punishment a passive one, but its effect will be that humans will have no freedom to choose between good and evil. As has been assumed from the beginning of this discussion, pedagogy and purification are but two aspects—cognitive and volitional—of the same process. With regard to both aspects the process has two phases and the second phase seems to be a passive one, not involving free effort and leaving humans without the freedom to sin.[91]

However, although the distinction between this life and the next in terms of free choice is certainly there, the inference which might be drawn from this—that there is no room at all for freedom in the afterlife—is false. It is possible, when reading Gregory's theology, to see a distinction between, on the one hand, the freedom expressed in choices between actions in the pursuit of virtue in this life and, on the other hand, the freedom expressed in the unimpeded rise of the soul to God. Although Gregory does not make this point explicitly, he appears to assume that the latter sort of freedom from sin and death, and not freedom of choice, is true freedom or the more important sort of freedom. Because humanity was created in the image of God and because like is attracted to like, the experience of being drawn towards God, despite sounding passive, is in fact the truest expression of humanity's real nature. This is true freedom because the inability to rise to God is a restriction. In order to understand this concept of freedom, one must therefore put into the background any conception of human freedom which is based on freedom of choice and the ability 'to do otherwise'. Freedom of choice *is* important for Gregory in this life, for it is necessary for virtue, but after death another, truer and more valuable, freedom takes its place. Since they are once again perfectly conformed to God's image, humans have divine freedom: they, like God, are not free to sin. Just as this is not seen as a restriction of God, neither should it be seen as a restriction of

[91] See Figure 1 for a diagrammatic representation of the relation of the cognitive and volitional apects of salvation in this life and the afterlife.

humans. Gregory appears to believe, then, that it is valid to express the conviction that all will be saved and at the same time to say that all will be free. They are not, admittedly, free to reject God, but for Gregory the availability of such an option is the very opposite of true freedom. The merits and problems of this view of freedom will be discussed in the concluding chapter in comparison with the eschatology of Karl Rahner, which will be the subject of the following chapters.

Karl Rahner

4

The Background to Karl Rahner's Eschatology

A. THE LIFE OF KARL RAHNER (1904–1984)[1]

Karl Rahner's upbringing was, by his own account, unremarkable. He was born into what he describes as 'a normal, middle-class, Christian family', did not shine at school and seemed only to stand out from his contemporaries because of his early-developed interest in Christian spirituality.[2] This interest was one of the factors which influenced his decision to enter the novitiate of the Society of Jesus after he left school and the Spiritual Exercises of Ignatius of Loyola played a central role for the rest of his life: their influence can be detected in his theology as well as in his less academic writings, and in later years he was much in demand as a director of the Exercises.[3]

Rahner's career as theologian and philosopher began as part of his Jesuit training.[4] Besides a thorough grounding in Aquinas, his philosophical studies focused in particular on Kant and the Jesuits Pierre Rousselot (1878–1915) and Joseph Maréchal (1878–1944). Of the latter, Vorgrimler writes:

> Maréchal had opposed Thomism to the philosophy of Kant and tried to make Kant's transcendental method fruitful for Thomistic epistemology. However, he was also very much concerned with questions of mysticism and mystical experience and in this connection, by asking

[1] This biographical discussion is indebted to the following works: Herbert Vorgrimler, *Understanding Karl Rahner* (SCM, London, 1986); William V. Dych, *Karl Rahner* (Outstanding Christian Thinkers Series, Geoffrey Chapman, London, 1992); Robert Kress, *A Rahner Handbook* (John Knox Press, Atlanta, Ga, 1982).

[2] See his description from *I Remember* (pp. 24 f.) cited by Vorgrimler in *Understanding Karl Rahner* (p. 47). Vorgrimler mentions Rahner's reading of *The Imitation of Christ* and other texts (*Understanding Karl Rahner*, 48 f.).

[3] Vorgrimler, *Understanding Karl Rahner*, 20.

[4] Between 1924 and 1934: this period also included several years practical experience and one year of retreat.

how 'modern man' was to be understood before God, was a great stimulus to Rahner.[5]

Through his training Rahner gained a good knowledge of the Church Fathers, particularly their writings on grace, the sacraments, spirituality, and mysticism.[6] His reading included writers such as Origen, John Chrysostom, Gregory of Nyssa, and Augustine as well as earlier authors.[7]

After his training for his order and for the priesthood was complete, Rahner was sent to study philosophy in Freiburg im Breisgau.[8] He was intended by his Jesuit superiors to teach philosophy, but their plans came somewhat unstuck when his doctoral thesis (an interpretation of Aquinas' metaphysics) was rejected by his dissertation supervisor, apparently for being too modern a treatment of the subject. However, Rahner's time at Freiburg was by no means wasted: his dissertation was later expanded and published as *Geist im Welt* and paved the way for his next scholarly work, *Hörer des Wortes*. Rahner also attended the seminars of Martin Heidegger, whose philosophy he much admired (albeit with major reservations) and some of whose ideas were later reflected in Rahner's own thought.

In 1936 Rahner moved to Innsbruck; after gaining his doctorate in theology in the same year and qualifying for teaching the year after, he was able to fulfil his superiors' revised plans for him to become a teacher of theology.[9] He began as *Privatdozent* in the theology faculty of Innsbruck University; however, after the Anschluss and the subsequent suppression of the teaching of theology by the Nazi regime (both at the university and in the Jesuit Order's own institutions), he accepted an invitation from the archbishop of Vienna to work in the Viennese Diocesan Pastoral Institute (1939). In a fashion typical of his career, Rahner wove together pastoral and academic concerns and continued to teach and lecture as much as possible during this period, both in Austria and in Germany.

[5] Vorgrimler, *Understanding Karl Rahner*, 51. For a discussion of Rahner's philosophy see pp. 118–29 below.

[6] Dych, *Karl Rahner*, 5.

[7] Vorgrimler, *Understanding Karl Rahner*, 52.

[8] Rahner was in Freiburg from 1934 to 1936.

[9] He held most of his posts in theology faculties, the one exception being the prestigious chair in *Christliche Weltanschauung und Religionsphilosophie* which Rahner held in the University of Munich (1964–7) as the successor to Romano Guardini.

When, in 1944, his work was again threatened by the Gestapo he went to serve in a rural Bavarian parish. Even after 1945, he continued to help those who had suffered from war and from Nazism, by combining pastoral work in Munich with a teaching post in the nearby Jesuit college at Pullach (1945–9).

As a churchman, the time which was perhaps both the high-point and the most testing period for him came towards the end of his time as professor at Innsbruck.[10] Over the previous years Rahner had gradually been gaining a reputation for innovation in theology: while in Vienna during the war he had written for the archbishop the 'Vienna Memorandum', defending the need for theological innovation against a letter from the archbishop of Innsbruck warning all his German-speaking colleagues of the dangers of new thinking.[11] Rahner's desire to see a renewal in theology was accompanied after the war by the growing conviction that a more general renewal in the Church was required, particularly in the light of the fact that many people were criticizing the Catholic Church's role *vis-à-vis* fascism. Rahner sympathized with this criticism, knowing it to be just, but feared that it might lead many to reject the Church completely.[12]

By the summer of 1962, the Vatican was concerned by Rahner's outspokenness to such an extent that it placed him under pre-censorship: that is, he had to ask permission before publishing his work or lecturing in public.[13] Within a month the three German-speaking cardinals (König, Döpfner, and Frings) had written to the Pope asking for the move against Rahner to be reversed. Meanwhile, the *Paulus-Gesellschaft* collected 250 signatures for a letter of protest to the Pope: the prominent people who signed it came from a wide variety of backgrounds, political and academic, from the sciences and the humanities. It was also endorsed by the German chancellor Adenauer. These protests had little short-term effect, but the practical impact of the censorship was diminished by the fact that Rahner quickly became involved in the Second Vatican Council.[14] He was appointed advisor to both Cardinal König and Cardinal Döpfner

[10] Rahner was professor of theology at Innsbruck from 1948 to 1964.

[11] In his later life, Rahner attributed much formative importance to his writing of this memorandum (Vorgrimler, *Understanding Karl Rahner*, 47).

[12] Ibid., 87–8.

[13] Kress, *A Rahner Handbook*, 8.

[14] Rahner was eventually released from the pre-censorship order in May 1963.

and towards the end of 1962 was nominated a council expert (*peritus*) by the Pope. His involvement undoubtedly was disapproved of in some circles as much as it was approved in others, but it left its mark on many of the council documents. William Dych lists the topics which particularly felt Rahner's contribution: ecclesiology, especially the role of the Pope and bishops; revelation, the inspiration of the Bible, and the relation between Scripture and tradition; sacraments and the diaconate; the relationship of Church to the modern world; the possibility of salvation outside the Church.[15] The last two themes in particular will be seen to be important in his eschatology.

Throughout his life, including the period after his retirement in 1971, Rahner wrote and lectured with great energy. His total output is very large: it includes the two early books mentioned above; hundreds of articles, now collected in the series *Schriften zür Theologie*; various monographs, and *Grundkurs des Glaubens: Einführung in den Begriff des Christentums*—the closest Rahner came to a thoroughly 'systematic' work.[16] He was also involved as an editor on many projects, including Denzinger's *Enchiridion* of dogmatic statements, the second edition of the *Lexikon für Theologie und Kirche* (for which he also wrote 135 articles), *Sacramentum Mundi*, *Handbuch der Pastoral-Theologie*, and the series *Quaestiones Disputatae*. These publications clearly reflect the breadth of his interests: even within the field of strictly dogmatic theology he covered a great number of doctrines. His concern with general reference works and the style of many of his monographs and short articles also reflect his desire to communicate the essence of the Christian faith to the ordinary believer.

B. PHILOSOPHY AND THEOLOGY

In his essay on Karl Rahner, J. A. Di Noia notes that there has been 'substantive debate' on the role which philosophy—and in particular Rahner's own particular philosophical method—plays in his theological works. Di Noia himself concludes:

[15] Dych, *Karl Rahner*, 13.

[16] Published in English as *Theological Investigations* and *Foundations of Christian Faith: An Introduction to the Idea of Christianity*, respectively.

it seems preferable to assess the theological essays on their own merits as systematic contributions to particular traditional debates rather than to view them as offshoots of the project adumbrated in Rahner's philosophical and foundational proposals.[17]

This indeed seems to reflect Rahner's intention. His main concern was to reinterpret theology, and particular doctrines, for people of today; not to put all the emphasis on a foundational layer of philosophy which would seem likely to obfuscate, rather than to clarify the issues. Nevertheless, there are certain concepts in Rahner's theology which seem to be particularly linked to the more philosophical aspects of his theology—concepts such as grace, freedom, and revelation for example. With regard to eschatology it will be seen that an understanding of the central idea of consummation is especially dependent on an understanding of these three. For this reason then, it would seem that even if Rahner's theological output cannot be seen as a fully systematic and exhaustive outworking of his philosophy, he at least closely interlinks philosophy and theology in many of his writings. This study is not the place for a detailed discussion of Rahner's complex philosophical views, but a brief comment on the most important features will serve as a useful introduction to the theological analysis of the following chapters.[18]

Rahner is frequently referred to as a 'Transcendental Thomist'. 'Thomist' refers to the fact that Rahner was profoundly influenced by Aquinas' thought, although he rejected the somewhat stale historicism of neo-scholastic debate in favour of what he saw as a more modern approach.[19] 'Transcendental' refers to

[17] J. A. Di Noia, 'Karl Rahner', in David Ford (ed.), *The Modern Theologians*, 2nd edn. (Basil Blackwell, Oxford, 1997), 127.

[18] The following is intended not as a defence or critique, but as a simple exposition in order to set Rahner's eschatology in context. For a detailed systematic and critical analysis of the philosophical and theological basis of Rahner's writings see: George Vass, *Understanding Karl Rahner*, i: *A Theologian in Search of a Philosophy*; and ii: *The Mystery of Man and the Foundations of a Theological System* (Christian Classics, Westminster, Md.; Sheed & Ward, London, 1985) and Karen Kilby, *The 'Vorgriff auf Esse': A Study in the Relation of Philosophy to Theology in the Thought of Karl Rahner* (Ph.D. thesis, Yale University, 1994).

[19] Vorgrimler cites an extract from Rahner's first book (on epistemology in Aquinas) *Geist im Welt*: 'If . . . the reader gets the impression that here an interpretation of Thomas is at work which derives from modern philosophy, the author regards such an observation not as a deficiency but as an advantage in the book, precisely because he did not know on what basis he could deal with Thomas other than the questions which concern *his* philosophy and the philosophy of the times' (Vorgrimler, *Understanding Karl Rahner*, 61–2; citing *Geist im Welt*, Innsbruck, 1939, 13 f.).

the original focus of Rahner's philosophical interests—that is, epistemology and in particular the investigation of the a priori structures of human nature which are the conditions of the possibility of all knowledge. The word 'transcendental' shows that Rahner has used the philosophy of Kant to create a synthesis with Aquinas' analysis of knowledge. However, Rahner's use of the word 'transcendental' means something in addition to the Kantian meaning of pertaining to the necessary or a priori conditions of the possibility of knowledge. In Rahner it also indicates that there is something about these conditions which is transcendent: that there is something which rises above and cannot be captured by categorial concepts. This transcendental analysis of human knowledge of Rahner's will be briefly summarized before its broader implications are examined.[20]

In their analyses of the human act of knowing an object, both Aquinas and Kant identified two factors at work: the subject's passive reception of the object and the subject's active participation. The reception of the object is through experience and is therefore an a posteriori factor. The subject's capacity for active participation, on the other hand, is claimed by Kant to be an entirely a priori factor. As the condition for the possibility of any act of knowing (i.e. the transcendental factor), it is shared by all humans.

Rahner asserts that the structure of the knowing subject him- or herself is an a priori for all knowledge. He describes this structure as 'self-possession' or 'self-presence' or 'subjective consciousness'.[21] Hence human knowledge is characterized both by the subject's 'possession' of the known object, but also by its 'possession' of itself. However, whereas 'possession' of the known object can mean an explicit, conceptualized comprehen-

[20] The sources for this summary are: Karl Rahner, *Foundations of Christian Faith* (= *Foundations*) (Darton, Longman and Todd, London, 1978) chs. 1, 2, 3; Di Noia, 'Karl Rahner', 121–6; Dych, *Karl Rahner*, 32–45; Peter Phan, *Eternity in Time: A Study of Karl Rahner's Eschatology* (Susquehanna University Press, Selinsgrove; Associated University Press, London and Toronto, 1988), 58–60; Vass, *The Mystery of Man*, chs. 3, 4, 5; Vorgrimler, *Understanding Karl Rahner*, 59–64; Karl-Heinz Weger, *Karl Rahner* (Burns & Oates, London, 1980), 11–34; Rowan Williams, 'Balthasar and Rahner', in John Riches (ed.), *The Analogy of Beauty* (T&T Clark, Edinburgh, 1986).

[21] Rahner, *Foundations*, 18–20. Rahner asserts that this phenomenon occurs at least in human spiritual knowledge (p. 18) and *par excellence* in 'the totality of man's spiritual knowledge' where it is 'the *reditio completa*, the complete return of the subject to itself, as Thomas Aquinas calls it' (p. 19).

sion it cannot in the case of the subject's self-possession: the latter is always unthematic, that is, unconceptualizable.

Self-possession is, then, the a priori for human knowledge; but there exists also an a priori structure for self-possession itself: this is, in Rahner's own words, 'pure openness for absolutely everything, for being as such'.[22] By this he seems to mean that it is only in the context of an awareness of being in general (or 'absolute being'—*das absolute Sein*) that the subject can possess itself as a particular being (and be aware of other particular beings). The awareness of, or openness towards, absolute being he sometimes calls the *Vorgriff* (preapprehension):

Man is a transcendent being insofar as all of his knowledge and all of his conscious activity is grounded in a pre-apprehension (*Vorgriff*) of 'being' as such, in an unthematic but ever-present knowledge of the infinity of reality.[23]

Rowan Williams explains why, in Rahner's thought, knowledge must have this basis:

[Rahner's epistemology is established] primarily on the basis of *Vorgriff*—formal 'pre-understanding', determining in advance the possibility of specific (categorial) knowledge. . . . This capacity can only operate if it has at its root the sense of difference between the concrete formal object . . . and the unlimited existential possibility 'underlying' it. Or, in other words, to understand *contingency* . . . is in the same moment to understand the entirely open-ended potential of being itself. . . . Agent intellect is a preapprehension, *Vorgriff*, of unlimited possibility, and ultimately of being-as-such, *esse*, the very act of existing, which is the universal ground of each and every specific possibility.[24]

Although Rahner sometimes speaks of the *Vorgriff* as 'knowledge', it is clearly not the same sort as knowledge of an object, but an unthematic consciousness which is, by definition, impossible to put into words, impossible to conceptualize. Rahner uses various analogies to express this difficult idea: for example, the

[22] Rahner, *Foundations*, 20 (*Grundkurs des Glaubens: Einführung in den Begriff des Christentums* (Herder, Freiburg, Basel, Wien, 1976), 31: *'die reine Geöffnetheit für schlechthin alles, für das Sein überhaupt'*).

[23] Rahner, *Foundations*, 33 (*Grundkurs*, 44: *'Der Mensch ist das Wesen der Transzendenz, insofern alle seine Erkenntnis und seine erkennende Tat begründet sind im Vorgriff auf das 'Sein' überhaupt, in einem unthematischen, aber unausweichlichen Wissen um die Unendlichkeit der Wirklichkeit'*—Rahner's emphasis).

[24] Williams, 'Balthasar and Rahner', 14–15.

experience of watching actors on a stage.[25] One focuses on the actors, not really seeing the stage, although without the stage one could not see the actors at all. Similarly, one has thematic knowledge of an object, whilst only being unthematically conscious of absolute being. (Where the analogy breaks down is that Rahner claims that one can never 'know' absolute being in the same way that one can know an object, whereas of course one can always shift one's focus to the stage.)

It is this double-sided phenomenon of self-possession and openness to absolute being which Rahner calls 'transcendental experience'.[26] It is called transcendental partly because it is the condition of the possibility of any knowledge and partly because in the experience the subject transcends itself:

> a subject which knows itself to be finite . . . has already transcended its finiteness. It has differentiated itself as finite from a subjectively and unthematically given horizon of possible objects that is of infinite breadth.[27]

It is unthematic because, both in its self-possession and in its openness to being as such, the subject transcends 'beyond any particular grasp of possible objects or categories'.[28]

Not only does Rahner assert that absolute being is the ground of transcendental experience which is in turn the condition of the possibility of any knowledge, but he also goes further to say that transcendental experience is the condition of the possibility of any human action, and indeed of human existence at all (hence the reference to 'all of his conscious activity' in the extract from Rahner quoted above). Thus, by extension, absolute being is the ground of human existence as a whole. An epistemological claim has been expanded into a much wider metaphysical claim. In particular, Rahner stresses that transcendental experience is the condition of possibility for freedom, willing, and loving.[29]

Because he has shown that transcendental experience is a universal feature of human life, Rahner can draw from his epistemological analysis various conclusions about human nature in general. Of particular importance is his claim that transcendental experience reveals humans as free, personal

[25] Weger, *Karl Rahner*, 29.
[26] See Rahner's definition of this term, *Foundations*, 20.
[27] Ibid., 20. [28] Ibid., 20. [29] Ibid., 65.

subjects. In his discussion in *Foundations of Christian Faith* Rahner deals first with personhood. Self-possession requires the horizon of absolute being, against which one experiences oneself as finite. However, according to Rahner, this very consciousness of one's finitude in contrast to infinity, shows oneself as a person, in that it reveals that one can in a sense stand outside oneself and make a judgement about oneself (albeit one which is usually unthematic). The paradigm of experiencing oneself as a personal subject is, according to Rahner, the act of asking questions about oneself: for in putting oneself into question one is in a sense standing outside oneself, transcending oneself. The answer to the question 'What am I?' must always be something more than simply an empirical account of one's physical structure, because in asking the question one has shown oneself to be more than the sum of one's parts. Needless to say, many anthropologies have answered the question 'What am I?' in purely empirical terms, but Rahner attributes this to the fact that the experience of personhood is overlooked precisely because it is a universal and constant factor in all experience, but a factor which cannot be objectified in empirical terms.[30]

Besides revealing human beings as persons, transcendental experience reveals them as free and responsible: for example, the very fact that one is able to put oneself in question exemplifies this. The action of transcending oneself, of seeing oneself in the context of the infinite horizon is, for Rahner, a free one. This is the root concept of freedom, although freedom is of course instantiated in particular actions in the history of the individual:

> Freedom is always mediated by the concrete reality of time and space, of man's materiality and his history.[31]

Because freedom is above all the freedom exemplified in transcending oneself, Rahner frequently emphasizes that freedom is *not* primarily 'the power to be able to do this or that' but is freedom in respect of one's whole self: 'the power to decide about oneself and to actualise oneself'.[32] This point will be re-emphasized when Rahner's concept of consummation is discussed.

In addition to personhood and freedom, a third important

[30] Ibid., 35. [31] Ibid., 36. [32] Ibid., 38.

feature of human existence which is revealed by Rahner's epistemological analysis is the unity of matter and spirit in each person. The a posteriori factor involved in knowledge—the passive reception of the object by the senses—reveals the knower as material; but the a priori transcendental experience of self-possession reveals the knower as spirit. Hence, the knower is, to use the title of Rahner's first book, 'spirit in the world'.[33] This reflects the point made above that although freedom is originally a transcendental experience it is inevitably instantiated in the world: a spiritual experience has a concrete material context.

Such are the anthropological conclusions which Rahner draws from his analysis of knowledge. What are its implications for theology? In order to answer this question, clearly one must locate the place of God in the epistemological and anthropological picture which Rahner has built up. Rahner equates God with what he calls absolute being. Hence, in every act of knowing, the a priori, transcendental experience can be described as self-possession and the non-thematic awareness of God.

> Hence the original knowledge of God (*die ursprüngliche Gotteserkenntnis*) is not the kind of knowledge in which one grasps an object which happens to present itself from outside. It has rather the character of transcendental experience. Insofar as this subjective, non-objective luminosity (*subjekthafte, ungegenständliche Erhelltheit*) of the subject in its transcendence is always oriented towards the holy mystery, the knowledge of God is always present unthematically and without name, and not just when we begin to speak of it.[34]

This leap from the concept of absolute being to God is problematic and it is grounded in too complex a layer of thought to be examined here.[35] However, one should avoid the conclusion that Rahner is arguing *from* human nature *to* the existence of God: his analysis of transcendental experience is not a type of natural

[33] Cf. Dych, *Karl Rahner*, 41; and Phan, *Eternity in Time*, 46.

[34] Rahner, *Foundations*, 21 (*Grundkurs*, 32). Peter Phan writes: 'Rahner calls this non-objective, unthematic knowledge of God who is co-known in every act of knowing, the *Vorgriff*, that is, the act of the intellect's self-transcending anticipation of the absolute being' (*Eternity in Time*, 34). See also Williams: 'In as far as [the] *esse* is presupposed (or pre-apprehended) as absolute and real, the *Vorgriff* of *esse* is a pre-apprehension of God—not as an object, but as the condition for grasping all objects' ('Balthasar and Rahner', 15).

[35] Di Noia, for example, attributes it to a Hegelian concept of absolute being ('Karl Rahner', 124).

theology.[36] Rahner seems to be asking: given that God is the ground of all experience, what does this say about human beings and their relation to God? The fundamental conviction that God is the ground of all experience and that God is known, yet mysterious, is prior to the assertions which are made about human nature. It seems to be based partly on scriptural assertions that humans can (or will) know God and that God is also Mystery, and partly on Rahner's own beliefs about what religious experience is like. In saying that experience of God is transcendental experience, he is asserting that it is direct but at the same time fundamentally unable to be objectified, that it cannot be grasped by human concepts and that it evades verbal expression. Hence, in this context Rahner speaks of the 'darkness of God', God encountering one 'in silence' and above all of God as the 'holy mystery'.[37] This view of the human experience of God is undoubtedly influenced by Rahner's own personal experience which he once described thus:

> I have experienced God directly. I have experienced God, the nameless and the unfathomable one, the one who is silent and yet near. . . . I have experienced God himself, not human words about him. This experience is not barred to anyone.[38]

Not only is this experience open to all, but it is to be found in every aspect of life: for example, in 'a state of "*aloneness*" . . .when everything is called into question'; in feelings of responsibility and guilt; in love and death.[39] As a Jesuit, Rahner attached great importance to the Ignatian instruction to find God in all things.

This emphasis on God as mystery has many implications for Rahner's theology: just three will be mentioned here. First, it

[36] On this issue see Vass, *The Mystery of Man*, 138–41. On proofs for the existence of God, Rahner himself writes: 'The peculiar situation of giving the grounds subsequently for something which does the grounding and is already present, namely, the holy mystery, is what constitutes the specific character, the self-evident nature, and the difficulty of giving a reflexive proof for God's existence. That which does the grounding is itself grounded, as it were, and what is present in silence and without a name is given a name' (*Foundations*, 69).

[37] Rahner, *Foundations*, 21–2; cf., 60, 65.

[38] Rahner, *Schriften zur Theologie* xv. 374 f.; cited (and translated) in Vorgrimler, *Understanding Karl Rahner*, 11. Di Noia comments: 'The soul's experience of God in prayer functioned as a kind of paradigm for Rahner's theological account of the Christian mystery' ('Karl Rahner', 119).

[39] Rahner, *Theological Investigations* (= *TI*) xi. 157–9; cited in Vorgrimler, *Understanding Karl Rahner*, 11–13 (cf. ibid., 35–6).

clearly shows the limits of human knowledge of God and reveals the character of human knowledge of God as being one of awe before the incomprehensible, rather than of mastery (or 'comprehension').[40] The mystery remains even in the eternal beatific vision[41] and is thus a positive quality: it indicates, one might say, that God is too 'full' to know, rather than too 'empty'.[42] Thus, secondly, because God is mystery, Rahner insists that hope is not just a feature of this mortal life but that it is, in Dych's words, 'a permanent element in our relationship to God'.[43] Thirdly, because Rahner indicates the human relation to God by these two concepts of hope and attempting to grasp the ungraspable, the *Vorgriff* is sometimes portrayed dynamically as a reaching-out for God. In his eschatology, this reaching-out is seen as a movement not just to God, but also to the future—in fact, Rahner seems to equate the two.[44]

However, Rahner goes further than saying that God is simply the static, apersonal horizon of all experience (albeit a horizon which is absolute being). He also asserts that God's relationship to humanity is one of 'self-communication' (*Selbstmitteilung*): this is the essence of Rahner's concept of grace. God is thus not only the horizon of human experience but through self-communication also becomes close to humanity. Rahner frequently describes the two aspects of God's relationship to humans as distant and close, respectively:

> And when we say that God is present for us in an absolute self-communication, this says . . . that this self-communication of God is present in the mode of closeness, and not only in the mode of distant presence as the term (*Woraufhin*) of transcendence.[45]

The close aspect, God's self-communication, one might also call divine revelation; Rahner stresses, though, that this divine

[40] Rahner himself makes this point in the passage from *Foundations* (p. 21) cited above on p. 124. See also Dych, *Karl Rahner*, 19. However, von Balthasar felt that in fact Rahner stressed 'mastery' over 'mystery' because of his use of anthropology (Williams, 'Balthasar and Rahner', 24).

[41] See Dych, *Karl Rahner*, 21.

[42] Di Noia, 'Karl Rahner', 124–5; again, von Balthasar doubted whether this implication actually followed from the basis of Rahner's theology (Williams, 'Balthasar and Rahner', 20).

[43] Dych, *Karl Rahner*, 24.

[44] Cf. ibid., 43; Rahner, *Foundations*, 126.

[45] Rahner, *Foundations*, 119. For the relation between the two aspects see Williams, 'Balthasar and Rahner', 16; and Vorgrimler, *Understanding Karl Rahner*, 60 f.

communication is of God's own self: it is not the gift of some object, nor is it a propositional statement about God. Mysteriously, and uniquely, God communicates God's self to humans without ceasing to be God. And because God remains God, God remains incomprehensible:

> Divine revelation is not the unveiling of something previously hidden. . . . Rather it means that the 'deus absconditus' becomes radically present as the abiding mystery . . .[46]

What is the point of such self-communication? Rahner describes it as being 'for the sake of knowing and possessing God in immediate vision and love', or as making 'personal and immediate knowledge and love of God possible'.[47] It is not a phenomenon *added on* to human experience but is best understood as relational: it is what *constitutes* the divine-human relationship. It can also be expressed as the indwelling of God in the individual.[48] Ultimately this relationship will be experienced as beatific vision; now it is experienced as grace:

> What grace and vision of God mean are two phases of one and the same event which are conditioned by man's free historicity and temporality. They are two phases of God's single self-communication to man.[49]

The beatific vision is thus the final and eternal fulfilment of God's self-communication to humankind: this is what Rahner means by the consummation of the individual. He often uses consummation and salvation synonymously, although strictly he seems to view consummation as the final achievement of salvation—as opposed to the progression of salvation-history.

It is because Rahner holds this view of salvation as the consummation of God's self-communication to humanity that Weger can write of Rahner's soteriology that 'Man is sanctified and saved because, in Christ, he *shares in God's life*' and Dych can speak of the human destiny as '*union with God in knowledge and love*'.[50] Rahner himself says that the person 'participates in God's

[46] 'The Hiddenness of God': *TI* 16. 238, cited by Dych, *Karl Rahner*, 21.

[47] Rahner, *Foundations*, 117–18, 122 ('*zum Erfassen und Haben Gottes in unmittelbarer Anschauung und Liebe*'; '*personaler unmittelbarer Erkenntnis und Liebe zu Gott*': *Grundkurs*, 124, 128).

[48] e.g. Weger, *Karl Rahner*, 88; Dych, *Karl Rahner*, 38–9.

[49] Rahner, *Foundations*, 118.

[50] Weger, *Karl Rahner*, 98; Dych, *Karl Rahner*, 131 (my emphases in both cases).

being'.[51] All these expressions seem to emphasize that God's self-communication or salvation are not events which happen to someone who is a passive recipient, but that the person participates in them. Rahner's most difficult assertion arises from this idea: he asserts that God not only affects a human person extrinsically but also becomes the individual's 'innermost constitutive element' (*das innerste Konstituierende*).[52] This concept of God's action is analogous to the notion of a formal cause, with the difference that God retains the divine essence intact and in freedom.[53] If one sees transcendental experience in dynamic terms, God is thus not only the end or goal of the movement but its source too, without ceasing to be God, nor the human person ceasing to be human.

Rahner thus emphasizes very much the fact that God's self-communication is not something 'added on' or extrinsic to the human being. He also insists that humans were from the beginning willed by God to be the arena for the communication of God's own self.[54] Hence he describes God's self-communication as an 'existential' (*Existential*), meaning, in Dych's words, 'an intrinsic component of human existence and part of the very definition of the human in its historical existence'.[55] For this reason, Dych concludes that (in Rahner's view) 'as the horizon of every person's entire existence, God's self-communication as grace and revelation are present at least unthematically in all human knowledge and freedom'.[56] In other words, Rahner is very clear that, in some sense, God communicates God's self to, or dwells in, each and every human individual. Although he is circumspect about whether the consummation of God's self-communication (that is, salvation) will actually be achieved for every individual, he is certain that that consummation is at least possible for all.

[51] Rahner, *Foundations*, 120.

[52] Ibid., 121 (*Grundkurs*, 128). Cf. 'inner constitutive principle of man': *Foundations*, 121 (*'ein inneres konstitutives Prinzip des Menschen': Grundkurs*, 127).

[53] Rahner, *Foundations*, 121.

[54] Ibid., 123.

[55] Dych, *Karl Rahner*, 36–7; cf. Weger: 'This state of being called by God . . . forms a permanent and ontological factor which determines man's being' (*Karl Rahner*, 87).

[56] Dych, *Karl Rahner*, 45; see also Phan, *Eternity in Time*, 95: 'Rahner suggests that the grace of faith in the mode of offer (the "supernatural existential") is not an intermittent intervention of God's part but a permanent existential of creatures endowed with spiritual faculties and of the world in general.'

The aspect of human existence which is open to God's self-communication is more precisely known by Rahner as the 'supernatural' existential (*übernaturliches Existential*)—indicating that God did not have to create humanity thus. In particular Rahner is keen to avoid what he calls a pantheistic or Gnostic conception of God inevitably emanating throughout creation. The crux of Christian faith is that God's self-communication 'is to be understood as the freest possible love because he could have refrained from this and been happy in himself'.[57] In traditional Christian language, one would express this idea by saying that God's self-communication is gratuitous. Rahner emphasizes that it is no less gratuitous because it appears in every human being: he rightly argues that although it is in fact the case that God's self-communication is universal, it need not have been the case, had God willed it otherwise. This argument is directed at those who see grace as something extrinsic, the gratuity of which is demonstrated primarily by the fact that not all humans have it.

To sum these ideas up, one might say that for Rahner consummation or salvation is the gracious fulfilment of the human relationship with God in which the individual will be related eternally to God in knowledge and love. The condition for the possibility of this relationship is human transcendental experience which not only includes an unthematic awareness of God as distant horizon but is also the realm of (or context for) God's close self-communication.[58] The self-communication of God, although universal and thus an existential of human existence, is not natural but supernatural and gratuitous.

Chapters 6 and 7 will deal with Rahner's concept of eschatological consummation in its individual and collective aspects, respectively. In order to understand Rahner's eschatology, however, one must first pay attention to the specific foundations on which it lies: his hermeneutics of eschatological assertions and his theology of history. These will be dealt with in the next chapter.

[57] Rahner, *Foundations*, 124; cf. Dych, *Karl Rahner*, 36–7.

[58] The relation between human self-transcendence and the supernatural existential/divine self-communication is not absolutely clear in Rahner's account and he notes that the two cannot be separated by introspection. However, he does say that human self-transcendence is the realm of God's self-communication (*Foundations*, 123), that it makes God's self-communication justifiable and intelligible (pp. 121–2), and that divine self-communication is a modality of human self-transcendence (p. 129).

5

Eschatology for a Modern World

In an article in *Sacramentum Mundi*, Rahner defines the 'last things' as 'the realities which form the limit—or lie beyond the limit—separating time, history of salvation or loss and free acts from their definitive and eternal fulfilment'.[1] This expresses the essence of Rahner's eschatology which is focused around the premiss that eternal life (both for the individual and for the world) is a fulfilment or consummation of life now. He accepts the general outline of the traditional elements of Christian eschatology, both those dealing with the end of an individual's life and those focused on the end of the world as a whole.[2] Into the former category fall the judgement of the individual, purgatory, heaven, and hell; into the latter fall the return of Christ to judge the whole world, the general resurrection, and the kingdom of God. However, it will be seen that his interpretation of these elements, whilst endeavouring to remain faithful to their essence, also tries to express them in terms relevant to a modern age and to purge them of unnecessary or unhelpful features. This chapter will examine the questions of why Rahner thinks a review of eschatology is necessary and what elements he considers to be required by it (section A.). It will then look in detail at Rahner's own treatment of two of these elements: a hermeneutics of eschatological assertions and a theology of history (sections B. and C.).

[1] Karl Rahner's entry on 'Last Things', in Karl Rahner et al. (eds.), *Sacramentum Mundi* (= *SM*), tr. W. J. O'Hara et al. (Herder & Herder, New York, 1968–70), iii. 274. This multi-volume work was issued simultaneously in German, English, Dutch, Italian, Spanish, and French. Rahner wrote many other entries, e.g. on beatific vision, death, eschatology, hell, and heaven.

[2] 'Last Things': *SM* iii. 274–5

A. THE REQUIREMENTS FOR A DOCTRINE OF ESCHATOLOGY

In his entry on eschatology in *Sacramentum Mundi* Rahner emphasizes that a review of doctrines about the last things is necessary for three main reasons.[3] First, he points to the rapid changes in the way in which humans view the world. The modern scientific view is not only one of a world in progressive development, but one in which humans see themselves as able to participate actively in that development by planning and recreating both themselves and their environment (even to the extent of widening human living space beyond earth).[4] This new world-view results, most threateningly for Christianity, in what Rahner terms 'modern militant political world-heresies of secular utopianism'[5]—in other words, the attempt to plan a perfect world while failing utterly to recognize God. Rahner complains:

> Christian eschatology has not yet been obliged to face up sufficiently to the secular and 'utopian' eschatology of the age beginning now, with its view of a single humanity, its hominisation of environment, and our manipulation of ourselves—a period in which a person's *practice*, as opposed to what was previously his *theory*, appears in a totally new way as his highest and as his specific characteristic.[6]

His warning is relevant to any secular ideology which claims to set before humans a precise blueprint for the future, but he seems to be thinking largely of Marxist utopianism. His emphasis on praxis and the future reflect changing contemporary approaches to eschatology, particularly among Protestant theologians. For example, Rahner's views coincide to a large degree with Jürgen Moltmann's analysis of history and hope: both theologians emphasize the genuine futurity of eschatological events, the action of God in them and the consequent impossibility of predicting or controlling them.[7] Rahner was in a closer dialogue, however, with Johann-Baptist Metz, a Roman Catholic priest and

[3] 'Eschatology': *SM* ii. 242.

[4] Ibid., 243–4. (Sputnik had been launched in 1957.)

[5] Ibid., 244. Rahner's views on secular utopianism will be discussed further in Chapter 7.

[6] 'The Second Vatican Council's Challenge to Theology': *TI* xi. 19f. (A speech first delivered in 1966, i.e. just two years before *Sacramentum Mundi* was published.)

[7] Cf. Jürgen Moltmann, *Theology of Hope* (SCM, London, 1967; first published in German, 1964) and essays 3, 6 and 7 in *Hope and Planning* (SCM, London, 1971; essays first published in German, 1962, 1965, 1966).

Rahner's former pupil.[8] Metz developed an eschatology which emphasized the importance of Christian praxis whilst at the same time seeing the kingdom of God as a divine gift, not a humanly created utopia.[9] It was perhaps this eschatology which had the most direct influence on Rahner: he welcomed Metz's attempt to bring a political focus to eschatology without diminishing the transcendence of the kingdom of God, and he tried to incorporate some of Metz's ideas into his own writing. Peter Phan concludes that of all recent theologians writing on eschatology, Metz is the most important with regard to Rahner's work, not only because 'Metz's criticism, on Rahner's own avowal, is the only one he took seriously, but also because Rahner enlarged the history of his own eschatology precisely in response to such criticism'.[10] However, Rahner's eschatology perhaps always has a more optimistic colour than does that of Metz.[11]

Secondly, Rahner is concerned that traditional eschatology has concentrated too much on the individual. A brief survey of books and articles on eschatology will bear out Rahner's claim: Christian theologians, with a few exceptions, have indeed tended to concentrate on ideas such as heaven, hell, and purgatory rather than on wider issues such as the transformation of the cosmos. Indeed, at the beginning of the twentieth century, especially in Britain and America, the focus was on philosophical investigations of the possibility of the immortality of the soul, rather than on broader theological themes. Consequently, Rahner felt that

A cosmic eschatology involving the whole of history has become very colourless and insignificant as compared with a doctrine of the

[8] For an account of Metz's influence on Rahner see Peter Phan, *Eternity in Time: A Study of Karl Rahner's Eschatology* (Susquehanna University Press, Selinsgrove; Associated University Press, London and Toronto, 1988), 31, 38.

[9] Cf. Francis Schüssler Fiorenza's comments on Metz's book of essays, *Theology of the World* (Burns & Oates, London; Herder & Herder, New York, 1969; first published in German, 1968): 'Whereas the first essay pleaded for Christian theology to take seriously the contemporary situation of secularization, the final essay proposed a political theology pointing to the inadequacy of secularized theologies' (Schüssler Fiorenza, 'Introduction' to Johann-Baptist Metz, and Jürgen Moltmann *Faith and the Future* (Concilium Series, Orbis Books, Maryknoll, N.Y., 1995), p. xii.) This mirrors Rahner's own attitude to theology's role in the modern world.

[10] Phan, *Eternity in Time*, 31. One of Metz's criticisms was that he saw in Rahner's anthropological method the danger of producing an individualistic, bourgeois religion.

[11] See Herbert Vorgrimler, *Understanding Karl Rahner* (SCM, London, 1986), 128: he notes that Rahner always speaks of what comes beyond and after suffering.

individual immortality of spiritual souls and of their individual destiny.[12]

Rahner claims that the effect of this emphasis on the individual is not only that there has been a one-sidedness to Christian eschatology, but also that scriptural eschatological statements which focus on the individual have been found very difficult to combine coherently with those that appear to express a cosmic consummation; consequently, eschatology has become 'bi-polar' because it 'has not advanced in theological reflection beyond a relatively superficial arrangement of the statements of Scripture'.[13] Rahner's main point is that the Church has not been able to come to terms with the fact that there are two different but equally important emphases in eschatology: interestingly though, he does not condemn the individualistic tendency outright, but rather suggests that it was a product of and was suitable for a particular age:

> it is quite possible that this *way* of proclamation—valid though its actual content may be—was in fact determined by the conditions of a particular age. It is therefore possible to ask whether that age is not now coming to an end and another one slowly emerging, one which by its own dynamic orientation towards the future will have a more direct relation to the cosmic eschatology of Christianity which concerns the whole history of humanity.[14]

It is worth remembering that *Le Phénomène Humain* by Rahner's fellow Jesuit, Pierre Teilhard de Chardin, was published in 1955, only a decade before Rahner set out these requirements for a review of eschatology in *Sacramentum Mundi*.[15] In his book Teilhard suggests a final positive summing-up of the whole world, and this schema, based on the concept of the 'Omega Point', is a notable exception to the dominant, individualizing eschatology of the day and may have been one stimulus to Rahner's own broad approach.[16]

[12] 'Eschatology': *SM* ii. 242

[13] Ibid., 243.

[14] Ibid., 242. This quotation usefully emphasizes the point already made that Rahner very consciously sees himself as reinterpreting eschatology in a manner appropriate for the times, but not as departing from Christian tradition.

[15] Pierre Teilhard de Chardin, *Le Phénomène Humain* (Éditions du Seuil, Paris, 1955).

[16] Teilhard's interest in evolution and his consequent dynamic anthropology may also have affected Rahner's later thoughts on human nature. It is difficult, however, to assess precisely what impact Teilhard's work had on Rahner. *Le Phénomène Humain* is cited in

Thirdly, Rahner asserts that there is a need to look again at eschatology in response to attempts to demythologize it. His critique of demythologized eschatology is clearly directed at Rudolf Bultmann and his school (although he rarely mentions any theologian by name). Although Rahner himself was sympathetic with the use of existentialism to illuminate Christian faith, and, like Bultmann, was influenced by Heidegger in particular, he was well aware of the dangers to which an existentialist interpretation could lead. Rahner's criticisms will be dealt with more fully later in this chapter in discussing his hermeneutics, but at this point it is useful to note that they closely reflect his second reason for looking anew at eschatology. He accuses the demythologizers of demythologizing eschatological statements in order that the individually focused ones fit easily with the cosmically focused ones, but protests:

the multiple ways in which tradition speaks of the last things cannot be simply and on principle reduced to one and the same 'demythologized' meaning.[17]

This may seem an odd criticism in the light of the fact that Rahner himself appears to want to achieve more coherence between the two sorts of statement; however, in the case of demythologization he makes it clear that coherence has been bought at too high a price: cosmic fulfilment is demythologized into 'the multiplicity of individual eschata'.[18] In other words demythologization is caught in the old trap of concentrating too much on the individual. Later it will be seen that, rather than wanting complete harmony between them, Rahner is more willing to hold individualistic and cosmic eschatological statements in tension and in a dialectical relationship—although this approach brings with it its own problems.

These three factors—a changing world-view prone to secularization, the individualization (and consequent bi-polarization) of

the bibliography of Karl Rahner and Paul Overhage, *Das Problem der Hominisation: über den biologischen Ursprung des Menschen*, 2nd expanded edition (= *Quaestiones Disputatae* 12–13) (Herder, Freiburg-im-Breisgau, 1961), but Rahner makes no explicit reference to it in the body of his text. It seems probable that Rahner had read *Le Phénomène Humain*, but—given the size of the bibliography—that he considered it to be just one of many books on the question of human beginnings and development. One might also hazard a guess that Teilhard's more speculative approach and free-ranging style was not altogether to the taste of Rahner, who preferred to see his theology always in the context of the official doctrines of the Roman Catholic Church.

[17] 'Last Things': *SM* iii. 275.

[18] 'Eschatology': *SM* ii. 243.

eschatological doctrine, and demythologization—clearly reflect Rahner's contemporary context. Writing shortly after Vatican II, which revealed a Roman Catholic Church more open to modern political and scientific thought, Rahner also reflects a general movement in both Catholic and Protestant theology away from individualistic, existentialist interpretations of the Christian faith towards more social and political concerns. Nevertheless, he does not completely abandon the former in favour of the latter. In line with his hope for a unified and balanced eschatology he can best be seen (to quote Peter Phan) as attempting to preserve a balance 'between presentist and existentialist eschatology (that of C. H. Dodd and R. Bultmann) on the one hand and eschatology as prolepsis and hope (that of W. Pannenberg and J. Moltmann) on the other'.[19]

Rahner not only presents three general reasons for a new look at Christian eschatology, but he also translates them into some specific requirements for 'a doctrine of eschatology as it ought to be'.[20] Because previous interpretations of eschatological statements have tended to either individualize or demythologize (or both), he insists on the necessity of a new hermeneutics specifically directed towards eschatology. Similarly, his concerns about new world-views and conceptions of the future lead him to call for a thorough theology of history (especially salvation-history) which would include a study of the connection between Christian eschatology and secular utopianism.

Furthermore, Rahner is keen that eschatology should be connected (perhaps one should say reconnected) to other branches of systematic theology. He is particularly insistent on the links between Christology (including soteriology), anthropology, and eschatology—for reasons which he makes clear in his hermeneutical discussions. He also wants to bring the following areas of theology into eschatological discussion: protology (the theology of creation and of the Fall), ecclesiology, the theology of grace, and the study of the doctrine of the sacraments. He also asserts the need for a proper analysis of certain terms, such as: beginning, ending, and fulfilment; history and time; the concept

[19] Peter Phan, 'Contemporary Context and Issues in Eschatology', *Theological Studies* 55 (1994), 515.

[20] 'Eschatology': *SM* ii. 244 (Rahner lists the requirements on, p. 243).

of eternity as fulfilment; the future, axiological and teleological presence of what is to come; judgement and place of beatitude. Finally, Rahner asserts that for a reinterpretation of Christian eschatology one must look at the eschatological attitude of the Christian in his or her daily life. What this means precisely is made clear in Rahner's discussion of hermeneutics, but even at this point it is apparent that Rahner is asking the theologian to look at the reappraisal of eschatology not simply as an academic exercise, but as a task which will yield a doctrine which will have relevance to Christian lives.[21] Eschatological doctrines should have existential and political significance or, to borrow one of Rahner's expressions, they should have a place in the heart as well as in the Catechism.[22]

The remainder of this chapter will examine his two fundamental requirements for a new look at Christian eschatology: a hermeneutics of eschatological assertions and a theology of history. The other requirements—a reconnection of eschatology to other areas of theology, an analysis of eschatological terms and the examination of Christians' eschatological attitude—are more difficult to discuss in isolation as they permeate the whole of Rahner's eschatology. They will feature in the following two sections insofar as they are connected to hermeneutics and theology of history, but they will also be considered in the following chapters in the course of examining Rahner's eschatology on its individualist and collective levels respectively.

B. THE HERMENEUTICS OF ESCHATOLOGICAL ASSERTIONS

Having seen why Rahner thinks that a new look at eschatology is necessary and what factors are needed for this reappraisal it is possible to turn to the most important of these factors: that is a

[21] For an examination of Rahner's hermeneutics of eschatology, see pp. 136–50 below.

[22] Rahner sometimes remarks with regret that some doctrines have become so obscure in their formulation that they exist in the Catechism, but not in the heart: e.g. 'Remarks on the Theology of Indulgences': *TI* ii. 175; cf. 'A Brief Theological Study on Indulgences': *TI* x. 150. One of Rahner's complaints against demythologizing is—ironically—that it renders eschatology 'non-existential'; see: 'The Hermeneutics': *TI* iv. 329, 321.

hermeneutics specifically related to eschatological assertions. Rahner's fullest setting-out of these hermeneutical principles is in a paper included in his *Theological Investigations* entitled 'The Hermeneutics of Eschatological Assertions'.[23] Similar points are also made in his much more general article on eschatology in *Sacramentum Mundi* and also in various articles in *Theological Investigations* which deal with specific eschatological doctrines: these will be referred to in order to clarify or confirm certain issues.[24]

For the theologian who wishes to reinterpret Christian doctrine in a manner suitable for contemporary readers, eschatology presents particular problems. First, many eschatological statements are highly pictorial, some—particularly those concerned with hell and punishment—employing vivid images even to the extent of appearing offensive. Rahner is sympathetic to those who would remove such images from use; however, it has already been seen that he cautions against trying to move too far in the opposite direction towards a fully demythologized eschatology. Secondly, as Rahner asserts in 'The Hermeneutics of Eschatological Assertions', eschatology has a specific epistemological problem attached to it.[25] This is that knowledge of the eschata cannot be simplistically associated with the knowledge of other divine truths because, however difficult it is to know about the incarnation, for example, it is a present not a future concept. The problem with the eschata is that they are in the future and thus one might argue that logically there cannot be any knowledge of them at all. This is the problem which Rahner sets out to answer explicitly and implicitly in his discussion of the hermeneutics of eschatological statements, looking at epistemological criteria for distinguishing not only between genuine and spurious eschatological statements, but also between the 'content' of a doctrinal formulation and its 'form' or mode of expression. His comments are arranged in the form of seven theses. (For the sake of clarity and ease of reference these are summarized in Appendix A.)

Rahner's first thesis shows that there is no possibility of a simple

[23] 'The Hermeneutics': *TI* iv. 323–46.

[24] There is an important section on demythologization in 'The Resurrection of the Body': *TI* ii. 208–10.

[25] 'The Hermeneutics': *TI* iv. 324.

answer to the problem based merely on the grounds that the eschata are not really in the future and therefore there is no logical distinction to be made between knowledge of them and of other events. This point is clearly made against the trend of demythologization and in particular against Bultmann, in whose demythologization, Rahner remarks, 'an attempt is made to existentialise the eschata in the individual instance of each particular believer'.[26] This comment fits with his criticism of demythologizing in 'The Hermeneutics of Eschatological Assertions':

> An interpretation of the eschatological assertions of Scripture, which in the course of de-mythising it would de-eschatologize it in such a way that all eschatological assertions of Scripture, explicit or implicit, only meant something that takes place here and now in the existence of the individual and in the decision he takes here and now, is theologically unacceptable.[27]

This criticism links demythologization with the individualization of eschatological statements which is one of Rahner's causes of complaint seen earlier.

Having emphasized, then, that the eschata are really in the future, Rahner must now rise to the challenge of explaining how knowledge of future events is both possible for and communicable to humankind. Thesis 2 puts forward his arguments for both these points. First, Rahner asserts that it is a 'strict truth of faith' that God's omniscience does include knowledge of the future.[28] Rahner's point here seems to be that since God knows the future, knowledge of the future is not in itself logically impossible. Furthermore, although God's knowledge of the future might not at first seem vital, it is important to note that Rahner claims that human knowledge of the eschata is not direct, but indirect and dependent on God's—in that divine knowledge is communicated to humans in their present experience.[29]

Secondly, Rahner asserts that such communication is possible because the eschata, although distant, are not alien to humankind, for they are realities which will concern the world and the people in it. As such they are therefore not intrinsically beyond

[26] 'Eschatology': *SM* ii. 244.

[27] 'The Hermeneutics': *TI* iv. 326.

[28] Ibid.

[29] However, at one point Rahner does suggest that direct knowledge of the future might be possible for humans, if clairvoyance is a natural phenomenon explained by parapsychology.

the power of human understanding (as the essential nature of God might be said to be). In theory, God could reveal *everything* about future events so far as they affect humanity. In fact, however, the revelation is restricted, Rahner asserts, not by God's inability to communicate, nor by our inherent inability to understand, but by our actual situation. This situation is dependent on God and specifically on salvation-history: hence God's particular will, and not human nature, determines what we 'hear' from God. So, Rahner remarks in an explanatory note to 'The Hermeneutics of Eschatological Assertions' that the subsequent theses 'do not lay down a priori laws as regards what is possible in itself and in general; they provide a norm which is itself already based on what God has de facto instituted in the concrete order of his salvific action'.[30]

Thesis 3 consists of two statements which further specify this limited nature of the sphere of eschatological assertions; the statements are, Rahner declares, in 'dialectical unity' with each other.[31] The first statement that 'the end has a character of hiddenness (*Verborgenheitscharakter*) which is essential and proper to it' is based on two different pieces of evidence.[32] Not only is it quite clear from Scripture that God has not revealed to humankind the day of the end,[33] but Rahner also believes that an examination of the theological concepts of hope and faith makes it clear that they would lose their full significance if the end were not to some extent hidden. He reasonably assumes that part of the definition of theological hope (or faith) is that it is based on something which is not completely certain or fully known. Since Scripture asserts that both faith and hope will remain, there must be something about the last things which will *always* be mysterious, even in the beatific vision.[34] Rahner does not think that eschatological events are unveiled or de-mystified in scriptural and dogmatic statements; rather, they are revealed 'precisely *as* a *mystery*', their hiddenness is affirmed.[35] Again this

[30] 'The Hermeneutics': *TI* iv. 327 n.

[31] Ibid., 329.

[32] Ibid., 329–30; *ST* iv. 408.

[33] See Matt. 24: 36; Acts 1: 6–7.

[34] See 'On the Theology of Hope': *TI* x. 247–9, esp. 249: the beatific vision 'is not the act in which the absolute mystery which is God is finally overcome and solved, but rather the act in which this truly unfathomable mystery in all its finality . . . must be sustained and endured as it is in itself without any possibility of escape into that which can be comprehended and so controlled . . .'.

[35] 'The Hermeneutics': *TI* iv. 330.

seems reasonable, since scriptural statements on eschatology are notoriously ambiguous and twentieth-century Christian theology appears to be no nearer to understanding all about the eschata than the Church Fathers, despite there being more dogmatic statements to study.[36]

The consequence of this essential quality of hiddenness which the eschata have is that it is easy to sift out genuine eschatological assertions from false ones, for the latter will wrongly attempt to give 'a prediction which presents its contents as the anticipated report of a spectator of the future event'.[37] Rahner confusingly calls this style of prediction 'false apocalyptic',[38] a term which has been criticized by some theologians because it appears to denigrate apocalyptic which they see as a genuine form of revelation.[39] However, Rahner does not assert that apocalyptic in general is an intrinsically faulty type of revelation, but that it is faulty when applied to eschatology in particular. This is because apocalyptic forms of revelation claim only to unveil truths which are fully present, although previously hidden (such as those about God's will, for example). Thus apocalyptic cannot unveil the eschata, because they are still genuinely in the future. Any apocalyptic revelation which claims to unveil the future as if it were present therefore not only leads to faulty eschatology, but also is 'false apocalyptic'.

The second statement of thesis 3 refers to 'the essential historicity of man'.[40] This is expressed fully by Rahner in the following way:

> If man is a being involved in history (*ein geschichtliches Wesen*), which means more than a temporal succession (*ein bloß äußere, reihende Zeitlichkeit*) such as holds good for physical objects, he cannot understand himself in any given present moment without an aetiological retrospect towards a genuinely temporal past (*eine echt zeitliche Vergangenheit*), and 'anamnesis', and without a prospect of a genuinely

[36] This reflects Rahner's view of the development of doctrine: dogmatic statements re-express Christian truths rather than add to a body of Christian truth.

[37] 'The Hermeneutics': *TI* iv. 330.

[38] Ibid.: 330; *ST* iv. 410: '*falsche Apokalyptik*'.

[39] For example, Peter Phan asks whether Rahner's characterization of apocalyptic is based on a sufficiently thorough knowledge of apocalyptic literature and whether he has 'sufficiently appreciated the positive impact of such literature on the struggle for liberation from an unjust social situation or persecution': Phan, *Eternity in Time*, 76.

[40] 'The Hermeneutics': *TI* iv. 330; *ST* iv. 410: '*die wesentliche Geschichtlichkeit des Menschen*'.

temporal future (*eine echt zeitliche Zukunft*). His self-understanding embraces beginning and end of his temporal history, both in the life of the individual man and of humanity. Anamnesis and prognosis are among the necessary existentials of man.[41]

It can be seen here that, for Rahner, history and time are inseparable from human experience. (Again, Rahner refers to demythologization asserting that it ignores the future aspect of human nature, despite claiming to be based on human experience.) Thus, this thesis means that one's present experience must reflect one's past and refer to one's future, but equally that a study of the future aspect of one's existence cannot ignore one's present or past. Hence, Rahner can draw the following conclusion:

But if the presentness of man's being is his being referred to futurity, the future . . . is not just something spoken of in advance. It is an inner moment of man and of his actual being as it is present to him now. And so knowledge of the future in so far as it is still to come, is an inner moment in the self-understanding of man in his present hour of existence—*and grows out of it.*[42]

Thesis 4 follows very closely on from this stating that:

if such real future is known and present, but as something hidden . . . [then] the content of this knowledge of the genuine future . . . is the element of the future yet to come which is necessary to the understanding of *present* existence. Knowledge of the future will be knowledge of the futurity of the present: eschatological knowledge is knowledge of the eschatological present.[43]

Consequently, eschatological assertions must deal with a future which is present as embryo in humanity but which is susceptible to human control or comprehension only to a very limited extent.

The fifth thesis expands on the fourth, stating that knowledge

[41] Ibid.: *TI* iv. 330–1; *ST* iv. 410.

[42] Ibid.: *TI* iv. 331, Rahner's emphasis; *ST* iv. 411: '*Ist aber die Gegenwart des Daseins des Menschen seine Verwiesenheit auf die Zukunft, ist die Zukunft . . . nicht ein nur Vorausgeredetes, sondern ein inneres Moment an ihm und seiner aktuellen Gegenwart in seinem Sein, dann ist die Erkenntnis der Zukunft, soweit sie noch ausständig ist, ein inneres Moment des Selbstverständnisses des Menschen in seiner Gegenwart und—aus ihr heraus*'.

[43] Ibid.: *TI* iv. 332; *ST* iv. 412: '. . . *Das Wissen um das Zukünftige wird das Wissen um die Zukünftigkeit der Gegenwart sein, das eschatologische Wissen ist das Wissen um die eschatologische Gegenwart.*'

of the future eschata 'is confined to such prospects as can be derived from the reading of his present eschatological experience'.[44] This eschatological experience is, for Rahner, the experience of salvation-history: God's revelation of salvation-history in the incarnation, crucifixion, and resurrection of Christ is an eschatological revelation, because it necessarily points towards the future and towards fulfilment. Hence eschatological revelation is not a preview, because it is drawing on something which is already present, that is, salvation in Christ. The eschatological future is already real, or present, only in the sense that it is already part of human self-understanding: the content of eschatological statements therefore is everything (but no more than that) which 'can be understood as fulfilment and definitive condition of that Christian human reality which revelation states to be present here and now'.[45] Rahner is very careful to condemn views which suppose that the future already leads of itself 'a supra-temporal existence (*ein überzeitliches Dasein*) of which history is only a projection on the screen of worthless time'.[46] Hence knowledge of the eschatological future is an 'inner moment in the self-understanding of man' in that 'the Christian man knows of his future in as much as he knows of himself and his redemption in Christ through divine revelation'.[47] This knowledge is not merely for comfort or to encourage Christian faith and hope; it is vitally necessary for an individual's spiritual decision of freedom.

The abstract expression of the previous theses makes them somewhat difficult to grasp; however, the specific points making up thesis 6 are distinctly easier. The first point asserts that since eschatology speaks of the fulfilment of God's salvation and of the personal decision of the individual it must speak of the possibilities both of the fulfilment and of the utter loss of the individual. This is because the future is bound up with human freedom, which would not be true freedom if humans were not free to decide against God. Hence Rahner writes:

true eschatological discourse must exclude the presumptuous knowledge of a universal apocatastasis and of the certainty of the salvation of

[44] 'The Hermeneutics': *TI* iv. 334.
[45] 'Eschatology': *SM* ii. 245.
[46] 'The Hermeneutics': *TI* iv. 337; *ST* iv. 419.
[47] 'The Hermeneutics': *TI* iv. 331, 335.

the individual *before* his death (*das angemaßte Wissen um eine universelle Apokatastasis wie um das sichere Heil eines einzelnen vor seinem Tod*). . . .all the eschatological assertions of Church and Scripture can be understood as affirming that damnation is a real genuine and inevitable possibility for the pilgrim.[48]

On the other hand, because God's grace must be seen as triumphant, the Church can (and should, and does) declare that some are saved, although it cannot say who is saved—except in the case of some saints and martyrs. Thus the Church can speak only of the *possibility* of damnation in contrast to the *certainty* of salvation and must reject the heretical notion of a double predestination. In Rahner's words 'It must be made clear in theology and in preaching that what is said about heaven and what is said about hell are not on the same plane.'[49] Furthermore, just as the victory of God's grace means that one should *declare* that *some* are already saved, it also means that one should *hope* that *all* are saved. Thus, Rahner rejects the *apokatastasis* only 'as a firm theoretical statement, as distinct from a hope that respects God's sovereign and unknown disposition and the openness of every history of freedom known to us'.[50] In fact, Rahner's own hope for universal salvation seems to have been very strong. This comes out partly in his discussion of Christian eschatological doctrine and in his theory of anonymous Christianity (as will be discussed in the following chapters) and partly in his own personal spirituality and pastoral attitude.[51] He also revealed in conversation towards the end of his life that he would have liked to have written something about the *apokatastasis* which would have been 'orthodox' and 'acceptable'.[52]

The next two parts of thesis 6 (b and c) are attempts by Rahner to show that his new hermeneutical approach can lead to the

[48] (Rahner's emphasis) Ibid.: *TI* iv. 338–9 and 339 n.; *ST* iv. 420. Rahner also rejects the *apokatastasis* elsewhere: see 'Hell': *SM* iii. 7, 8.

[49] 'Eschatology': *SM* ii. 245.

[50] 'Christian Dying': *TI* xviii. 236; cf. ibid., 241 and 'Profane History and Salvation History': *TI* xxi. 6. See also Phan, *Eternity in Time*, 152 ff; William Dych, *Karl Rahner* (Geoffrey Chapman, London, 1992).

[51] Vorgrimler records Rahner's view that 'Even if . . . humanity were to fall into the abyss, then I would still be firmly convinced . . . that even such an abyss always ultimately ends in the arms of an eternally good, eternally powerful God.' *I Remember*, 111, cited in Vorgrimler, *Understanding Karl Rahner*, 129.

[52] An interview by Leo O'Donovan published as 'Living into Mystery: Karl Rahner's Reflections at 75', *America* 10 (March 1979), 179, cited in Phan, *Eternity in Time*, 153.

resolution of some of the traditional conflicts between different emphases, a resolution which leads not to a bland homogenization, but rather to a balancing of opposite views. It has already been seen that eschatology is, in Rahner's eyes, a transposition of anthropology and Christology into the future. Since Rahner's anthropology firmly holds that human nature is a unity of spirit and body, it is to be expected that Rahner should assert that eschatological statements are about both facets. But he extends this to a further comment about individual and general eschatologies by connecting the individual specifically with his spiritual side and humanity as a whole with its material side:

> Eschatology is concerned with the fulfilment of the individual as individual spirit-person which comes with death as the end of the individual history. Eschatology is also concerned with the fulfilment of humanity in the resurrection of the flesh as the end of the bodily history of the world. But in each case it is concerned in a different way with the whole.[53]

The connections Rahner makes here are not totally clear, although the link between the body and the world may be explained by the fact that in his metaphysics Rahner sees the body of the individual in somewhat broader terms than one normally would: the person is not only a soul in a body, but is 'spirit in the world'. Rahner points to the tension between individualistic and collective strains among biblical and traditional eschatological statements: his plea is that this tension should be accepted, for its dismissal as contradictory all too often leads to a one-sided individualistic eschatology. The constructive tension may even, he suggests, explain such doctrines as that of purgatory.

Next, Rahner suggests that the apparent tension between imminent and distant expectations of the return of Christ should similarly be accepted as expressing different but not contradictory eschatological truths (6c). Rahner asserts that eschatology is an imminent expectation in so far as it is 'the assertion about present salvation as it tends to the future

[53] 'The Hermeneutics': *TI* iv. 341; *ST* iv. 423: *'Eschatologie als die im Tod als Ende der individuellen Geschichte eintretende Vollendung des einzelnen als einzelner Geistperson und Eschatologie der Vollendung der Menscheit in der Auferstehung des Fleisches als dem Ende der leibhaftigen Geschichte der Welt meinen je in ihrer Weise den* <u>*ganzen*</u> *Menschen'*, Rahner's emphasis.

fulfilment' and is a distant expectation precisely because this future is 'not yet' and incalculable and hidden.[54] As with the previous point, the tension is dialectical not contradictory, and individual scriptural assertions are not meant to be artificially rearranged or reinterpreted in order to produce coherence.

The next part of thesis 6 asserts that Christ is the central criterion for the validity of eschatological statements. This is because eschatology is based on the present experience of salvation—which is salvation in Christ:

> But this experience of salvation, the adequate source of eschatological assertions, is faith in the incarnation of the Logos, in the death and resurrection of Christ . . . It can therefore be said that *Christ* himself is the hermeneutical principle of all eschatological assertions.[55]

Finally, Rahner concludes his sixth thesis by saying that the above principles—together with a theology of history—allow one to say everything necessary to eschatology.[56] Indeed what Rahner calls 'the correct single principle' in his article on eschatology in *Sacramentum Mundi* can be said to summarize the essence of his first six hermeneutical theses:

> Eschatology is a forward look which is necessary to man for his spiritual decision in freedom, and it is made from the standpoint of his situation in saving history as this is determined by the Christ-event.[57]

Why does Rahner say that a theology of history is necessary in addition to the above principles? Above it was remarked that he saw salvation-history as essentially pointing towards the future and towards fulfilment;[58] earlier it was also seen that Rahner thought that an analysis of such concepts as beginning, ending, fulfilment, history, time, and eternity was a necessary partner to

[54] 'The Hermeneutics': *TI* iv. 342.

[55] Ibid.: 342–3. Cf. William Thompson, 'The Hope for Humanity: Karl Rahner's Eschatology', in L. O'Donovan, (ed.), *A World of Grace* (A Crossroads Book, Seabury Press, N. Y., 1980), 158.

[56] Rahner's suggestions for the basic content of eschatological assertions are given in Appendix B. They can be summarized as follows: time and history will end, and will end with the gracious victory of God. The period after the incarnation, death, and resurrection of Christ and before the parousia will be characterized by conflict between Christ and the world (or Anti-Christ). The end will be a consummation which can be expressed in many different ways; for example: as God's judgement, as the resurrection of the flesh and the transfiguration of the world, as the beatific vision in the kingdom of God, or as hell.

[57] 'Eschatology': *SM* ii. 244.

[58] See p. 142.

eschatology. These statements explain what a theology of history might be and why Rahner would feel it to be necessary: his whole view of eschatology rests on his concept of the dynamic, forward-looking nature of history in general and of salvation-history in particular (especially as experienced by the individual).

Rahner's study of the hermeneutics of eschatological assertions ends, in the seventh thesis, with a very practical interpretational principle for the reader approaching scriptural and dogmatic statements about eschatology. He declares that the above theses allow one to distinguish between the content and form of eschatological statements, in other words between what the statements mean and how they express what they mean. The distinction is important for the interpreter because Rahner holds that the content is what belongs to the common faith of the Church and therefore cannot be dropped, whereas the form is not relevant to heresy or orthodoxy. Hence, in discussing specific eschatological doctrines, Rahner often asks which aspects are 'dogmatically binding'[59]—i.e. what the content of the doctrine is. One example of how Rahner puts the distinction to practical interpretational use is his criticism of individualizing eschatology, which notes that it is a fault not of the *content* of eschatology but of its *form*.[60]

One must, however, be particularly careful not to assume that Rahner is suggesting that one can get to a doctrinal definition which is free from any metaphorical, mythological or other indirect means of expression, for he expressly denies the possibility of making 'a perfectly adequate and definite distinction between "thing" and "image"':

> This is impossible, for no other reason than that no other assertion about the thing is possible without some sort of image (*Bild*), and in this sense a 'myth' (*Mythos*) can be replaced by another, but not by language utterly devoid of images.[61]

Hence, although Rahner has shown eschatology to be anthropology and Christology on the plane of fulfilment, allowing for an anthropological and Christological re-expression of eschatological

[59] '"The Intermediate State"': *TI* xvii. 114; cf. 'Purgatory': *TI* xix. 181.

[60] See p. 133 above.

[61] Both quotations from 'The Hermeneutics': *TI* iv. 344; *ST* iv. 426 the first reads *'eine Scheidung schlechthin adäquat und eindeutig zwischen "Sache" und "Bild"'*.

assertions, this new approach cannot be said to reach a 'pure' concept, despite having the merit of getting rid of some of the more picturesque images commonly associated with eschatology.[62] One might label Rahner's own reinterpretation of eschatological statements, not as a demythologization but as a *re*mythologization. His criticism of demythologizing is not only that it tends to individualize eschatological statements and rid them of their future reference-point, but more fundamentally that the very word 'demythologization' asserts that myth can be got rid of completely and lays claim to an unattainable purity of expression. He writes:

> The 'critique' is, . . . of necessity, just as inadequate in relation to the criticized object in itself as the 'criticized' proposition.[63]

This does not mean that criticism is worthless, not least because some forms of expression are appropriate for one era and not another. Furthermore, Rahner asserts that there are some notions which are used to express doctrines 'whose representative element is of such a basically human and at the same time objectively unavoidable kind, that these notions, once they have been found, cannot really be replaced by any better ones'.[64] So while any expression is ultimately inadequate, some expressions are better than others and it is the duty of the theologian to find these.[65]

Rahner's hermeneutics of eschatological assertions raises several difficulties. One of these is his apparently ambiguous concept of the future. Despite insisting that it is genuinely future, he then seems to describe the future as part of an individual's *present* existence: is this not an outright contradiction? If one looks closer, it seems that he sees the history of the individual as a continuum in which the future grows out of the individual's present experience. Thus the future is present only in the sense that it is present in embryo form and in that it forms part of

[62] 'The Hermeneutics': *TI* iv. 345; cf. 'Last Things': *SM* iii. 276, where Rahner remarks that the doctrine of the last things must be connected to the rest of theology in order to prevent it from becoming a pallid 'philosophical kernel' with colourful biblical pictures added on.

[63] 'The Resurrection of the Body': *TI* iv. 209.

[64] Ibid.

[65] Cf. ibid., 209: when a theologian carries out the right sort of critique 'then he does not "demythologise", but does something which a theology has done and must always do'.

humans' current understanding of themselves. This relation between one's present and future existence also holds between one's present and future experience of salvation—in other words, Rahner is working with a model of inaugurated eschatology. The eschaton will be the fulfilment of the history of salvation, which is already present in the world. It is a model which preserves both the genuine futurity of eschatological events and also the reality of salvation in people's lives now—and in so doing does seem to be a faithful reflection of the general thrust of eschatological statements in the New Testament. The consequence of this model for Rahner's hermeneutics is that eschatology becomes more truly focused on salvation rather than on supposed eschatological 'events' and speculation. Humans have knowledge of past and present salvation-history by divine revelation, most especially in the incarnation, death, and resurrection of Jesus Christ; through this knowledge they have some sort of knowledge of the eschata. It is thus now obvious why Rahner insists that eschatology is inseparably linked with Christology and anthropology: knowledge of the eschata is simply knowledge of salvation in Christ and of human experience of this transposed into an expectation of their fulfilment.[66] Rahner is surely right to stress that this is what is most important in eschatology.

Other difficulties remain, however. Peter Phan is concerned, for example, that what he calls Rahner's 'anthropological reduction' may lose the sense of the new, which is vital to eschatology.[67] If eschatological statements are reduced to one's current experience, what has one gained above talking about salvation now? Rahner never takes such a rigorously reductionist and realized approach to eschatology: he always insists that eschata are fundamentally mysterious. The only things that we can know about the future are those which we can understand in terms of our present experience; but that is not all there is to the future. Phan also fears that Rahner's hermeneutics may yield too much information about the future—presumably by extrapolating too much information from one's present religious experience. However, one must emphasize that Rahner's hermeneutics is not *merely* an 'anthropological reduction': it is also Christological

[66] See Thompson, 'The Hope for Humanity: Karl Rahner's Eschatology', 159.

[67] For Peter Phan's criticisms of Rahner's hermeneutics of eschatological assertions, see Phan, *Eternity in Time*, 75–6.

(as Phan himself states) and this is the check on excessive extrapolation from one's current experience. Thus Christ, not humanity, is Rahner's central hermeneutical principle (see thesis 6d). Just as Rahner attempts to achieve a balance between views of eschatology which are centred entirely on the future or entirely on the present, so he also tries to balance the human and divine poles of salvation: salvation must be appropriated and experienced by a human individual, but it means nothing if it is not divinely granted. So in fact, Rahner's hermeneutic emphasizes that salvation-history in all its mysteriousness and unpredictability is at the heart of eschatology.

Phan's other major criticism of Rahner's hermeneutics of eschatological assertions is more weighty. He is concerned that in a search for 'meaningfulness' (presumably the existential significance to the individual) Rahner is in danger of compromising or distorting the meaning of the texts he examines. One might expand this criticism by pointing to two particular dangers. First, Rahner runs the risk of saying that eschatological statements mean something other than what their original authors intended them to mean—which raises awkward questions about the nature of the divine inspiration of both Scripture and magisterial statements. Secondly, Rahner may be able to duck the issue of apparently conflicting statements by insisting that they share the same core significance—but he would thereby be guilty of committing the same error as demythologizers. Clearly, the best way to assess whether Rahner has indeed fallen into these traps is to look at his eschatological writings in detail and this will be undertaken in the following chapters. However, a couple of preliminary remarks can be made now. His approach to hermeneutics is an honest attempt to re-express Christian eschatology in a form which is not just acceptable, but intelligible to the modern audience, without rejecting Scripture and tradition as the mainstays of Christian faith. To this extent (and apart from the obvious difference in attitude to the tradition of the Church) Rahner may be seen as sharing the same theological concerns as Bultmann. However, Rahner is well aware of the pitfalls of demythologization and therefore tries to express a theology which does indeed have existential significance for the individual but which is not theology reduced to that alone. He is not afraid of the transcendent dimension of eschatology—on the contrary his eschatology is centred on it—nor is he afraid of myth, provided that myth points to rather than detracts from what is truly important about human existence. It is this balance which is most attractive about Rahner's hermeneutics of eschatological assertions: balance between present and future, between the human and the divine.

A few other important aspects of his approach should also be noted. First, it is interesting that a Roman Catholic theologian is taking insights from Protestant theologians such as Bultmann and Moltmann and applying them to his own tradition. (For example he applies some of the techniques of the demythologizers both to Scripture and to the statements of the magisterium.) Secondly, this study reveals two beliefs which go far beyond being principles for the interpretation of eschatological statements and colour all of Rahner's thought on the last things and salvation: Rahner asserts that the *apokatastasis* is to be rejected as a certain dogma, but that one should hope for universal salvation; it has also been made clear that Rahner sees the eschaton in terms of fulfilment or consummation, rather than simply as the ending (or the continuation) of life as it is now.

Moreover, it has become clear that Rahner's list of necessities for a new eschatology ties in very closely with his new hermeneutics. In particular, the study of the eschatological attitude of the Christian in his daily life is important because eschatological statements can only be understood in relation to the present human experience of salvation-history. Similarly, the necessity for the connection of eschatology with other branches of theology is obviously due to the fact that eschatology is the expression in terms of fulfilment of the truths of Christology and anthropology.[68] Further, an analysis of eschatological terms will clarify the meaning of words such as 'future' which are central to his hermeneutics. Finally, a proper theological understanding of history is necessary, because knowledge of the eschata simply is knowledge of salvation-history in the mode of hope and consummation. This will be the subject of the remainder of this chapter.

68 Via these it can also be connected to other branches of theology.

C. THEOLOGY AND HISTORY

This section will deal with the fundamental features of Rahner's theology of history. First, it will show that Rahner believes it is the universal fact of death which shapes each human life and makes it into a history. Death is thus not seen simply as a end, but as a summing-up or a consummation, and the concepts of consummation and history are inextricably linked. Secondly, it will be seen that Rahner argues that consummation in this sense can apply not only to an individual life-history, but also to the history of humanity or the world. Finally, it will be useful to examine briefly Rahner's analysis of the relation between the history of the world and salvation-history.

i. Death and the History of an Individual

The most important source for Rahner's views on death is his monograph *On the Theology of Death* which appears as the second volume in the series *Quaestiones Disputatae*.[69] This work deals in turn with three aspects of death: its effect on human nature as a whole, its nature as the consequence of sin and the possibility of its transformation into a 'dying with Christ'. It is the first of these aspects which is most important for the present study of Rahner's eschatology.

Rahner claims that death affects human nature as a whole in three distinct ways.[70] First, it is universal—that is, that it affects the entire human race. Rahner denies that this statement is merely 'platitudinous', or just an empirical fact 'recognized by all as a matter of natural and common experience';[71] rather, he states that 'the universality of death is one of the affirmations of faith'.[72] In both *On the Theology of Death* and in the article 'On Christian Dying' he remarks that, as an empirical fact based on

[69] *On the Theology of Death* (Quaestiones Disputatae, Herder, Freiburg im Breisgau; Burns & Oates London, 2nd edn., 1965). This second edition, which is the text I use, has been revised by W. J. O'Hara and has different pagination and many minor changes from the original translation by C. H. Henkey in the 1st edn. (1961).

[70] As will become clear, the word which I translate as 'human nature'—*Mensch*—indicates both the human race and those facets of human nature as they are found in an individual.

[71] 'On Christian Dying': *TI* vii. 286.

[72] *On the Theology of Death*, 14.

the observation that so far in the history of humankind everybody has died, the universality of death could conceivably be an impermanent feature of human existence. Were there not a proposition of faith to the contrary, it would be conceivable either that the advancement of medical science might conquer death altogether or that death might be eliminated by divine intervention. The theological assertion of the universality of death is thus making an assertion about the necessary character of human existence—particularly with regard to sin and freedom, as will be seen shortly. Rahner stresses that it is not an abstract assertion but a message of faith which is addressed 'to each one of us as *individuals* as a truth which expresses the ultimate significance of the existence of each one of us taken as a whole'.[73]

The universality of death extends even to those who are thought of as still living at the Second Coming and who in tradition are imagined to be entering the kingdom of God 'alive': Rahner asserts that 'they will experience "death" in the sense that it is the consummation declared by God of their history of freedom'.[74] Similarly, he claims that Adam, had he not sinned, would have undergone a '"death" without dying'.[75] Instead of undergoing the process of physical break-up which humans now experience as the only way of death, Adam would have been able to have brought his life 'to its perfect consummation even in his bodily form through a "death" which would have been a pure, active self-affirmation'.[76]

This apparently trivial discussion of possible exceptions to the rule in fact highlights an extremely important distinction which Rahner makes between two sorts of death.[77] One is a consummation, or the transformation from this life to the next; it is this

[73] 'On Christian Dying': *TI* vii. 286.

[74] 'Christian Dying': *TI* xviii. 238; *ST* iv. 283: *'die von Gott verfügte Vollendung ihrer Freiheitsgeschichte'*; Rahner mentions this group as a problem for the assertion of the universality of death in *On the Theology of Death*, 14.

[75] *On the Theology of Death*, 34; *Zur Theologie des Todes* (Herder, Freiburg im Breisgau, 2nd edn., 1959), 33: *'der "Tod" ohne Tod'*. This death Rahner describes as 'a state of perfection in which (Adam's) bodily constitution would not have excluded that openness to the world in its totality which we now expect as the final result of the redemption and as the eschatological miracle of the resurrection of the body.' (Ibid. See ch. 9, section b. for a discussion of this 'openness to the world'.)

[76] *On the Theology of Death*, 34.

[77] This is rendered in the English translation as a distinction between 'death' and 'dying'; in the German Rahner sometimes uses *Tod* for both, and sometimes draws a contrast between *Tod* and *Sterben*.

which is absolutely universal. The other is the passive experience of death as physical breakdown; it is this imperfect sort of death which is the consequence of sin. This is now in effect universal, but need not have been so:

> death, as it is in fact suffered individually and universally by men, in the present economy of salvation stands in causal relation to sin, above all to the sin committed by the head and progenitor of the whole human race in his rôle as head. . . . Because man has lost the divine life in union with God by grace, his earthly existence also disintegrates.[78]

However, despite this apparently traditional approach, Rahner questions whether death should be seen more specifically as the *punishment* for sin, as has frequently been the case in the Christian Church. He asserts that the character of all death is hiddenness, because—despite a belief that one can actively take part in one's own death as the consummation of one's life—no-one knows whether it will *in fact* be possible to do so or whether death will actually be totally passive and the annihilation of one's self. This hiddenness and ambiguity is the result of original sin and the consequent absence of divine grace in human lives. Thus Rahner claims that the passive sort of death is not so much a punishment imposed externally by God; rather it is the intrinsic *consequence* of sin. For this reason, Rahner prefers to call death the 'expression and manifestation' (*Ausdruck und Erscheinung*) of sin rather than the punishment for it.[79] This distinction will be seen later to have interesting consequences for Rahner's concept of punishment and purification of sin after death.

[78] *On the Theology of Death*, 33 f.

[79] *On the Theology of Death*, 49; *Zur Theologie des Todes*, 45. Rahner's early insistence on the doctrine of monogenism—the view that all humanity was descended from one original couple—is an obvious problem for this interpretation of death. Rahner later rejected the doctrine, commenting that original sin is sin only analogously and that it is 'an historical and universal condition of man's freedom' ('Christian Dying': *TI* xviii. 236). Hence, Rahner came to believe that death is due to *individual personal* sins: 'Contrary to a widely held opinion, it must . . . be said expressedly that death in its hiddenness is not merely an expression and manifestation of that remoteness of God which humanity brought on itself by sin at the beginning, in "Adam" ' (ibid., 249). In 'Christian Dying' he notes that various New Testament statements about death show that it is the 'consequence of serious (unremitted) personal sins', a fact which, he claims, explains Paul's connection of death with the Law (pp. 249–50). The same claims are also found in *On the Theology of Death* (p. 51). However, Rahner does not seem to make the nature of the causal relation between individual sins and the universal phenomenon of death very clear.

These two sorts of death—consummation and physical disintegration—are not mutually exclusive: in by far the majority of humans they coincide, because both 'in the present economy of salvation' are universal. However, the former allows humans the possibility of adding an active self-consummating element to their death. This Rahner calls 'dying with Christ' (*Mitsterben mit Christus*), saying that one should follow the example of Christ in reacting to one's feeling of abandonment and the overwhelming passivity of the experience of death ('My God, my God, why hast thou forsaken me?') by abandoning oneself in hope to God ('Into thy hands I commend my spirit'). This self-abandonment is an act and a decision. Expressed in terms of freedom, one could say that dying with Christ amounts to, on the one hand, passively struggling under the limited character of freedom and, on the other hand, actively accepting and facing up to this. The description of this sort of 'good' death as consummation occurs frequently in Rahner's theology.[80] (It will be seen in the following chapters that Rahner believes that there is also the possibility of a negative consummation.)

The second way in which death affects human nature as a whole is that it affects both body and soul. This is implied by what has already been said in Rahner's emphasis on the psychological as well as physical aspects of death. For this reason he objects to the classical description of death as the departure of the soul from the body, for it implies that the soul somehow escapes death.[81] Equally consummation, the positive and active side of death, affects body and not just soul as is sometimes suggested by more spiritual understandings of the doctrine of resurrection.[82]

Thirdly, death affects human nature as a whole in the sense that it affects the whole life of each individual. Rahner asserts that death, rather than being simply the end of a series of events, is the completion or fulfilment of a life which gives a certain quality to that life *throughout* its duration. Most importantly for

[80] See, for example, 'The Body in the Order of Salvation': *TI* xvii. 88; *On the Theology of Death*, 30–1; 'Theological Considerations on the Moment of Death': *TI* xi. 315–20; 'On Christian Dying': *TI* vii. 287; 'The life of the Dead': *TI* iv. 353; 'Christian Dying': *TI* xviii. 226, 240, 243.

[81] *On the Theology of Death*, 17–18.

[82] Chapter 7 will discuss the effect of death on both body and soul in relation to Rahner's reinterpretation of the doctrine of the resurrection of the body.

his eschatology, death renders final and definitive the character of an individual's life—its decisions and actions. Thus death gives shape to a person's life: it is the consummation of that series of actions and events in each person's life which Rahner calls a 'history of freedom'. Above all, it is the consummation of those actions in which the individual relates to God. Rahner writes:

> Death brings man, as a moral and spiritual person, a kind of finality and consummation (*eine Endgültigkeit und Vollendung*) which renders his decision for or against God, reached during the time of his bodily life, final and unalterable (*zur endgültigen macht*).[83]

Decisions made in this life are made definitive in death because, Rahner asserts, eternity is not the infinite continuation of time, but the timeless consummation or fulfilment of time. Hence he writes that 'eternity is in time and emerges from it as it were as a ripened fruit growing out of it'[84] and that eternity is 'the plenitude of reality'.[85]

What is the 'decision for or against God' and when is it made? Rahner sometimes equates the decision with what he calls 'dying with Christ'; this might lead one to think that Rahner means that it takes place at the moment of death—particularly as there is in Catholic theology a strong tradition of believing in the possibility and importance of a death-bed commitment to God. However, Rahner recognizes that if the crucial decision for God could only be made at that point, this would exclude certain categories of people from making it, that is those whose death was sudden and unexpected or those whose death was preceded by a period of mental incapacity (for example, unconsciousness, senile decay, or extreme and debilitating pain). His argument is that although a decision for or against God takes place 'in' death, in fact death suffuses the whole of life:

> Christian dying (insofar as it is supposed to be not sheer suffering but a Christian deed of freedom) cannot simply and certainly be located in the last hours of a human being, since as human and Christian he may

[83] *On the Theology of Death*, 26; *Zur Theologie des Todes*, 26.

[84] 'Experiencing Easter': *TI* vii. 162; see also 'The Life of the Dead': *TI* iv. 348, where Rahner refers to eternity as time's 'mature fruit'.

[85] *On the Theology of Death*, 28; cf. Thompson, 'The Hope for Humanity: Karl Rahner's Eschatology', 160.

be no longer capable of such an act of dying . . . For this reason dying must be recognized as an event (*Vorgang*) that is taking place throughout the whole of life, even though at all times with varying intensity and with a fresh application of the freedom that accepts life or protests against it. . . .[86]

Rahner uses two sorts of evidence to support his claim that we are in effect 'dying all our lives'.[87] The first is his transcendental theory of human knowledge. He writes that the individual constantly experiences the finitude of his milieu because of 'the transcendental constitution of man, who in all his mental achievements of knowledge, freedom, production and in all other intellectual-personal achievements aims at a particular categorial object and at the same time . . . surpasses it'.[88] This transcendence, because it makes one aware of the finiteness of one's own existence, brings about an experience of 'disappointment' which is variously described as a 'presence of death', an experience of 'dying inwardly', or a 'basic mood permeating all things' which is a 'warning and herald of death'.[89] The second type of evidence is everyday experiences: for example, sickness. The infiltration of death into life is experienced in the patient's passivity: in a powerlessness to foresee or control illness, in the simultaneous feeling of isolation from society and dependence on carers, and in an inability to interpret the meaning of illness.[90] More generally, Rahner points to the many failures and disappointments of life in which humans are unable to foresee or control events.

One of the difficulties with this theory of *prolixitas mortis*, as Rahner calls it, is that it diminishes the importance of the biological moment of death as the focus of finality and completion. If death pervades life, how can it also finalize it? Rahner tries to avoid this problem by distinguishing between death in life and the moment of death; however, it is debatable as to whether the distinction he draws is clear enough:

[86] 'Christian Dying': *TI* xviii. 228; *ST* xiii. 271. Rahner notes that Ladislaus Boros (a former pupil) holds that a totally free decision for or against God must be made at the actual moment of death, but Rahner consciously distances himself from this position (*TI* xviii. 230).

[87] 'Christian Dying': *TI* xviii. 234.

[88] Ibid., 230.

[89] Ibid., 231.

[90] Sickness, Rahner writes, 'threatens and reduces even man's intellectual and free subjectivity, diminishes or withdraws from man the possibility of sovereignty' ('Christian Dying': *TI* xviii. 232).

> Life, therefore, is in a true sense a process of dying, and what we are accustomed to call death is the final point in this life-long process. Dying takes place throughout life itself, and what we call death when it comes is only the ultimate and definitive completion of the process.[91]

> [Death] constitutes the transition between the sort of being that is becoming and the sort of being that is final completion, from the freedom which has been given up to the achieved finality which is at the same time the moment of radical enfeeblement.[92]

Rahner emphasizes that it is not just the *prolixitas mortis* that affects the character of everyday life. In addition he claims that the finality which death gives to human decisions and the fact that the decision for or against God is made throughout one's life give this life its very serious quality. He criticizes religious theories which allow for second chances in a world beyond or in reincarnation into this world, on the grounds that they devalue decisions made before death. Hence, he strongly condemns the notion of the migration of souls into other bodies (metempsychosis or reincarnation) and the *apokatastasis*—presumably because both assume the possibility of some period after death in which new decisions for or against God can be made.[93]

Very curiously, however, Rahner also speaks of the possibility of further development after death, which seems to entail some sort of temporal afterlife. He writes that the statement that death is the finality of a life of freedom 'does not exclude totally man's further development after death (*'Weiterentwicklung' des Menschen nach seinem Tod*) nor does it presuppose a lifeless concept of man's future with God'.[94] Further development after death is suggested by the doctrines of purgatory, the resurrection of the body, and of 'the future consummation of the whole universe'.[95]

[91] 'On Christian Dying': *TI* vii. 290; *ST* vii. 277: *'Das Leben ist also der eigentliche Tod, und das, was wir Tod zu nennen pflegen, ist das Ende dieses lebenslangen Sterbens, das im Leben selbst geschieht und im Ende des Sterbens sich endgültig vollendet.'* Cf. '"He descended into Hell"': *TI* vii. 149.

[92] 'On Christian Dying': *TI* vii. 292; *ST* vii. 278 f.: *'[Tod] Übergang vom werdenden Sein ins vollendete Sein, von der aufgegebenen Freiheit in die getane Vollendung zugleich der Augenblick radikaler Ohnmacht ist . . .'.*

[93] See 'Christian Dying': *TI* xviii. 237. Note that Rahner rejects the *apokatastasis* only 'as a firm, theoretical statement, as distinct from a hope that respects God's sovereign and unknown disposition and the openness of every history of freedom known to us' (ibid.); cf. 'The Hermeneutics': *TI* iv. 338–9; 'Hell': *SM* iii. 7–8. See above, p. 185 and n. 48.

[94] *On the Theology of Death*, 26; *Zur Theologies des Todes*, 26.

[95] *On the Theology of Death*, 27.

One cannot defend Rahner against accusations of contradiction by claiming that such development is merely confined to a temporal intermediate period, for he continues to speak even of the ultimate state in terms which suggest linear time rather than eternity:

Even after the total consummation (*Gesamtvollendung*), it is of course impossible in a way to conceive the eternal life of the transfigured spirit in the immediate society (*in der unmittelbaren Gemeinschaft*) of the infinite God otherwise than as a never-ending movement of the finite spirit into the life of God (*eine unendliche Bewegung des endlichen Geistes in das Leben dieses Gottes hinein*).[96]

The following chapters will return to the problem of time in Rahner's eschatology; at this point it is sufficient to say that although Rahner sometimes speaks of eternity as allowing for some development in the individual, he certainly does not think that it allows for a change of decision *vis-à-vis* God.

The final point which should be made with regard to Rahner's analysis of death as affecting the whole person, is that there is an ambiguity in his writing as to whether death and eternity affect non-human life as they affect humans. One of his central assumptions is that time is heading in an unambiguous way towards a definite end; those creatures who possess a history of freedom are progressing specifically towards an end which will be a consummation of that history.[97] In the monograph *On the Theology of Death* Rahner writes that all the rest of creation shares with humanity 'a beginning through creation and a definitive end in the final transfiguration of the whole of creation before God':[98]

in which [end], the whole of reality, each creature according to its kind, will, in a way that we cannot more precisely conceive, participate in a created way in the eternity of God.[99]

However, when discussing eternity in the article 'The Life of the Dead', Rahner declares that it can only be understood as 'a

[96] *On the Theology of Death*, 27; (*Zur Theologies des Todes*, 26–7).

[97] See *On the Theology of Death*, 27: 'There is no eternal return of all things'; *Zur Theologies des Todes*, 27: *'Es gibt keine ewige Wiederkehr aller Dinge'*.

[98] *On the Theology of Death*, 27–8; *Zur Theologies des Todes*, 27: the phrase ends, *'ein definitives Ende in der Verklärung der Gesamtschöpfung vor Gott'*.

[99] *On the Theology of Death*, 28; *Zur Theologies des Todes*, 28: *'in dem die Gesamtwirklichkeit, je nach ihrer Art, einmal, in einer für uns näher nicht vorstellbaren Weise und in geschöpflicher Art, teilnehmen wird an der Ewigkeit Gottes . . .'*.

mode of the spirit and freedom, which are fulfilled in time'; as such, beasts, which do not have spirit nor freedom, therefore do not have the sort of time which gives rise to eternity.[100] Further, this implies that they are also excluded from the sort of consummation which takes place in eternity. This issue of whether the idea of consummation can correctly be applied to non-human life (and indeed to the history of the whole world) will be dealt with in more detail in Chapters 6 and 7.[101]

This brief summary of Rahner's theology of death has indicated three aspects of the universality of death. It affects the whole of the human race, the whole of human nature (body and soul), and the whole of a human life. This last fact (*prolixitas mortis*), combined with the fact of human freedom, means that death gives shape and meaning to a human life: it makes it into a history. More precisely, death renders final the free decisions of a lifetime. The facts that the decisions can be for God and that death can be a good one—a consummation—mean that a human history can become a history of salvation. This history of salvation is open to all in this way precisely because death and freedom are universal features of humanity. However, the connection of death with the fallen state of humanity is also important for his eschatology, because it means that death can never be an eternal positive consummation. Rather, the passive aspect of death is the consequence of (rather than the punishment for) sin and means that a human history is a history of enduring the consequences of sin, as well as a history of salvation. While Rahner's hermeneutics asserts that eschatology is the present experience of salvation translated into an expectation of its fulfilment, his theology of death reveals both what the character of our present human experience is (partial and doubtful, but with the possibility of decision still before us) and what the nature of its fulfilment or consummation might be.

Thus for Rahner history is much more than a simple succession of events in time: a human's life is 'truly historical' in that it moves unambiguously in one direction from a genuine beginning to a genuine end and that it is 'unique, unrepeatable,

[100] 'The Life of the Dead': *TI* iv. 348.

[101] For further criticism of Rahner's theology of death see Phan, *Eternity in Time*, 114–15. He is particularly critical of Rahner's anthropological methodology and his supposed alternative to the 'neoplatonic' dualistic idea of death.

of inalienable and irrevocable significance'.[102] As has been seen, the end is not a final term in a series but the consummation of the life of freedom before it. This is a repeated theme in Rahner's writings about death.[103] However, consummation is not a concept restricted to an individual human life: Rahner's more general writings on history show that it applies too to the history of the world.

ii. The Consummation of a History of Freedom

The word 'consummation' occurs frequently in Rahner's eschatological writings. Sometimes he appears to use it to mean the end of the world, sometimes the death and the resurrection of the individual; but he rarely gives a detailed analysis of what he means by the word. The one exception is his article entitled 'Immanent and Transcendent Consummation of the World'.[104] In this piece, Rahner first clarifies the five contexts in which the word 'consummation' (*Vollendung*) is used in everyday language. He notes that it can be applied to the following:

1. to a particular physical or biological event;
2. to the sum total of all such events, i.e. to the whole material world;
3. 'to the spiritual and personal history of an individual';
4. 'to all such spiritual and personal histories considered as constituting a unity' (*auf die Gesamtheit und Einheit solcher geistig-personaler Geschichten . . .*) which is more than 'a final amalgam in which they are all summed up';
5. 'to the real unity (here presupposed) of the material world together with the history of the spirit at both the individual and collective levels, in other words to the real unity and totality of temporal creation, of the "world" in the widest sense (*auf die (vorausgesetzte) reale Einheit von materielle Welt und*

[102] *On the Theology of Death*, 27; *Zur Theologies des Todes*, 27: *'einmalig, unwiederholbar, vor einer unaufhebbaren, nicht mehr rückgängig machbaren Bedeutung'*.

[103] Death is described as the consummation of the history of a human as a free being, and the definition of human life is given as a personal history seeking its own consummation ('Theological Considerations Concerning the Moment of Death': *TI* xi. 318, 314); death is seen as the end or the elevation into finality of a personal history of freedom ('Christian Dying': *TI* xviii. 234, 238–47); the consummation of a history of freedom is said to follow purgatory ('"The Intermediate State"': *TI* xvii. 119; 'Purgatory': *TI* xix. 164).

[104] *TI* x. 273–89.

Geistiger, individueller und kollektiver Geschichte, also auf die reale Einheit und Ganzheit von zeitliche Schöpfung, von 'Welt' überhaupt).'[105]

However, Rahner suggests that the word consummation has a different meaning in each case and that, in particular, the word is strictly inapplicable to the first two contexts, for '*the material world as such is in itself radically incapable of "consummation" (grundsätzlich unvollendbar)*'.[106] The reason for this is that consummation (at least in the specific sense that Rahner is using it) can only apply to a temporal event which has an end. This end must, moreover, produce a definitive result (*ein Ergebnis, ein Endgültiges*) which is different from the event itself and which is 'that for which the event considered precisely in its temporal development as event took place, that which it "sought" (*wollte*) and in which the event itself finds its meaning (*Sinn*) and its justification (*Rechtfertigung*)'.[107] A purely material event fails these criteria, Rahner claims, because no one stage of it—even the last—is qualitatively different from any other and a final stage is not 'sought': there is no will (*Wille*) to achieve a consummated state. Rahner's language here suggests that freedom is an essential element in consummation: what is expressed as decision in the case of the individual, here is described in more general terms as seeking and willing.[108]

Rahner thus describes the conditions for consummation in such personalistic terms that consummation by definition cannot be the conclusion of a purely material event. Indeed, it is not Rahner's concern so much to prove his claim that consummation cannot apply to the first two contexts in his list, as to set out a more specific meaning for the word 'consummation' as he uses it in his theology. One might say that Rahner is highlighting a

[105] 'Immanent and Transcendent Consummation of the World': *TI* x. 273–4; *ST* viii. 593.

[106] Ibid.: *TI* x. 274 (Rahner's emphasis); *ST* viii. 594.

[107] Ibid.: *TI* x. 275; *ST* viii. 594.

[108] For the connection between the consummation of the world and freedom, see e.g. 'History of the World and Salvation-History': *TI* v; 'Profane History and Salvation-History': *TI* xxi. The latter article in particular, in a section entitled 'The history of humanity as the history of freedom before God' (pp. 4–7), has an interesting analysis of history in terms of freedom. In this same article Rahner also emphasizes that freedom is directed towards finality. He explains that the possession of freedom does *not* enable one to make ever-renewable decisions, but rather is 'the capacity to commit an act of one's own that is ultimately irreversible' (p. 5).

more restricted 'theological' use of the word in distinction from its 'everyday' use in all of the five contexts which he describes. So when Rahner states that the concept of consummation can only be applied to 'that kind of history which is worked out in personal freedom', although he may appear to be making an unsubstantiated claim, in fact he is simply making a remark about his theological use of the word.

The fundamental problem for Rahner's concept of consummation is the relation of the last three meanings: what is the unity of all 'spiritual and personal histories' if it is not simply an 'amalgam' of them? and in what does the 'real unity' of the material world consist? These questions are of vital importance for Rahner's eschatology, for he must be able to explain why he is able to talk on the one level of individuals making decisions for or against God and on the other of the consummation of the world's attitude to God. Whereas the former is consonant with the possibility that some will be saved and others will not, the latter seems to suggest more of an 'all or nothing' outcome to the world. Hence, these questions are vital for an examination of Rahner's attitude to universal salvation. Is he hoping for all individuals to turn to God, or for a conversion, in some sense, of the whole world? Or is he able to hold the individual and the global meanings of salvation together? The following chapters will examine this question in more detail.

iii. Profane-history and Salvation-history

As has been demonstrated, Rahner's eschatology depends on the notion of individual human life-histories and universal world history heading towards consummation.[109] These histories have two aspects, which he labels salvation-history and profane- (or world-)history.[110] What is the relation between them?

[109] Rahner uses 'salvation' synonymously with 'consummation' in this article; for instance, he writes: 'salvation is indeed what brings the whole man to his perfection . . . Accomplished salvation is in no sense a moment in history but rather the culminating cessation of history' ('History of the World and Salvation-History': *TI* v. 97).

[110] In this context, 'world-history' means that aspect of history which is not salvation-history. It does *not* mean 'the history of the world as a whole', for it applies as much to an individual history as to the history of the world. Because Rahner tends, however, to discuss the relation of world- and salvation-history at a collective ('world') level, his terminology sometimes becomes confusing. 'The history of the world' can mean both 'profane-history' and 'the history of the world as a whole'. To avoid confusion the term 'profane-history' is used here as much as possible.

At root, salvation-history is the life of decisions in which an individual (or the world) accepts God's offer of himself. Rahner expresses a more complex relationship between this and profane-history in a detailed exposition which can be summarized in five main points. First, he emphasizes that 'salvation-history takes place in the history of the world'.[111] God's gracious self-communication of himself takes place in the profane world (pre-eminently and explicitly in Christ, but also in the prophets, for example)[112] and can only be accepted in this world:

> precisely this freedom of the corporeal, social and historical creature which is man is always and necessarily a freedom which is exercised through an encounter (*die Begegnung*) with the world—the community and environment in which man lives . . .[113]

Secondly, Rahner states that salvation is not itself profane, despite its profane context: it is 'an absolutely transcendent mystery'.[114] For this reason it is 'an absolutely fundamental heresy' for anyone to assert that any purely worldly state is his salvation.[115] Hence, although salvation can only be offered and accepted in the world, it is not fulfilled in the world; it is present but not as 'an object of possession or a produced effect':[116]

> the event of salvation is indeed contained in and achieved in profane history and yet is not present historically in its quality of saving event as such but is rather believed or hoped-for.[117]

One might say that salvation is present in the world eschatologically. Consequently, although one can be sure that God's salvation is available for all and is already effective in some, there can be no absolute certainty about the *details* of salvation—who is saved and who is not, what constitutes an acceptance or rejection of God, whether all will be saved. In particular, the events of profane-history do not reveal the content of salvation—an individual's actions are not so transparent that one can characterize them as involving an acceptance or a rejection of God.[118]

[111] 'History of the World and Salvation-History': *TI* v. 97.
[112] Ibid., 100.
[113] Ibid., 98 *ST* v. 116.
[114] Ibid.: *TI* v. 97.
[115] Ibid.
[116] Ibid.
[117] Ibid., 102; *ST* v. 120 f. *'ist das Heilsereignis in der Profangeschichte zwar enthalten, in ihr vollzogen, aber als solches nicht in seiner Heilsqualität selbst geschichtlich gegeben, sondern es ist geglaubt oder gehofft.'*
[118] Ibid: *TI* v. 100: 'profane history by and large does not permit of any unequivocal interpretation with regard to the salvation or damnation taking place within it'.

Thirdly, Rahner writes that not only does all salvation-history take place in profane-history, but that it is fully co-extensive with it.[119] In other words, God's offer of God's own self can be experienced in *every* aspect of each individual's worldly life and that the acceptance or rejection of God can be enacted in every aspect:

Every man exists not only in an existential situation to which belongs the obligation of striving towards a supernatural goal of direct union with the absolute God in a direct vision, but he exists also in a situation which presents the genuine subjective possibility of reaching this goal by accepting God's self-communication in grace and in glory. Because of God's universal saving purpose, the offer and possibility of salvation extend as far as extends the history of human freedom.[120]

This allows for the possibility of universalism but does not commit Rahner to asserting that all *will* be saved: the offer must be accepted; as yet it is only a possibility.[121]

Fourthly, Rahner recognizes that in Christ and the prophets, something about the relationship between the two histories has been revealed: where God's word interprets, salvation-history stands out in relief from profane-history. However, it is important to stress that the nature of salvation-history itself is always shrouded in mystery. For this reason, Rahner remarks that attempts to find an all-embracing pattern or 'meaning' in history are bound to fail. Despite their failure, Rahner at least understands what they are looking for and sympathizes with the search:

they are presuming that in the history being described something true and abidingly valid presents itself to us despite the historical contingency which no longer obligates us, and that this can be for us a challenge and a binding model.[122]

[119] 'History of the World and Salvation-History': *TI* v. 102–3.

[120] Ibid., 103; *ST* v. 121 f.: *'alle existieren nicht nur in einem Daseinsraum, zu dessen Konstitutiven die Verpflichtung auf ein übernatürliches Ziel der unmittelbaren Vereiningung mit dem absoluten Gott der unmittelbaren Anschauung gehört, sondern auch die echte subjektive Möglichkeit, dieses Ziel zu finden durch die Annahme der Selbstmitteilung Gottes in Gnade und Glorie. Heilsangebot und Heilsmöglichkeit erstrecken sich also wegen des allgemeinen Heilswillens Gottes soweit wie sich menschliche Freiheitsgeschichte erstreckt.'*

[121] The idea that God can be accepted and rejected in every human experience connects with his analysis of transcendental experience, as outlined in the previous chapter.

[122] 'Profane History and Salvation-History': *TI* xxi. 11.

Without being able to describe exactly what the pattern to history is and without the ability to express the meaning in concrete terms, at least Christianity is able to assert that history *does* have meaning, and that meaning resides in God—on the concrete historical level, in Christ.[123] According to Rahner, God is the meaning of history, or gives a pattern to history because God is both the guiding principle of history and its goal.[124] Nevertheless, this pattern cannot be fully expressed nor can it be used to predict the future, because of the radical incomprehensibility of God. Although there is a pattern, it is hidden, just as God's nature, although true, is obscure. Contrary to Christians who think that all history will be resolved 'in luminous brightness and transparency' Rahner warns that people need to trust in God's mystery:

> The ultimate meaning of history will only be brought about and attained when God in his grace grants it to free, finite subjects to abandon themselves in love in the incomprehensibility of God without the will to return again to the false autonomy of themselves.[125]

Nevertheless, fifthly and finally, salvation-history, whilst mysterious itself, does reveal some characteristics of profane-history by the very fact that it does stand out in relief from it. For example, through God's revelation, it reveals that the history of the world is not the history of God too, but is 'something created, finite, temporal and essentially referred to the Mystery which is something other than itself'.[126] It also reveals 'an antagonism' in worldly history which means that no element of it could consummate itself by its own power:

> Christianity knows of no history which would evolve of its own inner power (*aus ihrer inneren Dynamik heraus sich . . . entwickelt*) into the kingdom of God itself . . . The opposition between man and woman, the intellectual and the stupid, the rich and the poor, war and peace, rulers and subjects, and any other ineradicable antitheses of existence, may take different forms, may become more refined and more bearable, the effort to humanise these opposition may even be a

[123] Ibid., 12.
[124] Ibid., 10.
[125] Ibid., 8.
[126] 'History of the World and Salvation-History': *TI* v. 110.

duty for the human race . . . Nevertheless, the opposition will always remain . . .[127]

Although he admits that the antagonism may grow even more acute towards the end of the world, Rahner seems to assume that it will be overcome by the consummation ('always' thus refers just to time, not to eternity).[128] Furthermore, salvation-history reveals profane-history as relative and devalued, because God in his infinity 'outmodes' everything else:

Neither death nor life, nor things present, nor future possibilities are the ultimate, the finally significant, that which is salvation.[129]

This reiterates Rahner's earlier statement that it would be heretical to see anything earthly as salvation: any attempt to gain salvation here becomes part of history, is succeeded by the rest of history, becomes part of what is 'evil, godless and vain in history' because history is 'the realm of the provisional, the unfinished, the ambiguous, the dialectical (*der Raum des Vorläufigen, des Unvollendeten, des Zweideutigen, des Dialektischen*)'.[130] Nevertheless, as a balance to this rather pessimistic view of profane-history, salvation-history reveals the world as 'designed from the very beginning with a view to the Word of God become flesh'.[131]

It is clear then that Rahner sees salvation-history and profane-history as different, yet nevertheless co-extensive and mutually dependent. Profane-history can transcend itself into salvation-history, but the two will not become one unless at the eschaton God is universally accepted by the whole world: the whole *has the potential* to be consummated, but as profane-history moves towards the absolute future which is God, no-one can predict whether the whole world *will in fact* be consummated.[132]

Rahner summarizes the relationship of profane- and salvation-history by seeing the former as the condition of the possibility of the latter:

[127] 'History of the World and Salvation-History': *TI* v. 111–12; *ST* v. 131.

[128] See below, Appendix B, and Rahner, 'The Hermeneutics', 343–4.

[129] 'History of the World and Salvation-History': *TI* v. 113.

[130] Both quotations: ibid., 97 f.; *ST* v. 115.

[131] Ibid.: *TI* v. 114.

[132] The way in which Rahner speaks of *all* history as directed towards its consummation is confusing, but should be understood as meaning that all history reaches out to a consummation—but a consummation which it will not necessarily reach.

> Natural history in its material content and in its living form is the sphere which God puts before the finite spirit as the condition of its possibility—as the presupposition which transcends itself into the realm of the finite spirit by the dynamism of the absolute Spirit. So also the totality of the history of the world is the presupposition God has provided for salvation-history as the condition of its possibility transcending itself into it.[133]

Hence, just as there is a universal characteristic of human nature which is the condition of the possibility of the offer and acceptance of salvation, so there is a universal characteristic of profane-history which is the condition of the possibility of salvation-history. In both cases salvation/salvation-history is seen as a consummation of a previous history of freedom, whether that history is of the world or of an individual.

The next two chapters will examine the relation of Rahner's concepts of individual and collective consummation to his hope for universal salvation.

[133] 'History of the World and Salvation-History': *TI* v. 114.

6

The Consummation of an Individual History of Freedom

As has been seen from the analysis of Rahner's eschatological hermeneutics and of his theology of history, the concept of consummation plays a fundamental role in his eschatology. Its centrality can perhaps be compared to that of the idea of restoration to perfection in Gregory of Nyssa's eschatology. In each case the ideas have both personal and collective applications, and involve both divine and human agency. More importantly, each seems to suggest that humankind has been created in such a way that all humans are perfectible.

The next two chapters will examine in detail how Rahner's hope for the salvation of all is linked to the concept of the consummation of God's self-communication to all humans. The present chapter will analyse the basic meaning of Rahner's concept of consummation, that is with regard to eschatology and the individual; the following will examine how Rahner has tried to apply this concept of consummation to collective eschatology. Thus the basic structure of analysis—moving from a concept's core meaning to its universalistic implications—will reflect the previous analysis of Gregory's eschatology. It also reflects a development in Rahner's eschatological thought from—in Peter Phan's terminology—an 'individualist-existential' viewpoint to an 'interpersonal' and then a 'sociopolitical' perspective.[1]

This chapter will first analyse the theological basis of Rahner's concept of the consummation as the fulfilment of the human individual; it will then look at how this theory is reflected in his interpretation of the traditional Christian doctrines of heaven

[1] Peter Phan, *Eternity in Time: A Study of Karl Rahner's Eschatology* (Susquehanna University Press, Selinsgrove; Associated University Press, London and Toronto, 1988), 34–8.

(specifically the beatific vision) and hell. These doctrines raise problems for Rahner, some of which he tries to resolve by re-examining the doctrine of purgatory: an assessment of his success in this attempt will thus be the focus of the second half of the chapter.

A. CONSUMMATION AND INDIVIDUAL DECISION

i. Immanent and Transcendent Consummation of the Individual

In Chapter 4's analysis of Rahner's philosophy and theology it was seen that he considers human nature to be the condition of the possibility of divine self-communication and thus of consummation/salvation. Similarly, Chapter 5 showed that Rahner considers profane-history to be the condition of the possibility of salvation-history. In neither case is Rahner drawing a clear distinction between nature (human nature and profane-history) and grace (divine self-communication and salvation-history), for nature is always pervaded by and reaching out to the divine, through the creating and sustaining power of God. Nevertheless, Rahner does also wish to maintain that human decision is involved in the history of salvation, so he is faced with the challenge of explaining the interplay between human effort and divine grace—or, as he tends to express it, immanent and transcendent consummation.

The Introduction emphasized the tendency of traditional theology to try to balance the workings of divine grace and human effort in salvation, because an emphasis on one to the exclusion of the other has consequences which have usually been seen to be unwelcome.[2] Put simply, if grace is emphasized to the exclusion of human effort, God's gift of salvation either seems arbitrary, if only granted to some, or universalistic, if given to all. Both seem to deny human freedom; furthermore, to say that God's will is arbitrary seems to many to offend against the traditional picture of God as wise and good. Hence,

[2] In this discussion, the words 'salvation' and 'consummation' will be used synonymously: see 'Immanent and Transcendent Consummation of the World' (= 'Immanent and Transcendent Consummation'): *TI* x. 275, where Rahner equates the final (positive) consummation of 'the free personal history of an individual spirit' with 'salvation'.

nearly all Christian churches have rejected the doctrine of universal salvation and most deny the idea of a double predestination to salvation or damnation. However, if the emphasis is placed on human effort, in order to avoid those apparent errors, there is the danger of seeming to assert that people could earn their place in heaven through moral purity or human piety alone—an idea which most theologians have ruled out as simply impossible, besides being impious. Therefore, Christian theology has on the whole attempted to achieve a balance between the two.

In the article 'Immanent and Transcendent Consummation of the World', Rahner sets out this problem in his own terms:

> an *immanent* consummation is that which arises from the 'immanent' essential composition of the being which is in a process of achieving its consummation i.e. from the resources proper to it and through the intrinsic tendency of what is taking place towards a future goal. Immanent consummation is, therefore, considered precisely as the final outcome which has been worked out in time purely from within the event itself: the definitive finality of the freely posited event in itself . . . By contrast with this, *transcendent* consummation would in that case be a consummation which comes *ab externo*, being conferred upon the agent independently of the action he himself posits . . . it would be that which is given rather than the final and definitive state arrived at by the being itself in its process of reaching maturity.[3]

In terms of the consummation/salvation of the human individual, immanent consummation would be that achieved by the human in freedom; transcendent consummation would be that endowed by God's grace.

Where does Rahner stand on the issue of the balance between the two? It might seem from the analysis of Chapter 4 that he is taking a universalistic path in saying that God's gracious self-communication is imparted to all. However, he strongly denies that this necessarily entails universalism, for he insists that the individual is free to accept or to reject God. Hence, human effort

[3] 'Immanent and Transcendent Consummation': *TI* x. 277; *ST* viii. 597: '*so wäre eine immanente Vollendung diejenige, die sich von der immanenten Wesensstruktur des sich vollendenden Seienden aus, d.h. aus seinen eigenen Kräften und durch die prospektive innere Tendenz des Geschehens, eben als deren rein von ihm selbst her gezeitigtes Ergebnis darstellt: Endgültigkeit des freien Geschehens selbst. . . . Tranzendente Vollendung hingegen wäre dann eine Vollendung, die "von außen" käme, gleichsam unabhängig vom Geschehen selbst dem Geschehenden verliehen, somit eher das Gegebene als die Endgültigkeit des sich auszeitigenden Seienden selbst.*'

is involved, not in attempts to purify oneself (as in Gregory of Nyssa's theology), but in the determining of one's fundamental attitude to God.[4] Rahner explains the possibility of a decision about accepting (or refusing) God by asserting that God's self-communication is present in all humans *as an offer*:

> everyone, really and radically *every* person must be understood as the event of a supernatural self-communication of God (*das Ereignis einer übernatürlichen Selbstmitteilung Gottes*), although not in the sense that every person accepts in freedom God's self-communication to man.[5]

Although initially attractive, this idea is problematic because the concept of God communicating himself as an offer is so obscure, despite Rahner's efforts to clarify it. Rahner stresses that it 'must not be understood as a communication which could exist but does not exist', because this would imply that the success of God's communication (i.e. salvation) is dependent on some prior action or decision of the individual.[6] This might lead to the idea of the individual earning God's self-communication. Not only is this notion condemned by the Church, but it contradicts Rahner's central thesis that God's self-communication is an aspect of transcendental experience which is itself a prior condition for any human action. Consequently, Rahner rejects the idea that God's self-communication is merely a *potentiality* for the individual; rather, he holds that God's self-communication is an *actuality* in every individual. It is both in a sense present in the individual as the ground of human existence and also in a sense not yet present until the individual has said 'yes' to God.[7] God is both the gift and the condition of the possibility of accepting the gift.

This complex idea is an attempted solution to a difficult

[4] Rahner's basic concept here is that of a free 'decision' (*Entscheidung*) for or against God; elsewhere he speaks of: 'the freedom to say "yes" or "no" to God' (*Freiheit des Ja oder Nein zu Gott*); the free 'affirmation or denial of God' (*Bejahung oder Verneinung Gottes*); an individual's freedom to 'open or close himself to God's self-communication (*sich dieser Selbstmitteilung Gottes eröffnen oder verschließen*)'. All these seem to be equivalent to the idea sometimes described in Roman Catholic theology as the 'fundamental option' for or against God.

[5] Rahner, *Foundations of Christian Faith*, 127–8 (his emphasis); *Grundkurs des Glaubens*, 133.

[6] Rahner, *Foundations*, 128.

[7] See Karl-Heinz Weger, *Karl Rahner: An Introduction to his Theology* (Burns & Oates, London, 1980), 87: grace is 'a reality that is always present at the very centre of man's existence in knowledge and freedom and in the mode of an offer which must be accepted or rejected'.

problem. It is easy to see why Rahner feels led to a solution which tries to balance effort and grace in this way, but less easy to understand exactly what he means by it. If God is really communicating *God's own self*, how can God be related to an individual as an offer and yet simultaneously exist in that person as the precondition of accepting that offer?

The article 'Immanent and Transcendent Consummation of the World' adds another paradox. In the terminology of this article, one might express what has been said above thus: God is the transcendent consummation of the individual *both* in the gratuitous and universal offer of divine self-communication *and* in the gratuitous and universal divine presence in individuals as the condition of the possibility of them accepting this offer. That is, God is the transcendent consummation of the individual *and* the precondition of the individual's immanent consummation.

> The 'immanent' and 'transcendent' consummation of the spiritual creature is the same. It is one consummation in which the one aspect demands the other.[8]

However, he goes even further than this to say that there are *no* distinctions at all between the (human) immanent and the (divine) transcendent aspects of consummation. God is not only the gift, the one offering the gift, and the precondition for the individual accepting the gift; God also seems to have become the one accepting the gift. The paradox resulting from the identity of the (human) immanent consummation with the (divine) transcendent consummation is that:

> The nature (*Das Wesen*) of the spiritual creature consists in the fact that that which is 'innermost' to it, that whence, to which and through which it is, is precisely not an element of this essence and this nature which belongs to it (*ein Moment dieses ihrers Wesens und ihrer Natur*). Rather its nature is based upon the fact that that which is supra-essential, that which transcends it (*das überwesentliche, sie Transzendierende*), is that which gives it its support, its meaning, its future and its most basic impulse . . . (*Halt, Sinn, Zukunft und letze Bewegung*)[9]

Hence all pre-conceived notions about what is 'inner' and 'outer' to the human are broken down and one can say that a person's transcendence is his or her immanence.

[8] 'Immanent and Transcendent Consummation': *TI* x. 282.

[9] Ibid., 281; *ST* viii. 601.

In his emphasis of this point, that God 'has made himself an intrinsic principle (*zum inneren Prinzip*) of this world in that creature belonging to it which is endowed with spiritual faculties', Rahner seems to be heading towards panentheism.[10] Although he is not claiming that God is identical with the universe (pantheism), he is apparently saying that God is identical with the innermost feature of human existence. In the next chapter it will be seen that it is when this claim is interpreted on the collective level, so that consummation applies to the whole universe, that the problem becomes more acute. The main difficulty which panentheism presents for the concept of salvation is that it is very unclear where it leaves the role of the human individual. First there is the problem of freedom: Rahner appears to have tilted the balance so much in the favour of divine grace that the power of God's gift outweighs the ability of humans to refuse it. The next section will illustrate how he attempts to assert the freedom of the individual to refuse God. Secondly, even if humans are free to accept or to reject God, there is the question of what this acceptance consists in: is it faith, or virtue, or something else? This question will be dealt with in section iii.

ii. The Possibility of a Negative or a Rejected Consummation

Rahner thinks that the acceptance of God's offer of grace would only be free if a person was able to reject it, and he asks whether there could be a rejection of consummation on either an individual or a collective level. At some points in the article 'Immanent and Transcendent Consummation of the World', Rahner appears to be very tentative and merely suggests on the individual level a situation in which there might be an entirely natural, immanent consummation in which the supernatural and transcendent consummation was not attained by the person, or was even refused. He does, however, express doubt as to whether this 'definitive state which man arrived at entirely through the resources of his own nature' might truly be called a consummation—it would presumably be akin to the sort of purely material fulfilment which Rahner also refuses to call consummation.[11]

[10] Ibid.: *TI* x. 280; *ST* viii. 600.

[11] Quotation from ibid.: *TI* x. 283; a purely material state not a consummation, see ibid., 274 f.

In addition, Rahner explores the possibility of what he calls a '*negative* or *wrongly* worked out definitive state of freedom considered as the self-determination of the person to perdition'[12] and here he clearly comes to the conclusion that although a definitive evil state *is* possible it cannot properly be called consummation:

In any genuine ontology of freedom the good and bad outcomes of freedom are not ontologically equal as possible uses of it. It is true that in God's sight, freedom can reach its final outcome as consummation of the self in final and definitive evil (*Kann sich auch Freiheit . . . als Selbstvollendung in das endgültige Böse hinein vollziehen*). But still the nature of being, of good and therefore of freedom too, is such that this is not a possibility open to the free being which is ontologically on the same level. Such an outcome of the history of the free person as intrinsically involved as the final and definitive state he has reached is, on the contrary, to be understood as the final and definitive state of *non-consummation* (*die Endgültigkeit der Nichtvollendung*).[13]

Rahner also discusses the ability of the individual to reject God in *Foundations of Christian Faith*.[14] He first considers whether it is possible for someone to reject God if God were just the horizon of our existence (that is, if God were not also related to humans by divine self-communication). His answer is that in such an instance clearly one could reject God in a thematic way: that is, one could explicitly deny that God was the transcendent horizon of every human experience. However, Rahner claims that one could also deny God *unthematically*:

But since in every act of freedom which is concerned on the categorial level with a quite definite object, a quite definite person, there is always present, as the condition of possibility for such an act, transcendence towards the absolute term and source of all our intellectual and spiritual acts and hence towards God, there can and must be present in every such act an *unthematic 'yes' or 'no'* to this God of original, transcendental experience.[15]

Thus we encounter God 'everywhere', 'in all of the things of the world' and 'especially in our neighbour'; as such, God's presence

[12] 'Immanent and Transcendent Consummation': *TI* x. 276–7; *ST* viii. 596: '*die negativ oder schlecht gezeitigte Endgültigkeit der Freiheit als Selbstbestimmung des personalen Seienden in Unheil*'.

[13] Ibid.: *TI* x. 277; *ST* viii. 596–7.

[14] Rahner, *Foundations*, 97–106.

[15] Ibid., 98 (his emphasis).

can be unacknowledged, ignored, even rejected, in our very actions relating to our neighbour and the rest of the world.[16] This rejection is unthematic because it is non-conceptualized and non-conceptualizable. It creates a paradox, because at the same time as our actions reject God unthematically, God is the unthematically grasped ground of all our experience.

This would be true even if God were merely the distant horizon of all experience; it is more clearly true if God is also related to humans in the closeness of the divine self-communication:

> If the historical concreteness of our transcendence in grace . . . also consists in the offer of God's self-communication to us, and in the absolute closeness of this holy mystery as communicating itself and not refusing itself (*in der angebotenen Selbstmitteilung Gottes an uns und in der absoluten Nähe des heiligen Geheimnisses als des sich selbst Mitteilenden und sich nicht Versagenden*), then freedom in transcendence and in its 'yes' or 'no' to its ground receives an immediacy (*Unmittelbarkeit*) to God in and through which it becomes in the most radical way a capacity to say 'yes' or 'no' to God (*zum Vermögen des Ja und Nein zu Gott*).[17]

Nevertheless, Rahner asserts that although it is possible to deny God at these two levels, thematic and unthematic, and in these two aspects of horizon and self-communicated offer, it is in one sense impossible to deny God. This impossibility lies in the paradox just mentioned: because God as horizon is always the condition of the possibility of saying any 'no', so in making any denial one is silently affirming this horizon.[18] Hence, in denying God, one is caught in an 'absolute contradiction' (*ein absoluter Widerspruch*) in that one is denying and affirming God at the same time.[19] Rahner seems to suggest that this contradiction is self-destructive, because it is in effect denying the very ground of one's existence.[20] A life of such contradiction is one which would end in non- or a negative consummation; its paradoxical and destructive nature explains why Rahner says that the possibility of denying God is not 'ontologically on the same level' as accepting

[16] Ibid., 98–9.

[17] Ibid., 100–1; *Grundkurs*, 107.

[18] Rahner, *Foundations*, 99.

[19] e.g. ibid., 99; *Grundkurs*, 106.

[20] Rowan Williams writes: 'When the possibility of love has been opened up, there is a call to love unconditionally and radically and the refusal of such a call is the spirit's denial of its own nature': R. Williams, 'Rahner and Balthasar', in John Riches, *The Analogy of Beauty* (T & T Clark, Edinburgh, 1986), 16.

him.[21] Nevertheless, despite its apparently self-contradictory nature, Rahner is at pains to emphasize that such a possibility is a real one and that it lies before each and every individual because God is present to all, both as distant horizon and in the divine self-communication.[22]

iii. Unthematic Acceptance or Denial of God: 'Anonymous Christianity'

The main problem with Rahner's assertions about denying God is the concept of denying or affirming God unthematically. It is easy enough to understand that one can explicitly deny that God is the ground of one's existence, or that God has communicated the divine self to humanity—but what is involved in an unthematic denial of God as encountered in the world around one, or in one's neighbour? The question is an important one because of Rahner's expressed hope that all people might be saved: the possibility of an unthematic *acceptance* of God may explain how some who are not Christians might be saved.[23] However, there must also be the possibility of *rejecting* God unthematically, or the question of human freedom arises again: if everybody automatically accepted God at the unthematic level, this would contradict Rahner's belief that a free immanent consummation is part of the consummation of the individual.

A clarification of what Rahner means by an unthematic acceptance or rejection of God may be sought from his controversial concept of 'anonymous Christians' (*die anonymen Christen*).[24] In an article with this title, he argues that each

[21] 'Immanent and Transcendent Consummation': *TI* x. 277; cf. full quotation above, p. 174.

[22] In his discussion of saying 'yes' and 'no' to God, Rahner assumes throughout that what is possible for 'man' is possible for every individual (with perhaps a very few exceptions). For an explicit statement to this effect see *Foundations*, 103; see ibid., 106 for a brief mention of possible exceptions.

[23] The other explanation of the possibility of universal salvation would be a post-mortem means by which some gain salvation. This will be discussed in a later section.

[24] Rahner's ideas on this issue are controversial and the term 'anonymous Christians' particularly so. However, the term was not coined by Rahner himself. His article 'Anonymous Christians' was originally a review of a book by A. Röper called *Die anonymen Christen*. This review was broadcast by Westdeutscher Rundfunk in the summer of 1964; for publication in *Theological Investigations* references to this original context were removed and Rahner incorporated responses to possible objections. (See the details of the sources of articles at the back of *Theological Investigations* vi.).

human individual has the opportunity to hear and accept God because each is 'a being of unlimited openness for the limitless being of God'; however, this opportunity is not due to 'the mere fact of being human', but rather to God's grace.[25] So much is familiar. More surprising is his description of salvation as 'nothing less than the fulfilment and definitive coming to maturity of [faith in Christ]'.[26] It might seem impossible to have an unthematic faith in something specific, but in fact it becomes clear that Rahner is using the word 'faith' in a somewhat idiosyncratic way. First, it is faith in a revelation which can be *explicitly* expressed as Christian revelation, but which is more generally 'the revelation of grace which man always experiences implicitly in the depths of his being'.[27] Secondly, by faith Rahner means not cognitive assent to a proposition or set of propositions, nor an explicit commitment to a particular being, but rather a certain way of life:

> Prior to the explicitness of official ecclesiastical faith (*der Ausdrücklichkeit des amtlichen kirchlichen Glaubens*) this acceptance can be present in an implicit form (*in jener Unausdrücklichkeit*) whereby a person undertakes and lives the duty of each day in the quiet serenity of patience, in devotion to his material duties and the demands made upon him by the persons in his care.[28]

As this passage suggests, ideally this implicit acceptance of God will be made explicit,[29] but although it might 'strive for actuation' Rahner claims that 'an unfavourable historical environment may impose limitations in the explicitness of this expression so that this actuation may not exceed the explicit appearance of loving humaneness'.[30]

Rahner denies that this is salvation by works, or by a 'purely natural morality' (*ein rein natürliche Sittlichkeit*); instead he asserts that it occurs by God's grace, the grace of 'true faith'.[31] This concurs with his view in *Foundations*:

> [An unthematic] 'no' to God is not originally merely the moral sum (*das bloß moralische Fazit*) which we calculate from individual good or evil

[25] 'Anonymous Christians': *TI* vi. 392.
[26] Ibid., 391. [27] Ibid., 394. [28] Ibid.
[29] Rahner covers his tracks in *Foundations of Christian Faith* by asserting 'the necessity of making [an unthematic 'yes' to God] thematic', yet while asserting this he does not in the same place explain the reason for the necessity. (*Foundations*, 99.)
[30] 'Anonymous Christians': *TI* vi. 395. [31] Ibid., 398.

deeds, whether we treat all of these acts as having equal value, or whether we believe that in this sum what matters is only the temporally last individual act in our lives . . .[32]

Yet even if Rahner is arguing here that it is God's indwelling grace which enables the 'anonymous Christian' to act morally, he must acknowledge some human freedom exercised in a choice to act in that way—or his concept of anonymous Christianity would be tantamount to saying that all non-Christians necessarily do act with 'loving humaneness', which is clearly not the case.[33] In effect he is saying that a particular sort of moral virtue is sufficient for salvation in some cases, although this is not the ideal.

This study of his concept of anonymous Christianity elucidates Rahner's concept of the acceptance of God to a certain extent. At the least it can be a response of love to one's neighbour through which one is unthematically responding to God; ideally it is a fully explicit confession of Christ.[34]

The first part of this chapter has thus revealed that Rahner's idea of consummation is a complex one. At the most basic level, consummation is the perfection of a relationship with God which is based on knowledge and love. It is a possibility which is open to all individuals who have a personal history of freedom. However, consummation is also an event in which grace and human freedom interact, an event which is at once transcendent and immanent. Rahner's explanation of the exact nature of the relationship between these two poles of grace and freedom (or transcendence and immanence) raises important and difficult questions about the possibility of rejecting God.

[32] Rahner, *Foundations*, 101; *Grundkurs*, 108. The 'last . . . act' refers to the tradition of belief in death-bed confessions of faith. Rahner also emphasizes that one could never tell from a single act, or indeed even a lifetime, whether someone (even oneself) had said 'yes' or 'no' to God: *Foundations*, 101–2.

[33] Rahner writes: 'It would be wrong to declare every man . . . an "anonymous Christian"' ('Anonymous Christians': *TI* vi. 394).

[34] This section has used Rahner's discussion of 'anonymous Christianity' merely in order to clarify what he means by an unthematic acceptance of God. Of course, besides the problem of whether such an acceptance is possible, the major difficulty of Rahner's theory is whether an unthematic acceptance of God can truly be described as *Christian*. This issue is beyond the scope of this book, but for comments on Rahner's concept of 'anonymous Christians' see: Williams, 'Rahner and Balthasar', *passim*, esp. 12, 31; J. A. Di Noia, 'Karl Rahner', in David Ford (ed.), *The Modern Theologians*, 2nd edn. (Basil Blackwell, Oxford, 1997), 130–1; Weger *Karl Rahner: An Introduction to his Theology*, 95 ff.

The chapter will now turn to Rahner's discussions of heaven, hell, and purgatory, in order to see whether these answer those questions which his more theoretical work leaves unanswered or unclear. In particular, Rahner's analysis of the beatific vision sheds light on the question of what it is about the human that is consummated; meanwhile, his interpretation of the doctrines of hell and purgatory clarifies his view of the nature of human decision—especially the nature of rejecting God. Rahner's treatment of these three doctrines raises questions about the relation between individual and collective salvation, and consequently about human freedom, which will be dealt with in more detail in the next chapter.

B. PERFECT FULFILMENT AND UTTER LOSS

i. Heaven: The Beatific Vision

Rahner speaks of heaven in three contexts: in his hermeneutical discussions, in the context of interpreting the doctrine of the resurrection and in discussion of the concept of the beatific vision. As has been seen, in his writing on hermeneutics he claims that statements about heaven and hell cannot be made with equal certainty, but says little about the application of this principle to specific biblical or traditional statements about heaven. He is more interested in a general principle of interpretation, than in what heaven might actually be like. In fact, as William Dych points out, Rahner's way of interpreting eschatological statements *entails* that one cannot know what the consummation of the individual or the world will be like. For Rahner, scriptural images of 'eternal union with God' 'all point to that life with God which is not bestowed merely on an external reward from without, but is the very life and the very self one has created through time in grace and in freedom'.[35] In other words, one cannot predict the *precise nature* of the consummation; one can only make claims about its *existential significance*. In the words of William Thompson, according to Rahner's hermeneutics 'heaven and its beatific vision can . . . be said to be the

[35] William Dych, *Karl Rahner* (Geoffrey Chapman, London, 1992), 143.

experience of transcendence and grace in the mode of their fulfilment'.[36]

Hence, when Rahner refers to final salvation, it is usually in very general terms: for example, 'the victorious grace of Christ which brings the world to its fulfilment (*die siegreiche und die Welt vollendende Gnade Christi*)' or 'the victory of grace in redemption consummated (*der Sieg der Gnade in der vollendeten Erlösung*)'.[37] In his article on eschatology in *Sacramentum Mundi* he is more specific and draws two conclusions from the fact that salvation is the fulfilment of 'that Christian reality which revelation states to be present here and now'. First, there will be a resurrection of the flesh (although one 'cannot form any precise idea of the glorified body'): this emphasizes the material and collective aspects of salvation. Secondly, 'because there is a single saving history of mankind as such, its fulfilment cannot be *reduced* to that of the various individuals', but it will of course *include* individual fulfilment, which Rahner calls the 'vision of God'.[38] Heaven for Rahner is the fulfilment of the present experience of salvation which itself has its material-collective and spiritual-individual aspects; consequently, the two aspects of heavenly existence—resurrection and vision—are closely interconnected. This reflects Rahner's concern always to balance individual and cosmic eschatologies.[39] This chapter will deal with the former (the beatific vision, hell, purgatory) and the next with the latter (the parousia, the resurrection).[40] Since Rahner is clearly trying to work from within Christian tradition, his accounts of scriptural and magisterial statements will briefly be summarized before we turn to his own interpretations of the doctrines.

In his article on the beatific vision in *Sacramentum Mundi* Rahner cites scriptural references as evidence that the vision of

[36] William Thompson, 'The Hope for Humanity: Rahner's Eschatology', in L. O'Donovan, *A World of Grace* (A Crossroads Book, Seabury Press, New York, 1980), 160.

[37] 'The Hermeneutics of Eschatological Assertions': *TI* iv. 340; *ST* iv. 421–2.

[38] All quotations from 'Eschatology': *SM* ii. 245 (my emphasis).

[39] It was seen earlier, in the discussion of Rahner's sixth thesis in 'The Hermeneutics of Eschatological Assertions', that Rahner connects the bodily aspect of humanity with the material world in general and hence with a cosmic approach to eschatology. See above, Chapter 5, section B.

[40] In fact the beatific vision has collective aspects and resurrection individual aspects, so the division between them is not entirely clear-cut. However it serves as a useful general distinction.

God is gratuitous and direct.[41] Although statements of the magisterium are also usually very general, they do make three specific claims (which echo the biblical evidence): that the beatific vision is not natural, but gratuitous; that the directness of the promised vision does not contradict the fact that God's essence is held to be incomprehensible; and that the blessed who are without sin (i.e. have not sinned since their baptism, or since absolution and penance) enter upon the vision of God immediately upon death.[42]

Rahner's own exposition of the nature of the beatific vision follows these basic beliefs although not their exact expression. He describes the beatific vision thus:

> the full and definitive experience of the direct self-communication of God himself to the individual human being when by free grace God's will has become absolute and attained its full realisation.[43]

Thus, to answer one of the questions raised at the end of the last section, that which is consummated is not so much any part of the human being, but rather the individual's relation with God: his or her perfect reception of the self-communication of God. Nevertheless, Rahner does suggest that the vision does concern the individual's *spiritual* aspect in particular:

> As regards the ultimate essence of the beatific vision in the strictest sense, we must start from the position that the specific nature of created mind is spiritual knowledge and love which determine one another in radical unity. . . . And this knowledge and love exists in intercommunication between persons. It must also be noted that 'salvation' in its fullest sense means the perfect fulfilment of the spiritual person as such and as a whole, and therefore principally

[41] Gratuitous: 'Beatific Vision': *SM* i. 152 (1 Tim. 6: 16; John 1: 16; 6: 41; Matt. 11: 27; 1 Cor. 2: 11); direct: 'Beatific vision': *SM* i. 153 (1 John 3: 2; 1 Cor. 13: 12; Matt. 5: 8, 18: 10; 2 Cor. 5: 7).

[42] Rahner refers to Denzinger's collection of doctrinal definitions: Heinrich Denzinger, (ed.), *Kompendium der Glaubensbekenntnisse und kirchlichen Lehrentscheidungen* [= Denz.] The references below are to the most recent (37th) edition, edited by P. Hünermann (Herder, Freiburg-im-Breisgau, 1991). (Note that the paragraph numbers for editions before and after 1963 are different: the 1991 edition contains a conversion table at the back). General statements on the afterlife: see e.g. Denz., paras. 72, 76, 150, 801; vision not natural: e.g. Denz., 895 (= Errors of the Beghards and the Beguines, 5), 3028 (Canons of the Catholic Faith from the First Vatican Council 1869–70, 2 §3), 3238–40 (Errors of Antonius de Rosmini-Serbati, 38–40); incomprehensible: Denz., 800, 3001; immediate vision of God: Denz., 1001, 1316.

[43] 'Beatific vision': *SM* i. 151.

concerns his specific essence which distinguishes him from beings below the level of spirit.[44]

Not only does this mean that the self-communication of God is of love as well as of knowledge, but it also means that the communication is of God as Trinity, because the communication reflects God's triune nature as including the two 'processions' of truth in the Word of God and love in the Spirit of God. Despite this dual nature of the vision, however, Rahner admits both that the traditional expression 'beatific vision' has tended to emphasize the purely intellectual aspect of it and indeed that 'the beatific vision can best be described on its intellectual side' as a knowing and being known by God.[45] This implies that animals are excluded from this sort of fulfilment (as the extract above also suggests): the question of whether they are capable of any fulfilment at all will be dealt with in the next chapter.

Rahner's interpretation of the beatific vision rests on a teleological view of human nature as open in this life to a future fulfilment:

> The beatific vision is indeed the most perfect conceivable actuation of a spiritual creature inasmuch as the latter is open absolutely without limits to being, truth and value. But this unlimited transcendent capacity of man still has meaning and purpose even if it is not fulfilled by God's self-communication. For it serves to constitute meaningful, spiritual, interpersonal life in a freedom and history oriented towards a definitive possession of such a life, none of which is possible without such transcendence.[46]

However, despite the fact that this fulfilment can be the *only true* fulfilment of the spiritual person, this does not mean that the fulfilment is in any way owed to the person. Instead, it is entirely gracious. Nor does such a teleological concept of humankind imply that the capacity for God in humanity in general will inevitably be fulfilled as a whole, given God's omnipotence. This would be a dogmatic type of universalism, to which Rahner is very much opposed (i.e. universal salvation expressed in terms of

[44] 'Beatific vision': *SM* i. 152.

[45] Ibid., 151, 153: on the latter page Rahner notes: 'The parallel drawn between this knowledge [= seeing God 'face to face'] and being known by God (1 Cor. 13: 12) emphasizes the personal character of the mutual loving reception and self-communication as compared with purely objectifying cognition.'

[46] Ibid., 152.

inevitability and not hope). Confusingly, though, when Rahner does emphasize that the vision has a communal aspect, he expresses this in almost universalistic tones: he writes that since the individual is redeemed as part of humanity as a whole in Christ, the term beatific vision 'also implies in the concrete, if not formally, the unity of the redeemed and perfected in the perfect Kingdom of God, "heaven", as the communion of the blessed with the glorified Lord and his humanity, and with one another—the perfect accomplishment of the "communion of saints"'.[47] The question this raises is, if the individual is redeemed *qua* member of humanity as a whole, why is the whole of humanity not redeemed? This question echoes that asked of Gregory of Nyssa and will return with more force in the next chapter.

ii. Hell

In contrast with the beatific vision, which Rahner sees as the gracious fulfilment by God of the human capacity to receive God's divine self-communication, hell is the ultimate and definitive failure to attain this fulfilment.

Importantly, Rahner emphasizes that the nature of hell is due not to divine vindictive punishment (although it can broadly be seen in terms of God's justice) but to the nature of time and human freedom.[48] Hence he stresses that the character of hell as a place of punishment is not due to God's delight in causing pain, but is the consequence of a human rejection of God.[49] Similarly, its eternity is not due to God exercising the divine prerogative as judge and sentencing humans to infinite punishment for an infinite offence, but to the nature of death. Because human existence after death is timelessly eternal, any decision for or against God is rendered final. This applies no less to hell than to heaven: just as no-one can fall from heaven, so no-one can rise from hell.[50]

[47] Ibid., 151: this is one of the relatively few occasions on which Rahner speaks of 'heaven'. Rahner also refers to it as 'eternal life'.

[48] Thus Thompson describes Rahner's view of hell as 'the intrinsic possible result of our own possible obduracy' ('The Hope for Humanity', 161); and Dych notes: 'Judgment is understood not as a purely extrinsic "sentence" but as the intrinsic consequence of a person's fundamental option versus God' (*Karl Rahner*, 145).

[49] The nature of punishment in Rahner's eschatology will be further studied in the following section on purgatory.

[50] A further consequence of death being the end of time for the individual is that

Although he is clearly moving some distance away from traditional views of hell, Rahner is not advocating an entirely internalized interpretation. For example, he wishes to avoid two common misinterpretations of the traditional description of the punishment of hell as being by fire: the word should be interpreted neither in literal nor in purely psychological terms. The tendency to avoid the former has sometimes led to the latter, which Rahner objects to:

> [the word 'fire'] indicates the cosmic, objective aspect of loss which is outside the consciousness.[51]

That is, the 'fire' is in some sense external to the person experiencing it. Rahner emphasizes that 'fire' is a metaphorical expression for something which even if expressed in abstract terms would still be expressed in 'images'—this clearly ties in with his hermeneutical principle that it is impossible to get at a 'pure' concept.[52] Hell is thus more than the pain of a conscience awakened to its guilt: it is the experience of an ontological change which has an external source.

The problem is that some scriptural and doctrinal statements do tend towards a more literal interpretation of hell-fire.[53] How does Rahner deal with these? Summarizing the main references to hell in Scripture, Rahner seems to regard them all as 'threat-discourses', taking as his prime example the preaching of Jesus which was focused on a call to repent. Such threat-discourse is 'not to be read as a preview of something which will exist some day . . . it is rather a disclosure of the situation in which the persons addressed are actually to be found'.[54] Jesus' 'metaphors' are typical of his day and all indicate 'the possibility of man being finally lost and estranged from God in all the dimension of

doctrinal statements stress that those who die in mortal sin are said to descend to hell immediately—just as the blessed attain to the beatific vision immediately: 'Hell': *SM* iii. 7; Denz., 858.

[51] 'Hell': *SM* iii. 8 (§4a).

[52] Ibid. (§4a); 'The Hermeneutics of Eschatological Assertions', 344–6; and 'The Resurrection of the Body', 208–9. Rahner also rejects the concept of physical hell-fire in '"The Intermediate State"': *TI* xvii. 123.

[53] Hell-fire appears to be mentioned in Matt. 5: 22; 13: 42; 18: 9; Rev. 14: 10; 20: 10; 21: 8; see also Denz., 76 (*in ignem aeternam*). Most doctrinal statements refer more generally to punishment: e.g. Denz., 72 (*poenam pro peccatis aeterni supplicii*); 801 (*poenam perpetuam*), 839 (*aeternae gehennae ardoribus perpetuo cruciatur*).

[54] 'Hell': *SM* iii. 7.

his existence'.[55] Lying behind these remarks is Rahner's fundamental hermeneutical principle that Scripture does not predict history, but rather teaches us 'about our possibilities and our tasks':

> scriptural descriptions of the end both of the individual person and of the whole human race can be understood as statements about the possibilities of human life, and as instructions about the absolute seriousness of human decision.[56]

Dogmatic statements are to be read in the same way. Their focus on decision is illustrated by the fact that they refer to hell in very terse terms, often simply as the alternative to heaven. However, those that appear to mention the fire of punishment more specifically should also 'be read in the same way as the judgement-discourses of Jesus which they reiterate'—i.e. as using metaphorical language to underline the seriousness of decision.[57] The way in which Rahner deals with this controversial eschatological point is a good example of how his hermeneutics allow him to distinguish between the content (definitive loss) and the form (hell-fire) of a doctrine in a way which is not arbitrary or wishful-thinking, but which is guided by the belief that Scripture is addressed to believers now and is above all else relevant to their current experience of salvation-history.

Central to Rahner's interpretation of the doctrine of hell is his contention that it is a possibility for each human individual.[58] This is another way of stating the fact noted above that a negative consummation, as a result of saying 'no' to God, is possible for all people.[59] Because each individual is faced with this possibility, one can make *no* certain assertions about the fate of *all* individuals. This explains why Rahner denies the *apokatastasis*—by which Rahner means the absolute assertion that all people will actually be saved.[60] His denial of the *apokatastasis* has already been mentioned above in relation to his hermeneutical principle regarding statements about heaven and hell.[61] There it was seen

[55] Ibid. [56] *Foundations*, 103. [57] 'Hell': *SM* iii. 8.
[58] Ibid. (§4c). [59] See above, p. 176.
[60] Besides his own hermeneutical convictions, Rahner is undoubtedly also influenced by doctrinal statements condemning the *apokatastasis*. See Chapter 1, section D.
[61] 'The Hermeneutics of Eschatological Assertions': *TI* iv. 338–9: see above, Chapter 5, section B., on thesis 6(a); Rahner also denies the *apokatastasis* in 'Christian Dying': *TI* xviii. 236, 241.

that although hell was/is/will be a *possibility* for *all* people, yet one can say that *some* people *have* been saved (or one could not say that Christ's atonement had been effective). Thus it is a certainty that there are some people in heaven, but it is uncertain whether, at the eschaton, there will be anyone in hell. Hence Rahner writes:

> The Christian message says nothing about whether in some people or in many people evil has become an absolute reality defining the *final end result* of their lives.[62]

Indeed Rahner sees it as essential to Christian faith to have a pious hope that all might be saved and a belief in God's universal saving will—which are very different things from a dogmatic espousal of universalism.[63]

In holding to a hope in God's universal saving will and in rejecting the belief that certainly some are (or will be) damned Rahner is also denying the doctrine of double predestination which holds that some are predestined to heaven and others to hell. Hell must be (have been) only a *possibility* and not a certainty even for those who will be (are) in hell, if any.[64] Curiously, Rahner says in 'The Hermeneutics of Eschatological Assertions' that one *can* speak of *one* predestination, the content of which he calls 'the victory of grace in redemption consummated'. However, he has not in fact shown satisfactorily how he can speak of *any* predestination. If hell is a genuine possibility for everyone and if each human has genuine freedom, then hell is a possible destiny even for the saints and martyrs at some point in their lives. Rahner would appear to confirm this by his warning that it is presumptuous to declare in anyone's lifetime that he or she is saved. With this in mind it is difficult to see how anyone could be predestined to salvation—the problem cannot be avoided by saying that some are predestined but one does not know whom. The only way in which Rahner's claim will work is by watering down the meaning of predestination, so that it means 'it was/is predestined that some were/will be saved, but it was/is not

[62] *Foundations*, 103.

[63] In other words, Rahner says that one can say *neither* that all will be saved *nor* that some will not be saved.

[64] 'The Hermeneutics of Eschatological Assertions': *TI* iv. 340.

predestined that any particular individual was/will be saved'. This is indeed what Rahner sometimes seems to mean, but it is rather a forced meaning of predestination.

Associated with Rahner's belief that hell is a possibility for each, but a certainty for none, is his warning that each individual's decision for or against God is hidden. This is because 'freedom is the content of a subjective, transcendental experience and not a datum that can be isolated in our objective and empirical world'.[65] It is simply impossible to pick on an event or series of events in a life and say that there a decision for or against God has been made. The Christian must, therefore, resist making a judgement about another individual's fate:

> In certain circumstances it is possible that nothing is hidden beneath an apparently very great offence because it can be just the phenomenon of a pre-personal situation, and behind the facade of bourgeois respectability there can be hidden a final, embittered and despairing 'no' to God . . .[66]

This hiddenness applies even to one's own decision. Because the 'actual situation of a person's freedom is not completely accessible to reflection' one can never know with certainty whether one's actions—even if clearly evil—are such as to be an actual decision against God, or whether they are a necessary factor imposed on one which one endures passively.[67] In this respect Rahner is very realistic about the complexities of moral motivation and the real effect that biological and environmental factors have on human behaviour. That is, he is realistic not only in recognizing that certain circumstances do mitigate guilt, but also in asserting that in some cases these factors will be so complex that a certain human judgement regarding guilt (or attitude to God) is impossible. On the one hand, this assertion of the hiddenness of decision stands as a warning to oneself:

> We never know with ultimate certainty whether we really are sinners. But although it can be suppressed, we do know with ultimate certainty that we really *can* be sinners, even when our bourgeois everyday life and our own reflexive manipulation of our motives appear to give us very good grades.[68]

[65] *Foundations*, 101.
[66] Ibid., 102. [67] Ibid., 104. [68] Ibid., 104.

On the other, the recognition that one can never truly judge someone else should encourage open-mindedness and the abandoning of a condemnatory attitude with regard to the fate of other people. Throughout Rahner's eschatology these two ideas run in parallel: a hope in the salvation of all, tempered by the recognition of the seriousness of human sinfulness—particularly one's own.

iii. Problems Raised by the Notion of an Individual Consummation

Rahner's interpretation of the traditional Christian doctrines of heaven and hell follows his hermeneutical principles and, by describing the character both of its achievement and of its loss, illustrates further what he means by consummation. This confirms his analysis of consummation which was looked at in the first half of this chapter. His comments on both heaven and hell stress that it is a relationship with God which is fulfilled or lost and that the fulfilment or loss is expressed particularly at the spiritual level. 'Spiritual' is not, however, to be taken to mean 'merely psychological': the states of the beatific vision and hell both cause an ontological change in the individual. However, besides the problem set out immediately above, regarding Rahner's opinion of predestination, there remain the two general difficulties with the notion of consummation which were noted earlier. First, it is unclear how a consummation which has been expressed in such individualistic terms could extend to humans or to the world generally, despite Rahner's insistence on a balance between individual and collective eschatologies. This problem will be addressed in the next chapter.

Secondly, by presenting heaven and hell (or consummation and its absence) as alternative outcomes of a human history of freedom, Rahner raises the question of what is the precise nature of the free act which determines the definitive fate of the individual. Rahner faces a dilemma: either the act which says 'yes' to God is so general and widespread a phenomenon that he is led into universalism (or at least to rob a decision for God of its special significance beyond any other moral action), or it is so specific that certain individuals are excluded even from the possibility of consummation. Rahner clearly rejects the universalist path:

even in his discussion of 'anonymous Christianity' he is careful to emphasize that the unthematic acceptance of God through a loving life is universally possible, but not necessarily universally actualized.[69] This notion of an unthematic faith appears in Rahner's more theoretical discussion; interestingly, when he comes to interpret specific Christian doctrines, he chooses more often to talk of the human freedom to make a choice for (or against) God. The implication in the context of dogmatic discussion seems to be that such decision is explicit (thematic) and it is thus much more of a restrictive criterion for the possibility of salvation. Rahner's interpretation of the doctrine of purgatory is his attempt to solve the problems which this fairly narrow definition causes.

C. THE POSSIBILITY OF HUMAN DEVELOPMENT AFTER DEATH

The problem is that if salvation, or consummation depends on the freedom to make an explicit choice for or against God, some people would seem to be excluded from the possibility of making this choice. In the previous chapter it was seen that Rahner's analysis of death and eternity led him to emphasize the importance of a decision for God 'in' death.[70] But, because of his view of life as being-unto-death (his concept of *prolixitas mortis*), Rahner is not committed to saying that this decision must take place at the precise biological moment of death, so he does not exclude from the possibility of decision those whose death was sudden and unexpected or those whose death was preceded by a period of mental incapacity (for example, unconsciousness, senile decay, or extreme and debilitating pain). In effect he is saying that the decision must be *before* what is usually seen as the moment of death. However, this theory still appears to exclude those who are mentally *never* able to make such a choice (due to infancy or the sort of mental disability or illness which would make a choice of this kind impossible). Rahner's first solution seems to be that although consummation is the fulfilment of a

[69] See above, p. 178 and n. 33.
[70] Chapter 5, section C. i.

history of freedom, it is possible that some people do not have such freedom (although one could never state precisely who does and who does not).[71] Later in his career, however, Rahner returns to the problem and examines it in the context of a discussion of purgatory.[72] The rest of this chapter will first look at the development of his interpretation of purgatory by examining the three contexts in his *Theological Investigations* which deal with the subject: three articles on indulgences, one article on the intermediate state and finally one article on purgatory itself. It will then ask whether Rahner's attempted solution of the problem of decision in fact causes more difficulties than it solves.

i. Doctrinal Definitions

As ever, Rahner has previous Roman Catholic doctrinal definitions in mind as he studies the concept of purgatory. These are particularly vague and tentative, because of the lack of strong scriptural grounding for the doctrine; however several broad themes emerge. Most fundamentally, purgatory is connected to the doctrine that sin cannot be cleansed in this life a second time by baptism: instead penance is required. If a baptized person should die repentant but without having completed any allotted penance, purification after death will take place: in other words penance and purgatory are seen as two forms of cleansing, before and after death respectively. Hence, the fate of those who are in purgatory is contrasted with that of those who go immediately to hell and those who go immediately to heaven.[73] This clearly suggests that purgatory is a temporal state between this life and one's final destiny. This impression of a temporal state is further reinforced by the following statements: first that the purification is a temporary punishment (in contrast to the eternal punishment of hell), secondly that it can vary in length according to the individual, and thirdly that it can be lessened or hastened for some individuals by the prayers of the Church.

A further aspect of the traditional doctrine which is very important for an understanding of Rahner's interpretation is that although it is a state of healing, purgatory is not an

[71] e.g. 'Christian Dying': *TI* xviii. 237 (first published in German, 1976).
[72] 'Purgatory': *TI* xix. 181–93 (first published in German 1980).
[73] See e.g. Denz., 838, 856–8, 1304–6.

opportunity for the unrepentant sinner to turn to God. Finally, one should note that although the Council of Trent famously condemned Luther's criticisms of the doctrine of purgatory, it also warned members of the Roman Church against the dangers of describing purgatory too vividly, instructing preachers to avoid 'the more difficult and subtle "questions" . . . and those which do not make for "edification" and from which there is very often no increase in piety'.[74] This is very much the style of Rahner's reinterpretation: he is eager to maintain just the essential points of the doctrine and those elements which make for the building up—the edification—of the faith of the average believer. He is scrupulously careful to avoid anything which smacks of superstition and which might alienate the modern Christian.

From this brief survey it is clear that the doctrine of purgatory as traditionally expressed rests on three major presuppositions: that the punishment which it involves is purificatory, that it takes place in a temporal intermediate state, and that it is not a state in which someone can make a fundamental decision for (or against) God. Rahner's attitude to the first two issues will be examined before looking at his specific discussion of purgatory as an opportunity for decision.

ii. Divine Punishment: The Doctrine of Indulgences

Rahner's articles on the doctrine of indulgences reveal his concept of the nature of the punishment due to sin. He believes that an individual's actions do not affect merely what he calls the 'innermost "kernel"' (*dem innersten 'Kern'*) of one's personhood; rather, they have ramifications for a wider environment, where the person's acts of freedom are objectified and 'frozen into permanent form and preserved'.[75] In the case of sin these consequences are painful to endure—they are therefore

[74] The Council also instructs: 'Those matters . . . which tend to a certain curiosity and superstition, or that savour of filthy lucre, let them prohibit as scandals and stumbling blocks to the faithful . . .' Denz., 1820 (Council of Trent, Session 25, (3 and 4 December 1563): Decree on Purgatory).

[75] Both quotations from 'A Brief Theological Study on Indulgence' (= 'A Brief Theological Study'): *TI* x. 151; *ST* viii. 473; see also 'Remarks on the Theology of Indulgences' (= 'Remarks'): *TI* ii. 197. Elsewhere, Rahner also talks of the many 'layers' of the individual, which expression conveys the same point. Thompson writes that for Rahner purgatory is a state 'in which the finality of one's decisions penetrates the whole breadth of one's many-levelled being' ('The Hope for Humanity', 612).

also sin's punishment.[76] The punishment is eternal and unconstructive if the obdurate will refuses to acknowledge the sin committed, but temporal and medicinal if the sin is acknowledged and the consequences 'accepted and endured to the bitter end'.[77] These consequences have to be endured even if the sinner acknowledges the sin in repentance, because the ramifications of any human action are concrete and cannot simply be wiped out again. Penance is the active acceptance of these ramifications in one's lifetime; purgatory is the enforced experience of them after death. So, in Rahner's view, the punishment of purgatory is intrinsic in the sense that humankind and the world are so constituted that sin punishes itself; it is not extrinsically imposed by a vengeful God.[78] It is not however merely the feeling of guilt, but rather the experience of the definitive ramifications of one's sin.[79] As with the doctrine of hell, Rahner is avoiding a purely psychological explanation of punishment.

It is important to note that Rahner believes that the purgatorial experience of the consequences of one's sin is both punishment and purification, both painful and perfecting (in contrast to the punishment of hell). This is because he sees purgatory as an essentially *con*structive not *de*structive experience, frequently describing it as 'integration' (*Integration*). He believes that each person consists of many layers which are disrupted by sin; the consequent distortion of the individual is experienced as the contradiction between how one is intended to be by God and what one has allowed oneself to become.[80] The integrative nature of purgatory reverses this distortion.

Another important point is that just as traditional doctrine emphasized that purgatory was only an option for those who were eventually destined for heaven, so Rahner stresses that integration is only possible for those who have made a decision

[76] 'Remarks': *TI* ii. 196.

[77] Ibid. Rahner here seems to be equating a permanent refusal to acknowledge sin with a decision against God: the outcome of both is non-consummation/hell.

[78] Ibid. 196. Nevertheless it is clear that God is ultimately responsible for the punishment, having created the universe with such a constitution. Compare Gregory of Nyssa's idea of pedagogy, which relies on the notion that the consequences of sin are bad for the sinner, either because God imposes punishment directly, or because he has created the universe in such a way that sin is followed by painful effects (Chapter 3, section **c. ii.**).

[79] Ibid. 197.

[80] 'A Brief Theological Study': *TI* x. 153.

for God in their lifetime.[81] The decision is itself described by Rahner as 'the love that is based on faith and hope'—it is possible, therefore, that this might include the sort of unthematic decision which Rahner envisages as being made by an 'anonymous Christian'.[82] However, in the resultant integration of the individual, acceptance of God seems to become thematic, because the fulfilled state is based on 'that love in which God and his neighbour are loved with his *whole* heart and with all his powers'.[83] Put more fully:

> perfect love is that which has orientated 'all the powers', i.e. all the manifold levels of reality in the complexity of man's make-up (*alle pluralen Wirklichkeiten des vielschichtigen Menschen*) purely to God, so that these, without themselves being suppressed or deprived of their true natures, become the 'material', the 'expression' and the 'manifestation' precisely of this love.[84]

Remembering that Rahner defined the beatific vision in terms of knowledge and of love, it now becomes clearer that the consummation of the individual which is achieved through integration is focused in particular on the perfect fulfilment of one's capacity for love and knowledge of God. It also becomes clear why Rahner emphasizes that the purification of purgatory cannot simply be wiped out (either by God or by the Church through indulgences): it is a necessary process without which this coming to perfect love cannot be achieved. Rahner's point about indulgences is that they do not (and were not originally intended to have) a juridical function, releasing souls from specific periods of purgation; rather they should have an intercessory role, in parallel with prayers of the Church for those in purgatory. Such intercession should be conceived as asking that the integrative process might be smoother or shorter—but not that it might be altogether abandoned. Abandonment of the process would not only be impossible but also unwelcome.

However, a major problem with Rahner's notion of integration

[81] Ibid., 157.

[82] Ibid. This article was first published in 1955, the article 'Anonymous Christians' in 1964, so it is difficult to conclude with any certainty that in this writing on indulgences, Rahner was intentionally including the possibility of an unthematic decision.

[83] Ibid.

[84] Ibid.: *TI* x. 157; *ST* viii. 479.

or perfection is that it seems to imply a temporal progress. Indeed, Rahner emphasizes at one point that the punishments of sin are traditionally described as temporal because 'they must be endured in a process of development over a period of time, and can only be overcome in this'.[85] This difficulty cannot be resolved by suggesting that by 'temporal punishments' Rahner means those consequences of sin which one experiences in this life; this is because he clearly believes that the integrative process of enduring the consequences of one's sins can take place before *or after* death. Hence, Rahner would seem to be committed to believing in a temporal purgatorial state after death. However, in these articles he often refers to death as the end of time for each individual. A comparison of two passages from the end of the article 'A Brief Theological Study on Indulgences' illustrates the problem. First he writes:

> certainly according to Christian doctrine death is the end of that period in which an eternal destiny is worked out. What comes 'afterwards' is not a prolongation of the period or its continuation in an endless series of new ages, but rather the definitive fixing and the eternal validity of what has come to be in time (*sondern die Endgültigkeit und ewige Gültigkeit des in der Zeit Gewordenen*).[86]

But shortly afterwards he insists that:

> precisely upon a Christian conception of the history of man as an individual, we must recognize the existence of *a further period of time between death and the final consummation of all things*, during which the acts performed in freedom during man's time on earth are brought to their maturity . . .(*ein Zeitraum der Ausreifung des in Freiheit zeitlich Getanen noch zwischen Tod und der Vollendung des Alls*)[87]

It is difficult to interpret these passages in any way which is not plainly contradictory.

Thus, although Rahner's study of the practice of indulgences illuminates his view of purgatorial punishment as integrative and not destructive and offers further insights into his view of the nature of decision, it is confusing as to the issue of time after death.

[85] 'A Brief Theological Study': *TI* x. 153; *ST* viii. 474: *'sie in einem zeitlichen Entwicklungprozeß ausgelitten und so überwunden werden können'*; see also 'Remarks': *TI* ii. 197.
[86] 'A Brief Theological Study': *TI* x. 164; *ST* viii. 486.
[87] Ibid.: *TI* x. 164–5 (my emphasis); *ST* viii. 486.

iii. A Temporal Interim State?

This question of a post-mortem temporal state is taken up again in the article '"The Intermediate State"'.[88] This asks whether it is coherent to say that there is a period between the death of the individual and his or her full consummation. The article appeared in 1975, several years after the articles on indulgences which we have looked at above. In the meantime Rahner had published his monograph *On the Theology of Death*, which emphasized that death means the end of the individual's temporal existence and the end of the period in which someone can decide for or against God. Perhaps as a consequence of this study of the nature of death, and due to the development of his theology as a whole, '"The Intermediate State"' expresses considerably more caution over the concept of any sort of process after death than the articles on indulgences. This caution is clear in the way in which he opens the article by asking 'How dogmatically binding is the concept of what we call "the intermediate state"?'[89] His answer rests on his hermeneutical distinction between dogma on the one hand and, on the other hand, the terms in which it is expressed, or the assumptions which underlie its expression.[90] That is, he asserts that the concept of the intermediate state is not itself dogma, but is the underlying assumption of many dogmatic statements about eschatology: not being dogmatically binding itself, the concept can 'remain open to the free discussions of theologians'.[91] It is not *necessarily* a false concept, but Rahner's own conclusion is that it is just an 'intellectual framework' which contains, as he puts it, 'a little harmless mythology' (*ein wenig harmlose Mythologie*).[92]

His reasons for thinking that the idea of the intermediate state is merely an intellectual framework are both historical and theological.[93] He attributes the historical genesis of the doctrine

[88] '"The Intermediate State"': *TI* xvii; *ST* xii: *'Über den "Zwischenzustand"'*. The quotation marks in the title indicate that for Rahner it is only the so-called intermediate state.

[89] Ibid.: *TI* xvii. 114.

[90] See above, Chapter 5, section B.

[91] '"The Intermediate State"' *TI* xvii. 114.

[92] Ibid.: *TI* xvii. 114, 123; *ST* xii. 466. Peter Phan comments that, despite ostensibly keeping an open mind on the matter, Rahner in fact *does* appear to deny the reality of an intermediate state: Phan, *Eternity in Time*, 132–3.

[93] The other two objections focus on the historical genesis of the idea of the intermediate state and on the status of the human soul, respectively.

not to scriptural evidence (which is inconclusive) but essentially to the problem of the delayed parousia. The tension caused by the Church asserting both that the righteous individual is saved upon his or her death and that there will be a general resurrection at the end of the world was solved by the positing of an intermediate, temporal, and bodiless state between the two events. However, since this was only a means of trying to understand eschatology and was never a central doctrine, Rahner emphasizes that it should not now be accorded the same importance as, for example, the doctrine of the resurrection.[94]

A second reason for Rahner's view that the intermediate state is just an intellectual framework and not a central doctrine is that it carries implications about time which are unwelcome to him. Time is described by Rahner as one of the 'enormous intellectual problems' in the debate. He asks:

> How are we to think of time and the temporality of a departed soul, if on the one hand the soul is already with God in its perfected state (*ihre Vollendung bei Gott besitzt*), but on the other has 'to wait' for the reassumption of its function towards its own body?[95]

Attempts to deal with the problem by postulating a temporal intermediate state merely add further difficulties, Rahner claims, because they raise awkward questions about human freedom: he assumes that a temporal human existence entails human freedom and that freedom after death threatens his firmly-held belief that a decision for or against God can only be made in this life. Rahner tries to solve the problem by denying the existence of any temporal state after death at all[96] and he suggests that it would not be heretical to assert that the single and total perfecting of a person is immediate upon, or in, death and that the resurrection of the flesh and general judgement coincide with individual judgement.[97] This standpoint follows the position of his articles

[94] Consequently, Rahner thinks that 'the single and total perfecting of a person in "body" and "soul" takes place immediately in and through death', not in an intermediate state (Dych, *Karl Rahner*, 144).

[95] '"The Intermediate State"': *TI* xvii. 118; *ST* xii. 460.

[96] Ibid.: *TI* xvii. 118; *ST* xii. 460: Rahner remarks that there are difficulties with 'the question of "time" "after" death' which do not arise 'if the one and total person is removed from empirical time through his death (*wenn der eine und ganze Mensch durch seinen Tod aus der empirischen Zeit herausgenommen wird*)'.

[97] Ibid.: *TI* xvii. 115. It is very difficult to express such assertions in language which

on death, but the suggestion that individual judgement and general resurrection are contemporaneous brings with it difficulties for the doctrine of the resurrection itself. These will be discussed in the next chapter.[98]

Having rejected the notion of purgatory as a temporal interim state, Rahner's alternative seems, therefore, to be the consummation of the whole person in the moment of death. As a theological model for this he suggests (his own interpretation of) the doctrine of the assumption of the Virgin Mary, but beyond this he offers little clarification of the idea.[99] One issue in particular which needs elucidation is the nature of the purification involved in purgatory. If one is said to undergo an ontological change through experiencing the ramifications of one's sin, does it make sense to suggest that this change can be timeless? Does this not contradict Rahner's previous assertion that the consequences of sin 'must be endured in a process of development over a period of time'?[100] For further debate on the subject one must turn to his article on 'Purgatory', written some years later in 1980.

iv. Purgatory

The article 'Purgatory', but for the briefest of introductions, is written as a dialogue between two unnamed theologians.[101] Neither is explicitly or implicitly identified as Rahner himself, suggesting that he is distancing himself from each one's views because of his own ambivalence on the subject. The article has all the tone of an exploratory and conclusionless discussion rather than a piece of doctrinal exposition; nevertheless, it offers significant clues as to the direction in which Rahner's

reflects Rahner's belief that the consummation of the person is a timeless state. Although Rahner himself talks in terms of general and individual judgements coinciding, perhaps it would be more satisfactory to talk of the two theological concepts being the same, or expressing the same truth.

[98] See below, Chapter 7, section c.

[99] '"The Intermediate State"': *TI* xvii. 122–3. But there are problems with this—especially the difficulty of translating this model which applies to one person, to all the blessed. For a dogmatic statement on the assumption of the Virgin Mary (by Pius XII in 1950) see Denz., 3903.

[100] 'A Brief Theological Study': *TI* x. 153; see above, p. 194.

[101] Both theologians are anonymous in the text, but for the sake of clarity, they will be referred to as 'first theologian' and 'second theologian' according to the order in which they speak.

ideas were heading. The first theologian's words express eschatological views which Rahner has already established in previous articles in *Theological Investigations*; these have been outlined above. In contrast, the second theologian's discussion is clearly an advance on what Rahner has previously been prepared to assert. But neither Rahner as the author of the dialogue, nor the first theologian offers an outright denial of what the second has to say. The dialogue form certainly indicates an uncertainty in Rahner's mind: it is in a sense a conversation with himself. But there is no need to think that he is completely disassociating himself from any of the views expressed in the article; indeed, the piece is best interpreted in a way which sees Rahner as having some sympathy with both theologians.

The first theologian shares the presupposition of Rahner's study of indulgences that an individual human is an inwardly plural being and that purgatory is the process which integrates these many layers.[102] He also insists that death is the end of temporality for the individual but that he or she nevertheless has 'permanency' (*Bleibendheit*) after death.[103] His reason for saying this is that 'it seems to me that things cannot simply go on after death in temporal extension (*in zeitlicher Erstreckung*), since that would mean that the finality of judgement at death (at least for someone who has come to a radical personal decision in his earthly life) is no longer credible'.[104] Although it is unclear what 'permanency' in a non-temporal context means, the idea that timelessness brings finality and completion does reflect that held by Rahner in *On the Theology of Death*; consequently, one should assume that the first theologian reflects Rahner's own metaphysical views when he says that time is 'far from being a determination of reality that is always and everywhere valid'.[105]

Up to this point then, all is familiar territory and the repetition of the above ideas emphasizes that they are central features of

[102] 'Purgatory': *TI* xix. 184–5.

[103] Ibid.: *TI* xix. 183; *ST* xiv. 437.

[104] Ibid.: *TI* xix. 183; *ST* xiv. 437–8. One should note, for its relevance to Rahner's doctrine of the decision for or against God, that the inclusion of the phrase 'at least for someone who has come to a radical personal decision in his earthly life' is a modification of his view in the earlier articles which were looked at in this chapter, which appeared to suggest that those who had made no decision for God were on a par with those who had made a decision against God.

[105] Ibid.: *TI* xix. 184; *ST* xiv. 438: '*noch lange nicht eine Wirklichkeitsbestimmung, die immer und überall Geltung habe*'.

Rahner's eschatology. However, a new element in the discussion is the first theologian's full realization of the difficulty caused by claiming that the integration of the individual can be both a process and timeless. He offers two possible resolutions of the problem. The first runs as follows:

> Perhaps the unintegrated elements in man are incorporated into the final personal decision, now become definitive (*endgültig*) in death, in a lengthy 'process' (*in einem längeren 'Prozeß'*) which (while maintaining what I said earlier about the release of the dead person from our time) might nevertheless be seen as analogous to the present time (*analog zu unserer Zeit)* in a way that by and large corresponds to the traditional idea of purgatory.[106]

There are two separate difficulties with this solution. First, the speaker is not clear about how he is using temporal words such as 'time', 'process', and 'lengthy'. Sometimes he seems to encourage us to think of their use as metaphorical, since he suggests that the notion of time as used in the traditional doctrine of purgatory does not refer directly to the properties of what we understood as 'real' time, but rather illustrates the complex plurality of each individual's structure.[107] Elsewhere, he appears to be thinking in terms of analogy, for example stating that the so-called process of purification should be 'seen at least analogously as taking place in time'.[108] If he is harking back to Aquinas' use of the idea of analogy, it is difficult to see how there can be such a thing as something a bit like, but not exactly like time as we experience it now. Two numerically distinct but qualitatively identical time-scales may possibly be conceivable, but something merely similar to 'our' time is not, because time would appear to be an absolute concept which either applies or does not; it admits of no half-way stages. If the first theologian means that purification will take place in a perfect state in which individuals experience time without the shortcomings of their earthly experience of time (such as decay or fleetingness), it is still *time* which they are experiencing: it is merely the context of that time which has changed.[109]

[106] Ibid.: *TI* xix. 185; *ST* xiv. 439.

[107] Ibid.: *TI* xix. 185–6.

[108] Ibid.: *TI* xix. 185; *ST* xiv. 440: *'auch analog zeithaft gedachtes'*.

[109] Similarly, the Platonic claims that time entails change and that change entails decay can both be challenged by saying that it is merely the current human experience of time which is impossible to divorce from the experience of change and decay. Time in

The second problem is that, despite the speaker's contention that the individual does leave the world, nevertheless he states that the subject 'can and must still continue in its own way to participate in the fundamental temporality and historicity of the world, even if it has reached its consummation in the immediate vision of God (*selbst sogar wenn es durch die unmittelbare Anschauung Gottes vollendet ist*)'.[110] It is very unclear how humans could participate in this 'fundamental temporality and historicity' unless they were themselves temporal.

The second solution offered by the first theologian is that the so-called process of purgatory occurs in the moment of death itself:

> Why could not the 'duration' of the event of purification (*die 'Dauer' des Reinigungsgeschehens*) be identified with the (diverse) depth and intensity of the pain that man experiences in death itself, since there is a terrible difference between what he actually is and what he ought to be?[111]

If by the idea of purgatory occurring in death the first theologian means that there was in fact no process and that purgatory should be viewed as timeless, this would be by far the more convincing solution (although it would still leave the problem of whether integration or purification could take place in a timeless state). However, the issue is again confused by an attempt to introduce an odd concept of time:

> If someone were to introduce an element of time into the very occurrence of death (in the withdrawal from the present world) (*in den Vorgang des Todes selbst (in der Loslösung von der irdischen Welt)*), which need not be regarded as a priori unreasonable, then it would still be possible to avoid the idea of a time in 'purgatory' 'after' (*'nach'*) death and there would be no need subsequently to qualify this idea with the statement that time in purgatory is only analogous to the time with which we are familiar (*nur 'analog' zu unserer bekannten Zeit*).[112]

itself remains the same, whether accompanied by change and decay or not. In contrast, an analogical interpretation of the concept of love, for example, must surely claim that there is a profound difference between divine and human love, although they are similar, and that this difference is inherent in the love itself, not just due to the fact that different subjects are expressing the love.

[110] 'Purgatory': *TI* xix. 185; *ST* xiv. 440.

[111] Ibid.: *TI* xix. 186; *ST* xiv. 441; this clearly echoes Rahner's suggestion towards the end of the article '"The Intermediate State"'.

[112] 'Purgatory': *TI* xix. 187; *ST* xiv. 442.

This raises more questions than it solves. How long is death? Is death seen as the moment of physical death as certified by a doctor, or as something else?[113]

The first theologian concludes his exposition of the doctrine of purgatory by asserting that what the doctrine really means for the ordinary believer: we surrender ourselves as imperfect humans 'into the hands of an infinite loving God who brings everything to perfection (*der alles vollendet*)'.[114] This apparent expression of a universal hope leads the second theologian to take what he claims to be a wider view of the doctrine of purgatory: one should indeed look at what it means for the individual believer, but in addition one should look at its wider context in beliefs about life after death as a whole—and not just Christian ones. He first notes that the traditional doctrine has tended to concentrate on the human individual and left the relationship of the soul to the world obscure; he appears to suggest that in the state traditionally called purgatory the individual shares in the consummation of the world and that therefore his or her relationship to the world in death must be reassessed.[115] This reflects what Rahner wrote in his earlier works about the 'pan-cosmic' relationship of the soul to the material world in death; the theme also occurs in Rahner's interpretation of the doctrine of the resurrection.[116]

However, the second theologian's main concern is the nature of the purification in purgatory. He first criticizes the tendency of Christian eschatology to assume that the individual, if he or she has decided for God, comes immediately to judgement and then to the beatific vision and thus that 'any further development of personal history is superseded'.[117] He admits that this view is tempered by the concept of purgatory, which he summarizes as follows:

It places between death and radical eschatology understood in the light of God a (brief) intermediate state in which, on the one hand, man's

[113] Rahner does not seem to be referring here to his idea that the whole of life is a being-unto-death, because he speaks of 'withdrawal from the world' (ibid.).

[114] Ibid.

[115] Ibid.: *TI* xix. 189. This may perhaps be intended to pick up on the problem of the soul's relationship to the world which was noted in the first theologian's exposition.

[116] See below, Chapter 7, section c.

[117] 'Purgatory': *TI* xix. 188.

radical consummation is not yet supposed to exist (whether this 'not yet' is imagined or contrasted with our normal categories of time) and in which, on the other hand, things do not simply go on as before.[118]

However, he objects to the traditional view of the nature of purgatory being the expiation of sin through suffering, because it is 'too formal and abstract' with no connection to the true nature of a soul.[119] He contrasts the Christian emphasis on a definitive state after death with the eschatologies of other religious traditions (left unnamed) which, although 'complex' and 'confining' and with a dubious concept of time, do 'have ideas of a further development of those who have died, partly even of wholly welcome further developments, of an enduring and active relationship with the world, the environment, and the milieu to which they formerly belonged (*von einem bleibenden und aktiven Bezug auf die frühere Welt, Umwelt und Mitwelt*)'.[120] The particular development which the second theologian is thinking of is that which would be involved in making a decision for or against God. He is not concerned with the possibility of recanting for those who have made a decision against God, but rather with the possibility of making any decision at all for those who were unable to do so in this life. He describes as 'dreadful' the idea that there might be people whom God does not, in effect, allow to make a decision.[121] His suggested solution is the following:

If there is such a state as purgatory which does not come into existence merely by an external (*äußeres*) decree and intervention of God, but is a conatural (*konnaturale*) consequence of the nature of the plural human being, then I could imagine that it might offer opportunities and scope for a postmortal history of freedom (*post-mortale Freiheitsgeschichte*) to someone who had been denied such a history in his early life.[122]

This might not at first sight appear to fit with traditional Roman Catholic doctrine, but the second theologian concludes that the Christian eschatological dogmas which assert the necessity of turning to God before death do not apply to *all* humans (as has traditionally been assumed) but merely to 'those who have

[118] 'Purgatory': *TI* xix. 189.
[119] Ibid.
[120] Ibid.: *TI* xix. 189; *ST* xiv. 445.
[121] Ibid.: *TI* xix. 191.
[122] Ibid.: *TI* xix. 191; *ST* xiv. 447.

fulfilled themselves and reached finality in a free decision'.[123] The second theologian's view seems to be that the principle that 'with the death of a person his history of freedom is always and inevitably at an end, that he is definitely judged according to his works in this life' is correct, but simply has a narrower range of application than has previously been suggested.[124] He defends his departure from the usual interpretation of purgatory by pointing out that the doctrines of limbo and the salvation of baptized infants show that in the past Christians have been willing to make exceptions to the rule that salvation is dependent on a personal decision. His reference to works leaves open the possibility of an unthematic decision for God; however, this is not his direct concern since he is more interested in those who have no opportunity to make any sort of decision at all.[125]

Peter Phan suggests that because the second theologian refers to the eschatologies of other traditions, Rahner is attempting 'to correlate the doctrine of purgatory and the doctrine of reincarnation' and is 'presenting a modified version of the doctrine of reincarnation as compatible with the Christian faith'.[126] This is to overstate the case. Reincarnation means the taking up of a further bodily life in this or another world. It usually carries with it the implication that this further life will be similar to any previous life or lives with respect to the opportunity for salvation. The second theologian does take from this tradition the notion of a 'post-mortal history of freedom', but he seems to imagine that this history of freedom will take place in an intermediate state very different from life on earth, rather than in a new life on earth. He does think that the individual 'in' purgatory will be in some close relationship with the world—but he also thinks that of those in heaven, so it cannot be equated with most notions of reincarnation. A close connection with the world should not be confused with a second life in the world. Furthermore, the second theologian expresses impatience with the idea of the 'migration' of souls (i.e. reincarnation) and he assumes that the opportunity for decision will occur *either* in an earthly life *or* in

[123] Ibid.: *TI* xix. 190.

[124] Ibid. 191.

[125] Since this article was written well after that on 'Anonymous Christians', it is clearly possible that Rahner did intend the reference to works to include those who lived a life of love but who had not received the Christian revelation in its particular historical form; however, if this was his intention, he does not make it explicit.

[126] Phan, *Eternity in Time*, 133–4.

purgatory. These two states are explicitly contrasted and indeed the whole point of the second theologian's argument is that the state of purgatory has such a nature that it will make a decision for God possible for precisely—and only—those who did not have that opportunity in their earthly life. All this seems to suggest that the second theologian is only correlating the doctrine of purgatory with the concept of reincarnation insofar as he is admitting the coherence of the concept of personal development (and thus of a decision for God) after death.

The second theologian's argument in favour of the possibility of a time after death in which those who had previously not had the opportunity might decide for God is an interesting example of the encounter between traditional Catholic theology and the pluralism of the twentieth century. It is implicitly motivated by beliefs in the value of each human soul and in the importance of freedom of decision in the human relationship with God. It tacitly assumes that it would offend the Christian notion of God as just and loving for some to miss salvation because they were not able to decide for God in their lifetime and that it would offend human autonomy for salvation to be imposed upon them without the involvement of the human will.

However, there are major difficulties with the second theologian's suggestions. The first problem is that the theologian who proposes the possibility of decision after death does not make clear the category of people to whom this opportunity might apply. He mentions infants and seems to exclude those who have positively decided against God, but is otherwise vague. Rahner himself suggests that very few people will lack an opportunity for decision: because of the possibility of saying 'yes' or 'no' unthematically, it is by no means restricted only to those who have heard the Christian gospel. On the contrary, Rahner believes that all who have freedom have the opportunity to decide. Thus, if he is following Rahner's general presuppositions about freedom, the second theologian's remarks would seem to apply only to those who lack genuine human freedom. In *Foundations of Christian Faith* Rahner suggests that the mentally handicapped might suffer this lack, but he is generally reluctant to speculate on who else might do so.[127]

[127] *Foundations*, 106.

Nevertheless, a second problem remains: if the logical and theological possibility of a decision after death is admitted and if purgatory 'does not come into existence merely by an external decree and intervention of God, but is a conatural consequence of the nature of the plural human being', it is difficult to see why it should be a possibility for some people and not for others.[128] Could it provide the opportunity for repentance for those who had previously rejected God? More dangerously, could it allow those who had chosen God in their lives to change that decision? This problem can be looked at from two points-of-view. On the one hand, some might want to put the charge that in opening the lock-gate to admit a trickle of souls (perhaps infants and those whose mental or psychological state prevents any decision), the second theologian has also admitted a flood (any souls who have not explicitly decided for God in their lifetime). It seems clear, however, that the second theologian thinks that there is something about a decision for or against God which is definitive. It has been seen several times that Rahner views freedom not as the ability to change one's decisions time and time again, but rather as the ability to make a definitive decision. Prime amongst such decisions is that for God. The second theologian appears to share such a view. The reason why the opportunity for decision can only be opened up to those who have not yet made one at all is not some arbitrary criterion, but is the fact that it is simply impossible for a definitive choice to be rendered non-definitive. On the other hand, if the second theologian's views reflect Rahner's own and given that Rahner has elsewhere clearly expressed the view that one should as a Christian hope for the salvation of all, others might argue that the second theologian does not go far enough. He opens up the possibility of salvation for those who did not have the opportunity to decide for God in their lifetime, but denies that opportunity to those who rejected God before they died. It could be strongly argued that if one is to have a realistic hope of the salvation of all it is precisely to this category of person that the post-mortem opportunity for decision must be granted. If a decision against God in this lifetime is absolutely definitive then the hope for the salvation of all is in fact hopeless.

[128] See above, p. 202 for the full quote and reference.

Thirdly, there is the question of time and eternity. The first theologian suggested that references to time, development, and process in the context of purgatory simply indicate the multi-faceted character of human nature and its need to be integrated, and that they do not imply a temporal framework equivalent to that of a human life. Even if this suggestion is coherent, it does not seem at all coherent for the second theologian to claim (as he does implicitly) that even the sort of human development involved in a free decision can also be timeless. For the concept of decision must surely involve a past and a present: a decision is a crux and a turning-point. Even if reached after a gradual process, the moment of decision marks the point at which what was a possibility has become definitive. It may be questioned whether this all-or-nothing character of decision is the appropriate way to describe faith in God, but given that Rahner has chosen this way and given that he continually emphasizes the importance of a definitive choice, it is difficult to avoid the conclusion that a decision must be made in time, whether before or after death. This, however, contradicts his belief that life 'after' death is a timeless eternity.[129] Moreover, if one considers that purgatory must be a state which is temporal or analogous to time, in order for the concept of decision to make sense, then the definitiveness of decisions made in this lifetime is under threat. For, in Rahner's view it is precisely the timelessness of death which renders them definitive. If there is a temporal state after the moment of death in which some can decide, there seems to be no strong reason why those who have already decided cannot change their minds. And so one returns to the first problem mentioned above.

This chapter has assessed the coherence of Rahner's individual eschatology, with a particular emphasis on the role of a decision for God as the immanent factor in the individual's consummation. His emphasis on the universality of God's self-communication together with the possibility of an unthematic acceptance of God and an explicit decision for God made in purgatory explains how he is able to express a hope that all people might be saved. However, it has been seen that in

[129] For a similar criticism, see Thompson, 'The Hope for Humanity', 166–7: 'If eternity were not so much "finality" as a limit toward which we tend, then it could be conceived in more processive and dynamic terms.'

whatever way this immanent consummation is expressed it brings with it various problems connected with human free decision and with time. These will be discussed again in Chapter 8. The next chapter will investigate the concept of decision for God in the context of the collective consummation of humanity and the world.

7

The Consummation of the World's History of Freedom

The previous chapter looked at Karl Rahner's concept of consummation in theoretical terms as the definitive outcome of a personal and individual history of freedom. It was then seen how Rahner reinterpreted the traditional doctrines of heaven, hell, and purgatory. This clarified the meaning of consummation to a certain extent, revealing a focus on human fulfilment in terms of knowledge and love of God. However, Rahner's interpretation of individual eschatology left several problems: in particular it highlighted the difficulty of understanding fulfilment or reintegration as a timeless state and the problems caused by claiming that reintegration is based on human decision. Rahner's concept of 'anonymous Christians' (with the related idea of an unthematic decision for God) and his exploration of the concept of purgatory (allowing for a post-mortem decision) were both attempts to solve some of the difficulties caused by an emphasis on human decision. A further question remains, however: if consummation is dependent on human decision, does this decision need to be made by an individual, or can it be made at the collective level? In other words, one needs to ask how the individualistic framework of consummation which was examined in the last chapter might be extended to a collective eschatology. The present chapter will focus on this issue in particular. Like the previous chapter it will move from Rahner's theoretical statements about consummation to his application of them to traditional Christian eschatology.

A. CONSUMMATION AS A COLLECTIVE PHENOMENON

In Chapter 5 it was seen that Rahner believes that the structure of human existence means that an individual human history is tending towards a meaningful end—a consummation—which is 'that for which the event considered precisely in its temporal development as event took place, that which it "sought" and in which the event itself finds its meaning and its justification'.[1] It was also noted that he consequently thinks that mere matter in isolation cannot be consummated, since it does not have a structure which is both material and spiritual, and therefore free and self-transcendent. Thus, the word 'consummation' is incorrectly applied to either an individual physical event or the sum total of these events. Rahner next asks whether 'consummation' can be used of all human personal histories considered as a unity or of the unity of the whole material and spiritual world. Can either of these be said to possess a 'spiritual and personal history' as an individual does?

Rahner explicitly states that all he has said regarding the consummation of the individual can be said about humankind as a whole and he emphatically asserts the unity of humanity:

> Mankind is not the final summing-up, at the conceptual level (*die nachträgliche, gedankliche Summierung*), of all the particular persons endowed with spiritual faculties and of their personal histories as free individuals. On the contrary, in respect of its origin, its existence and its determination (*in Ursprung, Sein und Bestimmung*) mankind constitutes a unity (*eine Einheit*).[2]

He also stresses that God's self-bestowal—in other words the divine offer of grace—is offered just as much to this unity as to individuals. This idea is given scriptural authority by the use in the Bible of such concepts as the 'people of God', 'covenant', 'communion of saints' and 'kingdom of God' which indicate God's offer of salvation or revelation to certain groups.[3] Nevertheless, Rahner needs more reasoning to support his claim that

[1] 'Immanent and Transcendent Consummation of the World' (= 'Immanent and Transcendent Consummation): *TI* x. 275. See above, Chapter 5 section C. i. and ii.

[2] Ibid.: *TI* x. 284; *ST* viii. 603–4.

[3] Ibid.: *TI* x. 284.

humans form such a unity, for it is far from obviously true. Among the more prominent of the difficulties of the view is the question of salvation: Rahner has talked much of a personal response to grace, but in what way could there be a collective response without the meaning of individual human freedom (which he elsewhere greatly emphasizes) being called into question?

The question of the consummation of the world considered as a unity of material and spiritual elements is even more complex. Rahner stresses at a general level what he has said about matter and spirit at the individual level:

> The physical world is not merely the outward stage upon which the history of the spirit, to which matter is basically alien, is played, such that it tends as its outcome to quit this stage as swiftly as possible in order really to achieve full and complete spirituality in a world beyond that of matter. In a metaphysical interpretation matter is considered rather as that other factor which is necessary, in which and upon which alone *a finite and creaturely* spirituality can be *precisely that which* it is of its nature, and can bring this to its fullness. And this is constituted by the attributes of self-awareness, transcendence and freedom (*eine endliche, kreatürliche Geistigkeit das sein und sich vollziehen kann, was sie im Wesen ist: Selbstbewüßtsein, Transzendenz und Freiheit*).[4]

> [Matter] endures as an intrinsic element of the spirit and of its history even in its consummation (*Sie bleibt als inneres Moment des Geistes und seiner Geschichte auch in dessen Vollendung*).[5]

His implicit reasoning would appear to be that if there is unity between matter and spirit at an individual level and if there is a unity of all individuals then it is appropriate to speak of a general unity of spirit and matter.[6] There are several problems with this. First, there is the difficulty of asserting the unity of all humans, as mentioned above. Secondly, a unity of all personal spirits and their bodies does not account for all the matter in the world. What about animals and inorganic matter? Can they be considered as part of a unity with the matter of human beings? The problem is exacerbated by the fact that, even when he is writing

[4] 'Immanent and Transcendent Consummation of the World': *TI* x. 285; *ST* viii. 605 (Rahner's emphases).

[5] Ibid.: *TI* x. 289; *ST* viii. 609.

[6] For a discussion of the unity of matter and spirit at the individual level, see above Chapter 4, section B.

in the context of the consummation of the whole world, frequently Rahner sounds as if he is just thinking about the unity of matter and spirit in the human individual:

Matter exhibits its 'spirituality' in that it appears as an intrinsic co-principle (*inneres Konprinzip*) in a spiritual and personal being, and shares in the destiny of this being.[7]

Presumably, Rahner assumes that this unity extends to all humanity, in so far as humanity is an organic whole of spiritual and material persons. However, Rahner does not appear to demonstrate how the same unity applies to the entire universe.[8]

One clue to a resolution of this particular problem may be in Rahner's view of what constitutes the human body as expressed in the article 'The Body in the Order of Salvation'.[9] In this he explains that the body, as expression of the spirit, does not (if one goes beyond everyday usage) stop where the skin stops, but is 'an open system (*ein offenes System*)'.[10] In a sense—and he admits that this is an exaggeration—all humans live in the one body of the world and one can say: 'Through bodiliness the whole world belongs to me from the start in everything that happens.'[11] Suggesting that the states of heaven and hell are distinguished from each other by the way in which humans accept the world they live in—by how humans live actively and suffer passively—Rahner explains how his extended view of the body elucidates the Christian view of consummation:

This one 'concrete' existence in which we consummate our own spiritual, final liberty (*wir unsere eigene geistige, endgültige Freiheit vollziehen*), is itself in a dynamic history which sometime ends in transfiguration (*in Verklärung*), in a reality not only of the spiritual person, but also of his common sphere of being (*ihres gemeinsam Daseinsraumes*). The question then arises: how do I accept the final

[7] 'Immanent and Transcendent Consummation': *TI* x. 287; *ST* viii. 607.

[8] Philip Geister argues that Rahner does offer a convincing account of a single albeit bi-polar reality (as opposed to a dualistic schema); the problem is that matter is portrayed as dependent on and inferior to human spirit, with the result that Rahner's claims to a cosmological eschatology and a move away from individualism are undermined. Philip Geister, *Aufhebung zur Eigentlichkeit: Zur Problematik kosmologischer Eschatologie in der Theologie Karl Rahners* (= *Uppsala Studies in Faiths and Ideologies*, 5) (Acta Universitatis Upsaliensis, Uppsala, 1996), *passim.*

[9] *TI* xvii. 71–89.

[10] 'The Body in the Order of Salvation': *TI* xvii. 87; *ST* xii. 426.

[11] Ibid.: *TI* xvii. 88, 87.

condition of the sphere in which I necessarily am? Do I accept it as the transfigured world (*das verklärte Welt*), or as what the Bible calls hell fire?

The body is therefore nothing other than the self-consummation of the spirit in space and time (*Der Leib also ist nichts anderes als das raum-zeitliche Sich-selbst-Vollziehen des Geistes*). But this self-consummation (*Selbstvollzug*) of everything except God is of such a kind that it is essentially ambiguous and takes place in a sphere of existence in which all men and women communicate with one another from the very beginning.[12]

This passage would seem to suggest that the rest of the world is consummated as the extended 'body' of the human spirit and fits with Rahner's description of the spirit being in the *world* not in a *body*.[13]

This conclusion raises the related question of what form the consummation of the whole world might ultimately take. Sometimes Rahner even seems unclear as to whether matter is the (albeit necessary) *context* for spiritual consummation or whether matter is itself consummated. The latter seems to be Rahner's usual view, although as to the quality of consummated matter he admits ignorance, emphasizing that it is the absolute mystery of God to which the world is moving and that the consummation is therefore profoundly incomprehensible. Referring to 1 Corinthians 15: 35–56, in which Paul emphasizes that the risen body will be 'spiritual'—both the same and yet not the same as the earthly body—Rahner states that 'we are totally incapable of forming any conception whatever of the mode of existence of matter (*der Seinsweise der Materie*) in the consummation of the free history of the spirit'.[14] This question of the form of the consummation of the world will be examined further in the following two sections.[15]

Finally there is the problem of freedom and responsibility. Often, when talking of the collective consummation of the world, Rahner puts a great deal of emphasis on the divine aspect of that consummation:

[12] 'The Body in the Order of Salvation': *TI* xvii. 88; *ST* xii. 427.

[13] Geister seems to confirm this hyposthesis, by arguing that the world is consummated as the body of the incarnate and risen Christ: Geister, *Aufhebung zur Eigentlichkeit*, ch. 4, esp. 57–8.

[14] 'Immanent and Transcendent Consummation': *TI* x. 289; *ST* viii. 609.

[15] See below, sections B. and C.

[The material world's] movement towards its consummation is, right from the start, sustained by divine power, which consists in the love which bestows itself absolutely in freedom. In that this is and remains that which transcends all that is finite (*das alles Endliche Transzendierende*), it is the most immanent element in every creature (*das Immanenteste aller Kreatur*).[16]

Particularly the identification of the transcendent with that which is most immanent might seem to threaten the concept of freedom in the world. However, it seems clear from Rahner's general concept of consummation that the world must be self-transcendent in order to be consummated and that freedom is the necessary condition for the possibility of that self-transcendence. The world must be free even to reject God:

this self-transcendence of the material world in spirit and freedom takes place in history, in a contest therefore, in which sin is also possible and which can lead to a radical refusal of God.[17]

But how can the world as a whole be said to reject God? Is Rahner suggesting that it is possible that no-one and nothing will be saved?—or that God's saving will, despite being universal, might be entirely ineffective? This is precisely what he denies in his eschatological hermeneutics: one *can* claim that *some* have already been saved, or one can make no sense of scriptural statements about Christ's victory.

Rahner sometimes implies that the freedom of the world is intimately connected (if not reducible to) that freedom which resides in individuals: this is conveyed by the use of the first-person voice in one of the passages quoted above: 'how do *I* accept the final condition of the sphere in which I necessarily am? Do *I* accept it as the transfigured world, or as what the Bible calls hell fire?'[18] But this raises a problem: if individuals are to some extent responsible for the transformation of the whole world, how is this transformation affected by individuals making different decisions (for or against God)? Could one person's decision affect the destiny of the world, or even of a part of the world beyond one's own body?

In other contexts, Rahner seems to suggest that the freedom of

[16] 'Immanent and Transcendent Consummation': *TI* x. 289; *ST* viii. 609.

[17] Ibid.: *TI* x. 288.

[18] 'The Body in the Order of Salvation': *TI* xvii. 88 (quoted above, pp. 211–12).

the world lies less in the decisions of human individuals, and more in the universal creativity found in the world:

> The material world as such, so long as it remains confined to itself, has no consummation . . . But it is perfectly possible to accept that the material world, by reason of its essential orientation (*wesentlichen Bezogenheit*) to the spirit, is sustained from the very outset by that creative impetus (*schöpferischen Dynamik*), implanted by God, by which it tends towards the spirit as the goal of the self-transcendence of the material element (*das Ziel der Selbsttranszendenz des Materiellen*).[19]

Rahner explains this 'impetus' as the impetus to create a material and spiritual world which is the subject of God's self-bestowal; in other words, he seems to be envisaging the world itself as stretching out to God in a continuous process of recreating itself as part of God's creation. In writing this, he might be taken to mean an impetus which is non-human, or at least not exclusively human. Nevertheless, it seems clear from his other writings that it is by virtue of humankind that the world recreates itself: for example, Rahner often makes the point that humans are involved in the process of the recreation of the world by the means of modern technology. This would suggest that, in saying that the world transcends itself, Rahner does not mean that the world is ever tending to a more spiritual existence in a way that seems divorced from human effort—he is not espousing a version of the Teilhardian idea of the universe tending in an evolutionary development towards an ultimate Omega point. The word 'impetus' (*Dynamik*) might seem to suggest an 'inbuilt' or natural impulse, but this meaning is in fact far from Rahner's intentions. Rather, creativity is very much dependent on human effort, and particularly human effort at a collective level.

The notion of the world's 'creative impetus' is thus an important one, for it specifies how the freedom of humanity as a whole is expressed, just as the concept of decision specifies how freedom in a human individual is expressed. Because creativity is grounded in human freedom, and because it is a God-given freedom which brings with it responsibility, Rahner often refers to this creativity as 'the Christian task'. As with the notion of decision in the individual, there is a complex relationship in Rahner's theology of the Christian task between human freedom

[19] 'Immanent and Transcendent Consummation': *TI* x. 288; *ST* viii. 608.

(immanent consummation) and divine grace (transcendent consummation). This relationship will be examined in the next section.

B. DIVINE CONSUMMATION AND THE CHRISTIAN TASK

It is particularly important to clarify what Rahner means by freedom with respect to humanity as a whole, because it has a direct bearing on his views about universal salvation. If he were to stress too much the human effort involved, he might run the risk of creating a new form of Pelagianism, being wildly over-optimistic about human powers—a danger which Rahner himself sees in secular ideologies and utopianism. Alternatively, if he were to stress human effort but with a very pessimistic attitude to human power to change the world he would seriously undermine his own professed hope for universal salvation. By contrast, if he were to over-emphasize divine grace in such a way that the whole world is viewed as heading inexorably towards (a positive) consummation, he would not only be led to an outright assertion of universal salvation, but would also deny the immanent and free aspect of consummation that he has elsewhere stressed as being so vital. This section will examine this difficulty by looking at Rahner's view of the nature, the limits and the divine fulfilment of the Christian task.

i. The Nature of the Christian Task

In order to investigate the interplay between transcendent and immanent consummation in a collective consummation, the precise nature of the task before humanity must be investigated (just as Rahner's concept of personal decision was examined in the previous chapter in relation to the individual consummation). Does Christianity prescribe a detailed programme of action, or any specific tasks, or does it only give general guidance about the sort of behaviour that is required? Is it to be undertaken collectively by the institution of the Church or by individual Christians in their respective walks of life? Is the task only to be achieved in a Christian context or in the secular world at large? Finally, is it the task of Christians alone or can it be shared by those of other faiths or of no faith at all?

With regard to the first of these questions—as to whether the task is general or specific—Rahner is quite clear that Christianity cannot make detailed predictions, programmes, or prescriptions for the future.[20] However, he does emphasize that the individual does have the moral law of nature and 'the abstract principles of the unchanging gospel' which he or she must translate into specific imperatives.[21] Perhaps the pre-eminent reason why Christianity cannot provide the believer with hard-and-fast rules is that the environment and historical context is constantly changing. In the twentieth century, humans have reached a stage in their development in which they can change their environment and even their very selves:

> The man of today and tomorrow is the man of technology, of automation and cybernetics . . . [He] fashions his own environment . . . [He] applies his technical planning power of transformation even to himself . . . Man is becoming his own creator.[22]

So, although one can establish *general* norms of 'God-conformed' human behaviour, there is also a need for specific imperatives and programmes determined by the historical context and derived from the general norms.[23] Hence Rahner refers to the Christian's intramundane task as a 'problem'—its nature is not immediately obvious and there may be false steps on the way towards finding and achieving it.[24]

The second question asks whether the task is a collective or individual one. From what has been said above, it is clear that to some extent Rahner would see it as an individual mission: the Church can talk in terms of general norms, but the responsibility for making decisions about specific action must lie with the individual.[25] However, the task is not purely an individual one.

[20] 'Christianity and the "New Man"': *TI* v. 138.

[21] Ibid.: *TI* v. 139–40, quotation from, 140.

[22] Ibid., 136, 137, 138. See also 'The Church and the Parousia': *TI* vi. 310–11; and 'Profane History and Salvation-History': *TI* xxi. 12. Rahner suggests as means of human self-transformation: birth control, eugenics, psychology, propaganda and advertising (ibid., 138).

[23] 'Ideology and Christianity': *TI* vi. 56.

[24] 'Christianity and the "New Man"': *TI* v. 139.

[25] 'Ideology and Christianity': *TI* vi. 56; cf. 'Christianity and the "New Man"': *TI* v. 151.

Rahner also speaks of the task of the Church as a collective institution: it too must take note of its historical context and this is all the more important in the light of the fact that over the last one hundred and fifty years the Church has become stagnant:

> [The Church] ought to think a lot more about how she can arrange her life and message so as to avoid creating *more* difficulties than is necessary for the man of today and tomorrow.[26]

The sort of tasks Rahner has in mind are quite specific: the reform of liturgy and of canon law, the adaptation of the life of the religious orders and reflection upon the problems posed to the Church as an institution by a modern, pluralistic, and increasingly secular world. This is in addition to its responsibility to re-express theology in a new context[27] and to make pronouncements on general moral norms.[28] Thus, when he writes about responsibility for decision, the contrast he appears to be drawing is not so much between the Church as a body and the individual Church member, as between the Church as an official and authoritative institution and members of the Church seen as the living body of Christ. The latter has responsibility for deciding upon particular, historically specific paths of action.

The third question as to whether the task is only to be achieved in an ecclesiastical context or in the secular world at large clearly links with the second: if the task was conceived *entirely* as one of reform within the Church, obviously it would have no relevance to a wider secular context. However, it is clear that this is precisely what Rahner is denying. The admonitions to individuals to apply general norms to their specific walks of life[29] and the admission that the Church can make advisory pronouncements of a political nature[30] point to the fact that Rahner sees the task of the Christian as taking place very much in the secular world. (It will be seen, in answer to the fourth question, that it even *involves* the secular world as co-agent.) Rahner makes it clear in several places that the role of Christians both individually and collectively is to 'impress the framework of

[26] 'Christianity and the "New Man"': *TI* v. 151.
[27] Ibid., 152.
[28] Ibid.
[29] e.g. 'The Church and the Parousia': *TI* vi. 312.
[30] e.g. 'The Idea of the "New Earth"': *TI* x. 262–3.

secular life with the stamp of their *eschatological* hope'.[31] This is most evident in his article 'The Theological Problems Entailed in the Idea of the "New Earth"' in which he discusses the Vatican II document 'Pastoral Constitution on the Church in the World Today' (otherwise known as *Gaudium et Spes*) and stresses the secular arena of the Christian task several times.[32] Rahner also implies that the Christian task in the world is so extensive that by carrying it out Christians are in a sense taking part in the work of God's creation.[33]

Rahner's emphasis on the secular arena of the Christian task also connects with the fourth question, which asks whether the task is one that can be shared by non-Christians. Far from asserting that only Christians can work for the right sort of earthly future, Rahner admits that in the past Christianity itself has been an obstacle to earthly progress.[34] Meanwhile, those from outside the Christian Church have often been exemplary in their actions. This view depends on Rahner's belief that the love of one's neighbour—whether from a Christian motivation or not—is in fact the same as love of God. So one can be an unknowing or anonymous helper in the divine task:

> Christianity . . . maintains by its very teaching about the oneness of the love of God and of neighbour that whenever someone serves man and his dignity lovingly and in *absolute* selflessness, he affirms his affirmation of absolute moral values and imperatives . . . but it does not maintain in any sense that this is possible only in someone who is explicitly a Christian.[35]

Rahner even goes as far as to say that such actions can 'fall under the impulse of grace':

> even in the case of non-Christians the ultimate motive force (*die letzte Dynamik*) behind their acts and decisions as a part of human history is

[31] 'The Idea of the "New Earth"': *TI* x. 260–1 (Rahner's emphases).

[32] Ibid., 261, 265, 271–2.

[33] This has implications for the question of the relation between humanity's task in the world and God's consummation of it, which will be looked at later in this chapter.

[34] 'Marxist Utopia and the Christian Future of Man' (= 'Marxist Utopia'): *TI* vi. 65. See 'On the Theology of Hope': *TI* x. 257 for his complaint that in the past Christianity has been an excuse for conservatism.

[35] 'Marxist Utopia': *TI* vi. 65. See also 'The Theological Problems Entailed in the Idea of the "New Earth"' (= 'The Idea of the "New Earth"'): *TI* x, throughout which Rahner assumes that the Christian's task can be shared with atheists who are of 'good will' e.g. 260–2.

still, even in their case, precisely *grace*, even though they do not recognize it.[36]

This idea is clearly connected with Rahner's concept of 'anonymous Christianity' which was discussed in the previous chapter, and it has the same advantages and faults.[37] The claim that the task is both Christian and yet shared by atheists is too simplistic and casts doubt on what Rahner insists is the genuinely *Christian* character of the task. His claim that love for God and for one's neighbour are unified, is initially appealing, but raises the question of whether one is truly loving God in loving one's neighbour, if one has consciously denied God's existence. It was seen in the discussion of 'anonymous Christianity' that there was a tension between Rahner's assertion that a decision for or faith in God was necessary for salvation and his apparent reduction of this decision or faith to moral action. This tension is heightened even more by his claim that atheists can share in the Christian task, for it too seems to explain faith (or love of God) in terms of moral action (love of neighbour). Nevertheless, for all these difficulties, the concept of the unity of love of God and love of neighbour at both an individual and collective level, does provide one explanation of how Rahner can realistically hope for the salvation of all people.

Rahner's picture of the Christian task is still rather hazy, but this is clearly due to his warning that there are no precise instructions which are universally valid. He does, however, give an indication of the values at which the task should aim: he seems to be in agreement with the document 'Pastoral Constitution on the Church in the World Today' in saying that in general humans should work for a world which is 'more humane', 'more just', and 'more peaceable' than it is at present.[38] He asserts that the Constitution does present the goal which Christianity itself demands when it declares:

[36] First quote: 'The Idea of the "New Earth"': *TI* x. 271; second quote: ibid., 261–2; *ST* viii. 581.

[37] See above, Chapter 6, section A. iii.

[38] 'The Idea of the "New Earth"': *TI* x. 263. The phrases are derived from the 'Pastoral Constitution on the Church in the World Today' (= *Gaudium et Spes*, Constitution of Vatican II, 7 December 1965; see Denz., paras. 4301 ff.). Rahner gives no exact references for these words, but refers his reader to the following paragraphs of the Constitution: 11, 15, 21, 23, 24, 26, 37, 38, 40, 41, 43, 55, 57, 58, 61, 63, 76.

[the future] must be permeated by a justice and a love which make possible the free unfolding of each individual man, which cause the unity of mankind as a family of brothers to develop, which wage war more effectively on the destructive spirit of egoism and other kinds of sinfulness etc.[39]

Similarly, the document is also presenting the Christian task 'when it further goes on to apply these basic principles in detail to concrete realities in the form of demands for a just polity, upholding the status of the family and so guarding the dignity of man, working out an economic system which is just, working for peace, etc.'[40] In another article Rahner mentions similar aims, such as a social order which is as perfect as possible and which recognizes the absolute value of each person.[41] He writes:

The rational and actively planning construction of an intramundane future, the greatest possible liberation of men from the dominion of nature, the progressive socialisation of man for the attainment of the greatest possible scope for freedom are regarded by Christianity as part of the task demanded of man by his divinely willed nature, a task to which man is obliged and *in* which he fulfils his real religious duty, viz. the openness of freedom in believing hope for the absolute future.[42]

Clearly, part of the task itself is deciding, for example, what justice is, what actions it consists of, and in what ways in can be promoted.

This section has dealt with the question of what prescriptions can be made for Christian action. It has therefore emphasized the immanent side of collective consummation: the role that humanity has in perfecting itself. Always in Rahner's mind however is the other side, that is transcendent consummation. This recognition of the superiority of this divine element in the consummation of the world leads to an awareness of the limits of human action. The next two sections will discuss the contrast which Rahner draws between Christian and secular views of the future on this point and will ask whether Rahner's own view is coherent.

39 'The Idea of the "New Earth"': *TI* x. 263.

40 Ibid., 263.

41 'Marxist Utopia': *TI* vi. 64.

42 Ibid.

ii. The Limits of the Christian Task

In order to show the limits of human action, Rahner contrasts it with the sort of action prescribed by secular ideology. It is clear that he uses the term 'ideology' in a negative sense to mean 'an erroneous or false system which must be rejected in view of a right interpretation of reality'.[43] This sort of false representation of reality has more than just theoretical implications: it results in wrongly directed practical action, when 'the conversion of a partial aspect of reality into an absolute takes place'.[44] Rahner describes three types of ideological viewpoint.[45] First, *ideologies of immanence* turn finite areas of our everyday experience into absolutes (e.g. nationalism, racism, materialism). Secondly, *ideologies of 'transmanence'* exaggerate the importance of the ultimate and the infinite to such a degree that the world of experience is devalued (this is a particular problem for religious or philosophical people and can lead to utopianism, chiliasm or quietism). Thirdly, *ideologies of transcendence* pay such attention to the overcoming of both of the first two sorts of ideology that this task becomes all-important, with the result that nothing is valued and there is no engagement with anything definite.

Rahner admits that the Church has in the past been guilty of the first type of ideology, using Christianity 'to justify social, economic, political, cultural and scientific conditions which cannot claim permanent validity'.[46] He also warns about the dangers of trying to objectify the transcendent (and thus unobjectifiable) mystery of God. It is important that Christianity expresses its faith in words, sacraments, and institutions; but it must be wary of those who attribute more importance to the medium in which the divine is objectified than to God himself, and thus being guilty of another sort of ideology of immanence.[47] In particular Rahner notes that because Christianity is not a body of timeless doctrines the specific historical forms in which it is expressed are provisional: that is, the form should not be mistaken for the content.[48] (It has been seen that this concern is very apparent in Rahner's hermeneutical discussions.) From

[43] 'Ideology and Christianity': *TI* vi. 43. [44] Ibid.

[45] Ibid., 44–5; *ST* vi. 60: *'die Ideologie der Immanenz / der Transmanenz / der Transzendenz'.*

[46] Ibid.: *TI* vi. 46. [47] Ibid. [48] Ibid., 46, 52–4.

what has been said already about the Christian task it is clear that Rahner thinks that Christianity is in one sense worldly, so must avoid the second type of ideology, but he naturally denies the claims of materialists who see *all* metaphysical speculation as ideologizing.[49]

Rahner's concept of ideology is not specifically eschatological, although because it is closely connected with practical action it clearly has relevance to the question of what sort of goals the Christian should be focused on. With regard to the Christian task, the contrast between Christianity and ideology makes two main points: first, Christianity is concerned with the world, not just with transcendent realities; secondly, the Church must not be tempted to ideologize any particular earthly state or action, because its action is set in a changing historical context and will itself change.

Rahner also contrasts Christianity with utopianism: this, unlike ideology, is a necessarily eschatological concept. In the article 'Utopia and Reality', Rahner uses the word to mean an ideal which is sought for, however difficult the quest, and which in some sense ought to be, or is morally required.[50] In other words, every utopia imposes a duty (or set of duties) on people under some moral code or other—although of course the code may be mistaken. Noting that 'humanity seems to be burdened with countless such utopias', Rahner gives some examples in the same article: biological, social and economic security; the achievement of knowledge and 'a *well-organised* picture of reality in our minds'; just and charitable relations with others; realization of our true selves.[51]

Clearly these goals are not bad in themselves; in fact, they bear some resemblance to the future state of the world which Rahner declares it is the Christian duty to bring about.[52] Consequently, although he sometimes forcefully denies that Christianity aims towards worldly utopian goals,[53] in fact a more accurate view of his position would appear to be that he sees Christianity as not

[49] 'Ideology and Christianity': *TI* vi. 45, 47.

[50] 'Utopia and Reality: The Shape of Christian Existence Caught between the Ideal and the Real' (= 'Utopia and Reality'): *TI* xxii, esp. 26–7.

[51] For this list see ibid., 27.

[52] See above, p. 220.

[53] 'The eschatology of Christianity is no intramundane utopia, it sets no intramundane tasks and goals' ('Christianity and the "New Man"': *TI* v. 139).

focused *entirely* on earthly goals: its worldly tasks are totally subsumed under the 'task' of loving God. Thus he writes:

> Christianity must unhesitatingly recognize that future plans and future utopias within this world are not only from the Christian stand-point legitimate, but are the destiny which God's providence has assigned to man, in the carrying out and suffering of which alone can he live his Christian calling genuinely and completely today.[54]

The problem lies in the way in which utopianism views its goals. One difficulty is that utopianism usually claims that a perfect state of the earth is completely achievable in this world by humans alone. Rahner rejects such claims for several reasons. Most importantly, they fail to recognize the transcendent element of humanity's perfect state, and thus ideologize the earthly goal:

> It would be an absolutely fundamental heresy for any given condition in the world, or any condition which man can realise by his own planning and action, to be regarded by man as his salvation . . . All utopian conceptions of salvation-in-the-world are to be rejected as doctrines meriting condemnation.[55]

Secondly, Rahner has deep scepticism as to whether a truly perfect state in material terms is humanly realizable. At times he even suggests that when utopias have supposedly been realized, it is only because political leaders have defined their own particular utopias in such terms that they are easily attained.[56] In other words, most utopianism has a tendency towards being self-fulfilling. A third fault is that most utopianism ideologizes goals to such an exaggerated extent that each utopia is seen as the only situation of great value, devaluing everything else, including the present situation. Finally, worldly utopianism gives no guidance as to what will happen when its end is won: the goal is finite and utopianism cannot see beyond it.[57]

To sum up, Rahner's hope is that Christianity—like much utopianism—can play a critical and forward-looking role in the

[54] 'The Church and the Parousia': *TI* vi. 311.

[55] 'History of the World and Salvation History': *TI* v. 97. In Rahner's terminology this would be an ideology of immanence.

[56] 'Christianity and the "New Man"': *TI* v. 146; Rahner's examples are clearly from contemporary Soviet history: e.g. the conquest of space, the surpassing of America's meat production.

[57] 'Profane History and Salvation History': *TI* xxi. 13.

world, rather than a conservative one; however he stresses that the Church should avoid ideology when choosing its goals and should resist the temptation to see these goals as forming an earthly utopia which is fully achievable by human effort alone.[58] Hence, it is quite clear that Rahner thinks that the Christian task must be completed by God. The next section will assess his explanation of how human and divine action work together.

iii. The Christian Task Fulfilled by God

In some places, Rahner stresses the necessity of the divine consummation to such an extent that he specifically states that the human task in the world will fail—i.e. it will never be completed by humans alone.[59] However, for the most part Rahner emphasizes a relationship between God's consummation of the world and the Christian's task in the world such that the latter is not devalued by the former, but is given great importance, by being seen as part of God's creative purpose. Hence Rahner asserts:

> man himself takes it upon himself as a task with which he has been commissioned to fashion it and so to complete, in a process of historical evolution, the creative work of God himself (*die . . . Vollendung der Schöpfung Gottes in einem geschichtlichen Werden*).[60]

Nevertheless, this notion is problematic in several respects. First, there is the question of what exactly is consummated, if God is said to consummate the human task: is it the physical effects of human labour or its moral value? It was seen above that Rahner sees the goal of the Christian task as the development of a world in which qualities such as justice and love are dominant and in which mankind is unified and at peace.[61] This might seem to imply that this world is just a moral proving-ground and that whereas the moral value of what is done will be taken up into heaven, what humans actually do in the concrete will have no lasting significance. However, Rahner rejects this idea on the grounds that 'it remains true that concrete human history, with all its physical aspects, is the dimension in which the final

58 'Christianity and the "New Man"': *TI* v. 153.
59 'History of the World and Salvation History': *TI* v. 111–12.
60 'The Idea of the "New Earth"': *TI* x. 266; *ST* viii. 586.
61 See above, p. 220.

consummation and the absolute future are made real'.[62] The view that only the moral value of actions remains devalues the Christian task, even though it does not dismiss it as completely useless. In addition, Rahner objects to the fact that if it were only moral qualities that mattered, it would be possible that some virtues could be exercised in a world which was much meaner and more unjust than it would be if people were more intent on changing their physical environment for the better.[63]

In contrast, Rahner emphasizes that, although it will be transformed, history will endure in its 'historical outcome (*geschichtliche Ergebnis*)', *not* just in 'the meta-empirical morality (*meta-empirischen Sittlichkeit*)' realized in it.[64] He writes:

That which endures is the *work* of love as expressed in the concrete in human history.[65]

Rahner justifies this assertion by referring to the idea that the consummation of the world will be its *re*creation or 'transformation' (*Verwandlung*), *not* its replacement.[66] The scriptural phrase referring to a 'new heaven and a new earth' is confusing because it can wrongly be interpreted as implying a substitution, not a renewal (particularly because the Church has traditionally stressed the fact that the 'new earth' will be a gift of God's grace). However, following the doctrinal document, 'The Pastoral Constitution on the Church in the World Today', Rahner stresses that since it is the current world which will be transformed and not replaced, then part of that which is to be transformed is the work of love, the 'fruits of human activity', the world which mankind itself has shaped.[67] These 'fruits' are seen in very physical terms:

What we are speaking of here is a final consummation to be wrought out in the substance of man and of matter merely as these have been fashioned by God himself. . . . Is human history at the material and

[62] 'The Idea of the "New Earth"': *TI* x. 268.

[63] Ibid.

[64] Ibid.: *TI* x. 269; *ST* viii. 589.

[65] Ibid.: *TI* x. 270.

[66] Ibid.: *TI* x. 269; *ST* viii. 589. See also Peter Phan, *Eternity in Time* (Susquehanna University Press, Selinsgrove; Associated University Press, London and Toronto, 1988), 47; W. M. Thompson, 'The Hope for Humanity: Karl Rahner's Eschatology' in L. O'Donovan (ed.), *A World of Grace* (Crossroads, Seabury Press, New York, 1980), 162–3; William Dych, *Karl Rahner* (Geoffrey Chapman, London, 1992), 139.

[67] 'The Idea of the "New Earth"': *TI* x. 264–5. Rahner refers here to the following paragraphs of the Constitution: 34, 38, 39, 57. (See Denz., paras. 4301 ff. for the text of the Constitution.)

physical level itself to become a part of this definitive consummation, albeit through a process of death and radical transformation?[68]

This confirms the conclusion drawn above that, although Rahner is unclear as to the exact nature of the material world in its consummated form, he does believe that it will be consummated.[69]

The second question raised by the idea that humans and God both have a creative role in the world is how the two roles combine. It is clear that human and divine action are mutually necessary for the final collective salvation or consummation:

the Christian is absolutely justified and qualified—and indeed to a certain extent obliged—to take an active part in working for the future (*Entwicklung*) of the human race and thus of the world, by developing his own immanent powers and those of the world. For the consummation (*Vollendung*) to be brought about by God does not, in the last analysis, expect a dead but a living humanity which has gone to its very limits and so is burst open by salvation from above by developing its own powers (*die ihre Grenzen erfährt und so aufgesprengt wird für das Heil*). For man's finiteness and the essential tragedy and fruitlessness of all human history, inherent in all finite development, becomes manifest more relentlessly in this way than it would in a purely static world.[70]

But how can both humans and God be agents not only of the continuing process of creation but also of its *final consummation*, given that elsewhere Rahner has said that the human task will cease or fail?[71] This contradiction can be perhaps explained as looseness of expression. It is clear from what Rahner has said in relation to utopia and ideology that humanity cannot truly be said to complete any state of the world: God is the only true perfecter. Nevertheless, Rahner does not seem to explore this issue in so much detail as he devoted to the relation of immanent and transcendent consummation in the individual. One must ask whether—given that he thinks that humans will always 'fail' to a certain extent—God would complete the human task

[68] 'The Idea of the "New Earth"': *TI* x. 267. (Rahner's answer to the rhetorical question in this context is 'yes'.)

[69] See above, p. 212.

[70] 'Christianity and the "New Man"': *TI* v. 149 (*ST* v. 174).

[71] The above pair of passages show that Rahner uses the term *Vollendung* both of God and of humans in this context.

regardless of how far it had advanced. What degree of failure in the task would count as a rejection of God? Where does this leave human responsibility? This problem is exacerbated by the fact that Rahner sometimes refers to God not only as the transcendent consummation of the world, but also as its immanent consummation:

> He is the 'transcendent' consummation, and therefore can and will, precisely as *God*, himself be the 'immanent' consummation and the 'immanent' principle of the movement towards this single real and uniquely fulfilling consummation that is the fullness of finality: God—all in all (*diese eine wirkliche und einzig erfüllende Voll-endung sein: Gott—alles in allem*).[72]

This parallels the problem between immanent and transcendent consummation at the individual level which was noted earlier.[73] Whereas that appeared to jeopardize the freedom of one individual, this threatens freedom on a much broader scale.

Moreover the quotation above illustrates a third difficulty: that Rahner at times seems to equate God and consummation. For instance, in 'Marxist Utopia and the Christian Future of Man' Rahner emphasizes several times that Christianity is 'the religion of the future' or 'of the absolute future' and furthermore that this absolute future is nothing other than God.[74] In a later article, 'Utopia and Reality', Rahner even specifically equates God with a good (i.e. non-ideologized) utopia.[75] However, at other times Rahner appears to see God as the *agent* of the consummation. This notion of God as agent of consummation seems to make much more sense: the idea of God bringing about a consummation which is God's own self is a very difficult one, as is the parallel idea that somehow God (in the sense of being consummation) is still not fully realized and 'not yet'. Furthermore, in his identification of God with both aspects of consummation, Rahner runs the risk of a thoroughgoing pantheism: the idea that God is not only present in all humans, but in humanity as a whole and in

[72] 'Immanent and Transcendent Consummation': *TI* x. 289; *ST* viii. 609, referring to 1 Cor. 15: 28, but apparently without thinking that it entails absolutely universal salvation, as Gregory of Nyssa does.

[73] See above, Chapter 6, section A. i..

[74] 'Marxist Utopia': *TI* vi. 59–62. See also 'Immanent and Transcendent Consummation': *TI* x. 278, where Rahner equates consummation and the absolute future.

[75] 'Utopia and Reality': *TI* xxii. 29–31.

the world as a whole. Many Christian writers—including Gregory of Nyssa—have used the phrase 'God will be all in all' to suggest that *at the eschaton* there will be a perfect relationship between God and the world, even complete unity. One might suggest, in Rahner's terms, that at the eschaton, in the achievement of that towards which the world is reaching out, its transcendence becomes its immanence. However, Rahner claims that this unity of transcendence and immanence takes place *now*. It is very difficult to understand what this might mean. The confusion seems to arise from Rahner's description of God as the horizon of all human existence towards which the individual and the world are reaching out in transcendental experience. It is when this concept is applied eschatologically, when the *Vorgriff* is described not only as an attempt to reach out to God, but also as an advance into the future, that the identification of God with the term of this *Vorgriff* seems to be incoherent.

Finally, there are unwelcome consequences of Rahner's description of the consummation or the ideal utopia as including *all* human possibilities. He uses this concept in contrast with secular ideologized utopias which value and aim at only one aspect of reality (material or spiritual): Christianity, on the other hand values both. Whereas this is an important point, the way Rahner expresses it is confusing, for in saying that the consummation will include all human possibilities he seems to be making a claim not about matter and spirit, but one which might include evil and egotistical human motivations. It is surely not his intention to imply that these will be fulfilled in the consummation. Again, the lack of clarity can be explained by the fact that Rahner is seeing God in terms of the horizon of absolute being behind the existence of the world, but there seems to be lacking an analysis of how 'absolute being' might be said to 'include all possibilities'.

This section has examined the problematic relationship between immanent consummation and transcendent consummation at the collective level, highlighting in particular the difficulties of equating God with consummation, of preserving a distinct role for human freedom and of ascertaining what it is about the world which will be saved. Rahner deals with the first two issues mainly in his more theoretical studies, but the last is more prominent in his discussion of specific eschatological doctrines. He equates the traditional Christian concept of the parousia with the transcendent, or the divinely effected consummation of the world, the result of grace. Applying this in particular to the Church, Rahner writes that 'the essential nature of the Church consists in pilgrimage towards the promised future', but that at the same time 'God . . . is coming to meet her in the Parousia and her own pilgrimage is taking place in the power of Christ's coming'.[76] Another important collective eschatological concept is that of resurrection: this is seen as the effect of consummation on humanity and the world.

C. RESURRECTION AND PAROUSIA

The third part of this chapter will now see how Rahner applies his concept of collective consummation to the interpretation of specific Christian eschatological doctrines, bearing in mind the problems mentioned above. As was seen in the discussion of his hermeneutics, Rahner criticizes the fact that previous Christian eschatology has tended to focus on the fate of the individual, almost to the exclusion of any interest in collective eschatology. By contrast, Rahner tries to give a collective interpretation to doctrines which were previously more individualistic; this is particularly the case with his reinterpretation of resurrection.

Although Rahner's account of the beatific vision has a communal aspect to some degree, it is only his study of the resurrection which brings a truly collective approach to the concept of heaven. Rahner's brief historical survey of the doctrine stresses that for a long time the concept of heaven was equated primarily with that of the beatific vision of God, and, as the vision was not seen to require a body (being an intellectual activity), it was assumed that those who were blessed would enter heaven immediately on their death, without having to wait for the resurrection of their earthly bodies.[77] This view clearly reflected the belief that the resurrection of the body would be the

[76] 'The Church and the Parousia of Christ' (= 'The Church and the Parousia'): *TI* vi. 298.

[77] 'In the history of this Dogma during the Middle Ages, the view of the end veers more and more away from the resurrection of the body to the soul's direct vision of God' ('The Resurrection of the Body': *TI* ii. 206) Rahner implies that this trend became particularly well-established during, but was not restricted to, the Middle Ages.

resurrection of the very same earthly body as 'clothed' the soul in this life and the empirical observation that the bodies even of the saints were still in the tomb. Thus Rahner claims that the resurrection of the body came to be seen to have a 'supplementary character', or to be 'an "accidental" increase in the essentially already fully realised beatitude of the soul . . .'.[78]

Furthermore, Rahner asserts that the emphasis on the individual soul has been reinforced by demythologization's failure to provide an acceptable interpretation of the resurrection. In Rahner's opinion, the demythologizers dismiss the resurrection of the body as too miraculous: they claim that even in the Bible the resurrection is merely an image expressing the eternal victory of God over death.[79] Rahner condemns this disregard for the material nature of man, because it 'stultifies and betrays the true reality of man'.[80]

In response to the failure of demythologization, Rahner's reinterpretation of the doctrine of the resurrection of the body aims to re-emphasize the doctrine's importance, to make it coherent with the concept of the beatific vision and to connect the perfection of the human individual with the perfection of the whole world. With these aims in mind, he interprets the biblical phrase 'resurrection of the flesh' (or 'resurrection of the body') to mean the resurrection of the whole man, body and soul:

> 'Resurrection' means . . . the termination and perfection of the *whole* man before God, which gives him 'eternal life'.[81]

Hence, heaven can be described as a place, because it will include material bodies with some sort of spatial extension.[82] This is qualified by Rahner's statement that one cannot ask *where* heaven is, because it does not have a location in our physical spatial world, and further by his assertion that our bodily nature will be spiritual and without the restrictions which characterize it now.[83]

[78] 'The Resurrection of the Body': *TI* ii. 207.

[79] Ibid., 208.

[80] Ibid., 215. It is important to note that Rahner also condemns those who reduce humanity to nothing but matter and thus see no future beyond the point when each human perishes.

[81] Ibid.: *TI* ii. 211; *ST* ii. 219: *'Auferstehung also die Endgültigkeit und Vollendung des ganzen Menschen vor Gott, die ihm das "ewige Leben" gibt'* (Rahner's emphasis).

[82] Ibid.: *TI* ii. 214–15.

[83] Ibid., 215: no location in our physical spatial world; 214: our bodily nature will be spiritual.

This affirmation of the value of matter is strengthened by Rahner's claim that after death and until the resurrection is completed individuals remain in a relationship with the material world. In a difficult but important passage Rahner writes:

the continuing reality of the personal spirit can already reach the direct communion with God (*unmittelbaren Gottesgemeinschaft*) by the event and moment which, looked at from its intramundane side, we experience as death. In so far as this union with God (*dieses Gottesgemeinschaft*) constitutes the innermost being of blessed completion (*selig Vollendung*), 'heaven' and 'eternal happiness' can already be given with death. Nevertheless, the deceased remains 'united' (*'verbunden'*)with the reality, fate and hence the temporal events of the world, however little we are able to 'picture' (*'vorstellen'*) to ourselves such a continuing belonging-to-the-world and however few immediately comprehensible statements on this matter are contained in the Scriptures.[84]

The reason for Rahner's insistence on the continued relationship with the world lies in the theoretical discussion of consummation which was outlined above.[85] It is because the human is spirit in the *world*, because the human body is 'an open system', because (to repeat Rahner's bold phrase) 'through bodiliness the whole world belongs to me from the start in everything that happens'.[86] Hence, in a strong and conscious contrast with some Platonizing early traditions of the Church which eagerly encouraged believers to sever the emotional ties between their soul and the world in order to make the soul's departure from this life easier, Rahner is explicitly denying that in death the soul leaves the material world. In his monograph *On the Theology of Death* he makes this denial in detail. He claims that 'the Neoplatonic habits of thought' which have restricted Christian thought for so long have tempted theologians to see the human body and soul as separable elements and consequently to interpret death on the model of an immortal soul quitting the dead body.[87] Rahner complains that this interpretation has led to the assumption that 'the appearance of the soul before God . . . stands in some direct opposition to her present relationship to the world as though

[84] Ibid.: *TI* ii. 211; *ST* ii. 219–20.
[85] See above, p. 211.
[86] 'The Body in the Order of Salvation': *TI* xvii. 87–8; cf. Dych, *Karl Rahner*, 140.
[87] *On the Theology of Death*, 28.

freedom from the world and nearness to God must increase by a direct ratio'.[88] Rahner's own view is simply that the soul *cannot* leave the world upon the death of the individual. Rather, the soul enters into a new 'pan-cosmic' relationship with the world: whereas in life the soul was related to the world via a specific human body, upon death it becomes open to the entire universe.[89] Rahner cautions against interpreting this to mean that the world becomes the soul's new body, as it were, or that the soul is omnipresent in the world. He writes:

Since the soul, in death, is thought to give up her determined space-time location within the world and within the mutual inter-relationships of individual beings, she should hardly be thought to be all present in these same dimensions.[90]

The problem is that it is difficult to envisage what the exact physical relationship between the body and the world is. On this Peter Phan writes:

Despite the fact that Rahner repeatedly reminds us that the resurrection is the fulfilment of human beings in their entirety, including their bodily dimension, and despite his valiant attempt to retain heaven as a space (not commensurate with our physical space), one can hardly overcome the impression that his interpretation of the resurrection does not allow him to give a full account of the corporeal quality of the risen body.[91]

The resurrected person is not, however, related to a static world: an important consequence of Rahner's notion of the 'pancosmicity' of the soul is that the process of perfection which the individual endures in death is inextricably tied up with the process of perfection of the world:

the personal spirit, precisely as human spirit is a material, mundane, incarnate . . . spirit. And so the end of the world is participation in the perfection of the spirit: the world remains, beyond its previous history, as the conatural surroundings of the achieved spirit which has found its

[88] *On the Theology of Death*, 27–8; cf. 'The Resurrection of the Body': *TI* ii. 211: '"separation from the body" for the soul in death does not by a long way need to mean *ipso facto* a greater nearness to God. Remoteness-from-the-world and nearness-to-God are not interchangeable notions . . .'.

[89] *On the Theology of Death*, 28–30.

[90] Ibid., 30.

[91] Phan, *Eternity in Time*, 179; he also asks 'Is [the glorified body] anything more than the material world to which the corrupted body returns?' (ibid., 133); cf. ibid., 115.

finality in the fellowship with God and achieves its own history and that of the world at the same point.[92]

The end of the world—or its consummation—is 'the perfection and total achievement of saving history', the manifestation of the victory gained by Christ in his resurrection. It is also the perfection of the individual—the resurrection. Together, the perfection of individuals and the fulfilment of the world are expressed by the Christian concept of 'parousia':

> [Christ's] Second Coming takes place at the moment of the perfecting of the world (*bei der Vollendung der Welt*) . . . in such a way that he . . . will be revealed to all reality.[93]

Hence, Rahner attempts to connect the resurrection directly with an unquestionably collective eschatological concept—the parousia—in order to emphasize that the resurrection too is a collective experience. It is not the perfection of the individual, but of all the blessed; furthermore, this coincides with that of all the world.

However there are problems with Rahner's interpretation of the resurrection and parousia, regarding his concept of time. The way in which Rahner describes the resurrection as a 'termination and perfection' reminds one that he thinks that death is not a gateway between two temporal lives, but that it ends and completes the individual's existence in time. But, at the same time as asserting that life 'after' death is timeless, Rahner claims that because humans are many-layered beings, each individual's perfection cannot take place all at once, but is a process: the moment of perfection of each layer will not be the same.[94] (This is another expression of the same claim made in his interpretation of the doctrine of purgatory.[95]) Although he does not say so explicitly, Rahner is presumably thus equating purgatory and resurrection: the two words perhaps stress different aspects of the same phenomenon. Resurrection thus shares with purgatory the problematic concept of a timeless process.

[92] 'The Resurrection of the Body': *TI* ii. 213; *ST* ii. 221–2. In German the second sentence reads: '*so ist das Ende der Welt Partizipation der Vollendung des Geistes: sie bleibt, jenseits ihrer bisherigen Geschichte als konnaturale Umwelt des vollendeten Geistes, der seine Endgültigkeit in der Gottesgemeinschaft gefunden hat und seine und ihre Geschichte am selben Punkt vollendet*'.

[93] Ibid.: *TI* ii. 213; *ST* ii. 222.

[94] Ibid.: *TI* ii. 211.

[95] See above, Chapter 6, section C. iv.

The assertion that the resurrected enjoy a continued relationship with the world makes the temporal problem even more difficult: not only is Rahner suggesting that there is some sort of process in death, but he is claiming that the individual is still implicated in earthly time. No longer can Rahner turn to the concept of a heavenly time which is merely 'analogous' to earthly time, or claim that temporal words used of heaven are merely images.[96] Nor can he defend himself with reference to the idea that a timeless God can relate to a temporal world: God's relationship with the world is characterized by the fact that (assuming God is timeless, as Rahner appears to) God always has been and always will be timeless; by contrast the relationship between the soul and the world seems to be the continuation (in some sense) of a relation between two previously undoubtedly temporal things, both of which are still changing. If a soul is still in the sort of relationship with the world that Rahner implies, it must surely be in earthly time itself, not in something analogous to earthly time. So, in sum, it is not just that Rahner says that life after death is timeless and then describes it as a process leading up to a final resurrection that is the problem, but also that he claims that the soul is simultaneously in a state which he consistently holds to be essentially timeless (the beatific vision) and in a state which is essentially temporal (the continued relationship with the world).

However, the problem is not just a philosophical one: the temporal question has theological repercussions. Just as one needs to ask how an individual can be in time and not in time, so one needs to ask how one can simultaneously be perfect and not perfect. For the previous chapter made clear that Rahner saw the beatific vision as a state of perfection and fulfilment.[97] However, he also emphasizes with equal force that the human is not perfect until the resurrection:

> The history—which has remained within the framework of the world—of those who by their lives have already effected their personal finality (*Endgültigkeit*), reaches its real completion and explicit expression (*Ganzheit und Ausdrücklichkeit*) together with the consummation (*Vollen-*

[96] These two solutions to the problem of an atemporal process are made by the first theologian in the article 'Purgatory': *TI* xix. 187. See above, Chapter 6, section c. iv.

[97] See 'Beatific Vision': *SM* i. 152: 'The beatific vision is indeed the most perfect conceivable actuation of a spiritual creature . . .'.

dung) of the world. True human beings now become achieved as totalities with soul and body, and their perfection, already begun in death, becomes itself perfected, tangible in the world, embodied (*und ihre im Tod schon begonnene Vollendung wird selbst vollendet, welthaft griefbar, leiblich*).[98]

Previously, theology had solved this sort of difficulty, either by tending to ignore the resurrection or by asserting an individual resurrection at the moment of death. Rahner's resurrection is however clearly at the end of the world. By stressing the perfection of the beatific vision and the fact that the blessed achieve the vision immediately in death, Rahner is in danger of committing the very fault which he criticized in earlier theologians: that is, of giving the resurrection a 'supplementary character'. He guards against this, though, by constantly stressing that only when everything is consummated will God's salvation be perfected—even for those in heaven already.

Although there are grave problems then with the relation of resurrection to time, Rahner's reinterpretation of the resurrection does at least succeed in re-emphasizing the collective aspect of Christian eschatology: the notion that the individual is not fully perfected until the whole world is perfected is an extension of the more traditional idea that the joy of the blessed is not full until their number is complete. However, Rahner's vision of how the individual is inextricably interconnected with the material world raises the question of universalism: given that the universe—both its spiritual and its material elements—is apparently one web of interconnecting elements, how is it possible for everything *not* to be saved? Presumably, if every soul turned against God, there would be no salvation at all, but Rahner has explicitly ruled this possibility out. It is difficult, though, to envisage what happens if some individuals decide for God and others do not. One scenario which seems to make some sense is that the whole world will be perfected, however many individuals are saved: the question is then what happens to those who are not. It would be easy to suggest that their souls are 'lost', or fail to reach fulfilment, but given that Rahner is insistent that the human body is bound up with the rest of the world, he would seem to be committed to saying that the material side of those

[98] 'The Resurrection of the Body': *TI* ii. 213–14; *ST* ii. 222.

who reject God is perfected along with the perfection of the rest of the world. Furthermore, if each individual is a unity of body and soul, does that mean that the souls of those who did not decide for God are also caught up in this general restoration? Rahner leaves this question unanswered.

This chapter has tried to analyse Rahner's concept of collective consummation and to apply it to the notions of resurrection, parousia and the Christian task in the world. It has been seen how the application of the theoretical concept to particular doctrines clarified some matters (it is fairly clear that he thinks that the consummation of humanity and the world will include transformed matter), but raises still more problems (time and eternity, the exact relation of the human task and its completion by God, the possibility of failure and extent of human responsibility). These issues will be discussed in relation to Gregory of Nyssa's eschatology in the following, final chapter.

8

Comparison and Assessment

Both Gregory of Nyssa and Karl Rahner structure their eschatologies around the promise that ultimately God will be all in all. Self-evidently, their respective theologies are expressed in distinct ways, use different philosophical language and respond to the diverse concerns of the ages they lived in. Furthermore, Gregory declares his expectation with certainty while Rahner is content merely to express a hope. Nevertheless, in the previous chapters it has become clear that the object of their hope is at least similar. The question remains of how close this similarity is: is it just linguistic or does it run at some deeper theological level? And is their shared hope a truly Christian one? Of course, in attending to the similarities, one must not fail to do justice to the contrast between Gregory's and Rahner's answers to the questions of whether and how all people will be saved. One is led to ask to what extent the differences are attributable to changing cultural and philosophical contexts and to what extent they are due to the stance of the individual theologian. One must consider whether Rahner's answers are preferable or whether there is something to be learned from Gregory's approach. Finally, if the expression of the doctrine has developed, what developments might one expect in the future and which issues are still left to be resolved?

In order to answer these questions, this concluding chapter will first compare Gregory's and Rahner's answers to the questions of whether and how all people will be saved, before moving on to a more general assessment of their eschatologies.

A. WILL ALL BE SAVED?

i. Gregory of Nyssa's Arguments for Universal Salvation

In Chapter 3 it was seen that Gregory presents two direct arguments for universal salvation: one based on the nature of evil and the other based on the unity of humankind. On the one hand, it is now difficult to accept Gregory's conception of evil as non-existence and his argument that evil will necessarily cease to exist, because of their basis in Platonic philosophy. On the other hand, his basic assumption that the eternal existence of evil is incompatible with the nature of God is still acceptable to many theologians today—indeed, it underlies many contemporary arguments for universal salvation. Gregory's argument is based explicitly on the premisses that God is infinite goodness and that in the end God will be 'all in all' (1 Corinthians 15: 28). If God is good, God cannot be *all* in things which remain evil; if God will be all in *all*, there will be no evil things left. However, modern opinions differ as to what the elimination of evil might mean: views range from universal salvation, to the annihilation of those who refuse to accept God, or to the eternal exclusion of such people from God—interpreted in such a way that that exclusion is not itself an evil. Thus Gregory's argument from the nature of evil is far from conclusive when separated from his particular conception of what evil is.

Gregory's argument from the unity of humankind is still more problematic and alien to the modern reader. As we have seen, some of the difficulties spring from the fact that Gregory himself does not use it consistently: whereas he sometimes argues that Christ reconciled the world to God by assuming it in the incarnation, uniting it with God in the resurrection, and submitting it to the Father at the eschaton, he elsewhere has a different soteriology based more on the individual's imitation of Christ. It thus seems that although he on occasion exploits the opportunity which the former 'physicalist' soteriology afforded to bolster his universalism, his belief in universal salvation is by no means based on it. The other problem with his argument from the unity of humankind is that people no longer think of humankind (or the world) as a unity in the same way that Gregory does. Few conceive of humanity as 'a single living being' or accept his belief that creation can become 'one body', except in a very loose sense. Nevertheless, there may be one aspect of Gregory's idea of the unity of human nature which can remain powerful today and that is the notion that humanity *as a whole* was created in the image of God. If we treat Gregory's concept of the first creation in terms of a divine plan or intention for humanity (and not in terms of the creation of an 'idea' or 'form' of human nature which later gives rise to actual human beings) it may still make sense to say that the Genesis myth indicates that God has a plan for the *whole* of humanity: 'God said "Let us make man in our image, after our likeness"' (Genesis 1: 26) and not 'Let us make man and let some be in our image and after our likeness'. As we have seen, Gregory certainly talks of the renewal established in Christ, the true likeness of God, as the restoration of this image, and in a couple of places he grounds this on the words of Colossians 3: 10 '[seeing that you] have put on the new nature which is being renewed in knowledge after the image of the creator' (itself a clear echo of the Genesis phrase).[1] This may give one some grounds for believing that this restoration will be universal (although it is not certain on the basis of Scripture as a whole).

Gregory's two arguments for universal salvation thus boil down to a fundamental belief in the impermanence of evil in the face of God's love and a conviction that God's plan for humanity is intended to be fulfilled in every single human being. These beliefs are identified with 1 Corinthians 15: 28 and Genesis 1: 26 in particular, but are derived from what Gregory sees as the direction of Scripture as a whole. Thus, instead of just looking at Gregory's philosophical and theological arguments, one must also examine his use of the Bible as evidence for universal salvation. In general, Gregory's exegesis of the Old Testament, although stimulating and imaginative, cannot be taken to be good grounds for the belief that all will be saved. Any passages which Gregory takes to be soteriological, he reads in the light of the New Testament, often employing typology, allegory and other exegetical techniques to show that the Old Testament is in many previously unrecognized places a revelation of the work of Christ. Although Gregory clearly thinks that

[1] Gregory of Nyssa, *De hom. opif.*: 30. 33; *Contra Eun.* 2. 1.

such linking is justified in the light of typology found within the New Testament itself (see, for example, John 3: 14) his own use of it goes far beyond that of the New Testament writers. Thus Gregory links the story of Moses banishing the plague of darkness from Egypt to Christ's death on the cross: just as Moses rid Egypt of the darkness, Christ's death means that the outer darkness of hell will be banished. This is complex exegesis: Gregory is not merely linking an Old with a New Testament passage, but he uses the story of Moses to link two passages in the New Testament, thereby drawing a conclusion about Christ's atonement which would otherwise not be at all apparent from taking the New Testament at face value. But precisely because of its complexity, such a technique must be regarded with suspicion if it is treated as proof for a doctrine—the same technique could too easily be used to achieve exactly the opposite result.

As we have seen in Chapter 3, there are some scriptural passages which Gregory takes to be more straightforward references to universal salvation: he uses the Psalms, the hymn in Philippians 2: 10, and the prayer in Ephesians 3: 18–19 particularly frequently for this purpose. These passages certainly express the power, love, and goodness of God, but not in a way which would allow one to draw from them any specific eschatological conclusions. The only passage which could be used as more substantial evidence for universal salvation is the one which runs throughout all Gregory's eschatological writings: 1 Corinthians 15. It is useful to note that although the phrase Gregory cites most is from verse 28 ('that God may be all in all'), the whole chapter is suffused with inclusive, if not universal, language. The resurrection of Christ is the 'first-fruits' of a general resurrection; 'as in Adam all die, so also in Christ shall all be made alive'; Christ will destroy 'every rule and every authority and power', and 'all his enemies'; 'all things are put in subjection under him'; 'we shall all be changed'. Given Gregory's technique of reading individual verses in the context of the chapter or book as a whole, it is not surprising that he (and Origen before him) took this passage to indicate universal salvation. The passage is given particular weight because of the way Paul introduces it as a synopsis of the gospel as he received it.

However, although it forms the strongest scriptural basis for a hope for universal salvation, 1 Corinthians 15 can ground no more than a faithful hope, partly because it is not explicit and partly because there are other references in Scripture which promise unbelievers everlasting punishment. There are three available resolutions to this apparent contradiction in Scripture. First, one can take references to punishment as subordinate to references to salvation; this usually involves either understanding 'eternal' punishment to be of ultimate significance, but not everlasting, or taking all such references as threats rather than infallible predictions. Secondly, one can subordinate references to salvation to references to punishment and explain 'all' in passages like 1 Corinthians 15 as referring only to all who are or will be saved. Thirdly, one can acknowledge a running inconsistency or tension in the biblical evidence and settle the question on grounds other than the complete unanimity of the scriptural witness. For someone with the hermeneutical assumptions of Gregory, for whom Scripture must be read as a completely coherent whole with a single divine *skopos* (aim), the last option is impossible. His choice of the first 'optimistic' option over the second one, is the result of prayerful meditation on texts which emphasize God's love and goodness.

This approach, however, has become increasingly difficult to accept, because of the advancement of modern biblical criticism. Although those modern theologians who believe in universal salvation do tend to support their belief by appeal to Scripture, few are so confident as Gregory in the absolute and detailed coherence of the message of Scripture. They do use Scripture as a whole as a witness to the revelation of God's victorious love in Christ, but rarely see this as a justification for using specific verses as proof texts. Several openly admit that although they see the prevailing direction of Scripture as being towards universal salvation, there are some dissenting passages which cannot easily be explained away. In other words, they take the third of the three options outlined above. There are some modern universalists who take a more optimistic view of the unity of Scripture and try, like Gregory, to make the first option work; however, it is harder than ever for them convincingly to interpret difficult passages in a way which supports their case.

For these reasons, Gregory's method (especially his use of

allegory) is bound to remain controversial. Are there any more resources in Gregory's theology which could lead one to a more definite assertion of universal salvation? An obvious candidate is Gregory's view of punishment. In Chapter 3 this was used as evidence to show that he himself believed in universal salvation, but it is also possible to construct a coherent argument for universalism around it. This can be set out systematically in the following way, based on four premisses.[2]

First, God is infinite goodness and love. It thus follows that God's creation is good—neither infinitely good, nor good in all respects, but fundamentally good (because nothing that God created can be *absolutely* evil). Because God is infinite love and creation is good, God loves all creation.

Secondly, the only form of loving punishment is that which aims at the good of offenders, i.e. that which reforms them. Because God loves all creation, God aims for the good of all sinners and thus divine punishment is reformatory.

Thirdly, since God is omnipotent as well as all-loving, divine reformatory punishment ultimately will be successful.

Fourthly, there are a finite number of humans and thus only a finite number of sinners (who are finitely evil, because nothing in creation is absolutely evil). Therefore, because God's punishment is reformatory and will be successful, all punishment will eventually cease and all humans will eventually be saved.

Although the actual logic of this argument from punishment is solid, it contains various premisses which are contentious. For example, although most modern theologians would agree with the first, third, and fourth premisses (that God is infinite goodness and love, that God is omnipotent and that there is a finite number of humans) many would dispute the second premiss that punishment is loving only if aimed at reform. They might also claim that although God aims for the good of the whole creation, this may mean sacrificing the good of recalcitrant sinners for the good of the rest. In other words, the aim of bringing about the good of justice for creation as a whole may mean that some suffer eternally in hell. Against these points, however, it seems reasonable to assert that to put the claims of a general justice above the good of individual people runs the risk

[2] In essence, this is a more detailed adaptation of the argument that if God is perfectly loving and omnipotent it is incoherent to suggest that the evil of sin will remain eternally.

of binding God to a rule external to God. Furthermore, it does not seem to reflect the revelation of God in Jesus Christ, who showed love not only to all individuals, but precisely to those whom society had excluded. If anything, the gospels and Pauline epistles appear to criticize, rather than affirm, the overly-rigorous application of a general human standard of justice. Of all Gregory's arguments the argument from the nature of punishment is the most likely to be appreciated by modern theologians, because it does not rely on a philosophy or a hermeneutics which they no longer share. However, it is important to note that this is an argument constructed from various suggestions in Gregory's theology, not one which he explicitly used himself.

ii. The Grounds for Karl Rahner's Attitude towards Universal Salvation

Rahner does not set out a formal argument for universal salvation, even as a hope; however, there are two areas of his theology which one might regard as possible grounds for universalism: anthropology and hermeneutics.

Rahner's anthropology deals with human self-transcendence and openness to God. If one were to ground knowledge of the existence and self-revelation of God in knowledge of a human potentiality for the transcendent, and if that potentiality were universal (i.e. the supernatural existential), it might suggest that the fulfilment of that potentiality would be universal—in other words, that all would be saved. However, on closer inspection, this argument is flawed in several ways. First, the human existential experience of reaching out to an apparently transcendent aspect of existence does not prove the existence of a personal, good, and loving God. Secondly, even if it did, and even if everyone had that experience, that does not prove that the experience will be *fulfilled* by God in all. In any case, Rahner did not intend his idea of the supernatural existential to form part of a natural theology, but to be the fulcrum of a transcendental argument: he is asking the question 'if God were to communicate the divine self to humans, what would be the condition of the possibility of that self-communication?'[3] Similarly, Rahner is not concerned to *prove*

[3] In *Foundations* Rahner prefers to say that human transcendence and the divine mystery are 'mutually dependent on one another for intelligibility' and not that the

that all will be saved—as his eschatological hermeneutics show, he is not interested in categorical predictions about eschatology at all. Thus, in Rahner's examination of 'anonymous Christianity' and his interpretation of purgatory the question underlying his analysis is 'if God has a universal saving will, how can that will be effective, given the current fallen state of the world?'—not 'how can we prove from the way that God's will functions, that it will save all?' Ultimately, then, Rahner's assertion that everyone possesses the supernatural existential, seems to be a *theological* assertion. Although he often appears to ground it on an analysis of human knowing, in fact its universality is based on faith in God's universal revelation and saving will. As such it can perhaps be traced back to such scriptural foundations as 1 Timothy 2: 4.

This brings one to the issue of Rahner's hermeneutics and in particular his hermeneutics of eschatological assertions.[4] This is the nearest he comes to a formal argument for the truth of universal salvation. Rahner asserts that humans can claim to have knowledge of their future destiny only in so far as that knowledge is derived from their present knowledge of salvation. Eschatology is Christology, anthropology, and soteriology translated into an expectation of consummation. Because of human freedom, and in particular the freedom to say no to God, hell is a possibility for *all* people. Furthermore, because of the complex and elusive nature of human decision, one cannot make pronouncements (at least not during someone's lifetime) about whether other people have escaped that possibility. One cannot even be absolutely sure that one is not a sinner oneself.[5] However, although hell is a possibility for all, one is not required to believe that any people have, in fact, been damned. In addition, it is certain, in light of the salvific work of Christ, that at least some have been saved (for example, saints and martyrs) and at a general level, one can be sure that God's grace will be effective. Thus it is possible that all will be saved: indeed Christians should hope for this outcome, based on the revelation

former proves the latter. As for the usual proofs for God's existence, he claims that they are not intended 'to communicate a knowledge in which a previously unknown and therefore indifferent object is presented to people from without', but 'to indicate that all knowledge . . . takes place against the background of an affirmation of the holy mystery' (pp. 68–9).

[4] See Chapter 5, section B. For the seven theses, see Appendix A.

[5] See Chapter 6, section B. ii. and Rahner, *Foundations*, 102 and 104.

of 'the victorious grace of Christ which brings the world to its fulfilment'.[6] Consequently, one cannot avoid speaking of both heaven and hell, but these two outcomes are not to be regarded in precisely the same light: as Rahner expresses it, they are not parallel.

This view is usually expressed by Rahner in terms of a hope (that all will gain heaven) and a possibility (that some may go to hell). For example, his claim that the words of Christ about hell are 'threat discourses' follows the principle that scriptural statements about hell express only a possibility for each human, not an actuality for some.[7] Similarly, he does not usually appear to take 1 Corinthians 15: 28 to mean that, necessarily, each individual will be saved, but seems to treat it as an expression of God's will for the whole world which the Christian hopes will be fulfilled. However, occasionally (and particularly in his later writings) he makes a blunter assertion which is seemingly a paradox. For example, in *Foundations of Christian Faith* he writes:

> the existence of the possibility that freedom will end in eternal loss stands alongside the doctrine that the world and the history of the world as a whole will *in fact* enter into eternal life with God.[8]

Here the second, apparently universalistic, claim is expressed in terms which go beyond hope.

This paradox in Rahner's eschatology can be treated in two ways: either one can assume that 'the world and the history of the world as a whole' does not in fact include absolutely every human individual who ever lived; or one can assume that Rahner is content to leave a tension at the heart of his eschatology. The fact that Rahner criticizes some theologians for reducing the varied ways in which tradition speaks of the eschata to one 'demythologized' meaning, suggests that he is happy with such a paradox, and indeed that an aim of his

[6] Rahner, 'The Hermeneutics of Eschatological Assertions': *TI* iv. 340.

[7] An additional problem is that Rahner sometimes takes texts to mean something radically different from what their authors took them to mean—for example, at least some New Testament writers (for example, the authors of the epistles of 2 Peter and Jude) appear to have thought that some people would be eternally separated from God and it is difficult to treat them as 'threat-discourses'. This suggests that Rahner is arguing from a conviction about the divine saving will to a hermeneutical principle and not vice versa.

[8] Rahner, *Foundations*, 444 (Rahner's emphasis).

eschatology is to show that there are some pairs of eschatological statements which are ultimately irreducible. Certainly, his discussion of eschatology in *Foundations of Christian Faith* makes it clear that he thinks that statements about individual and collective eschatology cannot be reconciled.[9]

There are two reasons for this belief in the incompatibility of certain pairs of eschatological statements. The first reason lies in Rahner's conception of the nature of Scripture and Church teaching and of theological reflection on them. Unlike Gregory of Nyssa, Rahner does not assume that Scripture is like a seamless garment in which every single thread is intimately interwoven with all the others. Instead, Rahner seems to treat Scripture more like a coat of many colours, with different pieces, weaves and textures. He is interested in the shape of the garment as a whole, but often seems to assume that this shape is given to the garment by certain key pieces of cloth and that there are many pieces which are less important. Underlying Rahner's attitude is the assumption that one can treat different pieces differently, according to such criteria as authorship and genre. He also appears to think that a pair of segments which clash or fit awkwardly together will not ruin the shape of the garment (indeed it may even be that together they contribute to its unique shape). One senses that for Gregory, if someone pulled a single thread from the cloth, the whole garment of Scripture would fall apart; Rahner, on the other hand, seems to be content with the fact that certain of the pieces do not fit neatly together. In other words, he takes what has been described above as the third option: Scripture as a whole points to universal salvation, but its message is not precisely coherent. Furthermore, Rahner thinks that the same applies to Church dogmas as to Scripture: each statement must be read as part of a whole, but within that whole certain pairs of statements may clash.

The reason for this attitude to Scripture and Church teaching is that Rahner believes that both reflect the truth of Christ rather than embody it precisely. Hence they are true in the sense that they correspond to the truth; but they are not true in every respect, in the sense that the body of Scripture or the collection of teachings of the Church can be treated like a list of

[9] Rahner, *Foundations*, 443.

precisely worded propositions related to one another by strict logic. In this he is surely right, and he also correctly stresses that the Bible and the body of Church doctrine are each the work of various human authors writing under different historical conditions. It is these differences in perspective which are at least partly responsible for the fact that the whole is not fully coherent. However, one might protest that although Scripture and Church teaching inevitably lack the coherence of a *magnum opus* of a master craftsman, yet it is the job of a theologian to reflect on the biblical and dogmatic material and draw a more systematic account of Christianity from it. It may well be true, as Rahner insists, that one can never distil pure theology from Scripture and dogma, leaving historical and cultural conditioning behind; however, it seems that one author, writing from a single historico-cultural perspective, should be able to avoid a thoroughgoing and unresolved tension in his theology.[10]

The second reason for Rahner's belief that certain pairs of eschatological statements are irreconcilable is evident in his hermeneutical principle: eschatological statements must be read in the light of the present experience of salvation, in the expectation of fulfilment. Rahner is right to stress that a person's present experience of salvation is indeed ambiguous; however, whereas he sees this truthfully reflected in the ambiguity of his eschatology, the question remains of whether Christian hope should transcend that ambiguity and produce unequivocal eschatological statements. This need not mean an outright prediction of universal salvation: an expression of hope is not a prediction, but it does eliminate paradox. In sum then, Rahner's view of universal salvation is coherent and attractive when expressed in terms of hope; but because he sometimes goes further than this and speaks both of the possibility of hell and of the certainty of God's world-wide victory in love, he leaves a tension in his eschatology with which it is difficult to deal.

iii. Hope: Between Prediction and Paradox

Although Gregory does put forward philosophical arguments that all will be saved, these are acceptable only to those who share his

[10] Keith Ward challenges Rahner on this point: *Religion and Human Nature* (Oxford University Press, Oxford, 1998), 296, referring to Rahner, *Foundations*, 443.

Platonic premisses; his argument derived from the nature of punishment, on the other hand, rests ultimately on his belief that Scripture reveals God as willing the good of all people. Similarly, Rahner's anthropology fills out, but does not ground his hope for universal salvation: Scripture (reflected in the teachings of the Church) is the foundation. Thus in comparing Gregory's and Rahner's grounds for hoping for universal salvation, one inevitably comes to compare their interpretation of the Bible.

It is reasonable to assert that Scripture at least leaves the possibility of universal salvation open—most Churches reject the doctrine of double predestination. Furthermore, both Gregory and Rahner convincingly show that the Bible gives good grounds for thinking that this possibility will be fulfilled. However, the two theologians then part company, Gregory believing that a universal consummation is a certainty, while Rahner expresses it as a hope or holds it in a paradoxical tension with the possibility of hell. To side with Gregory is to accept that Scripture is a fully-coherent whole in which apparent references to actual damnation can be explained away. However, this view, although attractive, is ultimately too optimistic about the possibility of the reconciliation of various biblical texts and does not do justice to their sheer diversity. On the other hand, accepting the paradox of heaven and hell as Rahner sometimes does means agreeing not only that there are tensions in Scripture, but that these are ultimately irreducible and are mirrored in the teachings of the Church and in theological reflection. This view is too pessimistic: whilst acknowledging that there are irresolvable tensions in Scripture, one can try to reflect upon Scripture in a more systematic way. Consequently, it seems most reasonable to assert that Christians should hope that all will be saved (whilst acknowledging the possibility that some may not) instead of either asserting the certainty of the universal victory of God's love or affirming both this certainty and the possibility of hell together.

B. HOW WILL ALL BE SAVED?

i. This Life: *Philosophia* and Decision

Both Gregory and Rahner recognize that, although divine grace is the fundamental cause of salvation, people must do something to accept that grace in such a way that it transforms them. For Gregory the key concept summing up human action is *philosophia* —a word which is perhaps best expressed in English as the pursuit of virtue. A life devoted to *philosophia* is one in which one trains oneself to recognize and to will those things which are truly good.[11] Rahner's key concept is that of decision—apparently a radically different view of the human element in salvation. Gregory and Rahner thus seem, at first sight, to be on either side of the divide between works and faith. As we have seen, however, the meaning which Rahner gives to decision includes, but goes beyond, a conscious explicit commitment of oneself in faith to God. As his writing on 'anonymous Christianity' shows, decision can be an 'unthematic' commitment to the mystery of God through a life of selfless love. Because Rahner believes that love of God and love of neighbour are one, loving one's neighbour is not *evidence* of an unthematic, even unknown, commitment to God; rather, it *is* such a commitment. If one sees faith as not just simple belief in, but worshipful commitment of oneself to God, one can appreciate that Rahner's analysis of decision attempts to mend the old dichotomy between faith and works: in his interpretation, the works involved in loving one's neighbour are instantiations of an unthematic love of, commitment to, or faith in God.

The notion of decision as loving commitment might seem to bring Rahner a little nearer to Gregory; but in fact there is still a gap between them, for there are two ways of conceiving of what 'works' are. First, one can think of altruistic actions: loving one's neighbour, or, as Rahner puts it, radically risking oneself for another.[12] Secondly, one can think of achieving moral and spiritual purity or, to use Gregory's Greek word for this, *apatheia*. Thus the problem is that Gregory seems to be advocating an ethic focused entirely on self-improvement, in contrast with Rahner's emphasis on altruism. Clearly, Gregory was writing in the context of the ancient world in which it was natural to structure ethics around moral character, specifically virtue, rather than around particular moral actions. Hence, it is

[11] As noted in Chapter 3, section C. ii., it does *not* mean philosophy.
[12] See 'A Brief Anthropological Creed', in *Foundations*, 456.

unsurprising that Gregory connects *philosophia* with the attainment of virtue. Nevertheless, although this may explain why Gregory expresses himself in this way, it does not necessarily justify such an approach. Although virtue ethics have always been popular with theologians in the tradition of Thomas Aquinas (who looked back to and augmented Aristotle's concept of virtue) and have become increasingly influential in the twentieth century amongst theologians of many traditions (partly due to secular philosophers' interest), there is still a suspicion that virtue is another name for self-improvement and that as such it is selfish.

This complaint, however, is not fair for several reasons. First, although an ethic based on virtue may result in self-improvement, it is not the case that agents who act virtuously do so *with the aim* of self-improvement. This is clear, for example, with the virtue of generosity: we only call someone truly generous if he or she is willingly generous; we would not describe as generous someone who acted generously in order to become a 'good' or 'virtuous' person. Their true motive is important. So, although some would argue that all ethical actions must be altruistic and that the practice of virtue cannot be altruistic, in fact it makes perfect sense to say that altruism is a virtue, if one regards self-improvement as the result of and not the motive for virtuous action. Secondly, it seems fair to argue that if ethics aims at human good, it aims at the good for the agent as well as the good for the subject of ethical behaviour. Particularly in a religious context, it seems most peculiar to assert that, in the long term, ethical behaviour is not good for the agent. Again, it must be stressed that one is not talking here of reward: virtuous behaviour is not good for the agent because he or she will go to heaven; rather it is good simply because humans were designed to be virtuous. Gregory's concept of creation in the image of God, for example, seems to suggest this latter view. In this respect, then, Gregory is not so very far away from Rahner—although Rahner expresses the same idea in a negative sense in his eschatology: vicious behaviour is bad for people, not because they will subsequently endure punishment for it, but rather because sin is its own punishment and all people must live out the indelible effects of their sins. Finally, whereas the connotations of the term 'self-improvement' suggest improvement of oneself *by* oneself, Gregory assumes that ethical action is made possible by the Spirit of God. *Philosophia* is complemented by sanctification.

However, there are still troublesome elements of Gregory's concept of virtue. On the one hand, Gregory is at pains to stress that the life of *philosophia* includes care for the poor and sick. For example, in his account of the life of his sister Macrina he highlights her miraculous powers of healing. Furthermore, he describes the life of *philosophia* as active, that is, not just contemplative.[13] On the other hand, the virtue Gregory chooses to highlight—*apatheia*—seems to be singularly self-regarding and he does often give the impression that *apatheia* is not just the result of a good life, but is that towards which the good person is constantly aiming. This colouring may not have been intentional, but it is impossible to read Gregory from a post-Kantian perspective without being slightly suspicious about the role which motive plays in his ethics.

Rahner's interpretation of decision does not suffer from this problem—it also has a further advantage over Gregory's concept of *apatheia*. Because Rahner sees decision in terms of a commitment of love it is easier to understand how decision can also apply to humanity in a collective sense: humanity as a whole decides for God when it becomes co-creator of itself and of its environment in a way which is loving and responsible. In contrast, it is more difficult (although perhaps not completely impossible) to envisage how humanity could collectively cultivate *apatheia*. Yet as soon as one ascribes a task to humanity collectively, the question of self-interest fades away: the goal of the co-creation of humanity includes me, but is not restricted to me. Thus although it is clearly good for humans both as individuals and collectively to decide for God, this does not necessarily involve a dubious selfish motive.

For these reasons, Gregory is mistaken in his interpretation of the role of human works in accepting the grace of salvation in the course of this life. Yet a question about Rahner remains: in trying to bridge the gap between faith and works, has he in fact abandoned the true sense of faith? Rahner, however, firmly and consistently denies the idea that faith, or decision, is a purely

[13] Gregory of Nyssa, *De vita Mac.: SC* 178, §6, 162.

epistemological concern. He is not just saying that faith is a commitment, rather than a mere assent, to a particular belief. Nor is he just saying that that commitment cannot be regarded as true unless it is revealed in the action of the one who has faith. Rather he is asserting that certain behaviour (radical love of neighbour) is in itself a commitment to (or love of) God. This is not denying faith or decision any cognitive content at all: merely denying that it always has thematic content. Thus although the 'anonymous Christian's' unthematic decision for God should ideally become thematized and explicit so that the person has faith in Christ in the way one would normally understand it, this is not necessary for salvation.

Rahner's analysis possibly arises partly from his reflections on the psychology of decision. However, it is also, and perhaps primarily, prompted by the demands of his strong belief in the universal saving will of God, which forces him to ask the question of how people who have not heard the gospel of Christ can be saved. Similarly, such scriptural concepts as 'the people of God' and 'covenant' motivate him to ask how humanity might be said to respond to God collectively. Thus Rahner's interpretation of the human response to God not only does justice to the complexity of decision as a cognitive, volitional, and behaviour-related concept, but it is also coherent with the rest of his theology and eschatology. Its great advantages over Gregory's notion of *philosophia* are that it gives a proper role to faith and that it can be more easily applied to humanity collectively as well as to individuals.

ii. This Life: *Sunergeia*; Immanent and Transcendent Consummation

Whereas the previous section dealt with the relation between faith and works in the human reception of divine grace, this one will compare the views of Gregory and Rahner on the interrelation of divine and human action. To a certain extent, it is true to say that both theologians regard this interaction as mysterious: they state that salvation has both a divine and a human dimension, without delving too deeply into the question of precisely how these two fit together. Of the two, Rahner is perhaps the more precise, not so much because he feels he can delineate the precise relation between divine and human action, but more because he wishes to rule out some possible false readings. Whereas Gregory's notion of *sunergeia* runs the risk of being (mis)interpreted to mean that God responds to (and thus rewards) an initial human effort, Rahner is very clear that God is the source of any human reaching out to the divine: God is both the gift of salvation and that which makes the acceptance of the gift possible. Thus, Rahner rules out any interpretation which might hint at Pelagianism, whereas Gregory, writing before the Pelagian controversy, does not have the same awareness of the possible implications of his more loose explanation. Rahner's explanation has the additional advantage that it is consistent with the perception of many Christian ethicists who would insist that the true ethical enterprise begins after, and indeed springs from, the reception of God's offer of the grace of salvation: because of Rahner's idea of God's universally present grace he is able to say that truly ethical action is not the result of but is co-extensive with decision.

The problem is that in his eagerness to avoid the impression that humans earn salvation, Rahner sometimes comes close to saying that salvation is imposed upon them. If the source of all human movement towards God is itself divine, how can humans be said to be in any way responsible for responding to God? The answer must be that for Rahner human freedom is not absolute autonomy (in other words freedom *from* God), but rather living in the manner for which humanity was created: a life in and with God (freedom *in* God). This is a view which stresses the all-pervading influence of God on the world and sees it not as a constraint, but as the very life-force of creation. That it does not contradict true human freedom is ultimately a datum of faith for Rahner, just as it is a matter of faith for Gregory that the soul's inevitable eschatological participation in God is an expression of true freedom. In itself Rahner's is a coherent view of freedom in a theological and eschatological context, although clearly not one which is likely to win universal consent. The problem with his conception of the interrelation of divine and human action is thus perhaps not so much that what he advocates is not real freedom, but that the sort of freedom which he advocates seems to be heading towards an ultimate and inevitable positive resolution: universal salvation. But this conflicts with his frequent insistence that humans can reject God. This difficulty over the concept of freedom, then, is linked to Rahner's paradoxical language about salvation and the possibility of hell, which was noted earlier: the ambiguity of individuals' present experience of salvation is due to the fundamental ambiguity of freedom and decision.[14] Again one must ask whether Rahner is correct in being content with this paradox.

iii. After Death and in Death: Human Freedom and Life in God

A major difficulty in comparing Gregory's and Rahner's eschatologies lies in their very different conceptions of what life 'after' death is. Gregory consistently stresses the progress of the soul after death and is clear that all those who did not turn to God in their lifetime will do so afterwards. The very idea of progress after death implies a temporal state and Gregory's concept of perpetual progress suggests that this temporality will be permanent. However, humans will not experience time after death as they did before it: time in eternity will not bring decay.

By contrast, Rahner (at least early in his career) is adamant that there is no time 'after' death: rather death is the gateway to timeless eternity. In parallel with this idea runs his original conviction that no decision can be made after death. It is not clear whether the belief that death is timelessly eternal is due to his belief that a decision for God can be made only in this lifetime, or vice versa. Although he sometimes sounds as if the timeless nature of life after death is logically prior, there is good reason to suggest the opposite: in his later writings, the more Rahner considers the possibility of a decision after death, the less committed he seems to be to utter timelessness after death. Thus in his discussions of purgatory, he speaks both of certain people having the opportunity for decision after their death and of purgatory possessing a temporality which is analogous to time in this life. In this respect, it appears that there is a significant development in Rahner's thought and that changes in his beliefs about salvation alter his metaphysical convictions about time

[14] See section A. ii. above.

after death.[15] The issues surrounding death and time do not seem to be fully resolved in his theology. Of the two positions, Gregory's is the more consistent and coherent.

Notwithstanding this difficulty, is it possible to make any comparison between Gregory's and Rahner's views of the individual's relation to God after or in death? As we have seen, Gregory stresses the role of punishment as both revealing the effect of sin and purifying people from it. He stresses the passivity of this experience, in contrast with his emphasis on freedom as autonomy for action in life before death. One can therefore argue that this is the means by which Gregory reconciles the certainty of the outcome of salvation with the importance of human autonomy in this life: God will bring about universal salvation by imposing post-mortem punishment on those who did not repent in their lifetime; because God is loving and omnipotent this punishment will not fail to reform. As argued in Chapter 3, one can view the result of this punishment as a sort of freedom, in the sense that Gregory seems to believe that true freedom is the freedom to be able only to love God. This is perhaps a stronger form of the idea of freedom in God (as opposed to independence from God), which was discussed earlier in relation to Rahner's concept of decision.

Rahner agrees with Gregory to the extent that he denies the view that divine punishment is retributive, although he stresses more than Gregory the idea that post-mortem punishment is the experience of the intrinsic consequences of sin, rather than something imposed extrinsically by God.[16] Hell, if it exists for anyone, is the timelessly eternal suffering of the consequences of sin; in purgatory some people suffer the effects of their sin in such a way that it causes a change in their fundamental attitude to God, whereas others who have already decided for God suffer the effects of sin in a way which makes them ready for an eternal relationship of love with the divine. Hence, Rahner's view of purgatory may be compared to Gregory's view of post-mortem

[15] Although he seems to consider the possibility of purgatory being in some sense temporal, Rahner appears always to view the ultimate state (heaven, the beatific vision, resurrection) as timeless.

[16] The difference between God actively imposing punishment and God creating the world in such a way that sins are eventually visited upon the sinner is not very significant: in both cases, God intended sin to have a certain effect.

punishment, in the sense that it both reveals the effects of sin and causes the sinner to change. On the whole, Rahner's account of the experience of punishment stresses its passivity, but he does think that those in purgatory who have not yet previously had the opportunity to decide for God must make this decision in freedom. Freedom here, however, must be understood in the same way as Rahner views freedom in life: that is, not as autonomy in the sense of Gregory's view of freedom before death, but as a complex relationship between the transcendent and immanent in the individual. In the beatific vision, or resurrection, freedom seems to be an irrelevance, according to Rahner: for him freedom means freedom to decide, and in eternal bliss individuals will have neither the need nor the ability to decide. That this fulfilment of human life is a desirable and a permanent state is beyond doubt though, so perhaps it can be regarded as equivalent to the postulated idea of true freedom in Gregory's eschatology. This interpretation of Rahner's and Gregory's views on freedom can be summarized in Figure 2.

Gregory thinks that humans have more autonomy in this life than Rahner believes them to have; after death this autonomy is replaced negatively by a passive experience of punishment and positively by the freedom only to love God. Rahner thinks that both in this life and in purgatory the freedom to decide is not a freedom which allows autonomy from God, but is an imperfect form of freedom in God. This freedom to decide is perfected after death and eventually consummated, so that freedom becomes irrelevant in the eschatological life with God. As has been noted, Gregory's view of the possibility of change after death is more consistent than Rahner's. On the other hand, Rahner's concept of decision is more subtle than Gregory's. This subtlety does run the risk of becoming obscurity on the issue of how free humans are to say no to God, but it does do better justice to modern awareness of the various constraints on human freedom in decision and to the theological belief that all life is lived, to some extent, within the divine presence. Both theologies are united, however, in showing that the human journey moves from imperfect to perfect forms of the human relation to God—that is, towards a resolution of that tension between divine grace and human freedom which exists in this life. Fundamentally, the differences between Rahner's consummation of freedom and

	Gregory of Nyssa	Karl Rahner
this life	All have **freedom to act.** (= co-operation *with* God (*sunergeia*); but to some extent this is also freedom *from* God, or autonomy)	All have **freedom to decide.** (= freedom *in* God—*not* autonomy—but as yet not perfectly fulfilled)
after/ in death	**No freedom to act.** Punishment is imposed on those who are not already transformed.	Purgatory: a few have **freedom to decide**; others live out the consequences of their sin. (= freedom in God being fulfilled)
	Result: all have **freedom to love.** (= perfect freedom *in* God)	Ultimately, **freedom** an irrelevance in a timeless state. (= fulfilment of a history of freedom)

Figure 2.

Gregory's freedom only to love God are differences in nuance alone: their shared conception of a final perfect relationship between humanity and the divine is their way of expressing the truth that God will be 'all in all'.

C. CONCLUSIONS

This comparison of two interpretations of the idea of universal salvation has rested on the assumption that one can make some kind of distinction between the basic content and the form or expression of an idea. Thus, at the most simple level, both theologians express a similar object of hope or expectation—that God will be all in all—but Gregory uses Platonic and other ancient philosophical ideas to express and defend it, whilst Rahner's account is greatly influenced by existentialism and Transcendental Thomism. Returning to the metaphor used in the introduction, one may be tempted to compare the idea of universal salvation to a stream: the content (water) stays the same, even though it may change in form over its course, being in turn perhaps a swift-running rivulet, a waterfall, and a broad but sluggish river.

However, it is now time to examine this underlying assumption more rigorously. First, is there in fact a *substantial* common content to Gregory's and Rahner's ideas of universal salvation? and if there is, can it be described as genuinely Christian?

Secondly, are the differences in the two theologians' views attributable merely to changes in form—or has the content changed too? and in either case, what factors are responsible for this development?

i. Similarities: Is Universal Salvation a Christian Doctrine?[17]

The first and most striking similarity between the two treatments of universal salvation studied in this book is that they both structure eschatology around the central idea of fulfilment. This is expressed by the word ἀποκατάστασις (restoration) in the case of Gregory, and *Vollendung* (consummation) in the case of Rahner. As we have seen, for Gregory ἀποκατάστασις does not mean the return to an actual state of perfection which humans possessed before the Fall, despite what the basic meaning of the Greek word might suggest. Rather, in the light of his doctrine of the two creations, it means the achievement of a perfection which was always intended by God for creation. This did in a sense exist from the beginning as the form of (or potentiality in) creation, but will only be actual at the eschaton. Gregory often expresses this idea by means of the concept of the image of God: humankind was always intended by God to be in the divine image; however, because of human fallibility (represented by the Fall) it can never fully possess that image until the eschaton. Rahner too works with the idea that humankind was created for a relationship with God, towards which it is presently aiming and which will finally be perfected. So, both theologians have a

[17] The quest to retrieve a core belief or beliefs from different accounts of the universal salvation to a certain extent follows Rahner's own treatment of various Christian doctrines. However, while Rahner performs this task in the specific context of the Roman Catholic Church with the aim of establishing which elements of Church teaching are dogmatically binding, this study will limit itself to the less specific and more ecumenical question of whether the core can be said to constitute a truly Christian doctrine.

teleological view of creation (or of humanity, at least) heading towards the eschaton as its consummation, fulfilment, and perfection. All three words (which I take to be synonymous) refer equally well to both Rahner's concept of *Vollendung* and Gregory's idea of ἀποκατάστασις.

It is clear, then, that these two theologians see the eschaton as continuous with the present history of the world in some way (although Rahner would disagree that it is the *temporal* continuation of world history). Divine consummation, fulfilment, or perfection means that God will make an already-present reality as whole, complete, or good as possible—not that God will bring about an altogether new and different reality. Evidently, neither Gregory nor Rahner are proposing an eschatology in which 'a new heaven and a new earth' come about as a radical break with the old. Nor are they advocating a realized eschatology—neither in the sense that they believe that the perfection of the world has already been completed in the incarnation, life, death, and resurrection of Christ, nor in the sense that they give the 'vertical' axis of the believer's relation to God overwhelming importance over the 'horizontal' axis of history's movement towards the future. Rather, both can be seen as proponents of an inaugurated eschatology: the grounds for the fulfilment of the universe were established in creation and re-established in Christ after the Fall; thus a process of perfection has begun in him through the Spirit, but will not be completed until the end-times.

A second similarity is that in addition to agreeing that humankind is created for fulfilment, Rahner and Gregory also concur to a certain extent on what that fulfilment is. To simplify somewhat, Gregory talks of the perfection of human love and knowledge of God; Rahner expresses similar thoughts through the image of the beatific vision, which he construes not as a merely intellectual perception of God, but as an activity of faith, hope and love. Because both theologians believe that the eschaton will bring the perfection of what has gone before, they both see this final relationship with the divine as the perfection of the experience of salvation in this life. Rahner makes this point explicitly in his discussion of hermeneutics; Gregory seems to be affirming the same thing in his use of the concept of participation (μετουσία)—the soul can participate in God in this life, but will only be able to do so in an unimpeded way in the next. Indeed, it is tempting to draw a close comparison between the role of participation in Gregory's theology and that of the *Vorgriff* (understood in the context of God's self-communication) in Rahner's: although they rest on different philosophical and psychological assumptions, both concepts express a dynamic movement of the human person towards God which is present to some degree in all individuals, which occurs (at least partially) through grace, and which can only be fulfilled by grace. Gregory has no concept directly parallel to Rahner's supernatural existential, but his idea that all humans are created in the image of God fulfils a similar function, expressing both the universality and the graciousness of that which makes possible a human's relationship with God.

Importantly, both theologians stress that despite this gracious but innate tendency toward the divine, God can never be fully grasped by the human subject. God is, and always will be, divine mystery: both writers interpret this to mean not an emptiness, but a fullness of being. Put another way, God is too great, not too distant, to know. The result of this is that the dynamic movement of the soul is not so much an infinite movement towards an object which never can be reached, but an infinite movement *within* God (without implying that the soul is completely identified with God).[18] Gregory's and Rahner's depictions of the mysterious relationship between humanity and God are undoubtedly fuelled by their own lives of prayer and are reflected in their spiritual works: for example, the role Gregory gives to darkness in the encounter with God (symbolized in the *Life of Moses* by the cloud on Mount Sinai) is parallel to the place of silence in Rahner's writings on prayer.[19]

Connected with their accounts of the fundamental human relationship with God are Gregory's and Rahner's concepts of time and materiality in the afterlife. Here one can find a third similarity—albeit rather a broad one. Gregory's detailed account

[18] See Rahner, *Foundations*, 129: '[God's self-communication] means nothing else but that the spirit's transcendental movement in knowledge and love towards the absolute mystery is borne by God himself in his self-communication in such a way that this movement has its term and its source not in the holy mystery as eternally distant and as a goal which can only be reached asymptotically, but rather in the God of absolute closeness and immediacy.' For Gregory of Nyssa's doctrine of perpetual progress see above, Chapter 2, section A. iii.

[19] See, for example, Rahner's *Encounters with Silence* (Burns & Oates, London, 1975).

of the resurrection of the physical body in *De anima et resurrectione* shows that he takes the materiality of the eschatological state very seriously; furthermore, his idea of the perpetual progress of the soul suggests a concept of eternal, but perfect, time. For Rahner also, the human being is both spiritual and material. Materiality is not just an aspect of those people who still need to be perfected, nor will it be abandoned at the eschaton: heaven already contains some glorified bodies (e.g. those of Jesus Christ and the Virgin Mary) and, at the end, all spirit and matter together will be consummated, so that 'it will then be equally correct to call the one new reality a new heaven or a new earth'.[20] Rahner is much more cautious than Gregory about the idea of time after death, but some notion of temporality seems to be suggested by his notion of the 'pan-cosmicity' of the human soul (its association with the whole world) in death and, in his later theology, by his interpretation of purgatory. In any case, for Rahner, eternity is the fulfilment or the perfect fruit of time, rather than its negation. Thus, despite the obvious differences between them, Gregory's and Rahner's interpretations of resurrection do at least have the same purpose in mind. Each seeks to answer the question: what will human life be like when it has been released from the present deficiencies of material existence, without leaving materiality completely behind? With Gregory's concept of the perpetual progress of the soul and Rahner's idea of the atemporality of life 'in' death, each is seeking to express the possibility of some sort of human existence apart from an experience of time which is inevitably wed to decay. They both appear to believe that the rest of creation will be included in universal salvation, although neither is very interested in this issue: the implication is that humanity is the apex of creation and that other material things will be saved by virtue of the salvation of humanity. The differences in Gregory's and Rahner's answers to questions regarding materiality and temporality can be explained partly by changing scientific understanding and partly by different opinions as to what must be retained when human nature is fulfilled and what can be abandoned. However, these do not seem to be fundamental theological differences.

Fourthly and finally, as the first part of this chapter showed,

[20] Rahner, 'The Resurrection of the Body': *TI* ii. 215.

both Gregory and Rahner see the hope or expectation of universal salvation as grounded in the overwhelming love of God, revealed in Jesus Christ and witnessed to by Scripture. They both concur in the belief that God's purpose will be worked out through an interaction of divine love and human freedom, although they disagree as to the exact relation between these two factors.

Hence, if one were to try to retrieve a central core of belief about universal salvation from the eschatologies of Gregory and Rahner, one could perhaps state it as follows.

- The world was created by God in order to be wholly fulfilled by God. In particular, God wills all people to be saved.
- To this end, humanity was created with a gracious, but innate, tendency to reach out to God; however, this tendency was damaged in the Fall. Christ's life, death, and resurrection transfigure human life so that people are able once more to reach out to God.
- Salvation is a mysterious interplay of grace and response: the initial human tendency towards God is itself gracious; revelation, and the offer and fulfilment of salvation, are due to divine grace. In this life humans should individually or collectively accept divine grace in freedom in order that it may transform them.
- However, from human experience of the world, it seems very likely that some people do not have the opportunity to turn to God in their lifetime (because they die in infancy or appear to lack the capacity to respond to God), or fail to take up that opportunity (because they appear to die faithless or unrepentant of great sin). Because of the divine wish for the world to be fulfilled in its entirety, God allows at least some people to respond after, or in, death. However, this freedom to decide about God is a freedom of a somewhat curtailed sort; consequently, a change of heart about God (together with the unresolved effects of sin) will be experienced after death as judgement and punishment.
- The result of a decision for God in this life or punishment in the next is the truest freedom: a life lived in union with God. This is not a radical break with the current human relationship with God, but the fulfilment of the experience of salvation now; hence, despite the ambiguity of the present life, the

experience of communion with the divine in prayer is an intimation of the future life with God.

- Salvation does not affect humanity alone, because the whole cosmos is aiming towards a divine consummation—a tendency which was created and is sustained by God. This notion of the eschaton as the goal of the universe does not imply human moral advance from one century to another: rather it suggests that God is the consummation towards which all people and all aspects of the universe at all times are directed. In the end, the Christian can expect, or hope, that God will indeed be 'all in all'.

Is this a Christian doctrine? The framework of creation, fall, redemption and consummation is common to all Christian belief. The interpretation of this framework by Gregory and Rahner suggests that Christians are right to expect, or hope for, a universal consummation, given what has been revealed to them about God's love in creation and redemption. This may lead some theologians to accuse them of underestimating the damage caused by human waywardness, epitomized by the idea of the Fall. Human freedom, it may be argued, inevitably leads to sin. However, neither Gregory nor Rahner fails to take evil and sin seriously: Rahner in particular, living in the centre of Europe, and experiencing two world wars and most of the Cold War, was acutely aware of the human capacity for evil. His doctrine of purgatory is not just about allowing an opportunity for some people to decide for God after their deaths; rather it is primarily the context in which the effects of sin are experienced even by those who have turned to God. It is thus an acknowledgement that much sin can remain unresolved in this life. Gregory can be accused with more reason than Rahner of being too optimistic about the human condition, but his more pastoral writings show that he does not underestimate suffering and it can be argued that his eschatological optimism springs precisely from a pessimistic view of the current evil in the world. More fundamentally, however, to the extent to which Gregory and Rahner are optimistic, their optimism is based not on human capabilities, but on divine power and love.

Indeed, other theologians might want to argue that Gregory's and Rahner's hope for universal salvation is not Christian, because it rests too heavily on divine power and love to the exclusion of human freedom. Faith is meaningless, they would argue, unless it is completely free. However, although this may be true if one sees faith as a purely cognitive commitment, it has been seen that neither Gregory nor Rahner sees the response to God in those terms. Indeed, the complexity of Rahner's concept of decision forces one to ask whether humans ever have that sort of absolute autonomy to decide which many theologians assume. Furthermore, the suggestion in Gregory's writings that the truest freedom is living in union with God (and thus having lost the freedom to decide against him) must be considered seriously: although certain sorts of freedom are valuable, is there value in the sort of freedom which allows the creation ultimately to fall short of God's intention for it? Those who think that there is not, can affirm with Gregory that God's plans for the positive fulfilment of the whole world will come to fruition, albeit through punishment which may appear coercive. Others may feel that room should be left for an individual commitment of faith which is free in some meaningful sense, although not completely autonomous. They can express a prayerful hope that all people will use this freedom to decide for God and that the whole universe will be fulfilled.

A third criticism which might be raised is that neither Gregory nor Rahner gives an appropriately central role to Christ. In particular, this might appear to be the case in the light of the accounts given of Gregory's and Rahner's eschatologies in this book. However, although it is true that Christ is not so prominent in the writing of Gregory and Rahner as he is in some other theologians, such a criticism is not completely fair. In the first place, the present study has concentrated on soteriology only in its eschatological dimension and eschatology mainly in its universal scope. Neither theologian doubts that Christ died for all: the question, as they see it, is whether all will benefit from his death and resurrection. Thus the debate has centred on the human reception of the divine grace of salvation through Christ and not on Christ's atoning death and resurrection in themselves. Although, as we have seen, even the human response to God is itself infused with the divine, this presence of God is seen more in terms of the Spirit, if it is assigned to one member of the Trinity at all. (Rahner, in his discussion of decision, tends to talk of God, rather than of Father, Son, or Spirit.) Secondly, Christ does appear in the account each gives of specific eschatological doctrines: for example, Gregory's interpretation of Philippians 2: 10 suggests that the experience of bowing the knee to Christ is to be linked with both judgement and punishment. Rahner is more hesitant about assigning a specific eschatological role to Christ, largely because he moves away from the more pictorial expressions of eschatological events such as the parousia. However, although he does question the usefulness of some of the traditional imagery, he does not attempt to deny the eschatological presence and action of Christ—for example, both Gregory and Rahner connect their accounts of the resurrection with that of Christ, the 'first-fruits' of all creation. Finally, Christ has an important structural role in the eschatologies of each. Clearly, for Gregory, 1 Corinthians 15 is vital: all things will be submitted to Christ and he will then submit them to the Father. Thus the end of the universe is linked with the beginning in that all things were created through the Word and all will come to their end through him. For Rahner, Christ is the hermeneutical key to all eschatological assertions. Consummation is the fulfilment of the experience of salvation now and that experience is precisely 'faith in the incarnation of the Logos, in the death and resurrection of Christ'.[21] Thus Rahner is right to emphasize that eschatology must be Christology and anthropology transposed into a hope for their fulfilment. The reason why this book has concentrated more on the anthropological issues is because it is precisely the human response to salvation which is in doubt, not the potentially universal effectiveness of Christ's salvific acts.

Clearly, there will be differing opinions as to what the criterion of a Christian doctrine is and this is not the place to discuss that issue in detail. Nevertheless, although Rahner and Gregory express a belief with which not all Christians would agree, there are good grounds for thinking theirs is a Christian belief—particularly if it is expressed as a hope rather than as a certain prediction.

[21] Rahner, 'The Hermeneutics of Eschatological Assertions': *TI* iv. 342–3.

ii. Differences: The Nature and Causes of Change

Despite the broad similarities highlighted above, which one can take as the core content of a doctrine of universal salvation, nonetheless there are clearly many differences between Gregory's and Rahner's interpretations of the idea of universal salvation. The question thus arises of the nature of these differences: are they merely a matter of form or also of content? If the differences between them are in form alone, there seems to be no easy way to judge which theologian's answers are better: we can only say that one expresses himself more clearly or convincingly than the other, or perhaps that each author's interpretation is appropriate to his own context. Another important question is why changes of this sort are such a notable feature of Christian doctrine. The metaphor of a river changing from rivulet to waterfall to river as it runs over different terrains perhaps encourages one to think that doctrine spontaneously and inevitably changes according to context, with little or no creative input from the theologian. Again, if this were true, it would undermine our attempts to judge between Gregory's and Rahner's ideas, because we could only say that their respective theologies are good examples of how doctrine adapts to fit its environment. It would suggest that only one response to a particular context is possible.

The first two parts of this chapter (sections A. and B.) highlighted some of the most important differences between Gregory's and Rahner's answers to the questions of whether and how all people will be saved. It is clear that at least some of these differences affect the content of the idea of universal salvation. For example, advances in scientific understanding mean that Rahner's explanation of the resurrection is radically different from Gregory's. Although the precise nature of the resurrection body does not constitute the central part of the doctrine of universalism for either theologian, nevertheless it is part of each man's explanation of how all will be saved, and of the nature of that salvation. It thus is clearly more than a difference in expression. Differences between the two not only involve their specific conceptions of the nature and means of salvation, but also have ramifications for the grounds they give for believing in universal salvation. Advances in the understanding of the historical genesis of Scripture mean that Rahner is unable to treat biblical evidence in exactly the same way as Gregory; similarly, he cannot use the same philosophical arguments for universal salvation as Gregory does. As we have seen, one of the consequences of these differences in argument is that while Gregory states with complete confidence that all will be saved, Rahner is opposed to such a dogmatic assertion. Hence, even if Gregory and Rahner were to agree completely on what universal salvation would be like, their doctrines would be different in content, since the former theologian would be asserting that Christians should expect such an outcome and the latter that they should hope for it.

It is perhaps less clear that the expression of a doctrine in one philosophical language rather than another affects its content. Indeed, Rahner himself often seems to be assuming that it does not; thus he feels that he is able to re-express traditional dogmas in ways which are intelligible to the modern believer, without undermining the idea that the teaching of the Roman Catholic Church is unchanging truth. Nevertheless, it seems from an examination of his eschatology at least that this view is mistaken. Most obviously, the previous chapters have made clear that the metaphysical framework of Rahner's eschatology, and in particular his conception of time, is intimately connected to his idea of decision, which in turn has important implications for his views about the possibility of universal salvation. Earlier in this chapter it was suggested that one could draw tentative comparisons between various pairs of theological concepts used by Gregory and Rahner: ἀποκατάστασις and *Vollendung*; the image of God and the supernatural existential; μετουσία and the interaction of the *Vorgriff* with God's self-communication. However, the philosophical background to the concept or word in each case means that each pair points to a difference between the two theologians' eschatologies which is subtle, yet more than simply a change in expression. For example, whereas μετουσία and *Vorgriff* both focus on the human agent, the concept of God's self-communication clearly emphasizes divine agency. This makes it clear that although Rahner is able to say that 'man . . . participates in God's being', he emphasizes that this is so only by virtue of the fact of 'the communication of God's Holy Spirit'.[22]

[22] i.e. God's self-communication; quotations from Rahner, *Foundations*, 120.

In other words, one is reminded that while Gregory is usually content to emphasize just the human side of the divine-human relation in salvation, Rahner either emphasizes both aspects or the divine side. This surely has implications for the content of each writer's version of eschatology, although it is mainly a difference in emphasis. Even the fact that Rahner feels that he has to rule out various possible misinterpretations means that his doctrine has a subtly different content from Gregory's: for instance, his concept of what it means to decide for or turn to God carefully avoids hints of Pelagianism or world-denying asceticism. It may even be the case that the metaphors used by each of the two theologians to illustrate the same doctrinal point affect the content of that doctrine in some subtle way.

It would be going too far to suggest that the above types of change undermine our earlier attempt to identify a common core content in Gregory's and Rahner's eschatologies: although most, if not all, forms of reinterpretation have implications for doctrinal content, that is not to say that the central contentions of the idea of universal salvation have changed beyond all recognition. If this were the case, there would be little sense in speaking of Christian tradition (or traditions) in eschatology at all. Nevertheless, it is equally disingenuous to claim that the changes have no effect at all on the content, as if each generation can hand on to the next a package of ideas totally unaltered. Consequently, the differences between Gregory and Rahner are worth comparing and discussing seriously with regard to their relative merits. They do affect the content of the idea of universal salvation, they do involve questions of truth and falsity and are thus not simply translations of the same idea into different conceptual languages.

The second question asked about the creative role of the individual theologian in the process of doctrinal change. Some models of the development of doctrine, hastily expressed, can give the impression that doctrine spontaneously adapts itself like a chameleon to each new environment—Rahner's own model is a case in point. However, on closer inspection it is clear that although Rahner regards doctrinal change as inevitable, he also thinks that its specific direction is the responsibility of the theologian: there can be more than one response to each particular context and thus it is the duty of Christian thinkers to reinterpret doctrine in the most truthful and meaningful way possible. It is not correct to treat doctrinal change as a phenomenon or force—even a divine one—entirely divorced from individual creativity. Rahner's own response to various developments in eschatology illustrates this point well: he is clear that theologians have the choice of reacting to existentialist interpretations of eschatology in three ways. First, they can travel wholeheartedly down the route of demythologization, with its emphasis on a thoroughly realized eschatology. Secondly, they can reject the influence of existentialism and continue to hold to the traditional more mythological expression of eschatology which is focused almost entirely on the future. Thirdly, they can seek to balance future hope and present experience, and to reinterpret eschatology in a way which elucidates the truth lying behind the mythological language, without hoping to get rid of it altogether. Thus, one can distinguish between the conditions for change (a strong interest in existentialism in the intellectual community) and the agents of change (individual theologians). Although the former are important, they are never the sole determinants of development in doctrine.

Consequently, it is fair not only to ask whether Gregory or Rahner gives better answers to the problems raised by universal salvation, but also to ask in each case why they respond to their context in the particular ways that they do and what theological priorities are revealed by their choices. Furthermore, because we are rejecting (at least with respect to the idea of universal salvation) a model of doctrinal change as an impersonal force, in favour of an analysis which sees the creativity of individual writers interacting with various conditions for change, it is also important not to assume any particular pattern of overall development. Eventually, it may turn out to be the case that there has been an overall pattern of progress in doctrinal change in eschatology. However, even if this does turn out to be the case, a historical study of the development of eschatological doctrine shows that it has already been a winding path with many detours, alternative routes, and—some would claim—blind alleys, precisely because of the creative input of theologians along the way. Consequently, one cannot *assume* that any one particular change is an improvement—in other words, that every way in which Rahner differs from Gregory represents progress.

Conversely, one cannot presuppose a uniform pattern of regress and regard patristic formulations as a pure form of Christian doctrine to be retrieved by the modern Church. Finally, because of the several possible directions of doctrinal change open to each theologian at any one time and because of the theologian's creative impetus in choosing between them, one cannot espouse a model which assumes on principle that no interpretation of a doctrine is objectively better than any other because each interpretation is 'only' a reaction to its context.

iii. Looking to the Future

This concluding chapter has aimed to find a common core content shared by Gregory's and Rahner's versions of Christian eschatology. It has also assessed the relative merits of Gregory's and Rahner's answers to the questions posed by the concept of universal salvation. Such a comparison is important because the differences between the two responses affect the content of the idea and are not simply changes in form. Furthermore, a critical yet constructive comparison between the two is possible because doctrinal change is the result of a creative interaction between thinkers and their environments: it is not an impersonal process in which every change is by necessity an instance of progress (or of regress), or in which one can only identify a process of value-neutral adaptation to environment. Hence one can identify valuable aspects in each thinker's interpretation.

If one compares Gregory's and Rahner's answers to the questions of whether and how all people will be saved, which set is the most convincing, relevant, and meaningful to people living out their faith in the twenty-first century? Where their replies differ, inevitably Rahner has the advantage. Not only does he write in a contemporary philosophical language and with an awareness of the modern scientific view of the world, but he addresses theological problems which have become pressing only in the centuries since Gregory died. There are some exceptions—notably Gregory's concept of time—but for the most part Rahner's treatment of these specific questions is the better.

However, although we take it for granted that some of Gregory's ideas have suffered from the passage of time, we may be inclined to overlook the fact that the same applies to Rahner. Nevertheless, because the approaches of both existentialism and Transcendental Thomism have been criticized, Rahner's own philosophical language is also likely to seem at least out-of-date, if not discredited. It must be remembered though that Rahner's own theology anticipates and answers such criticism. For, despite his own often overly-philosophical means of expression, the great theme of Rahner's theology is his aim to make Christian doctrines beliefs of the heart, not just of the mind. Most of the time implicitly, but sometimes explicitly, Rahner bases his theological writing on the idea that all Christian doctrines need *continual* re-expression in order for them to become meaningful for ordinary believers. This is both an admission and a challenge. It is an admission that his own 'theological investigations' will lose their relevance and meaningfulness. It challenges each new generation of theologians to re-express their beliefs in a creative response to new contexts, whilst keeping faithful to Christian tradition and learning from their theological predecessors.

How should we respond to that challenge now? What can we learn from these two theologians' approaches to eschatology in general and to the idea of universal salvation in particular? Although many of Gregory's ideas and expressions have now lost their original power and clarity because of the changing context, this has not irreparably damaged his main contentions—the core content of the idea of universal salvation, which he shares with Rahner. Furthermore, some of his metaphors and models have retained their significance, or are capable of developing expressive new facets of meaning. For example, one could usefully re-examine Gregory's powerful application of the idea of humanity being created in the image of God and his view of God as a personal judge and dispenser of punishment (in contrast with Rahner's emphasis on punishment as the inevitable consequence of sin).

A further illustration of one of Gregory's images which could be given a new level of meaning is his notion that human nature is 'one body'. While Gregory has a strong sense of the unity of humanity at the theoretical or ideal level, people in the modern world have a greater awareness than he of the interconnectedness of humankind at a practical level. First, technology has improved communications to such an extent that someone can travel to the other side of the earth in a day; moreover, news and fluctuations on the stock exchanges spread in seconds. Clearly such integration was unthinkable in Gregory's day, when even the furthest reaches of the known world seemed inaccessible to most people. Secondly, since the Enlightenment a growing emphasis on the moral equality of each human (often in conjunction with the recognition of human rights) has encouraged one to view humanity as a single ethical community, albeit composed of many other sub-communities. Although this perspective is threatened to a certain extent by moral relativism, in fact international political interaction depends on a recognition, at the most basic level, of common interest if not of common purpose. Again, modern technology has affected this sense of an ethical community: in the era of nuclear, biological, or chemical weapons and international terrorism, a war between two countries or even between two factions within one country necessarily becomes a concern for the wider international community. Similarly, large-scale ecological irresponsibility in one state has knock-on effects in others. Thus, there are very good reasons why one should continue to use Gregory's concept of humanity as a unified whole: even though the reasons for using this model are different, its theological (and eschatological) implications are still essentially the same.

One can be similarly inspired by Gregory's meditations on the Bible, adapting his imaginative interpretation and his bold application of scriptural imagery to new contexts. His focus on the Bible as a harmonious work with a single *skopos* will perhaps be particularly attractive to those who are disenchanted with historical criticism and are interested in other types of interpretation which focus on the final form of the biblical text—for Gregory assumes a radical unity in Scripture, while historical-critical methods have tended to emphasize the heterogeneity of the biblical corpus by drawing attention to the diversity of its human authors, sources, historical contexts and literary genres. One type of final form criticism which has attracted recent interest is the canonical approach to the interpretation of the Bible. This method recognizes that the man or woman of faith naturally reads the Bible as it has been received by the Church: that is, as a canon of certain texts which are read in the light of each other. This is certainly how Gregory reads Scripture; nevertheless his method differs from the canonical approach in at least one vital aspect. Even if they dispute some of the particular conclusions of historical-critical scholars, modern canon critics are unavoidably aware of the diversity in Scripture; yet despite this they attempt to read Scripture as if it were a whole. For Gregory, on the other hand, there is no 'as if': for him, the Bible really is the single coherent work of one divine author (albeit working through human intermediaries) and must be read as such.[23] According to Gregory, apparent inconsistencies are placed there by the Holy Spirit only in order to lead the reader to a higher meaning.

A second type of criticism which focuses on the final form is that based on postmodern literary techniques. Postmodern hermeneutics are complex and varied, but in general they represent a move away from an interest in the historical genesis of the text, and towards a focus on the text as it stands and on the reader's response to it as such. Consequently, what becomes important is the reader's interpretation of Scripture as a given whole, including the way in which he or she interprets a text both in the light of other biblical passages and in the light of his or her particular situation. In this respect, Gregory's method is very similar; nevertheless, the basic view of the text which underlies postmodernism is very different from Gregory's own. Whereas the postmodern focus on the reader's response is in direct contrast with (indeed, is a reaction against) a preoccupation with the author's original intended meaning, Gregory's approach depends on his central assumptions that God is the author of the text and that the Bible thus speaks a truth which is unchangeably and inherently its own. Whereas postmodern literary critics think that interpretations of the Bible are to be created in response to a particular context, Gregory believes that Scripture contains a truth which is there to be uncovered by the exegete. (Since it is the expression of God's own self, this truth is

[23] John Barton makes this point with regard to Patristic biblical criticism in general: John Barton, *Reading the Old Testament: Method in Biblical Study*, 2nd edn. (Darton, Longman & Todd, London, 1996), 99. I am also indebted to his analysis of modern canonical approaches to biblical criticism, with reference in particular to the work of B. S. Childs and James Barr (ibid. chs. 6 and 7).

mystery and will perhaps never be completely revealed; nevertheless it is there.)

Clearly, then, it would be unwise to exaggerate the similarities between Gregory's reading of Scripture and modern methods. It is also difficult to be sympathetic to some of Gregory's more detailed exegetical techniques: we have already denied that his use of allegory and typology can be said to show that Scriptures gives unequivocal grounds for a belief in universal salvation. Nevertheless, if one feels that attention to the final form of the text is at least one important aspect of exegesis, then one can be inspired by Gregory's approach, even if one rejects some of its results and his assumptions about authorship and intended meaning. In sum, the content of Gregory's eschatology is sometimes more convincing than Rahner's—for example, with regard to certain very specific issues, such as time. However, for the most part Gregory's eschatology will be more valuable in the future as a stimulus to creative and imaginative theological thought and expression than as a source for an entirely satisfactory doctrine of universal salvation.

When turning to Rahner, we have seen that there are a greater number of specific points in his eschatology from which we can usefully learn. In general, however, the most profitable aspect of Rahner's approach to eschatology is perhaps his attempt to identify the concerns of the age in which he lives and to reinterpret eschatology in a way which can engage with those concerns. How can we apply this method to eschatology in the future? Without attempting the impossible task of predicting what the world will become, one can perhaps point to some factors which a theologian working on universalistic eschatology will now have to bear in mind.

Perhaps the biggest change since Rahner's death has been the ending of the cold war. This has not brought in a new era of peaceful optimism, since the fear of impending nuclear war between the Superpowers has been replaced both by the fear of ecological catastrophe and by a growing realization of the smaller-scale, but more chaotic and pervasive presence of war and conflict throughout the globe. The term 'globalization' is increasingly being used both to describe the global scope of such crises and other human concerns, and also to explain their causes. (Globalization is not just an economic phenomenon, but has political, technological, and cultural aspects too.) However, ecological disasters and political crises can be prevented only by fully global co-operation; this may mean in turn a change in what is regarded as a properly global view. In other words, globalization ideally should direct the attention of the powerful towards the southern hemisphere and the east, away from the north and especially away from the predominantly Christian north-west, thus encouraging a recognition of the increasing independence and importance of so-called developing or formerly colonial countries. In turn, theologians need to respond with a more truly global conception of theology, which takes very seriously religious cultures throughout the world. This requires scholarly study and a recognition not just of the similarities, but also of the differences between them. With regard to eschatology in particular, these differences may prove challenging to Rahner's reliance on the notion of anonymous Christianity for his hope for universal salvation. In addition, Rahner's concept of the Christian task and its relation to the eschatological consummation of the world needs to be reassessed. His concept of the moral and political task was very much coloured by liberation theology, which is centred on the role of a Christian theology for the oppressed in countries which are predominantly Christian. But theologians today also need to ask what the human task is in relation to poor and unstable countries which have no substantial Christian population: is there a specifically *Christian* task in relation to those countries? And in what sense can those who are not Christian be said to be participating in the collective co-creation and immanent consummation of the world? Furthermore, how can those whose present experience of the world is one of suffering and oppression be said to be participating in an on-going consummation at all?

Thus an ever-increasing awareness of a multi-ethnic and multi-faith world (together with the issues surrounding secularization) and a recognition of the role of suffering demand, not necessarily an abandonment, but certainly a new look at Rahner's viewpoint on universal salvation. His firm insistence on the priority of humankind in the creation also needs to be reassessed, given the ever-increasing knowledge about humanity's origins and place in the development of this planet. In addition to the study of the earth in the light of evolutionary theory, the continued exploration of space questions the position of humans in the context of the vastness of the universe. Whereas Rahner often regards space-exploration as directed towards creating a new living-space for humans, it is now more often perceived as directed towards pure scientific research. The heady optimism of the 1960s, when it was popularly thought that humans could colonize space, has been replaced with a more realistic, or pessimistic, view of earth's position in the cosmos. This is not to deny that humanity has a special role on earth: humanity must be singled out among the rest of creation as being uniquely capable of ecological destruction (the very opposite of Rahner's concept of the Christian task of the co-creation of the world). However, this pre-eminence of humanity is often reinterpreted by contemporary theologians as one of power, not of value. Thus the role of humanity in eschatology must be reassessed: do humans still have a special place, or must the doctrines of creation in the image of God or the supernatural existential be abandoned altogether? Do the hints in both Gregory's and Rahner's works that the whole universe will be saved need to be amplified?

Furthermore, future scientific research into human consciousness may help to elucidate the nature of decision. This may help the theologian to convey more clearly, or in more accessible language, the nature of human response to grace—although it is unlikely to unveil what Gregory and Rahner saw as the essentially mysterious relation of divine and human action in this respect. Similarly, a clearer understanding of the relation of brain to mind would also help theological discussions of the relation of spirit and matter, although again it will not resolve all problems. These two last factors, that is reflection upon humanity in the universe and the mind in humanity, can perhaps be called investigations into human nature at the macro- and the micro- level respectively. They might thus aid further philosophical and theological reflection into the relation of the individual to humanity as a whole, which is one of the most complex issues in the whole eschatological debate—and one issue with regard to which Rahner's account is particularly open to criticism.

Finally, further research into the concept of time by physicists, mathematicians and philosophers will feed into deeper theological reflection on that issue—again one of the most difficult and crucial aspects of eschatology and an area where Rahner's interpretation is at its weakest.

These are just a few examples of the ways in which Christian eschatology could be developed in the coming years: learning from the more vivid and imaginative approach of writers such as Gregory; the development of a more truly global perspective; the recognition both of humanity's possible insignificance in the context of the universe as a whole and of humans' unique responsibility for their own planet; the incorporation into Christian dialogue of a clearer understanding of the human mind; the theological reflection upon philosophical and scientific concepts of time. Some theological re-expressions of eschatology will consist of relatively minor alterations to its expression and content; others may lead to major changes. Nevertheless, change of one kind or another is inevitable and it is up to the theologians of the new millennium to take up the challenge and creatively determine the direction of that change. With this in mind, this comparison of Gregory of Nyssa and Karl Rahner has illustrated not only the difficulties, but also the possibilities and potential developments of the idea of universal salvation. Most importantly, however, it has shown that these two Christian thinkers' shared assurance of the universal saving power of God transcends the differences between them, and this should encourage future theologians to express convincingly and meaningfully the prayerful hope that at the end God will be all in all.

APPENDIX A

Karl Rahner's Seven Theses for an Eschatological Hermeneutics[1]

1. The eschata are still in the future in a very ordinary and empirical sense.

2. God's omniscience includes his knowledge of future events; although man's situation affects the extent to which he can receive God's revelation of the eschata, such revelation is not of events which are a priori beyond human understanding.

3. The sphere of eschatological assertions is determined by:
- (a) the fact that the eschata are hidden;
- (b) man's historicity.

4. From Thesis 3 it can be seen that knowledge of the future is knowledge of the futurity of the present . . .

5. . . . hence eschatological statements are derived from man's present experience of salvation.

6. The following further consequences result:
- (a) eschatological assertions about heaven and hell are not on an equal footing;
- (b) eschatological statements are both individual and universal;
- (c) there need be no antagonism between imminent and distant expectations of the parousia;
- (d) Christ is the hermeneutical principle of all eschatological assertions;
- (e) the above principles, together with a theology of history, enable one to say everything about eschatology.

7. One is consequently able to distinguish between form and content in eschatological assertions.

[1] A summary of the six theses in 'The Hermeneutics of Eschatological Assertions': *TI* iv. 323–46.

APPENDIX B

Karl Rahner: The Content of Eschatological Assertions

A. LIST GIVEN IN 'THE HERMENEUTICS OF ESCHATOLOGICAL ASSERTIONS'[1]

i. The 'formal principles of a theology of history':[2]

- 'history is directed towards a definite end';
- 'it reveals an antagonism';
- 'the temporal, the historical is always ambiguous';
- 'the forces at work grow radically stronger';
- 'the forces and epochs of the history of salvation and catastrophe are represented by concrete persons';
- 'sin is encompassed by the grace of God'.

ii. From the above and from humanity's experience of Christ can be derived 'all that can and may be said objectively in the Catholic theology of eschatology'. *For example*:

- 'time will have an end';
- 'towards the end the antagonism between Christ and the world will grow fiercer';
- 'history as a whole ends with the final victory of God in his grace'.

This consummation . . .

- '. . . in so far as it is the incalculable act of God's freedom is called God's judgement'
- '. . . in so far as it is the fulfilment of the salvation already real, victorious, and definitive in Christ, is called the return and judgement of Christ'

[1] *TI* iv. 343–4.
[2] Not intended to be a complete list.

- '. . . in so far as it is the fulfilment of the individual . . . is called the particular judgement'
- '. . . in so far as it is the fulfilment of the resurrection of Christ . . . is called the resurrection of the flesh and the transfiguration of the world'.

B. LIST GIVEN IN THE *SACRAMENTUM MUNDI* ARTICLE ON ESCHATOLOGY[3]

- 'The intrinsically limited character of time and its historical configuration from genuine beginning to a genuine irreplaceable end';
- 'the uniqueness of every part of the saving history';
- 'death and the "change" effected as an event by God, as a necessary mode of genuine fulfilment of time (since the Fall)';
- 'the fact that the end has already come with the incarnation, death, and resurrection of the Logos made flesh';
- 'the presence of this end as constituting the fact of the victorious mercy and self-communication of God (in contradiction to a double outcome on an equal footing which would be specified by man's freedom alone)';
- 'the special character of time now still unfolding "after" Christ';
- 'the persistent character of this period as a conflict (with Anti-Christ) which necessarily becomes more intense as the end approaches';
- 'the question of the convergence of the natural and supernatural finality of man and the cosmos';
- 'the final removal of the cosmic powers of the Law, of death, etc.';
- 'the enduring significance of Christ's humanity for beatitude';
- 'the positive meaning of the inequality of the glory of heaven';
- 'the vision of God as the abiding mystery (the positive meaning of the incomprehensibility of God)';
- 'the relation between the heaven of the redeemed and the reprobate world of the demons';

[3] 'Eschatology': *SM* ii. 245–6.

- 'the positive significance of the persistence of evil and the nature of the latter';
- 'the metaphysical essence of the glorified body';
- 'the one "Kingdom of God" of angels and men';
- 'the true nature of the "intermediate state" . . . which must not be regarded as purely spiritual'.

BIBLIOGRAPHY

A. WORKS BY GREGORY OF NYSSA

i. Abbreviations for and Approximate Dates of Works Used

Dates are compiled from Daniélou's introduction to: *Grégoire de Nysse: La Vie de Moïse* (2nd edition, Du Cerf, Paris, 1955) and his article 'La chronologie des oeuvres de Grégoire de Nysse' (*Studia Patristica* 7 [= *Texte und Untersuchungen* 92] 1966, 159–69), the latter taking precedence where the two differ. He later changed his mind about the date of *De mortuis*, but his original opinion, as given here, seems more likely.

Date	Title	Abbreviations used
371	*De virginitate*	*De virg.*
	De mortuis oratio	*De mort.*
374	*De oratione dominica*	*De orat. dom.*
376–8	*In inscriptiones psalmorum*	*In insc. pss.*
378	*De beatitudinibus*	*De beat.*
379	*De hominis opificio*	*De hom. opif.*
380	*De anima et resurrectione*	*De an.*
381–2	*Contra Eunomium*	*Contra Eun.*
382	*De tridui spatio*	*De tridui*
	In sanctum et salutare Pascha	*In s. & s. Pasch.*
	De infantibus praemature abreptis	*De infant.*
386–7	*Oratio catechetica magna*	*Cat. or.*
390–394	*In canticum canticorum*	*In cant.*
392	*De vita Moysis*	*De vita Moysis*
Works of Unknown Date		
	Adversus Arium et Sabellium	*Adv. A. & S.*
	De instituto christiano	*De inst.*
	De vita Macrinae	*De vita Mac.*
	In ascensionem Christi oratio	*In ascen.*
	In Ecclesiasten	*In Eccles.*
	In illud: tunc et ipse Filius . . .	*In illud: tunc*
	In sanctum Pascha	*In s. Pascha*
Various Dates		
	Epistulae	*Epp.*

ii. Editions

Not an exhaustive list, but a record of those used for this book. Gregory's works are also to be found in *Patrologiae: Series Graeca Prior* ed. J. P. Migne [= *PG*] volumes 44–6. Many of his writings are now published by Brill in the series *Gregorii Nysseni: Opera* [= *GNO*]. Dates below refer to individual volumes in the series; names refer to the editor of the particular work (not to the editor of the volume or series). Some of Gregory's works have been translated in the collection *A Series of Nicene and Post-Nicene Fathers* [= *NPNF*] vol. v: *Gregory of Nyssa*, eds. H. Wace and P. Schaff (2nd series, Parker and Co., Oxford, 1893, reprinted 1988).

Adversus Arium et Sabellium, de Patri et Filio. Greek: *GNO* iii/1. 71–85, ed. F. Mueller (1958)

Contra Eunomium. Greek: Books I & II: *GNO* i; Book III: *GNO* ii, both ed. W. Jaeger (1960); English: *NPNF* v. 35–248, tr. W. Moore, M. Day, H. A. Wilson, and H. C. Ogle

De anima et resurrectione. Greek: *Gregors Bischofs von Nyssa Gespräch mit seiner Schwester Makrina über Seele und Auferstehung*, ed. F. Oehler (Leipzig, 1858); English: *NPNF* v. 428–68, tr. W. Moore

De beatitudinibus. Greek: *GNO* vii. 2. 75–171, ed. J. F. Callahan (1992); English: *St. Gregory of Nyssa, The Lord's Prayer, The Beatitudes*, tr. H. Graef (Ancient Christian Writers, 18, Newman Press, Westminster, MD; Longmans Green & Co., London, 1954), 85–175

De hominis opificio. Greek: *PG* 44. 125–256; English: *NPNF* v. 386–427, tr. H. A. Wilson

De infantibus praemature abreptis. Greek: *GNO* iii/2. 65–97, ed. H. Hörner (1987); English: *NPNF* v. 372–81, tr. W. Moore

De instituto christiano. Greek: *GNO* viii/1, 1–90, ed. W. Jaeger (1952)

De mortuis oratio. Greek: *GNO* ix. 28–68, ed. G. Heil (1967); Greek text and Italian translation: *Gregorio di Nissa: Discorso sui defunti*, ed. G. Lozza (Società editrice internationale, Turin, 1991)

De oratione dominica. Greek: *GNO* vii/2, 1–74, ed. J. F. Callahan (1992); English: *St. Gregory of Nyssa, The Lord's Prayer, The Beatitudes* tr. H. Graef (Ancient Christian Writers, 18, Newman Press, Westminster, Md.; Longmans Green & Co., London, 1954), 21–84

De tridui spatio (= *In Christi resurrectionem* Iin PG). Greek: *GNO* ix. 273–306, ed. E. Gebhardt (1967); English: *The Easter Sermons of Gregory of Nyssa: Translation and Commentary. The Proceedings of the 4th International Colloquium on Gregory of Nyssa*, in A. Spira and C. Klock (eds.), *De tridui spatio*, tr. S. G. Hall (Philadelphia Patristic Foundation, Cambridge, Mass., 1981), 31–50

De virginitate. Greek: *GNO* viii/1. p.215–346, ed. J. P. Calvarnos

(1952); Greek text and French translation: *Grégoire de Nysse: Traité de la Virginité*, Intro., text, tr., comm. M. Aubineau (*SC* 119, Éditions du Cerf, Paris, 1966); English: *NPNF* v. 343–71, tr. W. Moore; and *St. Gregory of Nyssa: Ascetical Works*, tr. V. W. Callahan (Fathers of the Church, 58, Catholic University of America Press, Washington DC, 1967), 3–75

De vita Sanctae Macrinae. Greek: *GNO* viii/1. 347–414, ed. V. W. Callahan (1952); Greek text and French translation: *Grégoire de Nysse: Vie de Sainte Macrine* Intro., text, tr., comm. P. Maraval (*SC* 178, Éditions du Cerf, Paris, 1971); English: *St. Gregory of Nyssa: Ascetical Works*, tr. V. W. Callahan (The Fathers of the Church, 58, Catholic University of America Press, Washington DC, 1967), 163–91

De vita Moysis. Greek text and French translation: *La Vie de Moïse*, ed. and tr. J. Daniélou, 3rd edn. (*SC* 1 ter, Éditions du Cerf, Paris, 1968); English: *The Life of Moses*, ed. and tr. A. J. Malherbe and E. Ferguson (Classics of Western Spirituality, Ramsey, New York; Paulist Press, Toronto, 1978)

Epistulae. Greek: *GNO* viii/2, ed. G. Pasquali (1959); English: (selection) *NPNF* v. 527–48, tr. H. C. Ogle

In ascensionem; Greek: *GNO* ix. 323–41, ed. E. Gebhardt (1967)

In canticum canticorum. Greek: *GNO* vi. ed. H. Langerbeck (1960); English: *Saint Gregory of Nyssa: Commentary on the Song of Songs*, tr. and intro. C. McCambley (Hellenic College Press, Brookline, Mass., 1987)

In Ecclesiasten. Greek: *GNO* v. 277–442, ed. P. Alexander (1962)

In illud: tunc et ipse Filius . . . Greek: *GNO* iii/2. 1–28, ed. J. K. Downing (1987)

In inscriptiones psalmorum. Greek: *GNO* v. 24–175, ed. J. A. McDonough (1962); English: *Gregory of Nyssa's Treatise on the Inscriptiones of the Psalms: Introduction, Translation and Notes*, R. E. Heine (Clarendon Press, Oxford, 1995)

In sanctum Pascha. Greek: *GNO* ix. 245–70 (1967); English: *The Easter Sermons of Gregory of Nyssa* in A. Spira and C. Klock (eds.), *In sanctum Pascha*, tr. S. G. Hall, 5–25 (Philadelphia Patristic Foundation, Cambridge, Mass., 1981)

In sanctum et salutare Pascha. Greek: *GNO* ix. 309–11, ed. E. Gebhardt (1967); English: *The Easter Sermons of Gregory of Nyssa* in A. Spira and C. Klock (eds.), *In sanctum et salutare Pascha*, tr. S. G. Hall, 51–3 (Philadelphia Patristic Foundation, Cambridge, Mass., 1981)

Oratio catechetica magna. Greek: *The Catechetical Oration of Gregory of Nyssa*, ed. J. H. Srawley (Cambridge University Press, Cambridge, 1903; repr. 1956); English: *The Catechetical Oration of Gregory of Nyssa*, tr. J. H. Srawley (Early Church Classics, SPCK, London, 1917)

B. WORKS BY KARL RAHNER

Abbreviations used in this book are given in square brackets after the English titles. German editions are given only if they are cited in the main body of this book.

i. Monographs

Inspiration in the Bible (= *Quaestiones Disputatae*, 1) tr. C. H. Henkey (Nelson, Edinburgh and London, 1961)

On the Theology of Death (= *Quaestiones Disputatae*, 2) tr. C. H. Henkey and W. J. O'Hara (Burns and Oates, London, 1962) from *Zur Theologie des Todes* 2nd edn. (Herder, Freiburg-im-Breisgau, 1965)

Hominisation: The Evolutionary Origin of Man as a Theological Problem (= *Quaestiones Disputatae* 13) (Herder, Freiburg-im-Breisgau, 1965) tr. from Karl Rahner and Paul Overhage, *Das Problem der Hominisation: über den biologischen Ursprung des Menschen*, 2nd expanded edn. (= *Quaestiones Disputatae*, 12/13) (Herder, Freiburg-im-Breisgau, 1961)

Revelation and Tradition (= *Quaestiones Disputatae*, 17) tr. W. J. O'Hara (Nelson, Edinburgh and London, *c.* 1966)

Spirit in the World, tr. W. V. Dych (Sheed & Ward, London, 1968)

Hearers of the Word, rev. J. B. Metz, tr. R. Walls (Sheed & Ward, London, 1969)

Foundations of Christian Faith, tr. W. V. Dych (Darton, Longman &Todd, London, 1978) from *Grundkurs des Glaubens: Einführung in den Begriff des Christentums* (Herder, Freiburg, 1976)

ii. Articles from *Sacramentum Mundi: An Encylopedia of Theology*

Ed. Karl Rahner et al., tr. W. J. O'Hara, et al. (Herder & Herder, New York, 1968–70):

'Beatific Vision'; i. 151–3

'Eschatology'; ii. 242–6

'Hell'; iii. 7–9 (§1 only)

'Last Things'; iii. 274–6

iii. Articles from *Theological Investigations*

Tr. various (Helicon Press, Baltimore; Darton, Longman & Todd, London, 1961–92) from *Schriften zur Theologie* (Benziger, Einsiedeln, 1954–84). Dates in parentheses indicate the first publishing of a work in German.

'Remarks on the Theology of Indulgences', *TI* ii. 175–201 (first published in German in 1948)

'The Resurrection of the Body', *TI* ii. 203–16

'The Life of the Dead', *TI* iv. 347–54

'The Hermeneutics of Eschatological Assertions', *TI* iv. 323–46 (1960) 'Theologische Prinzipien der Hermeneutik eschatologischer Aussagen', *ST* iv. 401–28

'History of the World and Salvation History', *TI* v. 97–114 (1962) 'Weltgeschichte und Heilsgeschichte', *ST* v. 115–35

'Christianity and the "New Man": the Christian Faith and Utopian Views about the Future of the World', *TI* v. 135–53 (1961) [= 'Christianity and the "New Man"'] 'Das Christentum und der "neue Mensch"', *ST* v. 159–79

'Ideology and Christianity', *TI* vi. 43–58 (1965) 'Ideologie und Christentum', *ST* vi. 59–76

'Marxist Utopia and the Christian Future of Man', *TI* vi. 59–68 (1965) [= 'Marxist Utopia']

'The Church and the Parousia of Christ', *TI* vi. 295–312 (1963) 'Kirche und Parousie Christi', *ST* vi. 348–67

'See what a Man!', *TI* vii. 136–9 (1955)

'The Scandal of Death', *TI* vii. 140–44 (1966)

'"He Descended into Hell"', *TI* vii. 145–50 (1957)

'Hidden Victory', *TI* vii. 151–8 (1966)

'Experiencing Easter', *TI* vii. 159–68 (1965)

'Encounters with the Risen Christ', *TI* vii. 169–77 (1955)

'He Will Come Again', *TI* vii. 177–80 (1959)

'The Festival of the Future of the World', *TI* vii. 181–5 (1961)

'On Christian Dying', *TI* vii. 285–93 (1959) 'Über das christliche Sterben', *ST* vii. 273–82

'The Second Vatican Council's Challenge to Theology', *TI* ix. 3–27 (1967)

'A Brief Theological Study on Indulgence', *TI* x. 150–65 (1955) 'Kleiner theologischer Traktat über den Ablass', *ST* viii. 472–87

'A Fragmentary Aspect of a Theological Concept of the Future', *TI* x. 235–41 (1966)

'On the Theology of Hope', *TI* x. 242–59 (1968)

'The Theological Problems Entailed in the Idea of the "New Earth"', *TI* x. 260–72 (1967) [= 'The Idea of the "New Earth"'] 'Über der theologischer Problematik der "neuen Erde"', *ST* viii. 580–92

'Immanent and Transcendent Consummation of the World', *TI* x. 273–89 (1968) [= 'Immanent and Transcendent Consummation'] 'Immanente und transcendente Vollendung der Welt', *ST* viii. 593–609

'Theological Considerations Concerning the Moment of Death', *TI* xi. 309–21 (1968)

'Ideas for a Theology of Death', *TI* xiii (1970)
'The Body in the Order of Salvation', *TI* xvii. 71–89 (1967)
'The Intermediate State', *TI* xvii. 114–24 (1975)
'*Über den "Zwischenzustand"*', *ST* xii. 455–66
'Christian Dying', *TI* xviii. 226–56 (1976) 'Das christliche Sterben', *ST* xiii. 269–304
'Eternity from Time', *TI* xix. 169–77 (1979)
'Purgatory', *TI* xix. 181–93 (1980) 'Fegfeuer', *ST* xiv. 435–49
'Profane History and Salvation History', *TI* xxi. 3–15 (1982) 'Profangeschichte und Heilsgeschichte', *ST* xv. 11–23
'Utopia and Reality: The Shape of the Christian Existence Caught between the Ideal and the Real', *TI* xxii. 26–37 (1983)

C. GENERAL BIBLIOGRAPHY

ALDWINCKLE, R. *Death in the Secular City* (George Allen and Unwin Ltd., London, 1972)
ALEXANDRE, M. "Le *de mortuis* de Grégoire de Nysse", in *Studia Patristica*, 10 (= *Texte und Untersuchungen*, 107) (1967)
—— La théorie d'exégèse dans le De Hominis Opificio et l'In Hexameron', in M. Harl (ed.), *Écriture et culture philosophique dans la pensée de Grégoire de Nysse* (1971)
ALTENBURGER, M. AND MANN, F. *Bibliographie zu Gregor von Nyssa: editionen, übersetzungen, literature* (Brill, Leiden, 1988)
BADHAM, P. *Christian Beliefs about Life after Death* (Macmillan, London, 1976)
BAERT, E. 'Le Thème de la Vision de Dieu chez S. Justin, Clément d'Alexandre et S. Grégoire de Nysse', *Freiburger Zeitschrift für Philosophie und Theologie* 12 (1965)
BAILLIE, J. *And the Life Everlasting* (Oxford University Press, London, 1934)
BAIRD, J. A. *The Justice of God in the Teaching of Jesus* (SCM, London, 1963)
BALTHASAR, H. U. VON *Pneuma und Institution* (Johannes Verlag, Einsiedeln, 1974) tr. in M. Kehl and W. Loser (eds.), *The Von Balthasar Reader* (T&T Clark, Edinburgh, 1982)
—— *Dare We Hope 'That all Men be Saved'?* with *A Short Discourse on Hell* (Ignatius Press, San Francisco, 1988)
—— *Mysterium Paschale* (Ressourcement, T&T Clark, Edinburgh, 1990)
—— *Presence and Thought: An Essay on the Religious Thought of Gregory of Nyssa* (Communio Books, Ignatius Press, San Francisco, 1995)

BARTH, K. 'The Humanity of God', in *God, Grace and Gospel*, Scottish Journal of Theology Occasional Papers (Oliver and Boyd, Edinburgh, 1956)

—— *Church Dogmatics* ii/2 (T&T Clark, Edinburgh, 1957)

BÉBIS, G. S. 'Gregory of Nyssa's "De Vita Moesis": A Philosophical and Theological Analysis', *The Greek Orthodox Theological Review* 12 (1967)

BENZ, E. *Evolution and Christian Hope* (Victor Gollancz, London, 1967)

BERTHOLD, G. C. 'The Cappadocian Roots of Maximus the Confessor', in F. Heinzer and C. Schönborn, (eds.), *Maximus Confessor* (1980)

BLANCHARD, J. *Whatever Happened to Hell?* (Evangelical Press, Durham, 1993)

BONDA, J. *The One Purpose of God: An Answer to the Doctrine of Eternal Punishment* (Eerdmans, Grand Rapids, Mich. Cambridge, 1998)

BOROS, L. *The Moment of Truth—Mysterium Mortis* (Burns and Oates, London, 1965)

BROWER, K. E. AND ELLIOT, M. W. (eds.), *'The Reader Must Understand': Eschatology in Bible and Theology* (Apollos, an imprint of Inter-Varsity Press, Leicester, 1997)

BULTMANN, R. 'New Testament and Mythology: The Problem of Demythologizing the New Testament Proclamation', in R. Bultmann, *New Testament and Mythology and other Basic Writings*, ed. and tr. Schubert Ogden (SCM, London, 1985)

CAMERON, N. M. DE S. *Universalism and the Doctrine of Hell*, Papers presented at the Fourth Edinburgh Conference on Christian Dogmatics, 1991 (Paternoster Press, Carlisle; Baker Book House, Grand Rapids, Mich., 1993)

CANÉVET, M. 'Exégèse et Théologie dans les Traités Spirituels de Grégoire de Nysse', in M. Harl (ed.), *Écriture et culture philosophique dans la pensée de Grégoire de Nysse* (1971)

CAPPUYNS, M. *Jean Scot Érigène: Sa Vie, son Oeuvre, sa Pensée* (Abbaye de Mont César, Louvain; Desclée de Brouwer, Paris, 1933)

CHARLES, R. H. *A Critical History of a Future Life in Israel, in Judaism and in Christianity*, 2nd edn. (Adam and Charles Black, London, 1913)

CHERNISS, H. F. 'The Platonism of Gregory of Nyssa', in J. T. Allen, H. C. Nutting, and H. R. W. Smith (eds.), *University of California Publications in Classical Philology* xi: *1930–3* (University of California Press, Berkeley, Calif., 1934)

CLEMENT OF ALEXANDRIA *Stromateis vii. Clément d'Alexandrie: Les Stromates: Stromate vii*, ed. A. Le Bolluec (*SC* 428, Éditions du Cerf, Paris, 1997)

COUTTS, A. *Hans Denck 1495–1527: Humanist and Heretic* (Macniven and Wallace, Edinburgh, 1927)

CROSS, F. L. AND LIVINGSTONE, E. A. (EDS.), *The Oxford Dictionary of the Christian Church*, 3rd edn. (Oxford University Press, Oxford, 1997)

CROUZEL, H. *Origen* (T&T Clark, Edinburgh, 1989)

—— *Le Fin Dernière selon Origène* (Variorum Reprints, Aldershot, Hants., 1990)

DALEY, B. E. '"Apokatastasis" and Honourable Silence in the Eschatology of Maximus the Confessor', in F. Heinzer and C. Schönborn (eds.), *Maximus Confessor* (1980)

—— *The Hope of the Early Church: A Handbook of Patristic Eschatology* (Cambridge University Press, Cambridge, 1991)

DANIÉLOU, J. 'L'apocatastase chez Saint Grégoire de Nysse', *Recherches de Science Religieuse* 30/3 (July 1940)

—— *Platonisme et Théologie Mystique*, 2nd edn. (Aubier, Paris, 1944)

—— *Origen* (Sheed & Ward, London, 1955)

—— 'La chronologie des oeuvres de Grégoire de Nysse' *Studia Patristica*, 7 (= *Texte und Untersuchungen*, 92) (1966)

—— Introduction to *Grégoire de Nysse: La Vie de Moïse*, 3rd edn. (*SC* 1, Éditions du Cerf, Paris, 1968)

—— *L'être et le temps chez Grégoire de Nysse* (Brill, Leiden, 1970)

DECHOW, J. F. *Dogma and Mysticism in Early Christianity: Epiphanius of Cyrus and the Legacy of Origen* (Patristic Monograph Series, 13, Mercer University Press, Macon, Ga., 1988)

DENNIS, T. J. 'Gregory and the Resurrection of the Body', in *The Easter Sermons of Gregory of Nyssa: Translation and Commentary. The Proceedings of the 4th International Colloquium on Gregory of Nyssa*, ed. A. Spira and C. Klock (Philadelphia Patristic Foundation, Cambridge, Mass., 1981)

DENZINGER, H. (ed.) *Enchiridion Symbolorum Definitionum et Declarationum de Rebus Fidei et Morum*, 37th edn. with German trans.: *Kompendium der Glaubensbekenntnisse und kirchlichen Lehrentscheidungen*, ed. P. Hünermann (Herder, Freiburg-im-Breisgau, 1991)

DILLON, J. 'The Descent of the Soul in Middle Platonic and Gnostic Theory', in B. Layton (ed.), *The Rediscovery of Gnosticism* i (Brill, Leiden, 1980)

DI NOIA, J. A. 'Karl Rahner', in *The Modern Theologians*, ed. D. Ford, 2nd edn. (Basil Blackwell, Oxford, 1997)

DUNSTONE, A. S. *The Atonement in Gregory of Nyssa* (Tyndale Press, London, 1964)

DYCH, W. V. *Karl Rahner* (Outstanding Christian Thinkers, Geoffrey Chapman, London, 1992)

EDWARDS, M. 'Origen's Two Resurrections', in *Journal of Theological Studies* n.s. 46/2 (Oct. 1995)

FERGUSON, E. 'God's Infinity and Man's Mutability: Perpetual Progress

According to Gregory of Nyssa', *Greek Orthodox Theological Review* 18 (1978)

Ferguson, E. and Malherbe, A. J. Introduction to *Gregory of Nyssa: The Life of Moses*, ed. and tr. id. (Classics of Western Spirituality, Paulist Press, N. Y., 1978)

Gaine, S. *Indwelling Spirit and A New Creation: The Relationship between Uncreated Grace and Created Grace in Neo-Scholastic Catholic Theology* (D. Phil. thesis, Faculty of Theology, University of Oxford, 1994)

Geister, P. *Aufhebung zur Eigentlichkeit: zur Problematik kosmologischer Eschatologie in der Theologie Karl Rahners* (= Uppsala Studies in Faiths and Ideologies, 5) (Acta Universitatis Upsaliensis, Uppsala, 1996)

Gilson, E. *The Spirit of Medieval Philosophy* (Sheed & Ward, London, 1936)

—— *The Christian Philosophy of St. Augustine* (Victor Gollancz, London, 1961)

Grant, R. M. *Gnosticism and Early Christianity* (New York, 1959)

Gray, T. J. *Hell: An Analysis of Some Major Twentieth Century Attempts to Defend the Doctrine of Hell* (D. Phil. thesis, University of Oxford, 1996)

Gregory of Nazianzus *Fourth Theological Oration* [= *Or. 30*] *Grégoire de Nazianze: Discours 27–31*, ed. and tr. P. Gallay and M. Jourjon (*SC* 250, Éditions du Cerf, Paris, 1978); *NPNF* vii: Cyril of Jerusalem, *Catechetical Lectures*, Gregory of Nazianzus, *Select Orations and Letters*, ed. P. Schaff and H. Wace (T&T Clark, Edinburgh, (1894) repr. 1988), 309–18, tr. C. G. Browne and J. E. Swallow

Gutiérrez, G. *A Theology of Liberation: History, Politics and Salvation*, 2nd edn. (SCM, London, 1988)

Harl M. (ed.) *Écriture et Culture philosophique dans la Pensée de Grégoire de Nysse*. Actes du colloque de Chevetogne (22–26 septembre 1969) organisé par le Centre de recherche sur l'Hellénisme (Brill, Leiden, 1971)

Harmon, K. J. *Temporally Excluded from God? Some Twentieth Century Theological Explorations of the Problem of Hell and Universalism with reference to the Historical Development of these Doctrines* (D. Phil. thesis, Faculty of Theology, University of Oxford, 1993)

Hartshorne, C. *Reality as Social Process* (Free Press, Illinois, 1953)

Heine, R. E. 'Gregory of Nyssa's Apology for Allegory', *Vigiliae Christianae* 38 (1984)

—— Introduction to his *Gregory of Nyssa's Treatise on the Inscriptions of the Psalms: Introduction, Translation and Notes* (Clarendon Press, Oxford, 1995)

Heinzer F. and C. Schönborn (eds.), *Maximus Confessor*. Actes du symposium sur Maximus le Confesseur, Fribourg, 2–5 septembre,

1980 (= *Paradosis: Études de Littérature et de Théologie Anciennes*, 27) (Éditions Universitaires, Fribourg, 1980)

HELM, P. *The Last Things: Death, Judgement, Heaven and Hell* (Banner of Truth Trust, Edinburgh, 1989)

HENNESSEY, L. 'The Place of Saints and Sinners After Death', in C. Kannengiesser and W. L. Petersen (eds.), *Origen of Alexandria: His World and his Legacy* (University of Notre Dame Press, Notre Dame, Ind., 1988)

HICK, J. *Death and Eternal Life* (Collins, London, 1976)

—— *Evil and the God of Love*, 2nd edn. reissued with a new preface (Macmillan, Basingstoke, 1985)

HILL, C. *Regnum Caelorum: Patterns of Hope in Early Christianity* (Clarendon Press, Oxford, 1992)

HÖFNER, J. AND RAHNER, K. *Lexikon für Theologie und Kirche*, 2nd edn. (Freiburg-im-Breisgau, Herder, 1957–67)

IRENAEUS *Adversus Haereses* [= *Adv. Haer.*]. *Irénée de Lyon: Contre les Hérésies Livres I–V*, ed. and tr. A. Rousseau, L. Doutreleau, et al. (*SC* 263, Éditions du Cerf, Paris, 1979); *Five Books of Irenaeus against Heresies*, tr. J. Keble (James Parker, Oxford, and London; Rivingtons, Oxford, London and Cambridge, 1872)

JAEGER, W. *Two Rediscovered Works of Ancient Christian Literature: Gregory of Nyssa and Macarius* (Brill, Leiden, 1954)

KELLY, J. N. D. *Early Christian Doctrines* (A&C Black, London, 1958)

KILBY, K. E. *The 'Vorgriff auf Esse': A Study in the Relation of Philosophy to Theology in the Thought of Karl Rahner* (Ph. D. thesis, Yale University, 1994)

KIM, DAI SIL 'Irenaeus of Lyons and Teilhard de Chardin: A Comparative Study of "Recapitulation" and "Omega"', *Journal of Ecumenical Studies* 13 (1976)

KLAUSER T. (ed.) *Reallexikon für Antike und Christentum* (Hiersemann Verlags, Stuttgart, 1950)

KRESS, R. *A Rahner Handbook* (John Knox Press, Atlanta, Ga., 1982)

LASH, N. *A Matter of Hope: A Theologian's Reflections on the Thought of Karl Marx* (Darton, Longman & Todd, London, 1981)

LAWSON, J. *The Biblical Theology of St. Irenaeus* (Epworth Press, London, 1948)

LE GOFF, J. *The Birth of Purgatory* (Scolar Press, London, 1984)

LEYS, R. *L'image de Dieu chez Saint Grégoire de Nysse: Esquisse d'une Doctrine* (Museum Lessianum: Section Théologique no. 49; L'édition Universelle, Bruxelles; Desclée de Brouwer, Paris, 1951)

LOUTH, A. *The Origins of the Christian Mystical Tradition from Plato to Denys* (Oxford University Press, Oxford, 1981)

LOVEJOY, A. O. *The Great Chain of Being* (Harvard University Press, Cambridge, Mass., 1936)

LUCAS, J. *A Treatise on Time and Space* (Methuen, London, 1973)

LUDLOW, M. A. *Restoration and Consummation: The Interpretation of Universalistic Eschatology by Gregory of Nyssa and Karl Rahner* (D. Phil. thesis, University of Oxford, 1996)

—— 'Universal Salvation and a Soteriology of Divine Punishment', *Scottish Journal of Theology* (forthcoming)

LYMAN, J. R. *Christology and Cosmology* (Clarendon Press, Oxford, 1993)

LYONS, J. A. *The Cosmic Christ in Origen and Teilhard de Chardin: A Comparative Study* (Oxford University Press, Oxford, 1982)

MACLEOD, C. 'Allegory and Mysticism in Origen and Gregory of Nyssa', in id., Collected Essays (Oxford University Press, Oxford, 1983)

—— 'ANALUSIS: A Study in Ancient Mysticism', in id., *Collected Essays*

—— 'The Preface to Gregory of Nyssa's *Life of Moses*', in id. *Collected Essays*

MACQUARRIE, J. *The Scope of Demythologising: Bultmann and his Critics* (SCM, London, 1960)

—— *Existentialism* (Hutchinson, London; Westminster, Philadelphia 1972)

—— *The Christian Hope* (Mowbrays, London and Oxford, 1978)

MAR GREGORIOS, P. *Cosmic Man: The Divine Presence: The Theology of Gregory of Nyssa* (A New Era Book, Paragon House, N. Y., 1988)

MAURICE, F. D. *Theological Essays* (James Clarke, London, 1957; f.p. Cambridge, 1853)

MAXIMUS THE CONFESSOR *'The Ascetic Life' and 'The Four Centuries on Charity'*, ed. P. Sherwood (Newman Press, Westminster, Md.; Longmans, Green & Co., N. Y., 1955)

—— *Selected Writings*, tr. G. Berthold (Classics of Western Spirituality, Paulist Press, New York, 1985)

MCCAMBLEY, C. Introduction to *St. Gregory of Nyssa: Commentary on the Song of Songs*, tr. id. (Hellenic College Press, Brookline, Mass., 1987)

MCFAGUE, S. *The Body of God: An Ecological Theology* (Fortress Press, Minneapolis, 1993)

MCGIFFERT, A. C. *A History of Christian Thought* ii (Charles Scribner's Sons, New York and London, 1954)

MEREDITH, A. *The Cappadocians* (Outstanding Christian Thinkers Series, Geoffrey Chapman, London, 1995)

—— *Gregory of Nyssa* (Early Church Fathers, Routledge, London and New York, 1999)

METZ, J.-B. and MOLTMANN, J. *Faith and the Future* (Concilium Series, Orbis Books, Maryknoll, N.Y., 1995)
MICHAUD, E. 'St. Maxime le Confesseur et l'Apocatastase', *Internationale Theologische Zeitschrift* (= *Revue Internationale de Theologie*) 10 (1902)
—— 'St. Grégoire de Nysse et l'Apocatastase', *Internationale Theologische Zeitschrift* (= *Revue Internationale de Theologie*) 18 (1910)
MOLTMANN, J. *Theology of Hope* (SCM, London, 1967)
—— *Hope and Planning* (SCM, London, 1971)
—— *The Coming of God: Christian Eschatology* (SCM, London, 1996)
MÜLLER, G. 'Origenes und die Apokatastasis', *Theologisches Zeitschrift* 14 (1958)
—— 'Die Idee einer Apokatastasis ton panton in der europäischen Theologie von Schleiermacher bis Barth', *Zeitschrift für Religions- und Geistesgeschichte* 16/1 (1964)
OGDEN, S. *The Reality of God* (Harper & Row, New York, 1963)
O'MEARA, J. J. *Eriugena* (Clarendon Press, Oxford, 1988)
ORIGEN *Contra Celsum iv Origène: Contra Celse, Tome ii (livres iii et iv)*, ed. M. Borret (*SC* 136, Éditions du Cerf, Paris, 1968) *Origen: Contra Celsum*, tr. H. Chadwick (Cambridge University Press, Cambridge, 1980)
—— *De Principiis* [= *De Princ.*]. *Origenes: Vier Bücher von den Prinzipien*, ed. H. Görgemanns and H. Karpp (Texte zur Forschung, Wissenschaftliche Buchgesellschaft, Darmstadt, 1976); *Origen: On First Principles*, tr. from Koetschau's text by G. W. Butterworth (SPCK, London, 1936)
PELIKAN, J. Introduction to *Maximus the Confessor: Selected Writings*, ed. G. C. Berthold (Classics of Western Spirituality, Paulist Press, New York, 1985)
PHAN, P. *Eternity in Time: A Study of Karl Rahner's Eschatology* (Susquehanna University Press, Selinsgrove; Associated University Press, London and Toronto, 1988)
—— 'Contemporary Context and Issues in Eschatology', *Theological Studies* 55 (1994)
PITTENGER, N. *'The Last things' in a Process Perspective* (Epworth Press, London, 1970)
—— *After Death, Life in God* (SCM Press, London, 1980)
QUASTEN, J. *Patrology* i–iii (Newman Press, Westminster, Md., 1960)
ROBINSON, J. A. T. *In the End, God . . .* (James Clarke & Co., London, 1950)
ROWELL, G. 'The Origins and History of the Universalist Societies in Britain 1750–1850', *Journal for Ecclesiastical History* 22 (1971)
—— *Hell and the Victorians: A Study of the Nineteenth-Century Theological*

Controversies concerning Eternal Punishment and the Future Life (Clarendon Press, Oxford, 1974)
RUETHER, R. R. *Sexism and God-Talk: Towards a Feminist Theology* (SCM, London, 1983)
—— *Gaia and God: An Ecofeminist Theology of Earth Healing* (SCM, London, 1992)
SACHS, J. R. 'Apocatastasis in Patristic Theology', *Theological Studies* 54 (1993)
SANDERS, J. *No Other Name: Can Only Christians be Saved?* (C. S. Lewis Centre, SPCK, London, 1994)
SCHLEIERMACHER, F. *The Christian Faith* (T&T Clark, Edinburgh, 1928)
SCOTT, A. *Origen and the Life of the Stars: A History of an Idea* (Oxford Early Christian Studies, Clarendon Press, Oxford, 1991)
SHERWOOD, P. *The Early Ambigua of St. Maximus the Confessor and his Refutation of Origenism* (= *Studia Anselmia*, 36) (Rome, 1955)
SIMON, U. *The End is Not Yet: A Study in Christian Eschatology* (James Nisbet & Co., Welwyn, Herts., 1964)
SIMONETTI, M. *Biblical Interpretation in the Early Church*, tr. J. A. Hughes, ed. A. Bergquist and M. Bockmuehl (T&T Clark, Edinburgh, 1994)
SORABJI, R. *Time, Creation and the Continuum: Theories in Antiquity and the Early Middle Ages* (Duckworth, London, 1983)
TEILHARD DE CHARDIN, P. *The Phenomenon of Man*, tr. B. Wall (Collins, London, 1959)
TELFER, W. 'The Birth of Christian Anthropology', *Journal of Theological Studies* n.s. 13 (1962)
THOMPSON, W. M. 'The Hope for Humanity: Rahner's Eschatology', in L. O'Donovan (ed.), *A World of Grace* (Crossroads Series, Seabury Press, New York, 1980)
TRAVIS, S. H. *Christian Hope and the Future of Man* (Issues in Contemporary Theology, Inter-Varsity Press, Leicester, 1980)
TRIGG, J. W. *Origen* (SCM Press, London, 1985)
—— *Origen* (Early Church Fathers, Routledge, London, 1998)
VASS, G. *Understanding Karl Rahner*, i: *A Theologian in Search of a Philosophy*, and ii: *The Mystery of Man and the Foundations of a Theological System* (Christian Classics, Westminster Md.; Sheed & Ward, London, 1985)
VORGRIMLER, H. *Understanding Karl Rahner: An Introduction to his Life and Thought*, tr. J. Bowden (SCM Press, London, 1986)
WALKER, D. P. *The Decline of Hell* (Routledge & Kegan Paul, London, 1964)
WARD, K. *Religion and Creation* (Oxford University Press, Oxford, 1996)
—— *Religion and Human Nature* (Oxford University Press, Oxford, 1998)

WEGER, K.-H. *Karl Rahner: An Introduction to his Theology*, tr. D. Smith (Burns & Oates Ltd., London, 1980)

WEISS, F. L. *The Life, Teaching and Works of Johannes Denck* (published independently at Strasbourg, 1924)

WHITEHEAD, A. N. *Process and Reality* (Cambridge University Press, Cambridge, 1958)

WILES, M. *The Making of Christian Doctrine* (Cambridge University Press, Cambridge, 1967)

WILLIAMS, R. *The Wound of Knowledge* (Darton, Longman & Todd, London, 1979)

WILLIAMS, R. 'Balthasar and Rahner', in John Riches (ed.), *The Analogy of Beauty* (T&T Clark, Edinburgh, 1986)

—— 'Macrina's Death-bed Revisited: Gregory of Nyssa on Mind and Passion', in L. Wickham and C. Bammel (eds.), *Christian Faith and Philosophy in Late Antiquity* (= *Supplements to Vigiliae Christianae*, 19) (Brill, Leiden, 1993)

WRIGHT, N. *The Radical Evangelical* (Gospel and Culture, SPCK, London, 1996)

YOUNG, F. 'Adam and Anthropos', *Vigiliae Christianae* 37 (1983)

ZACHHUBER, J. *The Universal Nature of Man in Gregory of Nyssa: Philosophical Background and Theological Significance* (Brill, Leiden, 1997)

INDEX